The Library Friends, Foundations, and Trusts Handbook

The Library Friends, Foundations, and Trusts Handbook

Diane P. Tuccillo

ROWMAN & LITTLEFIELD
Lanham • Boulder • New York • London

Published by Rowman & Littlefield
An imprint of The Rowman & Littlefield Publishing Group, Inc.
4501 Forbes Boulevard, Suite 200, Lanham, Maryland 20706
www.rowman.com

86-90 Paul Street, London EC2A 4NE

Copyright © 2024 by The Rowman & Littlefield Publishing Group, Inc.

All rights reserved. No part of this book may be reproduced in any form or by any electronic or mechanical means, including information storage and retrieval systems, without written permission from the publisher, except by a reviewer who may quote passages in a review.

British Library Cataloguing in Publication Information Available

Library of Congress Cataloging-in-Publication Data

Names: Tuccillo, Diane P., 1952- author.
Title: The library friends, foundations, and trusts handbook / Diane P. Tuccillo.
Description: Lanham : Rowman & Littlefield, 2024. | Includes bibliographical references and index.
Identifiers: LCCN 2023059046 (print) | LCCN 2023059047 (ebook) | ISBN 9781538179253 (cloth) | ISBN 9781538179260 (paperback) | ISBN 9781538179277 (epub)
Subjects: LCSH: Friends of the library—United States—Handbooks, manuals, etc. | Library fund raising—United States—Handbooks, manuals, etc. | Libraries—United States—Gifts, legacies—Handbooks, manuals, etc. | Libraries and community—United States—Handbooks, manuals, etc.
Classification: LCC Z681.7.U5 T83 2024 (print) | LCC Z681.7.U5 (ebook) | DDC 021.7—dc23/eng/20240206
LC record available at https://lccn.loc.gov/2023059046
LC ebook record available at https://lccn.loc.gov/2023059047

Dedicated to all the members and leaders of library support groups, past and present, along with the generous philanthropists who have founded libraries, funded libraries, and continue to aid libraries now and into the future.

Contents

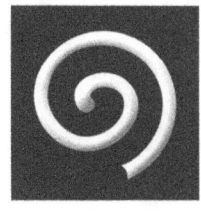

List of Figures ix

List of Appendices xi

Acknowledgments xiii

Introduction 1

CHAPTER 1 **Friends, Foundations, and Trusts: Roots, Purposes, and Envisioning the Future** 6

CHAPTER 2 **The Importance and Functions of School and Academic Library Support Groups** 26

CHAPTER 3 **Building or Revamping a Library Support Group** 36

CHAPTER 4 **Once a Friends of the Library, Foundation, or Trust Is Legally Established** 69

CHAPTER 5 **Righting Things That Go Wrong with and in Library Support Groups** 97

CHAPTER 6 **Virtual and Other Promotional Outreach for Library Support Groups** 111

CHAPTER 7 **Successful Member, Volunteer, and Donor Recruitment and Retention** 126

CHAPTER 8 **Fundraising for Library Support** 153

CHAPTER 9 **Additional Fundraising Ideas That Work!** 174

CHAPTER 10 **Donors: The Heart of Fundraising** 190

CHAPTER 11	**Library Support Groups Making Community Connections**	210
CHAPTER 12	**Library Support Groups Writing and Seeking Grants**	242
CHAPTER 13	**Distributing Funds to, Advocating for, and Otherwise Supporting Your Library**	252

Appendices	270
Selected Bibliography and Webliography	301
Webliography of Library Support Group Sample Websites	305
Index	309
About the Author	315

List of Figures

Figure 1.1. The Friends of the Poudre River Library in Fort Collins, Colorado, celebrate at the closing of a sold-out "grab bag" outdoor book sale in the parking lot of the Harmony Library branch in May 2020.   12

Figure 1.2. When the merger of the Friends of the Library and the Library Foundation was approved in Lawrence, Kansas, this graphic clearly depicted the benefits of the decision to combine into one group.   17

Figure 2.1. Student leaders are shown working at the 2017 Holiday Book Drive with assistance from the Barnes & Noble store agent.   30

Figure 2.2. Student leaders continued to carry the torch, raise the bar, and plan for the annual K is for Kids "From the Heart" teen fashion show for several years after Erin and Patrick Clawson entered college. Foundation founder and executive director Karen D. Clawson is at the far left, and her education partner and Barron Collier High School business teacher is at the far right.   31

Figure 6.1. The Friends of the Knox County Public Library's 2023 logo. For variety, there are also other versions: a dark blue, a lighter blue, and an outline version.   113

Figure 7.1. The Strategies for Youth Engagement graphic shows the various ways that youth involvement and leadership can make a difference.   130

Figure 7.2. Bumpers & Books, a literary trunk-or-treat created by the Junior Friends of the Groton Library, hosts over 500 people annually to see book-/author-themed cars. Here are a grandma and grandson, a Friend and Junior Friend, receiving the state award for Best Project from the Friends of Connecticut Libraries.   132

Figure 7.3. The graphic from the Junior Friends of the Library Penny Drive. 134

Figure 7.4. Two members of the Junior Friends of the Groton Public Library, Sabine Balentine (left) and Katie Houghton (right), wrap pennies donated during their Penny Drive fundraiser. 134

Figure 8.1. The Poudre River Friends of the Library in Colorado created a flowchart of their sorting and distribution process. Such a resource can be a valuable aid for those working with a library support organization's donation, sorting, and selling procedures. 162

Figure 8.2. One of the Friends of the Knox County Public Library book sales is held at Hi-Wire Brewing. 167

Figure 9.1. Plastic flamingos grace the lawn of a Flockin' Flamingos "victim" during the special fundraising event held by the Friends of the Austin Public Library in Minnesota. 175

Figure 9.2. At Party in the Stacks, one group posed in storybook princesses–inspired costumes. 184

Figure 9.3. Party guests mingle and enjoy food at Party in the Stacks 2022. The *Wizard of Oz* yellow brick road leads guests to the Emerald City décor. 184

Figure 9.4. Novel Tea flyer. 186

Figure 9.5. At the Novel Tea, community organizations pay to set tables according to that year's tea theme, a creative and fun element. 186

Figure 11.1. The Children's Book Festival poster promoting the event sponsored by the Atlanta-Fulton Public Library Foundation in Georgia is appealing and inviting. 219

Figure 12.1. Members of the Friends of the Knox County Public Library in Tennessee dressed up as characters from the book, *Little Blue Truck's Christmas* by Alice Schertle, for the station WIVK downtown Christmas Parade in December 2022. 248

List of Appendices

APPENDIX A — 270
Annotated Bylaws: What Should Be Included in Bylaws for Friends Organizations?
Compiled and written by Lisa C. Wemett. September 18, 2021. All rights reserved. Used with permission
Friends of Libraries Section, New York Library Association, Guilderland, New York

APPENDIX B — 275
Bylaws
Friends of the Weathersfield Proctor Library, Weathersfield, Vermont
Created January 30, 2006, most recent revision July 2015

APPENDIX C — 279
Board Member Position Description
The Friends of the Milford Public Library, Milford, Connecticut
Approved by the Board August 27, 2021

APPENDIX D — 281
Board of Directors Candidate Consideration Form
Friends of the Knox County Public Library, Knoxville, Tennessee

APPENDIX E — 283
The Ethical Dozen for Friends of the Library
Friends of Tennessee Libraries, Knoxville, Tennessee
www.friendstnlibraries.org
Adopted September 18, 2015

APPENDIX F — 285
Brochure and Membership Application
Junior Friends of the Library
Groton Public Library, Groton, Connecticut

APPENDIX G 288
Information and Membership Application
Junior Friends of the Uniondale Public Library
Sponsored by the Friends of the Uniondale Public Library, Uniondale,
   New York

APPENDIX H 290
Information Brochure and Membership Application
Friends of the St. Clair Shores Public Library, St. Clair Shores, Michigan

APPENDIX I 293
Information Brochure and Membership Application
Friends of the State Library and Archives of Florida
Florida Department of State, Tallahassee, Florida

APPENDIX J 296
Friends of the Library Used Book Sale Guidelines
Poudre River Friends of the Library, Fort Collins, Colorado
Revised April 2023

APPENDIX K 299
Brew & Bee Spelling Bee Program Instructions
Huntsville-Madison County Library Foundation, Huntsville, Alabama

Acknowledgments

This book could not have been written without the generous responses I received from library support groups, libraries, and related others around the country. Thanks to everyone who gave me permission to bring into play big and small ideas, information, quotes, photos, graphics, brochures, guidelines, and more, which they put to use within their own libraries and library support groups: Lauren Baas; Kimmerle Balentine and Sabine Balentine; Amanda Borgia; Mary Lou Britton; Jennifer Burgess; Elizabeth Carlton; Melissa Carroll; Julie Clark; Karen Clawsen and the former K is for Kids Foundation; Bethany D. and daughter Emily D.; Kathie Dooley-Smith; Robin Easter of Robin Easter Design; Adam Fletcher and The Freechild Institute for Youth Engagement; Lisa Fuller; Robin Gard; Monica Gavin; Jason Groendyk; Angela Houghton and Katie Houghton; Sarah Jacque and Abby and Andrew Jacque; Pamela Kempworth; Diane LaPierre; Terry Larson; Maggie McDonald; Beth McLacklin and Maisie McLacklan-Post; Mallory Nygard; Katy O'Neill; Onostasha Parfitt; Pam Pilla; Brooke Rawlins; Mark Richardson; Sheila A. Sullivan; Ariana Thomas of Flylight Creative; Robert Topolski; Virgie Townsend; Barbara Walton; Lisa Wemett; and Samantha Ye.

In addition to those named above, special gratitude is extended to the following libraries and library support groups: Atlanta-Fulton Public Library Foundation; Austin (MN) Friends of the Library; Denver Public Library Friends Foundation; Junior Friends of the Groton Public Library; Huntley Area Public Library Friends Foundation; Huntsville-Madison County Library Foundation; Friends and Foundation of the Lawrence Public Library; Friends of the Milford Public Library; Friends of Libraries Section, New York Library Association; Friends of the Olathe Public Library; Junior Friends of the Joseph H. Plumb Memorial Library; Poudre River Friends of the Library; Friends of the Knox County Public Library; Rancho Bernardo High School Friends of the Library; Friends of Tennessee Libraries; and Friends of the Weathersfield Proctor Library and Library Fundraising Committee.

As you can see, there are many people who responded to my inquiries and sent me details on how they do things successfully with their library support groups. I tried my best to include everyone here to whom I wanted to express appreciation, but please accept my sincere apology if I inadvertently left anyone or any organization out.

Again, thanks so much to everyone who helped me to make this book the best and most useful resource that I could.

—Diane Tuccillo

Introduction

IN 2005, I TOOK AN EARLY RETIREMENT PACKAGE offered at the City of Mesa Library in Arizona, where I had worked as young adult coordinator for twenty-five years. I began doing freelance workshops at libraries around the country on developing teen-participation programs, and I started teaching library-science courses virtually. I also decided to stay on at the library as a volunteer to help with certain teen-participatory library programs, and I joined the Friends of the Library. Additionally, I was elected to the Friends of the Library Board of Directors. I did all this for two years before moving to Colorado and being hired as a teen services librarian at the Poudre River Public Library District, which I did for ten more years.

During my time in the latter capacity, I often worked closely with the Poudre River Friends of the Library Board. I partnered with the Friends to recruit teenagers from our teen library advisory group to assist with book sales, promotional events, and advocacy. I also coordinated the selection of a teen from the group to serve on the Friends board as a teen representative. In turn, the Friends were very generous in providing funding each year for ten teens and two librarians to attend the Colorado Teen Literature Conference. This was in addition to the other special library programs and activities they supported monetarily for children, teens, and adults in our community, including author visits and music programs.

When I finally took actual retirement, the first thing I did was join the Poudre River Friends of the Library. Soon, I was nominated and elected to the group's board of directors. Our meetings included members of our board, plus the library director or other administrator; a representative from the library's board of trustees; and a representative from the Poudre River Library Trust. My participation helped me to learn a great deal about how the Friends function, the role of the Trust, the differences between Friends and trusts or foundations, and how these support organizations effectively partner with the libraries to which they are dedicated. To enhance my knowledge, I also joined the United for Libraries division through my lifetime personal membership in the American Library Association.

I served on the Poudre River Friends of the Library Board for three and a half years before recently moving to Tennessee. Once settled in our new home, I joined the Knox County Friends of the Library and immediately became involved.

Throughout all these years, I learned more and more about Friends, foundations, trusts, and their essential roles in making libraries vibrant, meaningful, and inviting places. I learned that their functions are not only monetary, but also as active, hands-on participants in the process of serving a community. Although these support groups are separate entities from the libraries they serve, their existence makes the libraries themselves more inviting and robust community centers.

Since I had already written five professional library resource books, I felt ready to write another that would cover the depth and breadth of library support groups, resulting in this book. It was written to help such groups hoping to pinpoint and expand their purpose; to revamp and improve their organization; to discover new and important ways to extend their support and advocacy; to ensure that their group is functioning at the best level possible; and more. Its particular focus is in being a useful tool for small, medium, and large public library support groups; for academic library support groups; and for various special and other library centers of support.

I also wanted to provide a resource for libraries that do not have a Friends group, foundation, or trust and wish to encourage local citizens eager to start these kinds of partnerships. In addition, university students of information and library science who need to learn about this vital facet of library-related work can discover a wealth of information here to aid in their future careers.

The elements of background, planning, operating, evaluating, enhancing, and maintaining library support groups, their purposes, and their activities are broken into sections for easy access as needed. However, it will be useful to read the entire book straight through to understand the information and concepts in order to consider, apply, and adapt them to individual library settings. There are focus boxes and testimonials that provide valuable background and details that enhance the content of each chapter and segment.

You will notice as you are reading that there are myriad ways that library support groups can be formed, adopted, adapted, and function. As you might consider ways to relate the information you encounter to your current group or a group ready to be founded, remember that you, your partners, and your stakeholders will need to decide exactly what approaches to take and how to integrate them with your own particular organization and locale. The ideas and examples given will provide a starting point. However, the myriad of further information about many of the topics that are addressed prohibits complete discussion and details about some of the suggested and useful auxiliary resources mentioned. If you find you want to delve deeper into any of them, web addresses are included in chapter endnotes, along with a selected bibliography and two webliographies at the end of the book.

The book begins with some background and history of library philanthropy and the growth of support groups. I am a firm believer that people cannot move forward in any undertaking without understanding from where they have come. This is as true for library support groups as it is with other significant endeavors. The foundational information you discover in the beginning of the first chapter bridges to discussions about the various types, formats, and functions of public library support groups. Finally, it concludes with information about the American Library Association division, United for Libraries, which is an indispensible auxiliary resource with which you will want to engage and refer to as your library support group starts off and/or moves in new directions.

The second chapter delves into the value and purpose of Friends of the Library and other support groups for elementary schools, secondary schools, and colleges/universities. These kinds of groups are rather uncommon, and it would behoove readers to consider how they might encourage the establishment of such organizations in their educational communities where no supplementary library support exists or to build up support that already may exist.

The third chapter addresses the creation and development of library support groups; the value and importance of mission, vision, other organizational planning steps to take; necessary documents to generate; and procedures to establish in order to demonstrate purpose, to describe policies, and to meet goals and expectations. From this point, the ways and means for Friends of the Library groups, library foundations, and library trusts to effectively organize themselves into cohesive units that meet the needs of their particular partner libraries or library systems, whether public, academic, special, state, or county, are discussed. You will also find guidelines for creating bylaws, which are *the* fundamental documents to get nonprofit organizations legally approved and which serve as a go-to tool for governance; coverage of the legal considerations and tax-exempt status requirements for nonprofit library support groups, including general information and advice; and further valuable considerations for launching new groups or enhancing already-existing ones.

In the fourth chapter, there is information on how to proceed once your nonprofit group is legally established. You will find job descriptions for all levels of library board members and leaders, from executive directors to committee chairs to teen or junior members. The process of approaching and designing a compatible and meaningful partnership with the library organization that is being served is also addressed in this chapter. Particular attention is given to strategic planning and key elements of budgeting and other nonprofit financial concerns.

In the fifth chapter, there are recommendations on how to handle challenging issues in library support nonprofits. These include dealing with group membership and participation decline and the possibility of group dissolution; having two factions, a Friends and a foundation or trust or a library support group and its beneficiary library that are in conflict with each other; conflict between members; and moving forward when a board or other significant resignation or forced dismissal may potentially occur or has been confirmed.

Because a Friends group, foundation, or trust is only valuable when it is carefully run and organized, chapter 6 addresses the development of a well-managed and viable social media presence; creating an active, ongoing marketing campaign to promote the group and help raise funds; addressing the recruitment and retention of wide age ranges of members, volunteers, and those serving on boards; and reaching out to potential donors and setting up methods to receive donations.

Chapter 7 is particularly relevant in concentrating on how to move groups forward positively into a contemporary library future. This means making sure to encourage participation from all age levels. When teens and even children are invited to pitch in and play significant roles, our reach is expanding to a lively and vibrant group of participants who can steer library support groups to what is new and current; who can encourage more youth to partake in library offerings; who will most likely grow into adulthood supporting, patronizing, and being involved in their libraries; and who will pass on a dedication to libraries, books, and reading to their offspring. Likewise, finding ways to include younger adults in the mix with retired folks is essential.

In this chapter, you will also be considering how, besides recruiting official members of all ages, library support groups will also do well to encourage an assortment of partnerships with clubs, organizations, and agencies that can contribute time and team efforts to their causes. And lastly, because recognition is such a strong motivator for retention, the chapter ends with ideas for special and ongoing methods of recognizing, thanking, and rewarding everyday members and partners—especially those who come through when they say they will and when they go above and beyond.

Although membership and activities are important, one of the primary reason Friends, foundations, and trusts exist and have existed is to raise funds for the libraries they support. We are all familiar with the traditional book sales, annual donation solicitations, and special events that these support groups sponsor to build up those funds. However, there are many other ways that today's groups can incorporate new and innovative methods and means to gain funds for their libraries, and chapters 8 and 9 present successful ways to employ traditional old standbys plus implement lesser-known fresh, creative, and even unexpected approaches.

Following that topic of fundraising, chapter 10 centers on donors as the heart of fundraising. This chapter addresses donor management and donor relationships; electronic giving to supplement traditional methods; capital funding campaigns; crowdsourcing; and auxiliary sources for donations.

Chapter 11 focuses on other ways groups can give library support, develop community connections, and engage in outreach activities. In addition to seeking funds for their libraries, groups can also contribute by boosting the pool of volunteers available to help their libraries; bringing author and other programs to their communities; partnering with schools, businesses, and other agencies for special programs and events; and helping to coordinate and run special reading activities.

Moving on, chapter 12 zeroes in on grants as a significant source of funding. Library support groups can do well by applying for, receiving, and putting grants into action to support their libraries. This chapter explores the many ways groups can discover suitable available grants; gives advice on creating an effective grant proposal; shows how to employ grant money received to aid the libraries being served; outlines the process of documenting grant progress and fulfillment; and explains the steps in navigating grantor reporting requirements.

After this, in chapter 13, there is advice on designing and implementing equitable and meaningful ways of distributing funds to libraries. This includes receiving library funding requests and wish lists; deciding what monetary support the nonprofit organization will be able to approve or must deny; setting a budget together with the library; and receiving feedback and follow up from the library after funds are given and put to use. There is also information on advocating for and raising public awareness about libraries in various manners; participating in special community events that can highlight libraries and their support organizations; participating in "library giving days" and other library appreciation activities; and, in turn, receiving appreciation from libraries.

At the end of the book, in the appendixes, you will find some examples of documents from successful organizations that can be emulated or adapted. To investigate further, once again, you are encouraged to examine the recommended related sources noted throughout the book in the textboxes and other areas by using the website titles for keyword online searching and the web links that are provided in each chapter's endnotes. You can also peruse and use the selected bibliography and two webliographies provided. Lastly, an index is included for locating or relocating various topics in the book as needed.

My hope is that this book will benefit those dedicated community members who institute, join, and participate in library support groups and that the knowledge gained will make those groups stronger and more effective. I also hope libraries that are the beneficiaries of group contributions will find the information useful as they develop solid working relationships and camaraderie with the dedicated support group members who truly care about doing their part to promote and build positive outcomes for them. Even though every library and library support group is unique and each must tailor their focus and approach to what works for their own particular community and organizational model, this book will provide direction, advice, inspiration, and motivation to adapt to their needs and make their relationships the best they can be to the benefit of all their library clientele.

I am a lifelong reader, library user, library supporter, and forever librarian. In my roles with library support groups as part of my professional mix, I learned and am learning a great deal about the extreme value of successful and hardworking library nonprofit support groups. However, I learned so much more as I researched widely for this book; heard from many wonderful, dedicated voices; and discovered myriad library support options from near and far that were new to me. My sincere wish is to pass on through these pages many of their examples, what I have witnessed and put into practice myself, and the wisdom others have bestowed upon me to keep library Friends, foundations, and trusts robustly moving into the future.

—Diane P. Tuccillo

CHAPTER 1

Friends, Foundations, and Trusts

Roots, Purposes, and Envisioning the Future

EVERY LIBRARY IN WHICH I HAVE WORKED and almost every library I have visited throughout my life has been the recipient of generous contributions in one way or another of library philanthropists. There was always a Friends of the Library group, a library trust, or a foundation raising funds behind the scenes, providing an impressive array of library programs, activities, special events, capital projects, collection additions, and much more. Every year, in the libraries where I was employed, the library staff had a long wish list of items and causes we dreamed of having funded, and even in the lean years, somehow at least part of each wish list was granted. It amazed me how community volunteers rallied time and time again to find the money to allow the libraries to have the ability to provide a high caliber of offerings beyond what a basic library budget could afford.

Now that I am participating in a Friends of the Library group for a third time and serving on the board of directors, in a third state, after having served on the boards of directors for two previous ones, and I have gotten to know and work with those who bolster the second library through a trust in addition to the Friends, my appreciation for library support groups has soared to a much higher level. What a meaningful, caring, and essential purpose these organizations serve! At the same time, I learned that these groups didn't always exist; that there are communities where they still do not; that the groups in some communities face obstacles and conflicts that keep them from being as effective as they could be; and that many groups suffer from the "aging out" of longtime members and need to encourage younger people to join in and step up.

I also discovered that, even though my library support group experience includes Friends and trust members partnering and connecting with one another as separate entities, some libraries have combined the two kinds of groups. Because of such combinations, this chapter will examine individual kinds of groups as well as those working in tandem.

To start off, though, I will briefly examine how these philanthropic library groups came to be. As I said in my introduction, I believe it is important to know some basic details about the origins of support groups to figure out how to move upward and onward from the groundwork they created. After I consider the roots of library support groups, I will begin to explore the many aspects and considerations of such groups that can make them well-planned, organized, and highly functioning. At the same time, it is important to remember that every group and every library is unique and that all support groups and libraries must devise their own organizational and partnering methods to target the needs of their particular communities.

How Library Support Came to Be

Before I consider the present and future ways of organizing and running a library support group, let us explore the value of their existence and take a look back at how such philanthropic efforts came to be. Although libraries receive financial support for annual budgets from sources such as local taxes or government-funded grants, in most cases budgets supply the minimal requirements to keep a library afloat. In order for any library—public, academic, or special—to provide a higher standard of collections, services, or facilities that communities hope for and often expect, additional monetary and other support is usually needed. Here is where Friends, foundations, and trusts come into play.

Many people, even some people who work in libraries, believe that the only role of these support groups is to supply additional funding. However, besides providing this funding, these groups can do much more. Simply having an active library support group or groups involved that boost a library's offerings and operations makes it more feasible for libraries to be awarded grant money. Friends groups can also supply volunteers and chairpersons for library programs and activities, purposes beyond funding. Furthermore, in a world where government officials and bureaucrats frequently seem to view libraries as archaic institutions that may no longer be necessary, library support groups stand up for them. Their advocacy as citizen volunteers adds power to that of library administrators as they are justifying their libraries' survival. It also promotes libraries to a general public that might not be aware of what their libraries can do for them. As representatives from that public and members of separate yet supportive entities from the library institutes themselves, their presence is influential.[1]

If you are curious about how and why such library support groups began in the first place, there is actually interesting history surrounding the formation and development of them. The histories of libraries along with the individual and group supportive contributions that created them, molded them, and helped them grow and flourish are inspiring and offer examples from which modern libraries and donors can learn.

The Establishment of Free Public Libraries

In the United States, the first libraries were subscription libraries, where patrons paid a fee to use them. The first was the Library Company of Philadelphia, which was started by Benjamin Franklin in 1731, and the second was the New York Society Library, which began in 1754.[2] When anyone thinks about today's *free* libraries, however, people usually identify them as tax-supported institutions that are provided at no charge to anyone patronizing them. Because libraries have been in existence in one form or another for centuries and extensive historical background would be exhaustive, my consideration of the topic will generally be limited to this latter definition.

In that light, the first such free institution was the one established as the Peterborough Town Library in New Hampshire in 1833. This town has a remarkable library history. It actually started its first library for members in the 1790s until the collection was literally worn out, discarded, or sold by 1830. In 1827, before its demise, a new Unitarian minister noticed the community need for a library serving everyone, of any age, and not just those who could afford the dues. On April 9, 1833, at the Peterborough town meeting, a free, tax-supported public library was proposed and approved, making it the first in the nation. Through the years, its location migrated from a general store, to the post office, to a pharmacy. By 1890, the need for a building became urgent, and citizens wanted to raise funds. Through the generous donations that were given, the actual library building was finally opened in 1893.[3]

As decades went on and the library progressed through and into the subsequent centuries, an active Friends of the Library group that was formed in 1979 was eventually followed in 2011 by the 1833 Society, a nonprofit trust, in partnership with the library trustees. Fundraising and seeking donors began in earnest to renovate, renew, and modernize their wonderful, historic library, which celebrated its grand reopening in September 2021.[4] This shows that, with the right support system in place, even a community of about 6,400 people can build up and have access to an outstanding library.

Returning to the time of the Peterborough Town Library's founding, consider that the second free public library did not appear until twenty-two years later, when the Boston Public Library was established by merchant Joshua Bates. Bates donated fifty thousand dollars to create a library that would, according to his wishes, fit up to 150 patrons at desks and that would be absolutely free.[5] Today, extending from that initial contribution, private philanthropy continues to greatly enhance what this large city library can offer to library users. This is accomplished via several support groups: the Boston Public Library Fund; the City-Wide Friends of the Library and affiliated groups in all its branches; the Associates of the Boston Public Library, which funds the conservation of special collections; and the Norman B. Leventhal Map & Education Center, which, as an independent nonprofit, supports its geographically oriented collection and promotes it to students and the general public.[6]

From these original roots, soon free public libraries in the United States were widespread, even though they often lacked dedicated buildings, as you can see through the early evolution of the Peterborough Town Library. They occupied spaces in unique varieties of places, among them city halls, old houses, spare rooms in stores, a ladies' restroom, a fire station horse barn, or a doctor's waiting room. As long as an available area existed, people had claimed them as library space.[7] Library access in these settings was, as you can imagine, way less than ideal, and again, as in the Peterborough example, donor advocates were needed to break the mold.

Library Philanthropy Grows and Flourishes

The New York Public Library provides one of the most outstanding and unique illustrations of philanthropic contributions making an immense difference in the world of free-to-the-public libraries. It was, and still is to this day, not operated under the auspices of the City of New York, but rather it remains a private, non-government nonprofit owned by the Astor, Lenox, and Tilden foundations. The generosity of the three richest men in New York—John Jacob Astor, James Lenox, and Samuel Tilden—provided the funds to build the first New York City library in 1854. Many additional city libraries followed, and the creative giving of the library system's founders inspired many other donors to fund important projects through the years to the present day.[8]

George Peabody, Enoch Pratt, and Andrew Carnegie also took up the cause of funding and creating public libraries starting in the 1850s. The most widely known advocate became Carnegie, when he stepped forward in 1886 to donate support. He required official requests from mayors, or sometimes city and town councils, that needed to include pledges of tax and building site assurances from the officials to gain approval.[9]

Carnegie personally offered these grants until 1911, when the Carnegie Corporation assumed the role. His gifts totaled $56,162,622 and paid for 2,509 libraries in English-speaking countries, of which 1,697 were constructed in 1,412 towns and cities in the United States, amounting to more than half of all American public library buildings by the time the final grant was given in 1919. As communities far and wide began to seriously depend upon public libraries, patrons were soon accustomed to taking the facilities and services for granted, and their expectations grew. Clearly, there became a need for more and more supplementary funding to satisfy library patron demands.[10] Luckily, there were additional people who stepped forward to take the reins at developing sources for that funding. Today, libraries and their users and supporters are the beneficiaries of the examples set by these early groundbreakers, leading to the development of the initial Friends of the Library organizations.

Every Library Needs Friends

The first organization to dub itself a library "Friends group" was started in France in 1913. However, looking forward in time and toward the United States, the first "Friends of the Library" group was begun in 1922 in Glen Ellyn, Illinois. Its first president was Mrs. Al Chase, and she led the new members as they raised money to buy books for the library by collecting $365 in dues. Later in 1922, another Friends group was established in Syracuse, New York.[11] This group may have been formed after taking note of the Illinois group.

Academic libraries also have needed and need Friends and other fundraising organizations for support and to serve as advocates. Quite a few college and university libraries today have Friends groups to help with special causes and activities, with the first-known such organization started in 1925 at Harvard University.[12] We'll be looking more closely at these kinds of library support groups later in this book. However, for now, there is another serious academically oriented concern to consider.

For years, libraries that serve younger students in schools have frequently lagged behind public libraries and those libraries supporting higher education facilities. Parent-Teacher Associations (PTAs) and similar support groups have traditionally tried to raise funds to help school libraries, but they prove to come up short when the funds gained must be shared with other "special" school functions like art and music. Unfortunately, school libraries are also regularly viewed as "non-essential," and administrators too frequently target them for staffing and budget cuts while allotting them a smaller share of the donation pie. Because PTAs must spread their advocacy between several school special functions, school libraries truly do need more well-organized Friends of the Library support groups to keep them strong by aiding them expressly and to highlight their value.[13] Further along in this book, I will discuss the prospects for making this happen.

In the meantime, I will take a look at the different kinds of library support nonprofits that are available overall and the best ways for them to organize and function.

Purposes of the Different Kinds of Groups

A key feature of successful, dedicated library support groups today is developing attuned, well-defined processes for partnering with their library organizations. Solid relationships that function with respect and good communication add value to libraries and to support groups themselves. Let us consider the central kinds of library support groups, their purposes, ways the groups can partner, and perhaps how and why they might merge while I connect descriptive examples to the options available in various settings and circumstances.

TEXTBOX 1.1

POUDRE RIVER FRIENDS OF THE LIBRARY

You will notice throughout the upcoming chapters and sections of this book where it mentions that you will need to consult legal counsel. In those cases, when you realize your organization needs to do this, you may wish to hire an attorney; you may have access to the attorney that works for your city or library; or you may know a local legal expert who has agreed to assist you for a nominal charge or without a fee. However, if none of those options is available, you may still be able to get pro bono assistance for your library support group at any stage of its formation or existence.

There are several ways you can find these kinds of free legal services through online resources offering help for nonprofits. You may be able to get pro bono legal assistance through such agencies as the TrustLaw program of the Thomson Reuters Foundation[1] or the National Council of Nonprofits.[2] In addition, the Lawyers Alliance of New York participates in an extended provider network of business and transactional legal services for nonprofit organizations around the United States. They supply an ever-growing and evolving list of contacts for pro bono nonprofit providers in various states and regions via their website.[3]

As you encounter information where legal guidance is recommended, you may wish to refer to these resources.

Notes

1. Nonprofit Management. July 8, 2022. "Get the Pro Bono Help You Need through TrustLaw," Taproot Foundation, https://taprootfoundation.org/get-the-legal-pro-bono-help-you-need-through-trustlaw/.
2. National Council of Nonprofits. 2023. "Pro Bono and Skilled Volunteers," https://www.councilofnonprofits.org/tools-resources/pro-bono-and-skilled-volunteers.
3. Lawyers Alliance for New York. 2023. "Pro Bono Providers Nationwide," https://lawyersalliance.org/providers-nationwide.

Friends of the Library Groups

The most well-known library support organizations are Friends of the Library groups, and there is a great chance that you already know what Friends groups are. Or do you? If you think that Friends just have book sales to raise money, think again. You might be surprised at the variety of accomplishments Friends groups can achieve! If you already have a group in your community, you might think about adding a few (or many!) of the options mentioned in this book that are not yet being put into play. If you are founding a group, you will want to consider all the ways that yours can be most effective by starting small and adding more options for group contributions and activities as you go.

To begin, here is a basic definition. Friends of the Library groups are nonprofit public charities that have members who are usually from a library's local community and serve as important library advocates. They complete a form and pay dues to join (although, at times, some Friends do not require dues, perhaps in areas struggling with economic issues or in the case of youth or "junior" members).

The main focus of the Friends is to raise money for a library to help build its collection or to offer funding for special library programs and events. Most of the time, groups have several officers—a president, vice president, treasurer, secretary, and additional members who serve with them on the board of directors, lead sub-groups as needed, and sometimes are tasked to be "officers in training" for when current officers complete their terms. The board works with the regular, non-board members to support the library in reaching a diverse audience through their dues; through donations of time, materials, and money; through fundraising projects, and even by securing small grants. Friends are completely independent entities from the libraries they serve, working as partners and not as employees. They sometimes receive perks and special honors for monetary contributions and essential roles they undertake.

As noted, Friends of the Library groups are historically very well-known for running book sales to raise funds. Sales can be annual, monthly, several times a year, special (such as a mystery book sale, a children's book sale, or a grab bag sale), or ongoing (such as via a library year-round book shop, a self-serve book sale display, or online). Books (and audio-visuals, though interest in buying these is waning in the public eye due to increasing personal electronic access) for sale are donated by the community or are given to the Friends by the library after they have been withdrawn from the collection. At this point, print books are still popular and in great demand, and used book sales remain quite profitable.

Friends are in charge of sorting the books and materials, pricing them, advertising sales, holding the sales, and dealing with other selling opportunities. Friends sale activities might also feature handmade items of interest to the public in addition to books, such as magnets, special bookmarks, and other money-makers, and sometimes they plan and run special fundraising activities in addition to the sales, for instance a gala after-hours library event with paid admission.

There are also Friends groups that go beyond those basic money-raising support modes. They may contact government officials, alert the local citizens about library issues, or promote supportive voting for library-targeted tax levies (which they can do within certain limits, unlike library employees). They can also make sure citizens know about what the library can do for them. Also, at times, Friends members may serve as library volunteers during programs and events like storytimes, author visits, summer reading challenges, marching in parades, and more. Because most Friends groups collaborate well

Figure 1.1. The Friends of the Poudre River Library in Fort Collins, Colorado, celebrate at the closing of a sold-out "grab bag" outdoor book sale in the parking lot of the Harmony Library branch in May 2020. *Credit: Jason Groendyk.*

with their library, staff members usually feel comfortable requesting funds for wish list materials and program offerings.

At times, Friends of the Library may write and publish an informative newsletter to bring attention to their activities and those happening in the library. Such newsletters also promote the library itself, provide Friends membership information, announce opportunities to help, and serve as public-relations tools so governmental officials and citizens alike can see and understand the value of the library to the community it serves.[14] In addition, Friends keep up with social media and have accounts for communication and advertising via the many platforms available while also regularly connecting for additional publicity opportunities with local newspapers, radio stations, and other promotional means.

Friends of the Library groups are dedicated to the library, library system, or network of regional libraries where the nonprofit is located. Depending on how the particular library or library system is set up, Friends can be town- or city-oriented, be county-oriented, or support libraries in all levels of academic settings. They can even be organized in support of a joint-use library/school facility, as in the case of the Gladstone School & Public Library in Michigan, where the school district operates the public library.[15] Many states also have state-oriented Friends and related kinds of library support agencies that are organized and function in various ways to assist groups throughout widespread locations.

Ordinarily, most Friends of the Library groups are founded to support a library in a particular community. There are several important steps to follow in forming such a Friends group:

- Hiring an attorney, finding out if the library's attorney can provide assistance, or, as noted earlier in this chapter, finding someone who may be willing to provide attorney services without charge.
- Convening a central group of Friends members to serve as the executive team or board who will be taking on the primary responsibilities of administrative work and strategic planning.
- Creating a joint operating agreement between the Friends of the Library and the library administration that carefully describes respective roles and positions of authority.
- Development of mission and vision statements, statements of purpose, other desired codes and policies, and determining priorities for service.
- Structuring a group formation/operation plan that includes whatever committees, task forces, or special assignments that will help the group accomplish its ongoing and yearly goals, including the development of an effective online presence.
- Constructing bylaws to provide group guidelines, establish the group as a 501(c)(3) tax-free organization, and allow legal acceptance of tax-deductible contributions.
- Having the attorney ensure that the correct documentation is completed for and receives approval by a group's particular state.
- Building a dues structure with any necessary exceptions for special circumstances.
- Setting a plan for membership recruitment and organizational publicity and promotion.[16]

Library Foundations

In addition to Friends groups or instead of them, libraries may have foundations offering library support. As a public charity, such a foundation is a nonprofit devoted to the altruistic purpose of supporting and addressing a library's unmet funding needs. The cash and other assets donated to fund the foundation can come from an individual, from a family, or through a business contribution, and it is tax-deductible. Once the foundation receives the assets, they no longer belong to the contributors and can be used to assist the designated library.

A foundation's legal organizational document lays out the purpose and intended activities of the foundation. Foundations need to be created with the help and expertise of a knowledgeable legal professional, which, as with Friends groups, may be hired or secured by less-costly means as previously indicated. The policies and procedures for creating a foundation, as well as the necessary documentation to become an official charitable organization, will vary state by state, and it is essential to learn the requirements for your particular state. The legal professional you consult and work with will be able to help you with the necessary vital steps. Your state library, state Friends organization (if there is one), or other related agency may also be able to give you good advice on getting started.

Once a library foundation targets the library as the nonprofit it legally serves, it uses its assets for the library's benefit. This may be to fund projects and satisfy other requests it receives from the library. The foundation may also propose a project it would like to fund to see if the library would consider accepting the offer.

Most of the time, donors give a sum of money to be used for what the library and foundation envision as the largest need, though at other times donors ask to have their money earmarked for a specific project or need they would like to support. A board of directors is in charge of overseeing the foundation and deciding which projects to fund with the assets it has available.

Since foundations that fund libraries are recognized by the Internal Revenue Service as public charitable organizations under the 501(c) (3) chapter of the tax code, they are exempt from federal income taxes. They are also usually permitted exemptions from excise taxes on net income from their investments since they are designated a public charity, but each foundation needs to check with its legal authority to ensure they are adhering to the rules on this matter. Both individuals and corporations can receive tax deductions by contributing to a library foundation.[17]

In order for a library foundation to succeed in its work on behalf of a library, it depends upon several factors, including:

- A clear mission and goals that mesh with those of the library it supports
- An open and mutually accommodating partnership between the foundation leader, the director, and other administrators of the library, as well as rapport with any Friends or other library support group that exists
- The ability to build strong organizational, business, community, and philanthropic connections that will glean financial donations in support of the library
- The foundation's director having a personal commitment to fulfilling the library's mission and vision and the ability to work well with other members of the board
- Extensive knowledge and background experience in fundraising and philanthropy[18]
- A clear plan for an effective online presence and the expertise and technological equipment to make it a reality

Library Trusts

Similar to and sometimes managed as part of Friends of the Library groups or foundations, a charitable library trust is formed when a grantor(s) titles property and assets in the establishment of a fund to support a designated library or libraries. Charitable trusts that support libraries can be found in a range of formats and for various purposes. For example, in 1999, the Poudre River Library Trust, Inc. was founded in Fort Collins, Colorado, by a group of library devotees to support the Poudre River Public Library District. Trust board members, honorary board members, and a small group of other private citizens committed startup funds to establish the Trust.[19]

In another circumstance, the Livingston County Library Charitable Trust in Missouri was created in 2013 to support library services and programs beyond the capacities of county funding. Its volunteer Trust Board is comprised of Livingston County Library Board of Directors and additional appointed members. Initial funding for the Trust was provided by a generous lead donation from the Lillian DesMarias Trust. DesMarias served as the library's dedicated, progressive library director from 1970 to 1980 and passed away in 2012. Since its founding, the Trust has accepted continual donations and allocates funds for library programs, materials, services, and capital projects.[20]

Like these Trusts, there are many others that have been founded as specific library support organizations of particular libraries or library systems. Overall, in the world of finance, charitable trusts have existed longer and have been more widely used than foundations, though in the library world, foundations and Friends groups take the lead, sometimes incorporating a trust within their donor and fundraising systems. The various kinds of trusts hold an important place in helping to secure and strengthen libraries financially. As previously recommended, check with a legal advisor when a singular library trust is being created or integrated into a Friends of the Library's or library foundation's set of fundraising and donor options to ensure proper legal documentation.

Even university libraries can have trusts established specifically for their benefit. At the University of Pennsylvania, the Delta Chapter of the academic honor society Phi Beta Kappa founded a library trust in 1970 that has grown extensively through the years. It has been used to supply the university library with unrestricted funds for scholarly materials in any field and to acquire essential research resources for faculty and students.[21]

On another note, sometimes a charitable trust is established by an individual or group intending to meet the needs of numerous libraries in designated regions. Donations are not associated with one particular library or library system but are given to those in the targeted state or area with the most need. One example of this is the J. Frank Dobie Library Trust. It was created in 1964 when the well-known Texas author and folklorist passed away, leaving most of his estate to establish annual Trust grants to help fund book purchases in small Texas libraries.[22]

Under the auspices of the State Library, another is the Trust for Montana Libraries, which was started in 2019 to increase private support for all libraries, including providing electronic Geographic Information Service, giving Montanans access to high-quality information and library services.[23] These kinds of far-reaching trusts supplement and add value to those localized town, city, regional, or county trusts that are one of the primary focuses of this book.

Merging Library Support Groups

Although this organizational design is less common, there are more and more Friends groups and library foundations that have combined or have originally been created as one entity in order to offer their complementary approaches of library support efforts in tandem. Depending on the circumstances, such an arrangement can be viewed as a technique to foster improved coordination and more efficient fundraising. What follows here are several examples.

In 1940, the Denver Public Library Foundation was created as a nonprofit to provide an avenue for donors who value libraries to help maintain excellence in the library system.[24] In addition, the original Friends of the Library group focused on book sales to fundraise for library support. Through the years until the 1980s, the two groups sometimes experienced ups and at other times experienced downs in compatibly communicating with and relating to one another due to differing perspectives on the most effective ways to support the library. To settle the differences, in the 1980s the two groups merged to present a united front to the community, to support the whole library, and to coordinate donor contacts and activity. At this point, the group was re-formed into one, the Denver Public Library Friends Foundation. Still, it took some more time for the two groups to repeatedly work effectively as a united team and in partnership with the library. Thankfully, there was a successful solution, and today, the Friends Foundation is extremely well run and coordinated, working effectively with the library system and the community. This solution came about in 2012 through a formal memorandum of understanding (MOU) between the Friends Foundation and the library through which any conflicts or miscommunications that still existed were finally put to rest and roles and relationships were clarified.

The person who was instrumental in coordinating the MOU accord was Diane Lapierre, now the director of the Poudre River Public Library District, and who had served during this time period as the Denver Library's director of community relations and the director of the Friends Foundation. The agreement was a key factor in bringing everyone into alignment. The appointment of Jeff Riley, an experienced nonprofit development professional, helped cement this positive end result.[25]

As you can see, the aforementioned MOU was a vital dynamic in getting the Friends Foundation on steady ground. Note that an MOU is not an exclusive device for library Friends, foundations, and trusts, but to the organizational and business world in general, and it is not unique to large library systems and their supporters. It can be a valuable document in any size library setting for many good reasons, and it is especially useful when merging and coordinating take place. More detailed information about this helpful instrument for achieving workable agreements will be addressed in chapter 3.

Today, the Denver Public Library Friends Foundation is an outstanding example of a positive outcome from merging two library support groups with differing perspectives. They have a well-rounded organization that pays for myriad programs and activities that are funded by donors and manned by volunteers; earns money by running a bookshop and online selling operation; and sorts donated books. Besides raising money, volunteering, and serving on the Friends Foundation board, members advocate for the library to the government and in the community.[26]

As this example illustrates, having both library support group factions acting as a single entity can be accomplished successfully under the right conditions and under the direction and guidance of good leaders, even if it takes time. A merger might be an excellent way to remedy confusion, issues of concern, and conflicting goals, and to streamline support functions for the benefit of all.

The following story additionally affirms this point. In 2020, the Lawrence Public Library Friends and the Lawrence Public Library Foundation in Kansas merged for numerous good reasons, one of the most important being avoiding the duplication of efforts. After the decision was made to move forward, a library website announcement appeared so the public would be aware of what was underway:

> **The Lawrence Public Library Friends & Foundation have each voted in favor of merging. We are full steam ahead!** Following overwhelmingly affirmative votes from the Friends' membership and from the Foundation board, the merger steering committee is happy to announce that the merged Friends and Foundation organization will take effect January 1, 2020. The past several years of forging a close relationship through joint support of the library's Summer Reading and Read Across Lawrence programs, a shared donor database, and distribution of an annual fundraising mailer and quarterly newsletter has prepared the two organizations to come together stronger than ever.[27]

After the introductory announcement, clear and careful explanations were added, further spelling out the merger. After such important decisions, when donor contributions are involved, it is wise to enlighten the loyal public regarding the reasons for this kind of decision. The Lawrence Public Library Friends & Foundation did this splendidly with full transparency.

First, they posted an easy-to-read graphic that depicted the reasons for their decision to a tee. It showed what each organization had previously been doing on its own and illustrated the overlap that the merger eliminated. Then a straightforward explanation complemented the graphic to enhance reader understanding. The draft merger document,

FRIENDS + FOUNDATION

Fund Current Needs
Run an online store
Book Sales
Recycle Books
Donate Books

Receive Donations
Recruit volunteers
Advocate for LPL
Increase LPL visibility
Create a community of library supporters

Fund Future Needs
Write Grants
Caddy Stacks
After Hours
Planned Giving

Figure 1.2. When the merger of the Friends of the Library and the Library Foundation was approved in Lawrence, Kansas, this graphic clearly depicted the benefits of the decision to combine into one group. *Credit: Angela Hyde.*

which included the proposed bylaws, policies, and procedures of the newly merged group, was also linked on the page along with a place for public comments.[28]

The new Friends Foundation explained to the community that their optimistically positive decision was based on the following:

- Combining the groups allows for more efficient administration, with one board, one board meeting, one tax form, one audit, and one accounting system instead of two.
- The dual group message presents a stronger presence with combined newsletters and annual appeals for donations, avoiding duplication and resulting in increased donations.
- The new format eliminates donor and membership registration confusion, which avoids lengthy explanations about the differences between the two organizations and ill will with those who simply want to help their library.
- Funding goals remain the same, with book sale committee finances, fund choices for contributions, and cherished community programs and annual library needs continuing as they were.
- All donors who contribute money or volunteer hours to the library cause in any way receive invitations to special membership events without leaving anyone out.
- The creation of one restructured board gives representation to all factions of the Friends Foundation, with thirteen board members filling positions, which include one representative for each standing committee of Finance, Book Sales, Internet Sales, Membership, and Fundraising.[29]

The new Friends Foundation website is also streamlined for clarity and easy access. On a single page, readers can find links to many individual topics of their choice as they incorporate a list of upcoming Friends Foundation events, several selections for offering donations and support, how to become a volunteer, and a list of what exactly is being funded for and at the library.[30] The same thing goes for the Denver Public Library Friends Foundation's website, which also offers clear and easily accessible information about all aspects of their fundraising, donation options, volunteer opportunities, events, and the nonprofit's impact on the library and community.[31]

Another motivation for merging a Friends group with a library foundation is when the number of residents served by a community library substantially increases. This is the case with the Huntley Area Public Library Friends Foundation in Huntley, Illinois. Their library was built in 1989 when about four thousand people were being served by it, and recently the building size more than doubled to meet the needs of a population that has grown to around forty thousand. As far as outside library support, in the late 1980s, the original Friends group was started by local women in a book club who had a vision of having an actual library district for the community. Their dedication to reaching that goal through fundraising resulted in the district being formed.

Because the library was supportive of the Friends group from the beginning, they have since then always ensured that a library staff person would serve as a liaison. In 2010, the staff person filling that role was newly hired Pamela Kempworth. Kempworth was tasked with converting the Friends of the Library, a basic volunteer and fundraising group, to an official 501(c)(3) public charity Friends Foundation so the group would be able to apply for grants to support reading and programming at the library. She found a local attorney who helped with the necessary procedures and filings, the original Friends of the Library group disbanded, and the new Friends Foundation was formed. From the very start and through all the years since, the library's collaboration has continued and has positively affected Friends Foundation accomplishments with members serving as volunteers, fundraisers, and ambassadors for the library.

The Friends' efforts had gleaned two to five thousand dollars per year for the library in the 1990s to around sixty thousand dollars a year in recent years, with a target goal of reaching a million dollars annually. Some of the events that contribute to the goal now include in-library book sales, two-day book sales four times a year, a fundraising breakfast, Minilinks@thelibrary, Bauble & Bling (gently used jewelry and bling), the Giving Tuesday Campaigns, Holiday Basket Raffles, and local restaurant fundraisers—quite commendable fundraising activity for a library serving a still-smallish population.[32]

Another successful yet unique merger undertaking took place in Glendale, California, when the Friends of the Library merged with the Glendale Library Foundation to form the Glendale Library, Arts, & Culture Trust in 2020. This merger preserves the mission commitments of the two original organizations and incorporates overarching support for the Glendale Library, Arts & Cultural Department of the City of Glendale. The trust conducts fundraising, special events, and other volunteer efforts that are designed to enhance resources plus aid community programming at the Glendale Central Library, its six branches, and the city's Brand Library & Arts Center.[33]

If you already have a Friends of the Library organization as well as a foundation or trust, you may find it valuable to investigate a merger if it appears that doing so might benefit both groups and the library—and perhaps even tie in other aspects of the community. If you are about to embark on creating a library support group in the first place, you may want to consider using the Friends and Foundation or other models. Evidently, there can be many good reasons to do it, although it does ultimately depend on each individual library and community need.

TEXTBOX 1.2

ADVICE FROM A FRIENDS FOUNDATION'S LIBRARY LIAISON

Our Friends Foundation has benefited from library support. Every director has supported the group and this new model. Without that support, we would not be as successful as we are. I believe every good Friends group needs the support of the director and board to thrive. If that support is not present, I would start with developing those relationships first.

Next, maintain an updated membership and donor list. Our group has membership dues, which I know can be controversial. For us, memberships work as another way to raise money and maintain an active donor mailing list. As a fundraising organization, we try to keep it fun; we like to say we put the *FUN in FUNdraising*.

Another recommendation is to form a group of Friends from nearby libraries. Have meetings at the other libraries and share your ideas with each other. Our group has adopted fundraising ideas from other groups, which have included Holiday Basket Raffles, Minilinks@thelibrary, and auctions for decorated watering cans and boxes.[1]

Pamela Kempworth
Head of Programming and Outreach/Friends Foundation Liaison
Huntley Area Public Library, Huntley, Illinois

Notes

1. Pamela Kempworth.

Friends, Foundations, Trusts, and Libraries: Special Organizational Arrangements

In some communities, the Friends, a library foundation or a library trust, and the library itself function separately but arrange interconnections legally. Each unit of the cooperative enterprise is independent but also relies on the others to successfully achieve goals instead of operating as a merged group serving a library or library system together. This arrangement is an option that may be especially practical for large, widespread library service areas.

An illustration can be found in the Fort Vancouver Regional Library District in Washington State. The Fort Vancouver Regional Library Foundation is a registered nonprofit, public charity incorporated in the state. Its articles of incorporation and bylaws specifically limit its activities to projects supporting the library district, as is required for any library support nonprofit. The relationship between the two organizations is contractual, through which the foundation has agreed to solicit and manage donations on behalf of the library in return for administrative support.[34] However, there is also a network of Friends of the Library groups throughout the twelve library district branches, each with its own officers, bylaws, dues structure, meetings, and activities, for which the Foundation serves as an umbrella organization that provides technical assistance and administrative support.

The Foundation hosts an annual Friends recognition event, offers training on fundraising topics, serves as a resource on group operations, and assists Friends in completing state and federal nonprofit reporting requirements. This relationship allows each individual Friends group to be as effective as possible in supporting their designated local library branch. By supporting the Friends groups, the Foundation is in turn supporting the library district according to its legal documents of foundation.[35] It is a win-win-win venture for all, suiting the particular needs of this community area.

Support for Membership Libraries and Small Libraries

Membership or subscription libraries were among the first libraries in the United States, and though the nonprofit versions remain in a small minority—about seventeen—these libraries still do exist. As nonprofits, they use the dues they collect to help run the library and are led by a volunteer board. As you can imagine, libraries like this still need outside assistance and therefore they are able to receive financial support from foundations and other sources of funding.

One such library is the Lanier Library in the foothills of the Blue Ridge Mountains in Tryon, North Carolina, which has a population of around 1,600. For most people in the community, the yearly fee is fifty dollars for an individual and seventy-five dollars for a household, there are higher levels of annual contributions that members can select—which gives them special perks—and, in addition, there is even an option of lifetime membership.[36] Non-subscription libraries usually depend on taxes, so a fairly priced, nonprofit *subscription* library like this one can be an acceptable bargain for residents when there are no other options.

This little, well-run library is able to provide most of the services that a free library offers—book groups, programs, events, a newsletter, and more—mainly because it receives outside support from public charities like the Polk County Community Foundation; the "small, yet mighty" Felburn Foundation[37]; other foundations, endowments, and trusts; book sales and annual fundraising drives; and bequests. Because of this support, it was even able to add solar panels to save library energy costs in 2021![38]

Yes, as you can see, small communities like the one in Tryon can have strong and active libraries and dependable supplementary support sources too. Before this example, you found out about the smallish public library in Huntley, Illinois, served by an active Friends Foundation. Another exemplary small town public library Friends group is from the Weathersfield Proctor Library in Vermont. This public library serves a population of about 2,900, and its Friends conduct many activities to give it a boost financially. Their Friends bylaws are included in the appendixes, and more details about the group are included in a later chapter.

Yet another Friends group that supports the Thompson Public Library in the village of North Grosvenordale in Connecticut (with an estimated community population of 1,500) illustrates what a small but mighty nonprofit can do for its library. This Friends of the Library group was started in 1989 and builds its library support fund through membership dues, book sales, and fundraisers. Financial assistance is given to the library for needs beyond the annual budget provided by the town, especially for children's services needs, and for larger technological projects to keep the library current into the future through its Next Chapter Fund.[39]

Small libraries, whether fee-based or free, can still be the beneficiaries of helpful library support sources like Friends, foundations, and trusts. Think back to the Dobie Library Trust mentioned earlier, which contributes funding to small libraries in Texas. You can see that, on a local level, depending on the libraries and their clienteles, much can be accomplished by dedicated citizens who devote time, money, and care to offer support to their libraries even in the tiniest communities. Look for information and examples from other small libraries in upcoming chapters.

School and Higher Education Library Support Groups

In addition to funding physical materials such as collections, materials, and equipment, these education-oriented library groups can help to enhance the profile of campus and school libraries through sponsoring programs and events. You have already encountered examples of a higher education Friends group and a university trust earlier in this chapter. There are more, such as at the University of Memphis in Tennessee, where the Friends of the University Libraries is comprised of volunteers from the campus and the surrounding community who wish to assist in fulfilling the libraries' mission. They develop public awareness of, appreciation for, and proper use of the libraries; serve in an advisory capacity when requested; assist in fundraising to maintain and expand the library facilities; and support the educational and programming goals of the libraries.[40] There will be more details about academic library support groups in the next chapter.

Likewise, a Friends group can have a positive impact on and supportive influence for a school library or media center. A school-oriented Friends group can supply volunteers; provide additional funding for special activities, books, and other library materials; and serve as a source for effective pressure when the library or media center funding is threatened. In a middle or high school library, a tween or teen Friends group could be organized to give students a sense of responsibility, a channel for promoting their school library, and an avenue to earn service learning credits. Having such a group would also be a positive way to encourage a love of reading and to develop a strong youth connection to their library, which can lead to lifelong library use and support.

In order to start such a group, parents, concerned citizens, and faculty—or even young people inspired to do so—need to consult and get the support of the school librarian or media specialist at the school, who would propose the Friends idea and get approval from the powers that be, before proceeding with the formation of a group.[41] This was the case with a parent and student–led school Friends of the Library and literacy promotional effort in Florida that you will read about, along with further school examples in chapter 2.[42] You will find more illustrations of academic library support groups and information about them in this upcoming chapter as well.

State Friends of the Library Groups

As noted earlier in this chapter, in addition to library trusts like the one mentioned at the Montana State Library, a number of states have Friends of the Library or similar organizations that offer guidance and help to libraries and library support groups on all sorts of topics, including fundraising within their states. Others offer information and assistance through state library association divisions and sections, and still others provide help through their state library itself. Two are state citizen-organized and -generated. If you would like to find out if your state has an agency you can turn to for aid with your Friends group or other kind of library support group, you can check the United for Libraries website that lists which states offer such services and the contact information for the ones that do.[43]

United for Libraries: An Essential Resource

To provide continuing guidance, as companions to this book and as go-to sources for library support group advice and information, you have seen and will see there are numerous online resources pointed out throughout it (with web addresses given in the endnotes), in addition to those included in the webliographies at the book's conclusion. The websites for the organizations listed are all helpful in their own ways; however, the most outstanding and useful one is the website from United for Libraries, due to its many offerings specifically targeted for those who volunteer in supporting their libraries in various ways.

United for Libraries boasts a rather complex history of organizational progressions to become the association that it is today—an active Division of the American Library Association (ALA). It all began in 1890, when the American Library Trustee Association was founded. That remained its name until 1999, when it changed itself to the Association for Library Trustees and Advocates (ALTA).[44] Notice that at this junction, the name brings library advocates—outside-the-library support voices—into play.

Before that time, a group called the Committee on Friends of the Library represented library support groups as part of ALA's Library Administration and Management Association (LAMA). In 1975, the Committee decided to compile a directory of known Friends of Libraries groups on campuses and in communities. In 1979, the incorporation of a separate entity—Friends of the Library USA (FOLUSA)—resulted from the project. After this, ALTA and FOLUSA continued to operate as separate organizations for a number of years.

In 2007, ALTA and FOLUSA entertained a proposal to become a united Division of the American Library Association, and in 2009 the members voted to become the Association of Library Trustees, Advocates, Friends, and Foundations, which eventually was changed to United for Libraries, a much more streamlined, meaningful, and memorable name. Today, members of these organizations work in tandem at the local, state, and national levels to effectively promote, speak up for, and strengthen the supportive voices that offer service and advocate for libraries; encourage the development and advancement of library foundations and other fundraising entities; and engage corporate contributions and involvement.[45]

If you are just discovering United for Libraries, you might speculate about what this ALA Division can do for you and your library support group through individual memberships. The answer is, a great deal, and while more specifics and actual costs can be found on the United for Libraries website, the staff of United for Libraries is also extremely responsive if you have questions or concerns about joining or other issues that the website does not fully address.

In essence, here is an overview of what memberships entail and offer for those who are thinking about becoming part of United for Libraries.

Personal members of ALA's United for Libraries Division must first join ALA and then add the division membership. A library support group might consider covering the cost for one or two personal members (most likely board members), who could then report back to the rest of the group about whatever they have learned. Once members of the group realize what membership gives them, you might find that they choose to join on their own. When current library support group members may already belong to ALA, it would be fairly simple to add the division membership to their annual dues.

Once people join, they will see that the benefits are great and worth the investment. Those benefits include membership discounts; access to online discussion groups; Learning Live monthly webinars; access to the e-learning site, plus its publications, tip sheets, and toolkits; a monthly e-newsletter; and access to the recently added BoardSource feature. Additionally, members who need one-on-one assistance with membership issues or who need more specific information on all topics relating to library support groups can get personalized help during United for Libraries' virtual "office hours" each week.

Another aspect is an annual three-day virtual conference each August, which does require registration, but those supporting libraries in several designated states receive it at no charge and those from a number of other designated states get discounted registration (the conference registration invitation indicates which ones).

One last feature is access to BoardSource, which is a valuable space for connecting to a huge amount of information and advice to keep Friends, foundations, or trust organizations ticking, especially for board officers. It usually costs a pretty penny to enroll, but with United for Libraries dues, it comes for free. The resource enables you to:

- Access all available papers on issues of fundraising, advocacy, recruitment, planning, orientation, and additional topics.
- Receive personalized guidance and support from governance experts through an "Ask-an-Expert" email service.
- Gain admission to the BoardSource Exchange, which is a collective, members-only information-sharing tool.
- Get emails offering "Resources & Solutions" for groups, plus downloadable tools, infographics, templates, and other materials.[46]

Although United for Libraries organizational memberships were discontinued in 2022, personal members receive all the benefits mentioned, and in addition they get a good discount on the purchase of additional seats for certain individuals—a fellow board member, the library director, or a library staff member—to access Learning Live sessions.

After you embark on founding, merging, or revamping your library support group, you may want to investigate the possibilities about what United for Libraries can provide for your group. Remember that even if joining officially through paying dues is not an option, their website is filled with free, valuable, and helpful information, advice, and details that can benefit your group without paying dues. Plus, about a quarter of all state libraries have purchased statewide admittance to United for Libraries resources for all library staff members, boards, and library support groups within their state boundaries. This offers access to a comprehensive collection of live and on-demand training, toolkits, tip sheets, publications, and more. You may want to check with your state library or on the United for Libraries website to see if your state is included.[47]

Notes

1. David Guion. October 19, 2019. "What Is Friends of the Library?" *Reading, Writing, Research*, https://www.allpurposeguru.com/2019/10/what-is-friends-of-the-library/.
2. James Stelle Gordon. Fall 2017. "Three Donors, a Trustee, and a Library." *Philanthropy Roundtable*, https://www.philanthropyroundtable.org/magazine/fall-2017-three-donors-a-trustee-and-a-library/.
3. Peterborough Town Library. 2022. "Early History" and "Creation of the First, Free, Tax-Supported Library," https://peterboroughtownlibrary.org/history-and-renovation-9330/location/peterborough.
4. Corrine Chronopoulos, and Tina Kriebel. 2021. "Peterborough Town Library Project: Recognizing Our Leadership and Donors." Peterborough Town Library, https://drive.google.com/file/d/1QGmDkxglci7XhOKOEXd2xBkOZPGQImQi/view.
5. Gordon.
6. Boston Public Library. 2022. "Support the BPL," https://www.bpl.org/about-the-bpl/support-the-bpl/.
7. Guion.
8. Gordon.
9. Gordon.
10. Guion.
11. Susan Cushman. September 6, 2019. "Friends of the Library, the History," https://susancushman.com/friends-of-the-library-the-history/.
12. Alfred Claghorn Potter. March 14, 1931. "'The Friends of the Library' Organization to Increase Number of Valuable Books in Widener." *Harvard Crimson*, reprinted 2023, https://www.thecrimson.com/article/1931/3/14/the-friends-of-the-library-organization/.
13. Guion.
14. K. T. Solis. October 20, 2022. "Who Are the Friends of the Library?" *Language Humanities*, https://www.languagehumanities.org/who-are-the-friends-of-the-library.htm.
15. Gladstone Area Public Schools. 2023. "Friends of the Library," https://www.gladstoneschools.com/school__public_library/friends_of_the_library.
16. Sally Gardener Reed. 2012. "Libraries Need Friends: A Toolkit to Create Friends Groups or Revitalize the One You Have." United for Libraries, https://www.ala.org/united/sites/ala.org.united/files/content/friends/orgtools/libraries-need-friends.pdf.
17. Mark Henricks. December 2, 2021. "Charitable Trust vs. Foundation: Key Differences." *SmartAsset*, https://smartasset.com/estate-planning/charitable-trust-vs-foundation.
18. Urban Libraries Council. Fall 2013. "Leadership Brief: Maximizing the Library-Foundation Partnership," https://www.urbanlibraries.org/assets/Library_Foundation_Part_Nov13.pdf.
19. Poudre River Library Trust. 2022. "Poudre River Library Trust," https://www.poudrelibraries.org/trust/.
20. Livingston County Library. October 31, 2013. "Livingston County Library Charitable Trust," https://www.livingstoncountylibrary.org/livingston-county-charitable-trust/. Reprinted from *Constitution-Tribune* (Chillicothe, MO).
21. Penn Libraries. 2022. "Phi Beta Kappa Library Trust Fund." University of Pennsylvania, https://www.library.upenn.edu/detail/givingfunds/phi-beta-kappa-library-trust-fund.
22. Texas Library Association. 2022. "J. Frank Dobie Library Trust: Grants for Texas Libraries," *TLA*, https://txla.org/awards-scholarships-stipends/grants/j-frank-dobie-library-trust/about/.
23. State of Montana Newsroom. January 4, 2022. "Trust for Montana Libraries Receives Six-Figure Donation." Montana.gov, https://news.mt.gov/Montana-State-Library/Trust-for-Montana-Libraries-Receives-Six-Figure-Donation.
24. Denver Public Library Friends Foundation. 2023. "Who We Are," https://www.dplfriends.org/who-we-are/.
25. Diane Lapierre, Email message to author, November 11, 2022.
26. Denver Public Library Friends Foundation. 2023. "If Books Could Talk, Oh the Stories They'd Tell," https://www.dplfriends.org/.
27. Lawrence Public Library. 2022. "Merger Information, Friends and Foundation," https://lplks.org/friends-and-foundation-merger/.
28. Lawrence Public Library.

29. Lawrence Public Library.

30. Friends & Foundation Lawrence Public Library. 2022. "Libraries Transform Communities and We Need Your Support," https://lplks.org/friendsfoundation/.

31. Friends Foundation Denver Public Library. 2022. "If Books Could Talk, Oh, the Stories They'd Tell," https://www.dplfriends.org/.

32. Pamela Kempworth, November 14, 2022. Email message to author.

33. Glendale Library, Arts & Cultural Trust. 2021. "Expanding Knowledge, Exploring Opportunities, & Enriching Lives," https://www.glact.org/.

34. Fort Vancouver Regional Library Foundation. 2018. "What Is the Relationship between the Library and the Foundation," https://www.fvrlf.org/what-relationship-between-library-and-foundation.

35. Fort Vancouver Regional Library Foundation. 2018. "Friends of the Library Groups." https://www.fvrlf.org/friends.

36. Lanier Library. 2017. "Lanier Library—More Than Expected," https://thelanierlibrary.org/.

37. Scott Mitchell. September 1, 2022. "The Felburn Foundation—Small but Mighty." *Ocala Style*, https://www.ocalastyle.com/the-felburn-foundation-small-but-mighty/.

38. Lanier Library Annual Report. 2021. "Letter from the President," https://thelanierlibrary.org/wp-content/uploads/AnnualReport2021-Final3.pdf.

39. Thompson Public Library. 2022. "Friends of the Library," https://thompsonpubliclibrary.org//about-us/friends-of-the-library/.

40. University of Memphis. 2022. "The Friends of University Libraries," https://www.memphis.edu/libraries/fol/index.php.

41. ilovelibraries. 2022. "Get Involved: Become a Library Friend," https://ilovelibraries.org/get-involved/become-a-library-friend/.

42. Karen Clawsen. 2022. "K is for Kids: Building Readers and Leaders." K is for Kids Foundation, https://www.kisforkids.org/.

43. United for Libraries. 2022. "State Friends Groups/State Friends Groups Contact Information," https://www.ala.org/united/friends/statefriends.

44. United for Libraries. 2022. "A Rich History." American Library Association, https://www.ala.org/united/about.

45. Peggy Danhof. June 2013. "A Short History of United for Libraries." Chicago: American Library Association Conference, https://www.ala.org/united/sites/ala.org.united/files/content/about/history.pdf.

46. United for Libraries. 2022. "Access Member Benefits." American Library Association, https://www.ala.org/united/membership/access#BoardSource.

47. United for Libraries. January 2023. "News from United for Libraries," https://americanlibraryassociation.informz.net/informzdataservice/onlineversion/ind/bWFpbGluZ2luc3RhbmNlaWQ9MTA4OTgyMTImc3Vic2NyaWJlcmlkPTExMjAxNDgyMDU=.

CHAPTER 2

The Importance and Functions of School and Academic Library Support Groups

AS MENTIONED IN THE PREVIOUS CHAPTER, libraries and media centers at schools for younger students, as well as libraries at higher education facilities, can benefit from the assistance provided by dedicated individuals who are organizing groups for recruiting volunteers and raising revenues. These efforts help to furnish supplemental items, activities, and enhancements that basic budget and staffing allocations do not cover. Just like library support groups at public library facilities, these organizations can make a difference in the quality of the library services being offered. Yet many people do not realize these types of library support groups can exist. Dedicated volunteers who care about libraries in traditional educational settings can create and run them for the same or similar outcomes as those serving public libraries.

I hope the examples and advice in this chapter and future ones in this book will enlighten anyone who has yet to see the benefits of pursuing the organization of such school and academic nonprofits; anyone who may already be trying to start a group for a library in an educational setting and who needs a starting point and ideas; or anyone who is already involved in such a group but understands that it needs a boost.

Academic Library Support Organizations

In general, public libraries have benefited from the financial and volunteer support of Friends and related groups for many more years than ones that are organized to back academic libraries, although a few academic libraries do have a lengthy Friends history. However, as additional academic libraries find it increasingly difficult to obtain the financial support they need to function optimally, the creation of new academic library Friends and similar organizations makes sense and can be a positive move for gaining the money and volunteers needed for support beyond what regular budgets can supply.

This is because a challenge academic libraries face today is that through time, their purpose has changed in the eyes of academic administrators. Though in the past they were viewed as a central hub and research center of an educational institution, today they are often considered an academic department subject to the same demands for accountability, assessment, and outcomes as other academic departments, which means they must often prove their value. Having Friends groups that are supporting academic libraries can be the key to helping the libraries demonstrate their value because they augment funding for the enhancements the libraries require to excel.

The most important factor in implementing academic Friends groups is the true commitment of academic library directors. Persons in this position work with and support the organizational volunteers and help define the purpose of the academic libraries' Friends, whether they serve as fundraisers, advocates, event planners, special volunteers, or public-relations representatives.

Academic Friends groups can usually be formed through the recommendations of academic library directors. The directors might collaborate with the development office or other university or college departments to help the group create bylaws; invite potential board members; aid them in establishing official nonprofit status; determine membership donation amounts; design membership brochures; and offer endorsements. However, it is highly suggested that directors wishing to establish support groups first get approval from the provosts or presidents of their colleges or universities.[1]

The following are some examples of active college and university library support groups that, if you are looking to start or expand a similar library support group, you may find inspiring:

- The Friends of the Duke University Libraries was started in 1930 and remains active to this day at this highly regarded private institution. Members are committed to strengthening and advancing library services by supporting and enhancing the library collections. They accomplish this mission through bequests and annual gifts as well as by accepting donations of books and other materials. Besides financial support, the Friends serve as advocates for the libraries and in turn promote the whole university community. Interested individuals are encouraged to join the Friends online through a fifty-dollar annually renewable membership contribution or with a one-hundred-dollar donation, which allows the giver to get a library card. The Friends also provide supplementary giving opportunities online through their Ways to Give page.[2]
- At the University of Northern Colorado (UNC) in Greeley, the Friends of the UNC Libraries, founded in 1973, is comprised of a dynamic assemblage of alumni, faculty, emeritus faculty, staff, students, and community members who advocate for, raise funds for, and promote the Libraries' services, collections, spaces, and programs. The Friends are an essential element in this state university's outreach efforts to obtain notable cultural and academic resources that cultivate both intellectual and artistic exchange. They have both co-hosted and piloted many of these endeavors, which include art exhibits, music recitals, speaker series, used book sales, and other fundraising projects. New members are always welcome, and the Friends leadership is particularly attuned to honing and revising its mission, needs, priorities, and governance guidelines to align with the university's strategic planning and to draw upon the interests, talents, and connections of its members. In addition to having an endowment fund, membership fees help to build the supportive coffers

with costs to join ranging from twenty-five to two hundred fifty dollars. Members receive invitations to special events, receive newsletters, have voting privileges, and are given several options for volunteer opportunities.[3]

- The Friends of the Allan Hancock College Library, a community college in Santa Maria, California, began in 2000 as part of the Allan Hancock College Foundation. The group fills an essential auxiliary funding role for the Library so it can expand educational resources for the students and the community as well as help build Library appreciation and enthusiasm. This is accomplished through contributions, donations, and special events that pay for materials, projects, and services beyond the regular Library budget. The Friends additionally support the literary works of students, faculty, and staff at the College; offer a Friends of the Library Book Club to all staff and faculty through which they can take part in timely discussions, develop relationships with peers and mentors, gain fresh perspectives, and reenergize as teams; and provide free lecture series on various topics. One unique partnership between Pacific Conservatory of the Performing Arts (PCPA, which offers an accredited program in acting and theater at the College), the Early Childhood Studies program at the College, the Orfalea Children's Center, and the Friends has been the "Spike & Friends Read Aloud" program to promote literacy and a lifelong love of reading. The volunteers who read and agreed to be videotaped and to have the videos posted on social media were comprised of PCPA students, Early Childhood Studies students, librarians, and other willing readers.[4]

- At Hilbert College, a small Catholic college in Hamburg, New York, its Friends of the Library's mission is to help financially support high-quality services, collections, and the library facility itself. Local adults may join the Friends for a twenty-dollar yearly contribution; Franciscan Sisters of St. Joseph may join for free; local high school juniors and seniors may participate in a High School Friends of the Library program; and College alumni may access the library without charge. Friends membership permits the user to also have a library card, which is renewable annually. The community is encouraged to sign up and contribute to take advantage of having ready access to a nearby college library.[5]

You will have noticed that the samples of Friends groups that are included in this section are from an assortment of college and university library types. This variety shows that academic libraries of any size can have a library support group as long as there are dedicated individuals who are willing to get the group established and running effectively, to work at fundraising, and to help finance whatever needs and desires the beneficiary library might have. This same principle holds true for elementary and secondary school libraries and media centers.

School Library Support Organizations

Once again, as mentioned earlier, school libraries often struggle to provide adequate service for their students. They can benefit from the support of Friends, foundations, or trusts, too. An organization might be called Friends of the "Little Town" School Library, or "Anywhere School" Library Foundation, "Our School" Library Trust (add a school name of your choice!), or any catchy name that indicates that the group is specifically designated to raise funds, take stewardship of monetary donations, seek grants, help get materials, and/or provide volunteer, hands-on aid for that particular school library.

You will recall the chapter 1 comments that Parent-Teacher Associations (PTAs) or Organizations (PTOs) also coordinate fundraising activities at schools, but they usually must spread the money they raise between all the special offerings of the school, including art, music, sports—and the library. However, these days, many school libraries are hurting for adequate funding to cover supplies, books and materials, and other kinds of assistance, and what PTAs or PTOs can provide is often not enough to make much of a difference. A solution to this issue could be the development of an independent "Friends of the School Library" or related kind of organization to aid in improving and enhancing a library that needs the backing.

The following textbox tells the story of a school-oriented Friends and Foundation that was in existence for many years. Even though it and its offshoot activities are no longer in operation (for sensible reasons), the story paints a clear picture of what such groups might accomplish with dedicated individuals at the helm.

TEXTBOX 2.1

K IS FOR KIDS: A STORY OF FRIENDS AND FOUNDATION SCHOOL LIBRARY SUPPORT

In 2001, siblings Erin Clawson and Patrick Clawson Jr. decided they wanted to help other students at their new school, Laurel Oak Elementary, when they moved to Naples, Florida. They were in second grade and kindergarten respectively, and both had observed there were items needed by both their teachers and fellow students. Soon, their mother, Karen Clawson, realized the reason for this was that budgets were tight for teachers and parents alike. She and her children enthusiastically met with the teachers and school staff to review their proposals to offer aid, and their ideas were put into action. Before long, Karen Clawson found herself volunteering full-time.

Because her children were avid readers who loved to check out library books, Clawson recognized that the large school library, despite having plenty of physical space as one of the most sizeable schools in Collier County, was lacking in materials and technology due to minimal funding. She met with the school principal to discuss what might be done as a remedy, and they decided that she would lead a local business partners' initiative to help raise money for library books.

Under the auspices of the newly formed Friends of the School Library, a flyer promoting the initiative reached business owners, who then contributed along with parents who joined the efforts. After the promising initial response, the Clawsons devised and hosted a kickoff book donation event—the Bring a Book, Bring a Friend Fun'raiser—which gleaned hundreds of new books plus funds to buy additional ones, and they delivered the books to the school library.

For three years, new families were recruited to host the events, and Clawson helped to organize and promote them. Local newspapers printed the stories, the community rallied to help, and businesses began to sponsor the events, which raised proceeds to almost ten thousand dollars in new books and monetary contributions. In addition, authors from the area sometimes participated. Clawson's children remained involved, thinking up enjoyable ways for children to take part by choosing which books their families donated; by delivering the books; by gathering photos to thank donors; and by assisting their school librarian at local bookstores to spend the funds that were raised.

(continued)

Through the years, the Clawson children remained involved and sparked new ideas for their school. They began a student-authored book project; built teams of on-location student reporters for the school's morning show promoting school events; and, with Clawson's help, printed full-color class newsletters for families with reports, interviews, contests, and columns, all student-created.

When project notoriety continued to spread, as you might imagine, six years later other schools and nonprofit organizations were requesting "fun'raiser" events to support their causes, too. Local leaders were encouraging Clawson to establish an official nonprofit organization after what had so far been accomplished, and the K is for Kids Foundation was born. Also, by this time, Clawson's children were in middle school and willing to expand their efforts countywide. They expressed a desire to have teenagers closely involved in the foundation's endeavors, and eager teen participants were placed in leadership roles. This gave those teenagers broad experience in business management or administration and helped them to explore potential career paths.

Soon, a newly formed Teen Advisory Team, consisting of the top student leaders, oversaw all teen volunteers and their foundation activities. These activities focused on giving needy children new books through "Bring a Book, Bring a Friend for Children's Literacy" and giving other teens chances to apply their skills in real-world settings through their teen-led "Readers and Leaders" program. Their efforts were recognized and honored by several local and state government officials.

Figure 2.1. Student leaders are shown working at the 2017 Holiday Book Drive with assistance from the Barnes & Noble store agent. *Credit: K is for Kids Foundation 2007-2018 as per founder Karen Clawson, used with permission.*

One of the highlights of their accomplishments was the K is for Kids Teen Fashion Show charity fundraiser, started in 2011, held annually for several years by teens, with a business teacher and Clawson guiding them. Held in a local high school, the countywide student community event was planned by teens and featured up to eighty models onstage promoting literacy and leadership for the Foundation. They accomplished it by showcasing fashions and accessories from a dozen area retailers. Related events included a reception, a silent auction, and talent acts, in addition to the fashion show itself.

Karen Clawson has received numerous honors and awards recognizing her as a trailblazer in literacy and education. After her children graduated from high school and following the well-over-two-year worldwide health emergency that impacted and impeded their efforts starting in early 2020, the Foundation has sadly needed to disband. However, due to the extensive timeline for this story, it still illustrates how grassroots endeavors can be brought to life by local volunteers who care enough to make a big difference in their schools and neighboring communities. The various facets of how the Friends of the Library and the K is for Kids Foundation functioned and evolved that are illustrated in this story may be inspiring for anyone who would like to bring similar literacy support projects to life today or in the future.[1]

Figure 2.2. Student leaders continued to carry the torch, raise the bar, and plan for the annual K is for Kids "From the Heart" teen fashion show for several years after Erin and Patrick Clawson entered college. Foundation founder and executive director Karen D. Clawson is at the far left, and her education partner and Barron Collier High School business teacher is at the far right. *Credit: K is for Kids Foundation 2007-2018 as per founder Karen Clawson, used with permission.*

Note

1. K is for Kids Foundation. 2010–2023. "K is for Kids: Building Readers and Leaders," https://www.kisforkids.org/.

As indicated in textbox 2.1, though the particular example of school literacy support, interrelated events, and bolstering activities described in it have been discontinued, it could offer motivation for a similar endeavor. Plus, you may be surprised to learn that there are already other organizations nowadays that are alive and well and helping to nurture the school libraries in their communities. Granted, school library support groups like these are few and far between, but maybe reading about them here can generate the creation of comparable organizations for school libraries that need them. If your library support group hopes to target or already targets a school library, you might want to pass on this information to your local parents, educators, and especially your school library media specialists or librarians. If the libraries featured next can do it, there is a good chance your community school libraries can benefit from such aid, too, when they learn it is truly possible.

One helpful example comes from Rancho Bernardo High School Friends of the Library in San Diego, California. Rancho Bernardo High School is a public high school in the Poway Unified School District of San Diego County. The school library functions like any good school library would, supporting student achievement with informational needs through print and electronic media and helping teachers develop projects that build critical learning and research skills. The school itself opened in 1991, and its accommodating Friends group began in 2007 to ensure the library is well-stocked with current books and technology and is fully operational. Parents and members of the community are urged to join the Friends to ensure the library's continued success.

A well-coordinated Friends of the Library group like this one functions in the same ways that other library support groups do, which will be described fully in upcoming chapters. It has an executive board of directors comprised of a president, vice president, secretary, and treasurer; a supporting board of directors; advisory members; and administrative members, who include the teacher librarian, principal, and assistant principal. It has a mission statement that says they are a "a nonprofit volunteer organization dedicated to supporting the library in meeting the intellectual, curricular, and technological needs of all the Rancho Bernardo High School students and staff through fundraising and advocacy." Their overarching vision is to build a strong library program for students to become information literate and lifelong learners. Meeting the vision and mission is achieved by aiming toward the following goals:

- To advocate for adequate funding, services, and staffing for the school library from state, district, and school site resources.
- To foster the development and effective use of modern information skills among the high school students.
- To enhance the collection of library resources for both students and staff.
- To increase awareness and support for the Rancho Bernardo Friends of the Library programs among parents and the community.[6]

This Friends group does not operate in a vacuum from the student body. In addition to the members of the school staff who serve on its board, they recruit student volunteers to serve as student board members. These students have assisted with money-raising projects, such as book sales and holiday gift–wrapping fundraisers. The Friends have also done other successful projects to raise money, such as an online auction along with a membership drive fundraiser among the parents of currently enrolled students.

Executive board president June Zhou offered advice for any other people who want to create a Friends group like theirs:

- You must have a core group of parent volunteers who are committed and who have a long-term plan to grow the organization.
- You need a dedicated grant writer on the board because a person with such a skill is crucial to raise money for any library support group. (Note: Stay tuned for specific details on the topics of grants and grant-writing for library support groups in upcoming chapters, especially chapter 12.)
- You must be sure to have the support of the school administration before proceeding and as your group evolves.[7]

Another, less complex, way that a Friends of the Library organization can shore up a school library is by creating a simple one that centers on donations to benefit building the library collection. At the Mill Springs Academy in Alpharetta, Georgia, a private K–12 school serving a small population of about three hundred students with learning differences or who experience attention deficit/hyperactivity disorder, the media center was in need of a support program to develop its specialized collection. In order to accomplish this, a Friends of the Library was formed. Members can choose to donate twenty-five or thirty-five dollars to participate, and the funds are used to purchase books, audiobooks, and books in digital formats. Donors' names are included on special book plates inside all new titles.[8] Despite the fact that this particular Friends model concentrates solely on the collection, perhaps contributors to a group such as this one could consider expanding their reach to become even stronger, more active supporters of their school library. However, a basic materials fundraising donor program might indeed be a good starting point from which to build.

With that in mind, here is another example from the Friends of the Library at the Double Eagle Elementary School in Albuquerque, New Mexico, which has already built an excellent library support organization with more intensive parental involvement. It is a school library Friends group that backs all aspects of the library, promotes community literacy, is completely donor-funded, and is run by volunteers.

There are many library volunteer opportunities available within this group because it is extremely active. They sponsor two Scholastic Book Fairs a year; a Battle of the Books competition; student book clubs; a visiting author program; a staff bookroom; a birthday recognition program; a DEAR event (Drop Everything and Read); a Literacy Fair; a schoolwide movie license; and subscriptions to the online learning websites BrainPOP, Raz-Kids, and Freckle.

Parents are encouraged to join and participate in this Friends of the Library group, which is, as noted on the group's application form, "not affiliated with the PTA." You might recall how, in the previous chapter, I gave reasons why this is an important differentiation.

Those parents who sign up as members pledge an annual monetary donation of their choosing. This money not only supports the library but gives the contributors an option to check out eight books at a time for a period of two weeks. The application for membership can be downloaded, or it can be picked up at the library. Friends meetings are held monthly in the evening and are open to members who are each invited to come and offer their support.[9]

Another school in Albuquerque, New Mexico, also has a very active Friends of the Library organization, which serves the library and students at the Georgia O'Keeffe

Elementary School. According to their bylaws, the purpose of the organization is to promote literacy at the school; to enrich the total resources and facilities of its Joyce Etulain Library (named after a former librarian at the school)[10]; and to enhance a love of reading among the school's students. The Friends accomplish a great deal by working to satisfy this mission.

The group's board of directors consists of the offices of president, vice president, secretary, treasurer, membership chair, fundraising chair, book club coordinators, Battle of the Books coordinators, and the school librarian. To become a member, applicants join at their choice of five different levels of donations: Fairytale member, ten dollars, receiving a Friends bookmark; Alumni member, twenty dollars, receiving a Friends magnet; Classics member, twenty-five dollars, receiving a Friends lanyard; Pulitzer member, one hundred dollars, receiving a dedication brick in the school courtyard, a lanyard, and a magnet; and Corporate Member, two hundred fifty dollars, receiving their business name on the school marquee for a month, business name and logo on the school Facebook page and school communications, and a magnet. The large corps of volunteers who aid the board in fulfilling the mission originates with those members who sign up and give contributions.

Thanks to those Friends of the Library members, a large number of books and other materials are added to the library each year, making it one of the best collections in the city. They also ensure that every student receives a library card, and through the author- and illustrator-visitation program, students get an up-close-and-personal look at how books are written and published while learning about some fascinating new reading choices to check out with their cards.

The Friends-sponsored book club programs introduce students to quality literature and encourage them to take pleasure in reading. In addition, the Friends offer other fun and exciting activities that promote the enjoyment and appreciation of literature, such as a read-a-thon, story writing contests, book fairs, reader awards, and Poetry Alive![11] presentations. As you can see, this is another pertinent illustration of what a school library support group can be.[12]

As a final point, if you are considering starting a school or academic library support group, keep these examples and the advice given here in mind as we progress through the following chapters. Remember that, as with any nonprofit library support organization, a school group—as well as one supporting a higher education library—can be highly functional, too.

Notes

1. Charles D. Hanson. August 2013. "Academic Library Friends: A Toolkit for Getting Started—You Can Do This!" United for Libraries, https://www.ala.org/united/sites/ala.org.united/files/content/friends/orgtools/academic-library-friends.pdf.

2. Duke University Libraries. [n.d.] "Friends of the Duke University Libraries," https://library.duke.edu/support/friends.

3. University of Northern Colorado. June 27, 2023. "Friends of the UNC Libraries," https://www.unco.edu/library/about_us/friends/.

4. Allan Hancock College. December 20, 2022. "Friends of the Library," https://www.hancockcollege.edu/library/friends.php?locale=en.

5. Hilbert College. [n.d.] "Friends of the Library," https://www.hilbert.edu/academics/library/library-services/friends-of-the-library.

6. Ranch Bernardo High School Friends of the Library. 2023. "Family. Friends. RB Community," https://www.rbhsfriendsofthelibrary.org/who-we-are/.

7. June Zhou. June 3, 2023. Email message to author.

8. Mill Springs Academy. 2023. "Friends of the Library," https://www.millsprings.org/academics/media-center/friends-of-the-library.

9. Double Eagle Elementary School. 2023. "Friends of the Library," https://doubleeagle.aps.edu/friends-of-the-library.

10. Mary Beth King. February 7, 2023. "History Professor Emeritus Etulain a Prolific Writer of History Books." University of New Mexico Newsroom, https://news.unm.edu/news/history-professor-emeritus-etulain-a-prolific-writer-of-history-books.

11. Academy of American Poets. [n.d.] "Poetry Alive!" poets.org, https://poets.org/listing/poetry-alive.

12. Albuquerque Public Schools. 2023. "What FOL Does," Georgia O'Keeffe Elementary School, https://goes-aps-nm.schoolloop.com/who-we-are.

CHAPTER 3

Building or Revamping a Library Support Group

I**N SOME COMMUNITIES,** a Friends of the Library organization, a library foundation, a library trust, or other library support nonprofit may not exist at all. In other communities, there might be one central nonprofit library support group, but those volunteers dedicated to the library see a need for each library branch to have its own group extending from the main one. In other cases, a community might have one nonprofit group for its library and recognize the benefit of adding a partner nonprofit to widen the scope of support. Then again, a community member might pass away and bequeath their assets as a library trust, and the trust is assigned to the Friends group for management. Another scenario might be that two existing groups, a Friends of the Library and a foundation or trust, choose to combine into one. Individuals who decide to get together to move forward in creating one or more of these kinds of library support groups are probably wondering how to begin the process and put their vision into action. At the same time, for groups already established, members may be trying to figure out how to grow and improve.

With any of these situations, whether you are starting a new library support group, changing or extending the format of the one you already have, or trying to develop a new organizational model, you need to have a plan along with pertinent documentation that can be accessed publicly. In chapter 1, there was some basic information on the varieties of groups and how such groups can find direction to set the wheels in motion, but in this chapter, there will be more in-depth detail on the steps needed to move forward, rules to follow to make a group official, and guidelines for optimum functionality. Before all that is covered, however—let us think about first things first.

TEXTBOX 3.1

HELPFUL, FREE ONLINE RESOURCES

If you are looking for means to assist you regarding how your nonprofit library support group can be founded, operate successfully, and grow, there are helpful, mostly free tools you can use. These resources are also included in the webliography at the book's end, but it is worthwhile to make special descriptive notations about them.

Blue Avocado[1]

Blue Avocado speaks for and to the people in community-based nonprofits. Although it is not specifically library support group–oriented, its focus on general information for nonprofits is valuable for Friends, foundations, and trusts, as it would be with all nonprofits. As an online magazine of the Nonprofits Insurance Alliance offering practical tools and tips by and for nonprofits, the free resource is fueled by a monthly newsletter created by nonprofit experts, practitioners, and funders. Through it, library support groups can find:

- Information about boards of directors
- Enlisting and working with volunteers
- Marketing and communications
- Fundraising and dealing with finances
- Further topics that also pertain to a variety of nonprofit operations

Candid[2]

This is a particularly useful resource for starting a library support nonprofit and includes elements such as checklists, nonprofit associations, help with developing a business plan, legal support, and government agencies. It also allows users to zero in on advice pertinent to each state. Candid:

- Offers an online assessment tool for those considering starting or having recently started a nonprofit
- Aids those who have not previously navigated the processes of incorporation and applying for 501(c)(3) status
- Gives advice for seeking funding to support a group project
- Helps to implement program ideas and in securing funding once the 501(c)(3) status is received[3]
- Offers a useful, free Seal of Transparency program for all fully registered nonprofits, including library Friends, foundations, and trusts that aids in group promotion, gaining funds, and even has an option to arrange for online donors and other payments using Apple Pay[4]

Library Strategies[5]

A nonprofit housed within a library foundation, Library Strategies believes that a dynamic library is at the heart of every great community. The organization works with libraries and library-supporting organizations to realize its vision. No matter what size community your library support group serves, Library Strategies provides:

(continued)

- Special sections on its website with free information for Friends of the Library groups and library foundations
- Free ideas, advice, and tips on such topics as fundraising, capital campaigns, strategic plans, grants, and more on its website
- A free e-newsletter with helpful advice
- Free webinars
- Consultants who are available to guide and assist you for a fee, if needed

Raise Funds[6]

This resource is a free knowledge base and virtual community center for philanthropic research and advice targeting the volunteer leadership and professional staff of nonprofit organizations. The content is created and selected, organized, and presented by experts in fundraising, marketing, communications, management, and governance. It can guide library support nonprofits in many aspects of their organizational and fundraising endeavors and efforts.

Notes

1. Blue Avocado. 2022. "Practical Tools & Tips for Nonprofits, by Nonprofits," https://blueavocado.org/.
2. Candid. 2023. "Get the Information You Need to Do Good," https://candid.org/.
3. Candid Learning. 2022. "Nonprofit Startup Resources." Candid, https://learning.candid.org/resources/nonprofit-startup-resources/.
4. Candid. 2023. "Introducing 2023 Candid Seals of Transparency," https://blog.candid.org/post/introducing-2023-candid-seals-of-transparency/.
5. Library Strategies. 2021. "Invest in Your Library. Strengthen Your Community," https://www.librarystrategiesconsulting.org/.
6. Raise Funds, https://www.raise-funds.com/about/.

First Things First: A Core Organizational Group

One essential first step for any new library support nonprofit is to establish the initial organizational group. This could be a team of local citizens, school or university library devotees, or other library supporters, depending on their beneficiary library's purpose, who instigate the founding of a Friends of the Library, a foundation, a trust, a Friends Foundation, or any format of library support society. Founding a group depends on the person or persons who serve as the catalysts in moving forward with the idea of starting it and bonding with the library the group will serve. Even in an economically challenged town, city, or region, citizens who get together with positive tactics to build a library support group can have success.

As you have noticed from some of the examples already shown in this book, the ways this might happen can vary. A new library support nonprofit might start with an enthusiastic group of locals deciding to pitch in and set up a fund for their neighborhood library, or a person might pass away and leave a trust fund earmarked for supporting a beloved library beyond its limited budget. Money designated for such a fund could be central to the establishment of a group to monitor, build up, and seek future donations for it.

At other times, forward-thinking library administrators might realize that their libraries would greatly benefit from the activities and additional funds from newly developed support groups and encourage their establishment. Yet again, a library might wish to encourage an outside group of library aficionados to organize as a supportive nonprofit for a particular capital campaign or other project. Often, groups like this that are formed to address short-term goals decide to continue their work once the target missions have been met by revising and building upon their previous functions to become ongoing financial contributors and to offer hands at the ready for the benefit of their libraries. Or a group of library devotees without a financial base to get underway may be able to garner startup money by engaging nearby businesses and neighborhood groups for donations, or by applying to organizations and agencies that offer grants for worthy community projects.

In whichever ways the seeds for library support groups are sown, there are certain items that initial planners need to take care of to get them started. Developing bylaws is one of the essential first steps, though there are other organizational points to complete before bylaws can be drawn up. A core group must exist, serving as the foundation to get things started, and when the group is still too small and unequipped to take action, developing a steering committee of a few core group volunteers is one method to begin the process.

A Steering Committee Can Get a Group Started

You can imagine how, when there are not enough people to tackle the various tasks necessary for a library support group to actually be formed, it presents many obstacles. Often, there is little that only a few people can accomplish to address the idea on their own, so drawing more people together before proceeding is the solution. With a promising goal that has been formulated by only a few as a catalyst, the answer lies in establishing a steering committee stemming from the initial interest group.

Before a steering committee can be convened, it is essential for the few grassroots organizers to consider up front what they are trying to accomplish in creating a library support group and to encourage and appoint one person to step up as spokesperson or leader. Then, they need to ponder several questions. Is the group's purpose to raise money to help fund library programs or capital expenses, assemble a corps of volunteers, advocate for the target library, provide public relations to inform and engage the community, offer a combination of these, or address some other purpose?[1] The answers to these questions will help to direct the initial organizers in designing a library support group and to decide who might be the best recruits. With the answers in tow, the next step would naturally be to further promote the cause by establishing a steering committee.

It is helpful to understand exactly what a steering committee does. A steering committee has governance in launching a new library support group by setting group direction, scope, timeline, budget, and other organizational processes. Another extremely important role is for the committee to seek out experts, authority figures, and stakeholders to buy in and say yes to joining the core group.[2] When new recruits are approached and persuaded to be involved, they should represent a variety of backgrounds and have diverse skills such as public relations experience, good knowledge of the library (perhaps a retired library staff member), familiarity with the law, financial experience, or any other number of qualities that offer additional abilities and talents. A campaign to enlist recruits can begin by aiming for the most logical and desirable candidates to enlist with your cause.[3] Once the steering committee builds a large enough group of interested and qualified people, it is time to plan a discussion meeting of everyone who has committed to moving forward. Besides inviting all those who comprise the founding group, for additional input any library staff or other community members who would be stakeholders once the library support group is formed should also be included. An organizational plan should be developed at the meeting, which is ultimately the meeting's purpose.

Once an organizational plan has been outlined by the newly formed library support group, the members will be ready to move on to the next steps toward legally becoming an active nonprofit, which are designating officers and creating bylaws. More about these topics are coming up ahead after some advice for convening effective meetings.

Convene a Well-Run Organizational Meeting (and Beyond)

As with any well-run meeting, an organizational meeting called in order to plan for becoming a legal nonprofit will be the most successful if it is devised to operate as efficiently and smoothly as possible. This is likewise an imperative goal for every meeting that follows once the group is established and progressing. For first-rate meetings to happen, it is an indispensable skill to know how to plan and run them, but many leaders lack this vital ability. The following advice can serve as guidelines to become accomplished at doing it correctly.

Keep in mind that when meetings are run carefully within the parameters of the agenda and by following a parliamentary authority that has been carefully chosen (more information about this coming up soon), those attending the meetings will enjoy and appreciate them, work will get done, participants will move forward with a sense of satisfaction, and they will feel that their time has been respected. Furthermore, members attending future meetings will look forward to them instead of dreading them. To help reach these outcomes, here are some general tips for arranging and running a successful meeting:

- Be clear about the purpose of the meeting and what issues need to be addressed. The person leading the meeting needs to do careful pre-planning.
- Create a list of attendees who will or may be able to benefit the group and invite them all to the meeting.
- Set an agenda and share it prior to the meeting with everyone who will be present, then remember to request any additional agenda items at the start of the meeting. Add any new topics to the items already listed.
- If needed, provide a video meeting link and record the meeting.
- Designate a person to take minutes (later this will be the duty of the secretary or other designated person or persons—see the following textbox).
- Be sure that those persons who have the floor are not interrupted, everyone gets a voice at the meeting, and cordial discussion takes place.
- Be ready to address any follow-up questions, and if answers are not at hand, research them and, depending on the weight of the questions, report back to the group with a message as soon as possible or at least at the next meeting.
- Plan for those who may need to attend remotely, welcome them, and be sure to include them as if they were there in person.
- Always start and end the meeting on time.
- Conclude the meeting with an action plan.
- Follow up the meeting with documentation, emails, and additional meetings if needed.[4]

TEXTBOX 3.2

CREATING EFFECTIVE BOARD MEETING MINUTES

The minutes from board meetings are legal documents that are the permanent records of the meetings. They record when the meetings took place, what transpired during them, and what action(s) resulted. It is traditional for the secretary of an organization to perform the task of taking meeting minutes, and it is fine to assign the person holding that office to do so. However, in today's board-meeting world, ideas about who takes minutes are evolving, and sometimes another board member takes on the duty, board members rotate doing the task, or a volunteer coordinator might be assigned to do it.

Some library support organizations prefer to have very formalized minutes, while others have chosen to go the more informal route. In any event, minutes can be used as reference resources about groups and their history, for legal reviews, for orienting new board members, or to openly share details about decisions and proceedings with the library and the public. They are not verbatim accounts or transcripts of meetings but meaningful and comprehensive overviews. Whatever the case may be for their usage, there are several elements that are expected be included in effective minutes:

- Name of the organization
- Date and start time of the meeting
- Names of the board members who are present, excused, or absent
- Noting whether a quorum exists
- Approval of the minutes from the previous meeting confirmed or corrected then approved
- The agenda for the present meeting approved or adjusted and approved
- Motions and decisions that are made during the meeting, who made them, and the reasoning behind them
- A brief description of the major points for and against debated topics without giving names or direct quotes, in order to preserve open opinions
- Voting results
- Names of abstainers and dissenters
- Descriptions of reports and documents that are presented and discussed
- Future action plans and tabled items
- The time that the meeting adjourns
- The name and signature of the secretary or other person who took and respectfully submitted the minutes, and possibly the president or chair as well

In special circumstances, library support organizations may decide to electronically record meetings in addition to taking written minutes for long and involved meetings. If oral or video recordings are made of meetings, boards of directors need to create written policies ahead of time about dealing with these formats to offer protection for board members from legal liabilities. If recordings will be destroyed later, the policies must state it.

Because meeting minutes are legal documents that can be used in court if questions about programs or policies crop up, they need to be accurate reflections of what happened at a meeting without raising concerns about legalities. For instance, when a board addresses a conflict-of-interest issue that has arisen against its organizational policy, the actions that were taken and any disagreements or dissents about them should be noted.

(continued)

After each meeting, the minutes need to be distributed to all board members prior to the subsequent meeting. Members must review them for mistakes or missing information, and any minor errors noted can be corrected before the document is finally approved at the next meeting. More serious corrections can be made at the next meeting itself, adjusted, and voted upon in its revised state for approval.

The final steps after the minutes are approved are to have the secretary, other notetaker, and the president or chair sign off on them and to then have them archived. The archives of meeting minutes should be carefully organized and easy to locate.[1]

Note

1. BoardSource. December 16, 2019. "Board Meeting Minutes," https://boardsource.org/resources/board-meeting-minutes/.

A Leadership Design Plan Is Key

For bylaws to be created, there must be a plan for leadership roles. The core group of persons who have convened to get a group started and who are chosen to fill these roles will be central in putting together the bylaws and gaining the new group its official designation as a nonprofit. There are many aspects to creating bylaws, but building a nucleus of positions to do the start up work first is imperative. These founders can align the core leadership positions and then build on them as the group progresses by including options in the bylaws for restructuring or adding positions as called for in the future. The considerations, requirements, rules, and details that a founding group of individuals needs to follow will be discussed in the rest of this chapter. In the meantime, the list below covers some points to think about when building a library support group leadership team. You will want to make note of the possible variations and arrange them to fit your particular circumstances.

For most Friends of the Library boards, the main officers will almost certainly consist of a:

- President,
- Vice president,
- Past president,
- Secretary,
- Treasurer,
- and at-large board members.

This list of officers and regular members is rather standard, and it is the easiest to put into place. However, groups serving larger communities will most likely need to create positions for additional board members and other types of leaders. For example, some Friends groups choose to designate some members as "officers-in-training" to prepare them to take on future leadership roles. It could be an assistant treasurer working with an official treasurer, or a substitute or assistant secretary learning the ropes from an official secretary. Doing this can be an effective tactic since the board will presumably then have someone in the wings, ready to fill the position in case of a sudden vacancy.

It also helps to have someone highly qualified and prepared who is ready to run for election when someone's term ends. A president may have a vice president (or president-elect) serving in this role as long as the vice president is willing to take the reins once the president's term is complete, and in some cases an immediate past-president might remain on the board to offer guidance. If a secretary has an understudy, that person being trained will be familiar with the job as soon as it is time to run for the office and then officially take it on.

The role of an assistant treasurer can be especially significant. It is a true plus to have a qualified trainee for the treasurer position waiting in the wings. Because a person in a financially oriented leadership position is directly involved with and in charge of the counting, depositing, paying out, and tracking of the group's income, expenditures, and library-cause donations, it requires a particularly confident, trustworthy, knowledgeable, dependable, financially savvy, and organized individual. A board treasurer and successor with all these skills can be hard to find!

As noted, depending on the size of the library or library system, a foundation, trust, or combined Friends and foundation may have a uniquely designed roster of officers. There may be a "chair" leadership position instead of a president or in addition, and maybe more than one chair if there are additional committees. There may be an executive director and a president. There may be a "staff" instead of "officers" or a "board," and, on the other hand, there may be several different "directors." Moreover, some library support organizations include a "student delegate," a "community member," or another person who supplies another aspect of representation.

For large libraries serving city or county communities, there may be an executive officer at the helm of the staff, followed by a group of directors of varying responsibilities in charge of such areas as philanthropy, special events, communications, book sales, finance, and database management. Medium and small foundations and trusts might be governed by a citizen's board that designates special roles to individual members. Ex officio members are also frequently included in the mix, usually in larger communities but also in smaller ones.

Ex Officio Board Members

The Latin phrase *ex officio* literally means "from the office." It refers to the position that the ex officio holds rather that the individual holding that position. Persons filling the positions of ex officio board members are usually not elected or appointed. They agree to serve in a position because of the contributions they can make through their experience, expertise, authority, or meaningful input. Although the idea of an ex officio board member is often misunderstood as meaning that one is bestowed with a lifetime, supporting, or emeritus membership status, there may still be some special benefits of membership carried with filling this kind of role.

The most notable way that a person serves as an ex officio board member is when bylaws dictate that a board chair or president is required to serve on all other committees or task forces. For instance, the president of a library foundation may sit as an ex officio member on the Friends board serving the same library. Sometimes, a member of the library staff, usually the director and/or the president of the board of trustees, may serve as an ex officio on a library foundation board. At other times, a library support group board may lack the expertise of a qualified treasurer and someone who is not a member but skilled at the task steps in as an ex officio to fill that need.

Ex officio members such as this only remain on boards as long as they still hold the positions or jobs that warrant their inclusion. If an ex officio member of a library support group, perhaps a library director, leaves the position that imparted their inclusion on its board, the next person to take on that position or to be hired for the job becomes the ex officio instead.

Usually, ex officio members are eligible to participate in the discussions and debates of the boards on which they serve, but their presence doesn't count for a quorum, and they often do not vote. However, this can vary depending on the particular bylaws of each organization, and an organization may choose to allow an ex officio to vote.[5] Voting status and whatever their other roles and privileges will be as part of the leadership group must be clearly stated in the bylaws along with commentary about how ex officios differ from full board members. At times, a director position on a board may be cast as ex officio, and again, how the position is laid out would be detailed in the bylaws.[6]

It is important to refer to the parliamentary authority a board chooses (details coming up about that soon) to address the issue of ex officio positions in whatever manner is deemed necessary when creating bylaws. It is also the responsibility of the actual board members to ensure that the bylaws regarding ex officio members are being followed.[7]

All positions for leadership on library support group boards need job descriptions so that everyone is on the same page, from the hiring or installing of the person in each position to the role each plays within the framework of the organization. In chapter 4, specific coverage is given on the development of such targeted job descriptions, and there is an example in the appendixes.

Organizational Rules and Components to Consider and Follow

Once leadership is established, it is time to undertake research and document creation for embarking on the process to become a certifiable nonprofit. Whenever the new leaders of a library support nonprofit are setting out to become an established organization, there are several important rules to follow and documents to think about adding. Some of these are legally necessary and others can be chosen by a group's leaders, members, and stakeholders to supplement and balance the required rules. There is a priority order for what organizational elements need to be considered and planned as a group begins the founding process. These next sections follow that priority order.

State Statutes and Federal Tax Rules for Nonprofits

Statutes are the rules enacted by a state legislature and they are where any new group should begin to ensure that the formation of the group meets state law. Often, state laws determine issues of quorum, notice, and more. Most states require a minimum number of board members, and you will want to know if your state does and, if so, what that number is.[8] An organization's documents must be in compliance with the laws in its state and those laws must be adhered to. An initial step would be to investigate the laws that would govern library support group nonprofits by checking in the statutes under "nonprofit corporations act" or similar law categories. A knowledgeable librarian from the library with which you would be partnering would be a wonderful resource person to assist you in finding this information for your particular state as a start. What you discover will aid in completing other documents such as your bylaws.

Likewise, a helpful librarian can assist you with retrieving pertinent information about applying for nonprofit tax status with the federal government. Even more so, conferring with your legal counsel will be instrumental in guiding you about receiving this status as you incorporate. Furthermore, the Internal Revenue Service (IRS) can be another guide to navigating the process of becoming a charitable federal tax-exempt nonprofit via its valuable website.[9] The organizers-in-charge as you move toward getting your group established will need to be the ones assigned to familiarize themselves with precise IRS information in addition to learning about the applicable statutes for your state.

Fundamentally, in order for a nonprofit to be tax-exempt and referred to as a charitable organization under section 501(c)(3) of the Internal Revenue Code, it must be set up and operated exclusively for the exempt purposes allowed by the section with no benefits to private interests or individuals. Also, the nonprofit may not be an "action organization" that attempts to influence legislation as a significant aspect of its activities or participate in any campaign for or against political candidates. Organizations that meet the criteria for 501(c)(3) are eligible to receive tax-deductible contributions in accordance with the Code's section 170.[10] Most library support nonprofits in existence meet these qualifications.

There is another rule to consider. The IRS says: "If a charitable nonprofit engages in an excess benefit transaction with someone having substantial influence over the organization, an excise tax may be imposed on the person or any organization managers agreeing to the transaction. An excess benefit transaction is one in which an economic benefit is provided by an applicable tax-exempt organization directly or indirectly, to or for the use of a disqualified person, and the value of the economic benefit provided by the organization exceeds the value of the consideration received by the organization."[11] Any Friends of the Library, library foundation, or library trust will need to be clear about this rule and consult with a legal authority about the process for dealing with an applicable situation if encountered.

The IRS offers online training that covers applying for tax-exempt status; the benefits, limitations, and expectations of tax-exempt organizations; and private foundations targeting charitable purposes. There are also numerous directional links for associated areas on the IRS website that can assist library support group organizers by providing helpful guidelines and instructions for all sorts of nonprofit tax-related inquiries. The main IRS page is a practical place to start.[12]

Charter or Articles of Incorporation

A document that declares your group is official is often a charter for a Friends of the Library group or articles of incorporation for a foundation or trust, although again, with the guidance of your legal authority, you will want to check to see exactly what it is called and how to complete the application documentation for your particular state. After completion and submission, the approval of the organizational certification is significant because it confirms the existence of your library support nonprofit group, clarifies the name of the group, and defines its purpose. The contents of these documents can serve as guidelines for issues that they address but that are not required by a state statute. Again, your legal authority can provide you with direction.

Bylaws

The distinctive features of your library support group, an explanation of its function and purpose as a nonprofit, and a description of the rights and duties of officers and members are covered in the bylaws that will be created as your new nonprofit is formed. They need to be carefully constructed and worded because they are meant to be longstanding and not readily changeable.

The nine essential elements that should be indicated in a nonprofit's bylaws are the group's name; its purpose; who are the members; details about who serves as officers and/or on the executive board; details about meetings; what committees may be formed; the selected parliamentary authority; and procedures to amend the document. More precise details about the actual development and publicizing of a group's bylaws are covered later in this chapter and examples of library support group bylaws can be found in the appendixes. For now, keep in mind that having bylaws is a fundamental element in attaining approval for legal nonprofit status.

Parliamentary Authority

Every new group must choose a rulebook to guide organization governance that is not covered by state law, charter, or bylaws. The set of published rules that is selected outlines the rules of parliamentary procedure that a nonprofit will implement and follow, and this is defined as "parliamentary authority."[13]

The most frequently recognized and used for group discussions, smooth functioning, and effective decision-making is the popular *Robert's Rules of Order*, now in its twelfth edition.[14] Most library support groups use this guide. However, another choice might be *The Standard Code of Parliamentary Procedure*, now in its fourth edition,[15] or the *American Institute of Parliamentarians Standard Code of Parliamentary Procedure*.[16] Different parliamentary manuals fill different niches depending on the size of the organization, its complexity, and its function. Remember that a group is usually locked into the parliamentary style that is chosen since it is used to create the group's bylaws language, which can be challenging to change, so it is important to choose carefully.[17] It may be useful and time-saving to contact an already well-established library support group similar to the one you are working to launch to find out what resource they are using, why they chose it, and if they can recommend it.

Special Rules and Customs

It helps to consider special rules and customs because they allow a group to fine-tune certain points of the official rules that have been chosen. You might think, "When would special rules apply, since there are already rules to follow? What would be the reason to add rules when there are already enough of them?"

The answer to both is that when a group realizes a parliamentary authority does not cover a rule as fully or in the precise manner that is necessary, the rule can be tweaked, and a special rule can adapt it to fit a particular need. The same goes for customs. To clarify, some group practices might fall into the category of traditions that inspire the comment, "Well, it has always been done it this way." Creating special rules or continuing to follow customs is acceptable as long as they do not conflict with the higher hierarchy of rules in bylaws, charter, or parliamentary authority. On the other hand, if a custom does break a higher rule, the group could decide to end the custom or adopt a special rule to allow for it.

To illustrate, suppose your group has the practice of allowing members to speak as often and for as long as they wish. *The Standard Code of Parliamentary Procedure* does not address speaker frequency or length of time speaking at all. Because it is silent on this topic, your group could create its own special speaker rules or choose not to cover it at all. However, if your group has chosen *Robert's Rules of Order* as its authority, the rule in it states is that anyone gets to speak twice for ten minutes for each motion. If your group decides that ten minutes is too long, members could adopt a rule to limit how long someone has the floor within those rule parameters instead of continuing the unlimited speaking time custom.[18]

Standing Rules

The last set of rules is a group's very own. They cover a group's management and administrative matters and are outside the realm of the parliamentary procedure rules they have chosen. These standing rules can address whatever a group needs them to address, whether it be requiring to wear special group tee shirts for events, the process for counting money after a book sale, the frequency of board meeting times, the way records will be stored, board membership termination, or any other "laws of the land" and group practices that need to be documented and followed.[19]

TEXTBOX 3.3

POUDRE RIVER FRIENDS OF THE LIBRARY STANDING RULES

This is an example of standing rules adopted by a Friends of the Library group in Colorado:

1. Funds from dues and sale of books can be used to enhance and support the library as outlined in the bylaws, encourage literacy within the community, and for the administrative expenses of Friends of the Library.
2. The Friends of the Library provide supplemental funding for library needs outside of the Poudre River Public Library District budget. Annually the library staff submits requests for activities and materials that fall outside the parameters of the library budget. The Board then considers the requests and approves what it wishes to fund. Library staff will provide a quarterly update and possible revisions based on changing needs.
3. The operational/fiscal year is January 1 through December 31.

(continued)

4. Dues are payable January 1 as follows:
   Student: $10; Individuals: $15; Family: $25; Patron: $100; Lifetime: $200
5. The Board of Directors meets monthly. If there is no pressing business, the Board may vote to skip occasional meetings at its discretion.
6. In addition to the president, vice president, past president, secretary, and treasurers, the Board of Directors shall include from five to ten members at large to serve in Ways and Means, Membership, or Public Relations Activity Areas.
7. When action is required prior to the next scheduled Board meeting, action may be taken by a majority of the Executive Committee of the Board of Directors (president, vice president, secretary, treasurers) and reported at the next Board meeting.
8. The Board of Directors shall monitor financial reports in relation to income to ensure the financial health and safety of the organization, approve the annual budget each January, and authorize an annual review by at least two members of Friends of the Library with knowledge of accounting procedures or by a professional accountant.
9. Each member of the Board of Directors, each book sorter, and each Harmony Shop volunteer will be required to sign a Conflict-of-Interest Statement. Anyone who volunteers to sort books for the Friends of the Library may not sell for personal profit any items obtained through their association with the Friends, including discards.
10. All members of the Board of Directors will be required to undergo a Level 2 background/criminal history check, to be paid for by the Friends of the Library. At least two members of the Board will see all results. If there is a response that indicates a concern, the administrators (the president and at least one other Board member) will review the information to help determine what action, if any, is required.
11. A director may be removed from the Friends' Board based on neglect of duty, conduct tending to injure the good name of the Friends, or conduct that disturbs the Friends' organizational well-being or hampers its work. A volunteer's association with the Friends may be terminated at the Board's discretion for conduct that disturbs the Friends' organizational well-being or hampers its work.
12. The treasurer and assistant treasurer of the Friends of the Library shall divide responsibilities between themselves and may appoint others to collect and deposit shop, donation shelf, and book sale receipts.
13. All financial accounts will have four (4) Directors as signers (treasurer, assistant treasurer, president, and vice president) and require two signatures for any check over $2,000, except checks payable to the Library District. Funds in excess of $5,000 will be transferred to interest-bearing accounts at least quarterly if interest rates warrant it. Any new investment strategies will be brought to the Board for approval.
14. The president will appoint a person to maintain the archive records. That person will keep a copy of retention guidelines and will be consulted before disposal of FOL information, records, or news articles.
15. These standing rules may be amended by a majority vote of the Board of Directors.[1]

Note

1. Poudre River Friends of the Library.

Mission, Vision, Values, and Other Important Statements

Following the organizational rules, a group will need to establish important statements about their purpose and function. To provide focus for and allow public knowledge about any present-day library support group, it is wise to have both a mission and vision statement. In addition, it can be a good idea to append a values statement. Although some people view these types of statements as important specifically in business and work environments, they can also be helpful for nonprofits working for and with libraries. Even so, some businesses and nonprofits discount them and choose not to include them at all while others prefer to combine them. The best advice is to have separate statements without combining, which is a more effective method that carries more weight.[20]

A set of statements might be written for each individual element of a library support group—the board members, or the regular members, or any additional/special non-member volunteers. That could be a useful choice for large support groups serving a sizeable community library or library system. On the other hand, having an overarching set of statements to include everyone under the membership umbrella is also an acceptable option for any size library support group. Deciding what approach to take is up to each organization and its particular community focus.

After he studied a large number of library mission and vision statements, Dr. Chris Drew, an educator and creator of the blog, *The Helpful Professor*, noted:

> Library mission statements are personal to the context in which they're located. If you're a library situated in a diverse city, it's probably imperative that you focus on diversity in your mission and vision statement. Similarly, if you're a school, your school library mission statement will be full of information about students and learning.[21]

That is wise advice, and important to think about. You will be reading here about the value of mission—and vision and values—statements with tips on how to write them, but you want to reflect on the goals of the library support group(s) in your own community as you consider how you will actually devise or revise the statements pertaining to your needs. Every set of statements is or will be unique to the organization for which it stands. With that in mind, let us take a closer look at what these kinds of statements mean and entail.

Mission, vision, and values statements are created and developed to enhance the journey everyone in the group takes as they target, reach, or reevaluate anticipated outcomes. It is important for the statements to avoid being too wordy and complicated, which is a mistake that organizations often make. It is equally important to avoid accidentally switching the mission and vision statements, an easy oversight. The advice given later in this section will help to clarify what it takes to make streamlined and effective statements that will aim, as a unit, to be a guiding light.

TEXTBOX 3.4

HUNTLEY AREA PUBLIC LIBRARY FRIENDS FOUNDATION

Here is a straightforward, easily understood example of all three statements given in the most logical and meaningful order from the Friends Foundation in Huntley, Illinois.

Our Mission

The mission of the Friends of the Huntley Library is to raise funds to support and promote the many resources available at the Huntley Library.

Our Vision

The Friends of the Huntley Library are community members who are book lovers, readers, listeners, and information seekers who value the Huntley Library as a vital community resource. We offer our support for the many resources available at the library by advocating for the library, raising funds, sharing our expertise, and volunteering our time.

Our Values

- We value the Huntley Library as a vital community resource and are proud to be advocates for the library.
- We value the diversity of the Friends membership and our unique backgrounds and expertise.
- We value integrity, transparency, and open communication in our organization.
- We value the ideals of good stewardship and pledge to be good stewards of all donations.[1]

Note

1. Huntley Area Public Library Friends Foundation. 2022. "We Are the Friends . . . ," https://huntleylibraryfriends.org/.

When library support groups build and use these three statements as a guiding light for establishment and moving forward, especially when they form a foundation for a group's strategic plans, it takes time and patience to see the results of their effectiveness. Likewise, when library support groups choose to affix codes of ethics, conflict-of-interest statements, online privacy notices, or any other pertinent declarations to their operations, their acceptance and use needs to be embraced by their boards of directors, their membership, any special volunteers, and others to whom the policies relate.

As any of these statements are being developed, it makes sense to engage the partnering libraries in conversations to give input and feedback on the development of them to ensure they gel with what both the supporting nonprofits and the libraries see as compatible values and goals. It is important to ensure last draft buy-in for the written statements by all stakeholders before finalizing and publishing them. Again, when library support groups ultimately develop strategic plans for themselves—a prudent idea—some of the statements could be part of the planning process, and each might lead to a different objective.[22] The statements can serve as useful guidelines as strategic planners work.

You will find more coverage ahead about strategic planning for library support nonprofits. For now, I will take a closer look at creating mission, vision, and values statements tailored to your group's functions and principles.

Mission Statements

A mission statement is a concise explanation for a library support group's reason to exist. It illustrates the group's purpose and its general objectives while supporting the vision and clearly communicates those to the members, board, donors, service and funding recipients, and whatever other stakeholders there may be.[23]

A good mission statement zeroes in on what is most important to the organization and what is achievable in brief, informative, simple, and direct language. It avoids fancy or lofty language, clichés, and generalizations; it emphasizes outcomes; and it is realistic.

Think about and discuss the following when creating a mission statement:

- What does our library support group do?
- Whom are the people we serve?
- What are we trying to accomplish?
- What impact do we want to achieve?[24]

Essentially, a mission statement is a concise single sentence or, at the most, a brief paragraph that not only serves as a guide for those directly involved in the organization but also highlights the purpose of the group in membership recruitment and other promotional materials geared toward the library community it is aiding.

TEXTBOX 3.5

EXAMPLES OF MISSION STATEMENTS

Here are some examples of the mission statements of library Friends, foundations, and trusts from various parts of the country that support libraries and library systems of various sizes. Notice how each statement succinctly tells the reason for the group's existence without saying how they aim to fulfill it:

- West Palm Beach Library Foundation, West Palm Beach, Florida: "Our activities financially support the library and its free programs, services, and resources that enrich and strengthen our diverse community."[1]
- Stillwater Public Library Foundation, Stillwater, Minnesota: "to engage the community and its resources to expand the reach and impact of the Stillwater Public Library."[2]
- Friends of Snow Library, Orleans, Massachusetts: "to support the Snow Library, its Trustees, and staff with programs, activities, books and equipment not provided by town appropriations."[3]
- San Carlos Branch Chapter of the Friends of the San Diego Public Library, San Diego, California: "The mission of the Friends of the San Diego Public Library is to enhance the [library system] so that it may fulfill its literary, educational, technological, community, and cultural purposes."[4]
- Poudre River Library Trust, Fort Collins, Colorado: "The Trust collaborates with the Library District Board of Trustees and staff, Friends of the Library, and donors to grow and manage funds to generate innovative Library programs, projects and services."[5]
- Tulsa Library Trust, Tulsa, Oklahoma: "The mission of the Tulsa Library Trust is to increase the Tulsa City-County Library's capacity to provide the highest quality programs and services to citizens for lifelong learning."[6]

Notes

1. West Palm Beach Library Foundation. 2022. "Mission & Vision," https://www.wpblf.org/index.php/who-we-are/mission-vision.
2. Stillwater Public Library Foundation. 2022. "Mission & Vision," https://www.stillwaterlibraryfoundation.org/mission-vision.
3. Friends of Snow Library. 2022. "Mission Statement," https://friendsofsnowlibrary.org/about/mission-statement/.
4. Friends of the San Diego Public Library. 2022. "SCFOL Mission Statement," https://sancarlosfriendsofthelibrary.org/mission-statement/.
5. Poudre River Library Trust.
6. Tulsa Library Trust. 2022. "Tulsa Library Trust: Why We Do What We Do," https://tulsalibrarytrust.org/.

Vision Statements

A vision statement projects what a library support organization hopes to be in the future and what might be achieved in the long term to meet its mission. Although it is inspirational and motivational, it also offers direction by mapping out where the organization is going. Essentially, it is a guide for deciding upon both current courses of action and future expectations. It is meaningful, concise, unambiguous, forward thinking, inspirational, and targets expected outcomes. While a mission statement pinpoints what a groups aspires to be for as long as it exists, a vision statement can change and adapt to whatever are currently the best goals for completing the mission.[25]

Consider asking these questions when creating a vision statement:

- As we move forward, where are we heading as a group?
- What goals do we want to achieve and what contributions do we want to make to build a positive future for the library we serve?
- How do we imagine the library we serve in the future?[26]

When you set out to write, polish, and complete your vision statement, it will be helpful to follow these best practices:

- Collaborate with key members of your group's leadership to brainstorm.
- Working together with the leadership, write down any brainstormed ideas, streamline them, and edit afterward.
- Write a draft without using jargon and opting for plain language that your fellow group members, library staff, and the general public will readily understand.
- Distribute the draft to other members of the group who will need to give their feedback to be considered for the final version.
- Write the final version, assuring that it feels aspirational, not overly ambitious, and makes sense.
- Bring the final version to the stakeholders and, if needed, make any finishing adjustments.[27]

A useful point to remember is that a mission statement and a vision statement are not easy to create. They require much thought and planning even though writing them may seem simple. It is easy to confuse them, mistake one for the other, write too little, or write too much. Some good rules of thumb for developing and releasing the statements are to:

- Create the mission statement first, label it as such, and have it come first in any written informational material about your group that is being put together.
- Add the vision statement following the mission statement, label it as the vision statement, and use honed wording to describe or list the ways to see the mission through.
- Keep in mind that, in the future, the mission and vision statements can be revisited and revised when needed. It might be helpful to review the statements each year to make sure that they are still accurate and on target.

TEXTBOX 3.6

EXAMPLES OF VISION STATEMENTS

Below are some vision statements from library support groups that offer helpful examples by telling what the groups do to address their purpose:

- Friends of the Sunnyvale Public Library, Sunnyvale, Texas: "[We support] the library in ways not possible with Town of Sunnyvale budget allocations alone. The Town of Sunnyvale provides salaries, utilities and operating expenses for the Library. Additional support from Friends aims to:
    - Provide volunteer support
    - Raise private funds
    - Support children's programs
    - Promote literacy and the love of books
    - Sponsor cultural and literacy events
    - Promote library advocacy in the community and on legislative issues"[1]

- Metropolitan Library System Library Endowment Trust, Oklahoma City, Oklahoma: "[The trust was established as] a way for people to give to the library and to designate funds to help meet future library needs such as renovation or construction. The Trust raises funds each year by making requests to the community and hosting an annual fundraising dinner, Literary Voices®."[2]

- Leander Library Foundation, Leander, Texas: "To accomplish this [mission], the Leander Library Foundation works to increase awareness about the library and its importance to the community, and to raise funds through individual gifts, corporate sponsorships, and foundation grants. It also operates a used bookstore on the library grounds, which is run by volunteers. All funds received are used to provide library programs, equipment, educational materials, books, and facility improvement."[3]

Notes

1. Sunnyvale Public Library. [n.d.] "Friends of the Library," https://www.sunnyvalepubliclibrary.org/supporting-the-library/friends-of-the-library.html.

2. Metropolitan Library System. 2022. "Welcome to the Library Endowment Trust," https://supportmls.org/let/.

3. City of Leander Texas. 2022. "Library Foundation," https://www.leandertx.gov/lf/page/leander-library-foundation.

The Importance of Nonprofit Board Culture

Establishing a mission and vision statement provides a good start to developing focus for any new or revamped library support group. These can form the foundation for continuing to build a solid group culture. There are several reasons this is valuable.

First of all, bear in mind that the culture of any nonprofit board encompasses its values, beliefs, and the expected behaviors of the group and by clearly defining that culture it can greatly affect the organization's success. In essence, when a library support group, like any other nonprofit, identifies and follows the premises of their particular board culture, it becomes the basis of governance, decision-making, and overall relationships between the board, the organization's members, the library being served, and any other stakeholders. The principles of a particular board's culture is covered in the various documents a board might create, such as its mission and vision statements, bylaws, values statement, conflict-of-interest policy, and any other documentation that aids in guiding how the organization functions.

I have started our investigation of this topic by examining the importance of mission and vision statements. In this section, I will further explore the importance of library support group culture, publically acknowledging it, and putting it into action by creating values and other statements that openly express group intentions in order to use those statements as guidelines. Before I do, I will begin with some reasons why quality board culture is important:

- To start with, it channels decision-making, especially when a group is facing difficult choices. When a board has established values and beliefs, those can serve to effectively weigh options and help choose the ones that align most closely with the organization's mission and vision.
- Next, it leads to group accountability. When values, beliefs, and expected behaviors are documented, it holds everyone on the board responsible for their contributions and actions and determines the consequences for violating the culture.
- It promotes positive interactions, fosters respect, builds trust, and encourages open communication as members feel at ease sharing ideas and concerns.
- It attracts the most qualified and dedicated people who share the organization's values and beliefs, promoting a stronger sense of commitment and engagement and leading to enhanced outcomes.
- It also supports organizational success by promoting collaboration, innovation, and a sense of purpose. This in turn builds solid group morale, strengthens stakeholder relationships, and increases effectiveness.
- Finally, a strong nonprofit board culture can lead to a better focus on diversity, equity, and inclusion throughout the library support organization and the library it serves.[28]

Picking up where creating mission and vision statements left off, I will give you an overview of the various kinds of statements your group may wish to consider and design as you continue building and documenting for your own positive organizational culture. Throughout the rest of this book, you will find information and examples that demonstrate how you might choose to effectively put the culture you design (or redesign) for your group into place. I will begin by examining the significance of values statements and how to create them.

Values Statements

Writing a values statement or a statement of core values for a library support group is a way to expand the content of a mission and vision statement. Because mission and vision statements are usually very short and to the point in explaining to people what the group is targeting and what it expects to accomplish as it proceeds in its work, a well-written values statement better connects the mission to the vision, and it deepens the understanding of goals for those looking into what the group stands for.[29]

This could be for the benefit of library staff wanting to be informed about the attitudes and scruples the support group intends to incorporate to help them. It could be for anyone wishing to join the group or contribute to the cause and desiring foreknowledge about the mind-set of the people they are supporting. It could also be for community members interested in knowing how their library and its advocates think and function as they pay taxes toward the library, or they consider selecting the library support group for a grant. What a group chooses to value most highly says a great deal about the organization.

The initial step in writing a values statement is to recognize how it will gel with the nonprofit's mission and vision statements. Once written, the statement lets interested parties see the reasons that the mission and vision should be fulfilled, it explains a group's motivations, and highlights the worldview under which the nonprofit operates. Through a values statement, the operational culture is defined for volunteer group members and boards, for the library itself that a group supports, and for support group donors. All of these perspectives are essential, and they need to be considered and addressed as the values statement is created.

In the process of writing a values statement, there are several steps to follow to make sure it is on target:

- It is important to get input from the people to whom the statement matters by convening a committee. This committee could include representatives from the library staff, library support group volunteers and board members, donors, and perhaps even a member or members of the demographic that the library serves.
- Committee members can be directed to write their own value statements that they would like other members to consider. Under the direction of a facilitator, themes can be discovered during presentation and discussion. The central themes can be put into a narrative that defines group stances reflecting how the organization's mission and vision will be fulfilled.
- Once targeted values are determined, the narrative can be revised into short, clear, stand-alone sentences. Once the committee agrees that each sentence represents a unique aspect of the values and there in no duplication in ideas or language, the values statement can be reviewed independently by other stakeholders who were not part of the process.[30]

After everyone has agreed upon and approved the values statement, it can be included with the mission and vision statements or other documents to more fully express the group's purpose.

TEXTBOX 3.7

EXAMPLES OF VALUE STATEMENTS

Although this chapter covers the import of such statements and how to produce them, they are not commonly created by many library support groups. Nevertheless, remember that having them expressed along with mission and vision statements can enhance the understanding of a group's purpose and presence, so they should still be considered for inclusion. Notice that each example given here uses a somewhat different arrangement for their values statement, and likewise, you can feel free to be inventive with yours.

Friends of Williamsburg Regional Library Foundation, Williamsburg, Virginia

Core Values

- Trust—We work hard to earn trust through engagement, accountability, and transparency.
- Stewardship—We honor the philanthropic priorities of our donors. We value and steward their gifts.
- Civility—We respect and listen to each other's views and opinions.
- Innovation—We employ innovative approaches to help our library face challenges, develop new programs, and plan for the future.
- Collaboration—We bring people together to support our library. We partner with others to amplify our efforts.
- Future-Focused—We fund the vision of the library now and into the future.[1]

Middle Country Library Foundation, Centereach, New York

Values Statement

The Middle Country Library Foundation values public libraries as primary resources for individual members of society to realize literacy. To fulfill its mission and vision, the Foundation values the power of innovation and creativity; the necessity of financial integrity; [and] the imperative to respect and prize diversity in all its forms.[2]

Library Foundation of Los Angeles, Los Angeles, California

Core Values

- High achievement: We set high bars for performance.
- Accountability: Each of us is responsible for our individual and team outcomes.
- Empathy: Our work is defined by caring for others.
- Learning: Learning enables growth.
- Curiosity: Brave, bold questions help us evolve.
- Adaptability: We welcome change.
- Partnerships: We do our work by building bridges.
- Collaboration: Respect and communication build successful teams.

(continued)

Friends of the Joseph T. Simpson Public Library, Mechanicsburg, Pennsylvania

Core Values

The Friends of the Joseph T. Simpson Public Library Board of Directors adheres to the following values, in alignment with the Library Board of Trustees (Note that in this example, the Friends are agreeing with and applying the core values that the Trustees have developed.):

- Lifelong Learning—Providing comprehensive services, programs, and collections that encourage educational and intellectual development throughout people's lives and providing opportunities for discovery in settings that are stimulating and engaging in support of literacy and lifelong learning.
- Community—Providing a welcoming environment for people and groups to gather and interact with others and experience learning opportunities.
- Service—Providing and delivering excellent service to all by staff who are friendly, knowledgeable, helpful and approachable.
- Access—Providing access to a wide range of viewpoints, opinions, and ideas, so that all individuals have the opportunity to become lifelong learners.[3]

Notes

1. Williamsburg Regional Library. 2019. "Friends Vision, Mission, and Core Values," https://www.wrl.org/give/friends-mission/#.
2. Middle Country Library Foundation. [n.d.] "Mission/Vision & Values," https://middlecountrylibraryfoundation.org/about/mission-vision-values/.
3. Friends of the Joseph T. Simpson Public Library. August 6, 2021. "Friends of the Joseph T. Simpson Public Library Strategic Plan for 2021–2023," https://www.cumberlandcountylibraries.org/sites/default/files/SIM/Documents/Friends/Friends_Strategic_Plan_2021-2023.pdf.

Library Support Group Ethics Statements

After values statements, another kind of statement to think about creating is an ethics statement. Library ethics statements stem from a history that is enlightening. Starting in 1939, in order to provide guidance for professionals offering information services, library staff, and library trustees, the American Library Association (ALA) devised an official Code of Ethics, which was updated in 2008. After the creation of such a code, the United for Libraries division of ALA adopted an amended Public Library Trustee Ethics Statement so that library boards of trustees would have documentation to make their ethical obligations clear. Following these codes and statements, ALA created further statements such as Freedom to Read, The Library Bill of Rights, and Freedom to View. Based on these documents, many libraries nationwide adopted similar codes and statements to guide work responsibilities, to stand behind positive points of view within the profession, and to reinforce trust concepts among their staff members. The groundwork of these documents eventually inspired many library support groups to formulate and model their own codes and statements to guide ethical behavior.

Until 1994, there was no national ethics statement that Friends of the Library groups could abide by. In that year, Tennessee libraries developed a statement, revised in 2013, that compared the responsibilities of trustees, library directors, regional libraries, and Friends of the Library. From this base, the Friends of Tennessee Libraries chose to clarify Friends' responsibilities and help them make better decisions by developing and adopting a final version of the Ethical Dozen for Friends of the Library in 2015. The twelve points in this statement offer a clear ethical path for Friends and other types of library support groups to follow.[31]

These ethics statements could be adapted for an organizational ethics statement by any Friends, foundation, or trust group by applying any particular group requisites and fully acknowledging the Friends of Tennessee Libraries as their source in the document. You will find the full text of The Ethical Dozen for Friends of the Library included in the appendixes (used with permission).[32]

Conflict-of-Interest Policies

To further reinforce a library support group's code of ethics, it can be very helpful to have a conflict-of-interest policy to accompany it. Any nonprofit group that is going to be seeking and accepting donations of materials, money, and volunteer time from any source can keep its trustworthiness and honesty at the forefront by not only attesting to a code of ethics but also by augmenting the code with a well-crafted conflict-of-interest policy. Such a policy also provides guidelines for group members so they can be certain their roles, goals, and activities are completely on the up and up.

Of course, while a board, group members, and any stakeholders work toward adding a conflict-of-interest clause to their nonprofit's policies, it is important to follow similar steps for creating the other kinds of statements mentioned in this chapter so far. The policy can first be drawn up by a committee; then be circulated among those benefitting from the policy to get feedback; and eventually be finalized through the agreement of all parties before becoming official.

TEXTBOX 3.8

SAMPLE CONFLICT-OF-INTEREST POLICY

This example of a conflict-of-interest policy from the Poudre River Friends of the Library in Fort Collins, Colorado, can serve as a suggested format for any library support group as they develop their own document.

Conflict-of-Interest Policy

The standard of behavior at the (full name of group) is that all volunteers and Board members scrupulously avoid conflicts of interest between the interests of the (full name of group) on one hand, and personal, professional, and business interests on the other. This includes avoiding potential and actual conflicts of interest, as well as perceptions of conflicts of interest.

(continued)

The purposes of this policy are to protect the integrity of the (full name of group)'s decision-making process, to enable the public to have confidence in its integrity, and to protect the integrity and reputations of volunteers, Board members, and our libraries. The policy is meant to supplement good judgment, and members are expected to respect its spirit as well as its wording.

No Board member or volunteer shall use his or her position, or the knowledge gained, in such a manner that a conflict between the interest of the organization and his or her interests arises. Each Board member or volunteer has a duty to place the interest of the (full name of group) foremost in any dealings with the organization and has a responsibility to notify the Board when a conflict arises.

In the course of meetings or activities, Board members and volunteers shall disclose any interests in a transaction or decision where the member, his/her business or other nonprofit affiliations, family, employer, or close associates will receive a benefit or gain. If a situation arises that requires discussion by the Board of Directors, the member may be asked to leave the room for the discussion and may not be permitted to vote on the question. The meeting minutes would then reflect the discussion, the vote taken, and any abstentions.[1]

Note

1. Poudre River Friends of the Library. 2022. "By-Laws and Standing Rules," http://www.prfol.org/board/.

Honoring, Respecting, and Acknowledging the Gifts of Donors

When donors provide gifts to Friends, foundations, and trusts, it is imperative to recognize and show appreciation for what has been given. Most groups do just that, but it reinforces the sentiment when a statement of respect and appreciation is expressed up front, before a donation may even be given.

As an example, the Friends Foundation of the Birmingham Public Library openly supports and promotes the Donor Bill of Rights that was created as a collaboration of several nonprofit organizations that are credited along with the text of the document featured in the next textbox. Other library support groups may wish to follow suit. To use this statement, a library support group must include the exact credits given following the document.

This document is significant in that it demonstrates to donors up front how library support groups value their generosity. It would be a positive step for any library support group to show their gratefulness and appreciation for donors' contributions by likewise posting this statement. As the Friends Foundation of the Birmingham Public Library declares along with the statement's inclusion on its website:

> Philanthropy is based on voluntary action for the common good. It is a tradition of giving and sharing that is primary to the quality of life. To assure that philanthropy merits the respect and trust of the general public, and that donors and prospective donors can have full confidence in the not-for-profit organizations and causes they are asked to support, we declare that all donors have these rights.[33]

Consider adopting the Donor Bill of Rights and adding it to your group's website, donation requests, and/or other publicity for your cause.

TEXTBOX 3.9

DONOR BILL OF RIGHTS[1]

I. To be informed of the organization's mission, of the way the organization intends to use donated resources, and of its capacity to use donations effectively for their intended purposes.

II. To be informed of the identity of those serving on the organization's governing board, and to expect the board to exercise prudent judgment in its stewardship responsibilities.

III. To have access to the organization's most recent financial statements.

IV. To be assured their gifts will be used for the purposes for which they were given.

V. To receive appropriate acknowledgment and recognition.

VI. To be assured that information about their donation is handled with respect and with confidentiality to the extent provided by law.

VII. To expect that all relationships with individuals representing organizations of interest to the donor will be professional in nature.

VIII. To be informed whether those seeking donations are volunteers, employees of the organization, or hired solicitors.

IX. To have the opportunity for their names to be deleted from mailing lists that an organization may intend to share.

X. To feel free to ask questions when making a donation and to receive prompt, truthful and forthright answers.

Note

1. The text of this statement in its entirety was developed by the American Association of Fund-Raising Counsel (AAFRC), Association for Healthcare Philanthropy (AHP), Council for Advancement and Support of Education (CASE), and the Association of Fundraising Professionals (AFP), and adopted in November 1993. (Used with permission via this acknowledgment.)

Social Media Presence

In today's library support group world, employing social media platforms can be essential in connecting with library users, potential and current members/volunteers, and in seeking donations. Most libraries themselves now have a social media presence and some add a social media mission statement that provides a general picture of a library's social media efforts as well as links to pages for whatever library support groups with which they may partner.

Reflect upon how the Pima County Public Library in Arizona dedicates an entire page on its website to "The Library on Social Media" and gives a link to the library system's "Social Media Community Guidelines." The page also lists and links all the social media platforms that library users can access to connect to the library virtually as of this writing—Facebook, Instagram, Tik Tok, Twitter, YouTube, Flickr, and SoundCloud. Additionally, it gives a list with links for many of the library's online "Services, Teams, & Programs" and to the individual Facebook pages for each branch library.

Beside the library-specific lists and links, the website provides links to several "Library Friends Groups on Social Media" in the county along with a note that the pages listed are "not maintained by library staff."[34] This is a crucial notation since library support groups are independent entities apart from the actual library system, a detail that needs to be stressed to the public. However, even though such groups are separate from library organizations themselves, there is usually no issue with libraries providing online links to the Friends, foundations, and trusts that aid them. However, to be certain, when your library support group is included on the library's website with a link, be sure it indicates to online users that they will be directed to an outside website as the library is a separate entity and does not maintain that site. Following these rules for user awareness is imperative to avoid confusion about the differences between an independent nonprofit that benefits the library and the library itself.

Ultimately, social media is a wonderful way to promote library support group mission and vision statements, plus other particulars. This might entice interested parties to join as they explore what's new and peruse group activities and accomplishments. Later on, in chapter 6, you will get more details and advice concerning social media and library support groups. In the meantime, I will address another side of the use of social media among library support groups.

Online Privacy Notices

Despite how essential and beneficial data storage and online communication has become, and despite how carefully your library support group protects its online resources, it is unfortunately all too easy to realize how electronic security can be breached and ways that underhanded people can take illegal advantage of the records they gain. The practice of doxing—the compilation and dissemination of personally identifying information and facts about individuals' lives in order to sell it, usually online—has become rampant. Data infringements are common and frequently in the news. The public has become more aware and wary of this dilemma, and rightfully so.

Under these circumstances, when upstanding people are interested in joining a library support nonprofit group, paying their dues, and giving money and time to causes, they need to be assured that it is as safe as possible to do so in such an environment. Therefore, in this era of all varieties of virtual communication and payment, it behooves any library support group to include an online privacy notice for those signing up as new members as well as for those who become donors. This can provide a sense of security and personal control for those participating in a nonprofit cause as well as for the nonprofit itself. It can also offer some protection from retribution if someone manages to gain illegitimate access to personal information via any social media platform or virtual communication tool that a library support group is using.

Essentially, to generate a privacy notice, engage those who are members of the library support nonprofit, board members, library personnel, or any stakeholders in helping to fashion such a notice in order to get feedback and, in due course, to give final version approval. Be sure to include the privacy notice in group publicity and on sign-up forms or add a notation to let group donors and participants know how they can get a copy online or in print if they wish.

> **TEXTBOX 3.10**
>
> **SAMPLE ONLINE PRIVACY NOTICE**
>
> This privacy notice discloses the privacy practices for www.prfol.org, the webpage for Poudre River Friends of the Library.
>
> ### Information Collection, Use, and Sharing
>
> We only have access to/collect information that you voluntarily give us via email or other direct contact from you. We will not sell or rent this information to anyone. We will use your information to respond to you regarding the reason you contacted us. We will not share your information with any third party outside of our library organizations. If you join the Friends of the Library, we will use your email information to announce our book sales, events, and annual meetings, to send membership reminders, and other occasional library-related issues.
>
> ### Your Access to and Control over Information
>
> You may opt out of any future contacts from us at any time. You can do this by contacting us at fol@prfol.org. Each email also gives an opt-out option.
>
> ### Security
>
> If you join online, your credit card information is processed via PayPal. We do not retain that information. For the PayPal policy, see: https://www.paypal.com/us/webapps/mpp/ua/privacy-full.[1]
>
> ### Note
>
> 1. Poudre River Friends of the Library.

You may also want to direct any concerned members or donors to resources they can use to protect their online and other personal information. A librarian at the facility your group serves will be able to help you gather materials to share with anyone who needs it. There is a good chance the library has already assembled such information in the research section of its website or as a pamphlet. It would behoove any library support group to ask for this help.

One resource you might review and recommend to concerned individuals is an impressive page set up on the San Jose Public Library's website. Its Virtual Privacy Lab is an exemplary collection of toolkits, some most pertinent to locals but with others being useful to anyone who needs assistance. Toolkits include links, tips, and resources to empower users to customize their online identity and covers online privacy, social media and online sharing, internet security, data sharing, information footprints, anonymity and tracking, and other tools.[35] This webpage might also be of interest to library support group leaders to evaluate the safety of electronic communication methods and social media platforms their group may be utilizing.

Memorandum of Understanding

Another practical document is a memorandum of understanding (MOU). You may already be familiar with this kind of document but are unsure of how to arrange for its use for your particular situation, or based on what you read about it in chapter 1, you may be wondering about more details regarding what this document is and what it does in the first place. In either case, let us look at the role it can play in keeping things running smoothly within library support groups and between groups and the libraries they are aiding.

You may recall that the Denver Public Library and the Friends Foundation with which it partners entered an MOU, which put both the library and the library support group devoted to it on the same track. From the story that was relayed regarding the creation of this document in the example, you may have basically gathered what defines an MOU and when it might be useful. However, there is much more to it, and if you are not already familiar, what follows is information that can clarify what an MOU is, its purpose, and how you can successfully develop and use such an agreement.

An MOU is a written agreement between parties that expresses their aligned will, and it details the intent of a common line of action. This kind of document can be bilateral between two parties, or it can be multilateral, between more than two. Essentially, an MOU is a means for all involved parties to express that they agree to move forward toward their common goals. It indicates a mutual understanding based upon clear information and the important stances each party holds. These should be agreed upon prior to the creation of the document to ensure it is unambiguous and effective.

Although an MOU is not legally binding it signifies a serious declaration. It is less formal than a contract but more official than a handshake. Despite the fact that it might sound like a contract, which is legally binding and enforceable by a judge, it is not. It is the same as a letter of intent in United States law and basically demonstrates each party's willingness to agree. It also acts as the foundation for negotiations, it discusses a mutually beneficial goal(s), and it expresses the desire for both/all parties to work together toward attaining the goal(s). To ensure that an MOU addresses all goals, intentions, and expectations in a straightforward document that all parties can agree to and understand, it is essential that formulating its content be guided by an experienced lawyer. As indicated in chapter 1 for other circumstances, a group could hire an attorney, find out if their partner library's attorney can provide assistance, or if they can locate someone who may be willing to provide attorney services to a library support nonprofit without charge.

In general, an MOU should include in its scope details about targeted intended actions, the names of the parties involved in the agreement, and the respective responsibilities of those parties. Other key elements to incorporate are timing for the start of the agreement, the length of the agreement, and how the agreement may be terminated.[36]

As with other documents that library support groups might wish to develop along with the input from their partnering library or library system, the best place to begin is by having all parties prepare their own draft of what they anticipate the document might deal with regarding ideal expectations, desired outcomes, a list of any potential outcomes they would not compromise upon, and a statement on how they believe all stakeholders would benefit from the MOU. Comparing initial positions is a useful way to begin discussions on developing an MOU. Whether a Friends organization, a library foundation or trust, or even a short-term, specially formed committee or task force, that library support group and the library recipient of its efforts can benefit from having an MOU when there is any conflict or confusion about each other's roles, responsibilities, and requirements. This can be true for a large library system as well as a small-town solitary library.

Overall, there are more benefits than disadvantages to creating an MOU agreement. The advantages include establishing mutual goals and objectives; reducing uncertainty that prevents the possibility of future disputes; setting a foundation for future goals; allowing for easy dissolution of the non–legally binding agreement if terms are not being met; and establishing a clear record of terms agreed upon for later evaluation. The main disadvantages are that either party can usually exit the agreement or not meet expectations without suffering negative consequences. However, despite these disadvantages since it is not legally binding, such an agreement is still viewed as a significant step forward. Recognizing the time and effort put forth to create the document, learning what is important to others involved, and understanding the importance of working together to progress all help to ensure its success and a cordial mutual working environment.

Whenever libraries or library systems and their dedicated library support groups are having difficulty perceiving each other's purpose or in being compatible as partners in building trust, commitment, mutual goals, and understanding, positive agreements can be achieved by using MOUs as focal points for solidarity.[37]

Establishing Governance: Creating Bylaws for Library Support Groups

Once a potential library support foundational group has been convened and is ready to make their group official, the next step is absolutely critical. Creating bylaws for the group provides a complete organizational outline for the newly forming organization that is part of the mandated charter, articles of incorporation, or other document each state legally requires. It is an operational guide for a nonprofit that does fundraising and donor-seeking to benefit its designated library or library system. Small, medium, and large library support groups should create their bylaws in a standard style and format that is clear and straightforward.

Some people might think that bylaws are just dusty old documents that were initially required but that will eventually become unused and almost forgotten as time passes. However, bylaws are essential to the existence and operation of any library Friends, foundation, or trust organization. By knowing about, referring to, and applying library support group bylaws, all members and stakeholders can clearly comprehend how the organization is governed. Furthermore, because bylaws are legal documents that dictate how an organization must be run and function, failure to follow their stipulations can potentially inflict overwhelming negative consequences on an organization and its board.

In order to meet the legal demands of a properly created set of bylaws, a newly formed library support organization, or a currently functioning one that wishes to revise their bylaws, will do well to follow these suggestions:

- Get assistance for creating new bylaws, or amending bylaws already in effect, from a professional with solid experience in nonprofit matters. Cutting corners and using an advisor who is not an expert is an unwise choice. Even with expert legal guidance, it is still the responsibility of the board to have input into the provisions and to vote to approve the final document.

- When working on bylaws, focus on the basics. These will include such topics as organizational purpose; board structure; officer position descriptions and roles; terms of board service; officer and board member succession and removal; official meeting requirements; membership provisions; voting rights; conflict-of-interest policy; a provision for future amendments; additional non-negotiable areas that may be judged as necessary; and notations of adoption, revision, and amendment dates. Aim to avoid provisions that might tie the hands of future boards—be "forward thinking."
- Be sure to know about and understand all the provisions of your bylaws, whether newly created or revised, and follow them carefully. It is a good practice for board members to review the bylaws annually and to ensure that all new board members have read and understand them. This is important because a board member is obligated to follow the bylaws and a court of law will side with your bylaws in any dispute that is brought forth by another board member, a volunteer, an employee, or a beneficiary of the group's help. If you are uncertain about anything in your bylaws, consult a fellow board member or a legal professional to aid you.
- Be prepared to review, update, revise, and amend your bylaws if and when times and circumstances change. Make sure your amendments make sense in the long term and carefully follow the provisions in your bylaws to make the changes.
- Remember that your bylaws are not a policy and procedures manual. As mentioned earlier in this chapter, you will want to create separate standing rules for your group to follow that are detached from the bylaws and not in conflict with any of the provisions in it.[38]
- Keep in mind that you will need to include general descriptions of duties for the founding officers as part of your legally approved bylaws. You may also want to outline the responsibilities of regular members and volunteers. As long as you also address the ability to amend the bylaws later on, you can adjust the duties and add positions as need be, which is often desirable.
- Examine the bylaws included in the appendixes of this book for some useful examples to emulate. Also in the appendixes you will find a document (used with permission) from the Friends of the Libraries section of the New York Library Association called "Annotated By-laws: What Should Be Included in By-Laws for Friends Organizations?" The document is useful as a guideline in preparing your bylaws, but as usual be sure to check your own state's nonprofit requirements and consult with your legal expert to ensure your document meets the requirements of your particular locale.[39]

The diligent crafting or amending of library Friend, foundation, or trust bylaws is central to a new, merged, or active group's development and function. It offers structure to and security for a group's governance and eliminates guesswork. To conclude, consider this motto: "Good governance establishes a foundation for good work."[40] That is the essence of well-formulated and functional bylaws.

Notes

1. Montana State Library. 2023. "How to Organize a Friends Group," https://msl.mt.gov/libraries/consulting/online_publications/newlibrarydirectorshandbook/friends_volunteers/organizingfriends.

2. William Malsam. June 8, 2022. "Steering Committee: Definition, Roles, & Meeting Tips." Project Manager, https://www.projectmanager.com/blog/steering-committee-definition.

3. Montana State Library.

4. Sophia Barron. September 19, 2019. "12 Tips for Running a Successful Meeting."Owl Labs, https://resources.owllabs.com/blog/meeting-tips.

5. Jeremy Barlow. August 18, 2019. "What Is the Role of an Ex Officio Board Member?" Board Effect, https://www.boardeffect.com/blog/what-is-the-role-of-an-ex-officio-board-member/.

6. Kristin Skinner. October 20, 2021. "The Ex Officio Board Member Role Explained." Aprio, https://aprioboardportal.com/news/ex-officio-board-member-role-and-responsibilities/.

7. Jeremy Barlow.

8. Jess Wolwszyn. August 12, 2022. "Who You Need on Your Nonprofit Board." Classy Blog, https://www.classy.org/blog/who-you-need-on-nonprofit-board/.

9. Internal Revenue Service. 2022. "Exemption Requirments—501(c)(3) Organizations." United States Government, https://www.irs.gov/charities-non-profits/charitable-organizations/exemption-requirements-501c3-organizations.

10. Internal Revenue Service.

11. Internal Revenue Service. 2022. "Intermediate Sanctions—Excise Benefit Transactions." United State Government, https://www.irs.gov/charities-non-profits/charitable-organizations/intermediate-sanctions-excess-benefit-transactions.

12. Internal Revenue Service. 2022. "How Can We Help You?" United States Government, https://www.irs.gov/.

13. Sarah E. Merkle. October 23, 2019. "Organizational Rules for Nonprofits to Follow." BoardEffect, https://www.boardeffect.com/blog/organizational-rules-nonprofits-follow/.

14. Henry M. Robert III et al. *Robert's Rules of Order*. 12th ed. PublicAffairs, 2020.

15. Alice Sturgis. *The Standard Code of Parliamentary Procedure*. 4th ed. New York: McGraw Hill, 2000.

16. American Institute of Parliamentarians. *American Institute of Parliamentarians Standard Code of Parliamentary Procedure*. New York: Mc-Graw-Hill, 2012.

17. Jim Slaughter. February 7, 2022. "*Robert's Rules of Order* vs. *The Standard Code of Parliamentary Procedure* vs the AIP Standard Code of Parliamentary Procedure." Law Firm Carolinas, https://lawfirmcarolinas.com/blog/roberts-rules-of-order-versus-the-standard-code-of-parliamentary-procedure-versus-aip-standard-code/.

18. Merkle.

19. Merkle.

20. Brex, Inc. 2021. "22 Vision Statement Examples to Help You Write Your Own," https://www.brex.com/blog/vision-statement-examples/.

21. Chris Drew. October 23, 2022. "31 Examples of Library Vision and Mission Statements." Helpful Professor, https://helpfulprofessor.com/library-mission-statements/.

22. Society for Human Resource Management (SHRM). 2022. "What Is the Difference between Mission, Vision, and Values Statements?" SHRM, https://www.shrm.org/resourcesandtools/tools-and-samples/hr-qa/pages/isthereadifferencebetweenacompany%E2%80%99smission,visionandvaluestatements.aspx.

23. Society for Human Resource Management (SHRM).

24. Bâton Global. 2022. "How to Write Mission, Vision, and Values Statements—100 Examples to Guide You through the Process," https://www.batonglobal.com/post/how-to-write-mission-vision-and-values-statements-with-examples.

25. David Gorton. June 27, 2022. "Mission Statement Explained: How It Works and Examples." Investopedia, https://www.investopedia.com/terms/m/missionstatement.asp.

26. Bâton Global.

27. Julia Martins. July 26, 2022. "How to Write a Vision Statement: Steps and Examples." Asana, https://asana.com/resources/vision-statement.

28. The Hive Collective. May 11, 2023. "6 Reasons to Focus on Nonprofit Board Culture," https://hivecollective.net/2023/05/11/6-reasons-to-focus-on-nonprofit-board-culture/.

29. Tony Russo. [n.d.] "How to Write a Value Statement for a Nonprofit." Chron, https://smallbusiness.chron.com/write-value-statement-nonprofit-73594.html.

30. Russo.

31. Donald b. Reynolds. October 12, 2015. "Ethics for Library Trustees, Staff, and Friends." Library Hotline, https://libraries.vermont.gov/sites/libraries/files/PublicLibraries/Trustees/Friends/Ethics%20Statement%20for%20Friends%20Library%20Hotline.pdf.

32. Friends of Tennessee Libraries. September 18, 2015. "The Ethical Dozen for Friends of the Library," https://www.friendstnlibraries.org/wp-content/uploads/Ethical-Dozen-FOTL.pdf.

33. Friends Foundation of the Birmingham Public Library. 2023. "About the Friends Foundation," https://www.friendsofthebpl.org/about/.

34. Pima County Public Library. 2022. "The Library on Social Media," https://www.library.pima.gov/the-library-on-social-media/.

35. San Jose Public Library. 2023. "Virtual Privacy Lab," https://www.sjpl.org/privacy.

36. ContractsCounsel. 2022. "Memorandum of Understanding," https://www.contractscounsel.com/t/us/memorandum-of-understanding.

37. ContractsCounsel.

38. Greg McRay. March 14, 2022. "Nonprofit Bylaws—The Dos and Don'ts." Foundation Group, https://www.501c3.org/nonprofit-bylaws-the-dos-and-donts/.

39. Lisa C. Wemett. "Annotated By-Laws: What Should Be Included in By-Laws for Friends Organizations?" New York Library Association, 2021.

40. McRay.

CHAPTER 4

Once a Friends of the Library, Foundation, or Trust Is Legally Established

IMAGINE THIS GREAT NEWS! Your library support group has finally had its charter or articles of incorporation legally approved, including, of course, your bylaws. It was a challenging task for the originating group members to take on and get done, but it was accomplished by following all the required or recommended nonprofit organizational steps covered in the first two chapters. Now, it's time to move forward into putting the steps into real action.

The next step to take is finalizing your executive board and any other leadership roles that need to be put into place. It is essential to select the best, most knowledgeable people who are interested in filling and available to fill each role. You may be thinking: Where is a good place to start? The answer is with a solid team of people dedicated to the idea of effectively getting the newly established library support nonprofit successfully off the ground and moving forward.

The Founding Core Group Job Descriptions

By now you know that the ideal place to begin is with the core group of individuals who make up the team that put your charter or articles of incorporation into place. This group can decide what additional members are needed, if any, and how to go about seeking them out. It can also develop the job requirements and duties for each role you already have in place plus those you want to fill to add to the core group, according to the bylaws. If bylaws need to be amended or revised to support the need for any new positions, the core group will have the ability to do this if the bylaws were created appropriately.

After you have chosen the positions that you require to lead your group, you will want to devise job descriptions for each individual's role. This will help the rest of the board to understand each fellow leader's roles and responsibilities and allow those filling each role to understand the expectations for their position. Here are some points you might want to think about incorporating in each of your job descriptions:

- Position: The official board member's title
- Function: The overall role, purpose, or authority of the position
- Duties and responsibilities: The specific activities and responsibilities of the position
- Qualifications and requirements: The expectations such as time requirements, meeting attendance, committee involvement, and so on, plus any qualifications, skills, knowledge, and experience needed to carry out the duties of the position
- Expected outcomes of the position: The specific results that the position is accountable for and to whom
- Orientation and training: What orientation/training may be offered, the time commitment to complete it, and the topics that will be covered
- Term: The length of time and dates for the position to be fulfilled and any options or limitations for serving additional terms
- Evaluation: If, when, and how performance and participation quality will be determined, and evaluations will be provided
- Benefits: Any rewards or perks that may come with the position such as memberships, payment of expenses, webinar fees, and so on
- Approval dates for the position: The date that the job description was approved or revised and if/when the position description may come up for review[1]

In your descriptions of duties and responsibilities, you may want to add the following basic expectations using whatever wording you like as long as the essential concepts are intact. These can be worthwhile additions because library support groups are, of course, legal nonprofits. As leaders of a nonprofit group, board members on all levels have three primary legal duties that are quite meaningful and common to all nonprofits:

- Duties of care: Obliges all board members to ensure prudent use of all assets, including whatever facilities are used as part of their work; positive actions for and attention paid to the people they work with and serve; and the promotion of the goodwill of the organization.
- Duties of loyalty: Guarantees that all the activities and transactions of the organization advance its mission; that conflicts of interest are recognized and disclosed; and that all decisions are made in the best interest of the Friends, foundation, or trust instead of private or personal interests.
- Duties of obedience: Requires compliance with all applicable laws and regulations; commitment to the group's own bylaws; and adherence to the group's stated purposes or mission.

Although the significant focal points of these three legal duties have been addressed in one way or the other in previous chapters, it can be beneficial to review the duties and keep them in mind as people are chosen for and/or elected to a nonprofit board. If you feel the need, you may also want to consult with your state attorneys general, state charity officials, and state-oriented nonprofit associations to locate other resources on board roles and responsibilities.[2] Plus, if you are a member of United for Libraries or have free access to the BoardSource Exchange from your state library or other source as discussed at the end of chapter 1, know that it provides an additional avenue for such investigation.

Further Descriptions of Duties for Library Support Group Boards

Remember that much of the information in this section depends on how large and/or complex your library support group may be, but it is provided so that you can pick and choose the topics and concepts that are most pertinent to your particular group's wishes and needs. Consider the library support group style and function for which you are nominating and selecting board members or officers as well as the type and size of the library community you will be serving. Is your organization a Friends of the Library, a foundation, a Friends foundation, a trust, or some other kind of nonprofit library support group? Is your group working to support a large city or regional library that needs the added value of an executive director and directors for targeted needs?

With your particular limitations in mind, such as if your library is small and/or serves a widespread rural area with a small population, your needs will probably be more basic. In that case, you might possibly decide to have a combined board member title like that of "secretary/treasurer." On the other hand, if your library serves a large urban area, you may need to recruit special managers and directors under an executive director to take charge of specific matters like database management or marketing.

Keeping in mind your particular needs, you will want to choose positions from the following list of potential roles and the duties that usually come with them. Even if you decide that your group functions would improve by having a different or additional focus as positions and roles are designed, this list can offer you a place to begin and to reserve for the future.

- Executive Director:
  - Exemplifies all aspects of an outstanding leader and fills the role of liaison with the library that is benefitting from the organization's efforts
  - Manages and effectively connects/communicates with internal (such as library staff liaisons and the library support group board of directors) and external stakeholders (such as partners, volunteers, the library community being served, and donors) who might play a role at any level of library support group activities and involvement
  - Oversees all of the processes used by the organization to fulfill its mission through its daily activities and functions
  - Takes responsibility for all aspects of financial management, conscientious stewardship, and effective business decision-making involving funding diversity, program expense allocations, and effectively filling nonprofit staffing needs
  - Creates an environment that fosters constructive future growth and sets a tone for adopting positive values, policies, and beliefs to reflect the identity of the library support organization
  - Possesses a firm understanding of the organization's mission and a clear vision to achieve it through strategies that align with its overall purpose of supporting the library it serves[3]

- President or chair:
  - Serves as the chief volunteer for the organization
  - Provides leadership for the other members of the board of directors in achieving the group's mission

- Schedules meetings, creates meeting agendas, and distributes agendas and other necessary documents to the board of directors with meeting announcements
- Plans and conducts meetings of the board of directors aligning with the chosen parliamentary authority
- For board consideration and approval, recommends the establishment of special committees to enhance or meet the group's mission and oversees the appointment of chairs for those committees
- Seeks volunteers for special committees and coordinates individual board member assignments
- Serves ex officio as a member of associated groups or with the leadership of the library that is being served as needed and attends their meetings when invited
- Makes certain that board matters are handled appropriately; committees are functioning efficiently; qualified new board members are recruited in a timely fashion; orientations are well-planned and run; and meeting preparations are completed properly
- Discusses the issues confronting the organization with the board and any important outside parties
- Guides and mediates board actions with respect to organizational priorities and governance concerns
- Monitors financial planning and financial reports
- Plans and facilitates group strategic planning
- Prepares an annual report which reflects the organization's achievements toward its mission and objectives
- Speaks to the media when needed, represents the organization to the community, and ensures that high-quality group publicity is being produced.
- At least annually, reviews matters of governance that relate to the board's structure, management, and relationship to the library being served

- Vice president or vice chair:
  - Acts as president or chair on behalf of the person currently in the role who may be absent
  - Reports to and works closely with the president or chair to assist with the presidential duties
  - May be assigned to a special area of responsibility such as membership, media, personnel, annual events, or other group causes
  - Performs other duties as assigned by the president or chair

- Treasurer:
  - Manages the finances of the organization by keeping clear and careful records of all financial transactions
  - Counts and double-checks all monetary proceeds from fundraising events and other income, and arranges deposit of the funds in the financial institution selected by the board
  - Pays the invoices of the organization and keeps track of all expenditures
  - Ensures that appropriate financial reports are made available to the board for meetings and otherwise as needed

- Reports, on a regular basis, to the board on key financial events, trends, concerns, and assessments relating to organizational fiscal health
- Provides an annual budget to the board for their approval and monitors the budget throughout the entire fiscal year
- Brings financial matters, procedures, and responsibilities to the board's attention for discussion, solutions, and approval as needed
- Trains other board members to assist with financial procedures as needed
- Recommends audits and the selection of an auditor, if required, and meets and confers with the auditor[4]
- Works with the board to find a bank that does not charge fees for community groups when possible, to choose who has signing authority, and to decide how many signatures are required (usually the treasurer and one other board member)[5]

- Secretary
  - Maintains documents and correspondence of the board and ensures effective management of the organization's records
  - Manages the notetaking, recording, and archiving of board meeting minutes
  - Distributes minutes for each meeting in a timely fashion prior to each subsequent meeting and revises minutes as needed after discussion and approval of the agreed-upon content
  - Demonstrates familiarity with the organization's legal documents in order to note their applicability during meetings

- Committee chairperson:
  - Researches, plans, and oversees the logistics of the committee's assigned purpose and operations
  - Reports to the president on the progress of or concerns with the committee's targeted goal
  - Presents committee decisions and recommendations to the board
  - Assigns duties to committee members
  - Ensures that all committee members have the information and training needed to fill their roles
  - Sets agendas and runs meetings to plan, organize, prepare for, and ultimately run the special event or activity assigned to the committee
  - Ensures distribution of committee meeting minutes and other appropriate documents
  - Coordinates with all those involved in seeing the committee objectives come to fruition
  - Evaluates the final outcomes and effectiveness of the committee's work in reaching its goals and objectives

- Board member or member-at-large:
  - Comprehends and expresses a commitment to the organization's mission and purpose
  - Keeps current with issues and trends that affect the organization
  - Prepares for meetings by reading agendas, minutes, reports, and other documentation in order to actively participate in any ways needed

- Regularly attends meetings and shares information and ideas with the president that may be addressed on subsequent meeting agendas
- Contributes skills and knowledge through active meeting participation and on any committee assignments
- Asks questions when explanations or more details are needed
- Understands and helps to monitor the organization's financial affairs
- Avoids any potential conflicts of interest
- Agrees to and maintains confidentiality whenever needed
- Is aware of legal and regulatory requirements and ensures compliance[6]

- Ex officio member:
    - Serves only on the board as long as they are not included on another board with competing interests
    - Willingly contributes knowledge, expertise, and experience to enhance the board's function
    - Adheres to the duties, responsibilities, expectations, rights, and limits of authority as dictated by the board's bylaws
    - Prepares for, attends, and contributes to board meetings regularly
    - Assists the board with appropriate outside connections and interests when needed to enhance the board's operations[7]

Again, when you are creating each job description, the general format you will want to follow is as follows:

- Position title
- Summary of the position
- Election process for and duration of the position
- Responsibilities
- Qualifications
- Date the job description was approved by the board of directors

If you would like to see constructive example of a job description, please check the appendices.

Recruiting New Library Support Group Leaders and Board Members

When a new group is formed, the core group members have been the ones to get things in motion to compose the bylaws and legally apply for nonprofit tax status. Once the new group is official and can begin to take more action, it is time for current core members to step into regular roles of leadership if they are willing and able, and they have not done so already.

It is also time to evaluate the board composition and figure out if additional positions are needed. Perhaps the core group decides that none of them is skilled enough to completely take on the role of treasurer and a willing and capable person needs to be found. Then again, it might become evident that, if more and better decisions are to be made and several upcoming committee chair and co-chair positions are required, adding a few (or more) at-large members would be wise. Or it might suddenly seem prudent to take the advice about adding "assistant" positions serving "in-training" with those in the core positions. No matter what the reasons may be, this is when recruitment for qualified new individuals comes into play.

There are many workable avenues to take to find and enlist new and eager community members to join forces with your board whether to shore up the board with new positions when first getting started, later on when vacancies occur, or when the board composition is reevaluated in the future and it becomes evident that additional positions are needed. Here are a few recommendations. It would likely be beneficial to have a discussion with fellow board members to consider these ideas and perhaps come up with some new ones.

- Evaluate your current board and determine what community connections, personal styles, and areas of expertise are already represented on it. Compare a list of open positions and/or positions you wish to create to those already available, then aim to fill the gaps.
- Discuss the parameters of meeting time(s) and location(s) and determine if these may be attendance barriers for those interested in joining the board. If adjustments need to be made, try rearranging meetings, and consider offering an option for board members to participate electronically.
- Make sure that your group reputation is solid by assuring that meetings are meaningful, well-run, inclusive, and productive.
- Incorporate several methods of promoting your board and its purpose through an easily accessed group website, social media platforms, and printed materials. Invite those interested in the board to apply online, by using a paper form, or submitting a letter of interest.
- As an example, the Friends of the Sun Prairie Public Library in Wisconsin posts a special notice on their website, with hyperlinks to the job description, questionnaire, and email contact, that says, "Are you interested in serving as a board member for the Friends of the Sun Prairie Library? The Friends are actively seeking new board members to bring fresh and diverse perspectives and help us grow our community, and we want YOU! What does a Friends board member do? Please read through the Friends Board Member Volunteer Job Description to find out. If you are interested in applying to serve on the Friends board, please fill out this Questionnaire for Prospective Board Members and return it to the Sun Prairie Library. Questions? Please email us."[8]
- Talk it up! Current members can readily share information with their contacts in conversations where interested parties might be drawn to apply once they understand the value of the board's work.
- If current board members know people who would fit the bill perfectly for a position on the board, fill them in with information about how they might serve and personally invite them to consider applying to join.
- Publicize the library support group and the board at library events, fundraisers, and other activities. Talk to people at the events to discover those who may be enticed, ask for their contact information, and connect later on to pursue their interest.[9] Make doing these things a priority.

TEXTBOX 4.1

APPLYING FOR BOARD MEMBERSHIP

We have questionnaires and applications for new board members. We use these to begin our process. Then our review committee examines the materials and passes them on to our Nominating Committee. The Nominating Committee interviews each candidate and, if the candidate passes the interview, nominates the candidate to the full board. The board then either fills an immediate opening or collects names for the annual meeting of our membership, when the members vote on enough candidates to fill open spots. Our current board includes thirteen adult board members and two junior board members, ages sixteen to eighteen.[1]

Cynthia J. Mestelle
President, Friends of the Sun Prairie Public Library Board

Note

1. Cynthia J. Mestelle. Email message to author, November 28, 2023.

Including Teenage Members on the Board

As you are thinking about potential members for your library support group board, consider the possibility of including high school age students to serve along with the adult members. For many good reasons, having youth representation on adult boards is a positive approach. However, before you decide to add a teen or teens to your board, be aware that states have varying laws addressing youth serving on adult boards. Reasons for laws involving youth on boards can range through a variety of issues and concerns. For example, there could be fears that minors could be held liable in potentially complicated legal situations; there could be apprehension about the possibilities of youth being manipulated by adults to secure votes; or there could be the worry that underage youth who are permitted to vote could threaten the validity of contracts or decisions made by adult boards.

If you learn that youth under the age of eighteen are restricted from full voting membership on adult boards in your state, there are still alternative options you might take:

- Teenagers might serve on adult boards as *non-voting members* who are not able to hold offices or chair committees. They may be allowed to attend meetings, discuss issues, share ideas, and assist as volunteers.
- Youth could serve in advisory capacities as *ex officio members* from their library-oriented teen council or advisory committee, participate in some discussions, share opinions, and report back to their youth cohorts and library staff advisors.
- Youth could be given limited opportunities for board participation as *teen representatives* to pass on details to the board about teen interests for analyzing potential youth programs to be funded; participate in mentor/mentee relationships with adult board members while aiming for full board membership when majority is

reached; help to secure youth volunteers to assist with book sales; or any number of "unofficial" but useful duties.

Even if your state laws restrict the participation of youth on adult boards, The Freechild Institute for Youth Engagement makes a clear argument for having youth serving on adult boards in any ways possible:

> The Freechild Institute believes that no matter who youth are, where they live, whatever they do with their time, and what they'll do with the rest of their lives, young people today can, should, and must become engaged everywhere throughout their lives and our society. Youth engagement fosters new thinking, new actions, and new solutions that can change the world in positive, powerful ways.[10]

The following are some instances that describe how I have seen firsthand that youth engagement on adult boards has positive outcomes. When I was a librarian at the City of Mesa Library in Arizona, there was always a teen representative serving on its Library Board of Trustees. The teens who served were members of the Young Adult Advisory Council at the library, and they ran for and were elected to this board position by the other teens on the council. Later on, after college, one teen, by then an adult, expressed interest and was elected to the board again, eventually becoming chair. Although this was a library trustee board position and not one on a library support group board, it shows that occasionally forward-thinking libraries have had the wisdom to include teenagers in their ranks when they are permitted to do so.

The same held true for the Friends of the Poudre River Library Board of Directors in Colorado where I lived after Arizona. Through the subsequent years that I was a librarian there, at the invitation of the Friends Board of Directors, our teen advisory group chose a teen to represent them on the board with the adult members. After I retired and was elected to the board myself, I worked with the teen services librarian at that time to recruit the next "teen representative" to serve on the board.

This is not common practice, but perhaps, according to the Freechild Institute, it should be. Inviting teens to participate on boards of directors gives them an opportunity to learn the process of serving in that capacity; teaches them about board procedures and planning; allows the adults to hear youthful perspectives; develops skills and builds self-esteem; shows them that adults respect them and their viewpoints; allows them to earn service learning credits if needed; gives them an excellent participatory experience to put on employment résumés and college applications; and best of all, makes them more connected and dedicated to libraries, books, and reading for life.

As explained, I have witnessed these benefits firsthand in my library work incorporating teens on boards. Here is further evidence akin to the Arizona example: One teen, who served on the Friends of the Poudre River Library Board in Colorado through high school as the teen representative, went off to college and received a marketing degree. After graduation, she decided she wanted to be elected to the board again, as an adult, so she could continue her board service. Her degree gave her outstanding skills working with computers and marketing, and once she was elected, she took on the task of managing the Board's website and social media. She completely revamped the Friends' website to make it more attractive, informative, and user-friendly. Her high school experience on the Board drew her to gladly come back and take on this subsequent responsibility, the story of which is relayed in the next textbox.

TEXTBOX 4.2

THE VALUE OF TEEN BOARD EXPERIENCE

My service as the teen representative on my local Friends of the Library (FOL) board was, at first, a learning experience more than anything. For two years, I went to all the monthly meetings, volunteered at the regular book sales, and spent one afternoon campaigning for a ballot measure to fund the library district. I didn't know much going into the role except that I loved the library, and I knew I wanted to be part of the group that supported it.

It was strange being a high schooler learning to read organization finances or trying to assist in drafting a new mission statement. Despite everyone's enthusiasm at having a young person on the board, I didn't feel as if I was contributing most of the time as much as I was playing catchup. But, looking back, that was probably the most vital impact it could have left on me.

My connection with the library was my first experience with organized community involvement. It was my first exposure to local governance and organization, the metrics and laws that dictate public funding, and most importantly, understanding where individuals like me fit into it all.

Once I graduated from high school, I could no longer be the FOL's "teen rep," but I did keep contact during college, even working with the FOL for some of my course web projects and continuing to patronize the book sales. While working as a student journalist at my college newspaper, I learned continually more about the impact of local involvement, and I couldn't help but recall the work those in the FOL were doing. That's why after graduating from the university, I knew I wanted to rejoin my FOL board as a full member, now with skills that could help grow the group's role and influence.

Today, I enjoy my role helping to maintain the FOL website and volunteering at the same book sales I did when I was a kid. I truly appreciate the type of community connection the FOL board offers me as a young adult because not only can I easily contribute ideas and hands-on work, but I can see the immediate impact our choices have on a place I care deeply about.[1]

Samantha Ye
Poudre River Friends of the Library Board of Directors
Fort Collins, Colorado

Note

1. Samantha Ye. Email message to author, January 19, 2023.

Here is another example from the Friends of the Sun Prairie Public Library in Wisconsin where the board of directors has been seeking new members to serve. As noted earlier, the board looks not only for adult candidates, but also for two high school students to serve as "junior" directors. Their application for junior director consideration is posted on their website along with a separate solicitation for adult positions. It says:

> The Friends Board has created two new positions for high school students to become junior board members. Do you know someone who might be interested? Please take a look at the Junior Board Member Job Description. Interested students can fill out the Junior Director Application and return it to the Sun Prairie Library or scan and email it to [us].

After clicking and opening the link for the junior director application, it states:

If you are as enthusiastic about the library as we are, consider applying to become a Sun Prairie Public Library Junior Board Member!

- Learn how a library operates.
- Receive volunteer hours
- Get experience working in a city library
- Meet interesting people[11]

Terry Larson from this Friends group explains, "The reason we want to have teenagers on the Board is that most of us on the Board are old enough to remember the 1950s and 60s! We want young people's perspectives and input on Board initiatives. It's good to have younger people in the room. The only challenge has been to fit meetings during times when the students are available."[12]

A beneficial opportunity like this to serve beside adults on boards of directors will give more teenagers a chance to walk the same path as the teens I knew in the past. However, as Larson mentions, keep in mind the school and extracurricular schedules of teens which can cause potential conflicts, and arrange board meetings to accommodate their time constraints. You may even want to consider virtual meeting access for them if they like that option and it can be put into place. By doing so, you may be able to keep them active and engaged despite busy personal agendas.

An exciting option to note is that, in addition to youth serving on boards, a few library support groups here and there have set up "Junior Friends of the Library" sub-groups or separate groups to encourage youth to become members who assist their libraries like the adults do. There will be further information in chapter 7 about junior library support groups and how the Freechild Institute can aid in envisioning and creating effective youth membership and involvement.

Training and Orienting Board Members

Before you have your organizational leaders chosen for roles and ready to work, an important course of action is to put together a new board member orientation packet. After some time, as the board settles into the individual roles and possibly expands, you might wish to create plans for special orientations and trainings with further written documentation that can be used to educate newbies, to which they can refer as needed, and which can be revised and updated in the future as need be. As part of that strategy, consider developing a "buddy system" through which new board members or officers are oriented and mentored one-on-one by longer-serving members of the group.

For potential items to include as you put together a new board member packet, this list of most materials I received from the Poudre River Friends of the Library in Colorado when I joined the Board there several years ago might help. It will give you a good idea of the documents you may choose to include in your introductory packet. You may also opt to create the "packet" in an electronic format that board members can access from their computers. Consider adding:

- A letter of welcome from the board president
- A list of general duties and expectations for all board members (along with job descriptions and expectations)

- A checklist of important board-related materials and other resources
- A description of the history and the roles and responsibilities of the library support group in relation to the library being served
- A chart of the year's board meeting dates, times, and locations
- A chart of special events, activities, and projects currently being planned and provided for the library throughout the year
- A current sample of a board newsletter
- A current example of a board agenda
- A membership list of board officers
- A current list of key board members describing their activities and responsibilities
- A current example of the actual and proposed annual budget
- The conflict-of-interest statement
- A sample of the support group's brochure for publicity
- The organization's bylaws
- The standing rules
- A current sample of a "wish list" from the library, requesting funds for the coming year
- A fact sheet about the group describing its purpose and accomplishments
- Additionally, a memorandum of understanding, if there is one

At the time of this writing, I was embarking on service beyond my volunteer work with the Friends of the Knox County Public Library as a new board member. I was introduced to the membership as a newly elected member at the large annual meeting. Also, at the first regular board meeting I attended, I was given an orientation handbook with information similar to that which I received from the Friends of the Poudre Library. At this first meeting, we did some "getting-to-know-you activities," then went through the handbook. From my own experiences, I know that it is quite beneficial to plan such introductory and orientation time for any new board members to make them feel welcome and appreciated.

If you have two or more new board members, you may decide that a group orientation and training is a sensible way to do it. That way, you can reach everyone at once and not have to repeat the information. You could include not only details but maybe add in a group tour of the library facility you will be serving, any areas specifically designated for group use, or places outside the library where, for instance, donated books or other group materials are being stored. A nice reason to do the training sessions with a group is that everyone gets to hear each other's pertinent questions and feedback that would be potentially missed when doing them one-on-one. However, individualized orientations have their benefits as well. More targeted attention can be paid to the one person being trained, the person can get to know a mentor better from the start, and some people may simply favor this approach instead. You can decide how to proceed by checking in with fellow members already on the board for their opinions and by asking your new members what they think about each kind of training and what they would prefer.

As all the preparation and orientation progresses, be sure to keep the library being served in the loop. Good communication during this time as well as after the group is more sturdily established is essential to positive future teamwork and knowing what to expect between the library and its support group partners. Coming up next, I will more closely examine these relationships.

TEXTBOX 4.3

LETTER OF WELCOME FOR NEW BOARD MEMBERS

You might be thinking about what to include in a letter of welcome for new board members. The following letter template, based on the one I received from the Poudre River Friends of the Library in Colorado, can serve as a guideline when you are writing a similar message:

Dear (name of new member), (office to which elected):

Welcome to the (name of the library support group). You have been elected at our (month, date, year meeting) held at the (name of library or other location).

All our board members have an advisory role in the business conducted by the (name of library support group). As (title of office), you may be asked to take on other specific duties after you have had some time to adjust to your role and to participation at board meetings. However, you can also always volunteer to take part in any other aspects of our organization. Those include (name pertinent individual activities/events such as book shop, sorting, fundraising, membership drives, etc.), or any other projects that come along.

You are encouraged to speak your mind often at board meetings or at other times to communicate your ideas and thoughts on improvements, changes, and any additional pertinent topics.

Your (name of library support group) service is considered to be a large asset and your contributions a great addition to our board. We are glad to have you with us!

Thank you,

(Name of board president or chair, title)[1]

Note

1. Poudre River Friends of the Library. December 18, 2018. "Letter of Welcome." New Board Member Orientation Packet.

Partnering with the Library

It is clear that a library and any library support group or groups assisting it are separate entities. However, that doesn't mean they cannot work as partners and collaborate and, under ideal conditions, that is exactly what they do. You have already seen the important role library staff members can make serving as ex officio board members of Friends, foundations, or trusts. You have seen how promoting each other on websites and social media is beneficial to both parties as long it is made plain that each operates independently of the other. In the following chapter, you will see how library staff members can temporarily assist a floundering library support group in an ex officio manner to help get it back on its feet, demonstrating that mutual cooperation and care are the keys to good library and library support group relationships. There are some important additional ways that this camaraderie can happen, and one of those ways is planning together.

Planning Together for Library Support

To achieve an optimum mutual relationship, a library being supported by a Friends, foundation, or trust organization will find it necessary to be in reciprocal, regular contact. Whether it is the library seeking volunteers for a program it is holding; the support group looking for young assistants from the library's teen council for an upcoming fundraiser; a trust offering to donate a new, meaningful sculpture for the library's entryway; or any myriad other possibilities, these cooperative interactions can only take place when the library and the support group have nurtured a cordial, collaborative joint relationship.

By regularly planning together, each organization cultivates its mutual cause to build a strong library community of readers, learners, thinkers, and all sorts of other users who rely on, support, and stand up for their library. This might include having library staff, library trustees, and library support group board members attending one another's monthly meetings to discuss an upcoming budget; having representation from all associated parties at long-range strategic planning sessions; or working together to organize a grand opening celebration for a newly completed support group grant-funded project. Because there are so many levels and types of planning needed to successfully fund and run a library, there are plenty of strategic plan variations to utilize.

Studies consistently show that nonprofit organizations with written plans double their probability of achieving success. However, according to research, only half of all nonprofit groups have strategic plans, and among those that do, too few of them actually put the plans to good use. No matter whether your library support group is new, well-established, growing, or struggling, carefully created strategic plans can direct your group toward successful outcomes and encourage it to thrive. Helpful tools like that are worth taking the time and effort to implement.[13]

The various methods of strategic planning that I will examine in the following sections can guide library support groups through completing everyday and yearly missions to reaching toward future goals for continued, improved, or innovative achievements several years into the future. To find out more about the various kinds of strategic planning formats—what they are, and what they are not—read on.

Strategic Planning Terminology for Library Support Groups

At times, you may notice long-range goal setting called "strategic planning," and at other times, it is called "development planning." Although strategic planning and development planning for nonprofit groups sound like two names for the same concept, those terms can be close, but not on point all the time. Yes, although both do indeed aim toward sensible, valuable, precise, and attainable goals that focus upon successful completion at the closing stages of a particular timeline, they are not always interchangeable because of differences depending on how the terms are used.

Personal development plans can be used to center upon an individual, so if your library support group created a development plan, it could be, for instance, in preparation for when a treasurer trainee wants to hone the skills required to fill the office when the current treasurer's term ends. It would be created in a format that builds strategic pathways aimed at one person's goals. A strategic plan, in contrast, generally focuses on the organization as a whole, targeting its overarching goals and various ways to achieve those goals, although other kinds of strategic plans could be devised for individual elements to meet the overarching goals such as a strategic plan for a singular fundraising program, a facility use conflict, or an effort to recruit new volunteers.

Development Strategic Plans (aka Fundraising Strategic Plans)

You can see that a strategic plan centers on an organization in part or as a whole, depending on its purpose. Nevertheless, a development strategic plan is an aspect of organizational plans which is also called a fundraising strategic plan that specifically targets raising money by nonprofits to build up (or develop) a funding base. When a library support group is mapping out ways to engage donors, arrange money-raising events, secure grants, solve fiscal problems to increase funds, or address any number of related objectives, a development strategic plan could be used to zero in on progressive steps to getting those funds.[14]

As a matter of fact, another central reason for having such a strategic plan is that grant makers often ask for an organization's plan or ask how a particular proposed project aligns with a set plan before awarding money. Your development strategic plan can also be an aid in determining whether a specific grant would be a good fit for your library support group's financial goals.[15] By and large, a development plan can be a useful tool to strengthen the organization itself, specifically to make it function more effectively as a steady channel for library monetary support.

Considering the import of such a plan, it would make sense to have a library being served to be involved and represented in the planning process for the development plan or any strategic plan directly impacting its functions. To begin producing a high-quality plan, the library director will usually share information about the library's needs which gives the support group a place to begin deliberating. Then there are several steps that can be followed to generate a development plan itself that fits the needs of the library:

- Identify strengths and what might need improvement in the library support group. This can be done by three or four board members and the library director working together or even with the help of a consultant if that is an option. Be sure to follow the recommendations for running a successful meeting from chapter 3 for a meeting like this or for another kind.
- Plan a retreat or workshop, perhaps for a half day but maybe longer, to critically examine the support group's current activities, to establish new goals and strategies, and to figure out if new activities need to be added. The library director would be involved in the retreat in addition to a representative from any trust or foundation that co-supports the library.
- Once the goals and strategies are listed, aim for a timeline of three years to tackle and complete them, which is a fairly standard timeline for development plans as it is with most long-term strategic plans. You can aim to have certain items completed in one, two, or three years within the plan, depending on the urgency of each item's intended accomplishment(s).
- Be sure to assign a particular person to be in charge of monitoring and supervising the end product of every action point in the plan.[16]

TEXTBOX 4.4

MEMBERSHIP NEWSLETTER EXCERPT

Here is an excerpt from the January 2023 membership newsletter of the Poudre River Friends of the Library. Although this is not the text of a completed development plan, it presents a good overview and example of the process and the results of a workshop to address future fundraising and related issues with a later step of putting a finalized development plan in place. You can see how this group applied some of the recommendations relayed in the section above to activate the process.

Meeting to Create Development Goals

In early December 2022, representatives from the Poudre River Friends of the Library Board of Directors, the Library District, and the Library Trust met for a workshop to "gain understanding and agreement on the roles and responsibilities of each entity; develop agreement regarding the joint purpose of all entities; and develop priorities and goals for fundraising work during 2023."

Topics included funding sources for all groups (Friends' include book sales, grants, and donations), use of the funds (Friends' is mainly for programs, particularly the Summer Reading Challenge), assets and strengths (Friends' is our volunteers, reputation as booksellers, work ethic, and advocacy), and liabilities and challenges (Friends' include rent for storage and stagnant board recruitment and membership—you can help with the latter two by volunteering to serve on the Board and by renewing your membership and encouraging others to join the Friends).

Current best practices for fundraising were also discussed at the workshop. Things already done successfully as well as things that need work were identified. A draft statement was written and is to be shared with each group's respective boards for review, and it is hoped, agreement.

The Friends Board was scheduled to go over the statement at their January 2023 meeting. Nevertheless, identified at the workshop and of interest is an overview of our 2023 activities. These include:

- Actively participate in and promote the Friends of the Library Week
- Develop an on-boarding class for volunteers and members
- Revise the membership structure
- Continue to evaluate book sales
- Secure free, convenient, and accessible long-term space for storing, sorting, and processing books[1]

With this initial groundwork at hand, the Friends would be able to move on to creating a true strategic plan that will facilitate progress toward positive goals.

Note

1. Poudre River Friends of the Library. January 2023. "Development Goals and Meeting." *Poudre River Friends of the Library Newsletter*, 3, https://mcusercontent.com/9a49e6d2f9f3b9dfd39b7e54d/files/2361ff32-5eea-ca93-9aea-3d2ebe50b12d/2023_01_Jan_Newsletter.pdf.

Other Types of Strategic Plans

Since they are step-by-step blueprints to fulfilling mission and vision statements, resolving problems, raising money, and positively moving organizations forward during a particular range of time and circumstances, choosing the right format for each plan is imperative.[17] In that regard, a strategic plan timeline might span several years, as noted in the development strategic plan description. However, other strategic plans can be for shorter, more limited periods with other purposes. Inherently, there are five basic kinds of strategic plans:

- Standard: For this plan, the goals and objectives are relatively stable, usually focus on the coming year, and are based on the status quo. Included in a standard strategic plan would be an anticipated annual budget based on the current one; forging a plan to replace a board officer set to leave during the next year with someone who has been in training; or other imminent but easily managed issues on the near horizon.
- Issue-based: This type of plan is frequently employed when a particular serious concern is occurring or reoccurring and needs to be directly addressed. To illustrate, if a library foundation targets certain funding goals and repeatedly does not reach those goals in time to pay for an anticipated project, an issue-based strategic plan may be a pathway toward a solution to solving the problem.
- Organic: An organic strategic plan is most likely used when the future is unclear or uncertain. In a way, it is a pre-strategic plan, aiming to get a group heading in the right direction by developing an original set of goals and objectives. A newly formed library support group, a Friends and foundation anticipating a merger, or a group completely revamping itself would most likely benefit from an organic plan in which leadership, the developing or revising of organizational documents, building a website, and other necessary organizational issues would be tackled.
- Real time: When something unexpected arises, a real-time strategic plan to meet short term goals may be in order. Suppose a library support group suddenly learns that the facility where the donations for an impending book sale fundraiser are stored, sorted, and priced is no longer available for their use and an alternative must quickly be found. Gathering board members to create a real-time strategic plan to find a replacement storage area, move the books efficiently, and configure the new area's workspace in a timely fashion would be an imperative first step to finding a suitable resolution.
- Alignment: The best strategic plan for developing compatible goals among separate organizations, such as a Friends group and a library trust that are serving the same library and that are working in tandem on a targeted project, is this one. When a library support group wants to assemble a forward-thinking, overall strategic plan for building an effective mutual operation or instilling overall growth during a set time period, it would be most helpful if there would be representation from as many associated parties and stakeholders as possible who would be aligned at the planning table, to create an aligned strategic plan.[18]

Strategic plans are most productively devised by using SMART goals. This acronym is a good way to remember the essential points in a well-rounded plan: S = specific; M = measurable; A = assignable; R = realistic; T = time-related. The best plans have goals that are specific, measurable, and sensible, with clear direction as to who will be in charge of each action along with reasonable timelines. Following this SMART formula allows the plan to be monitored to ensure the greatest success.[19]

To illustrate, imagine that a library trust would like to allocate capital funds to the library it supports for adding a children's amphitheater to the park area outside the library building. Its hypothetical SMART strategic plan might look like this:

- The ex officio trust member serving on the library's board of trustees submits a proposal for the project from the trust to the library trustees and the library administrators by January 20, after which the plan is approved.
- A sub-committee of the trust leadership team investigates costs and submits a detailed project budget request to the trust's finance team by April 1.
- The library trust's finance team reviews impending donations and allocates enough funds from donors who wish to earmark their contributions for outdoor capital library additions. Then the designated funding sources and amounts would be on the agenda for potential approval at the May 1 trust meeting.
- Once approved, the library trust finance team hires a construction company and decides with the library and trustees to contract for a workable completion date of May 1 the following year, in time for several summer reading challenge programs and activities to take place in the amphitheater that summer.
- The amphitheater is completed by the target date and the library staff plans a grand opening celebration which is held on May 5, two weeks before summer reading begins.

Of course, this is a very simplistic outline and a true version of such a plan would be much more precise. However, you can see that the plan includes three necessary elements:

- Each task is assigned to a specific person or group to accomplish.
- Each step has a deadline.
- Each step leads to the target goal of building the new amphitheater which could not have taken place without the previous steps first being met.[20]

By using a very detailed, step-by-step type of plan, any strategic document that you need to generate would be easy to follow, act as a checklist, and successfully take your library support group to the completion of a designated goal for your beneficiary library.

TEXTBOX 4.5

TOOLS TO ASSIST YOU IN CREATING STRATEGIC PLANS OF ALL KINDS

These two online resources can assist you with further information about creating strategic plans:

Nonprofit Strategic Planning: The Ultimate Guide + Examples[1]

On this webpage, you will find plenty of information about creating whatever kind of strategic plan or strategic development/fundraising plan that you need. Included are links to examples, marketing strategies for fundraising, and even instructions with a template for putting together your annual report in which goals achieved from your strategic plan can be touted.

YouTube[2]

Whether you want a quick overview on how to design and write a strategic plan, or you need a longer, more detailed video workshop, you will find several helpful, current choices on YouTube.

You may also want to refer to some of the other resources given in the selected bibliography and webliography at the end of this book for additional pointers about creating and using strategic plans.

Notes

1. Jay Love. 2023.
2. YouTube, https://www.youtube.com/.

Effectively Planning and Monitoring Library Support Group Finances

As mentioned earlier, one of the most valuable, yet often one of the most elusive persons to place on a nonprofit board of directors or executive board is a highly qualified treasurer, unless it is in a very large organization that may be able to afford a salary to fill the position. Longtime certified public accountant Dennis Walsh called treasurers of all-volunteer organizations "the unsung heroes of our times" based on all the impressive, donated work for which they are so generously responsible.[21] He is absolutely right, and I think you will agree after you learn about the expectations for someone in the position.

Because serving as a treasurer is usually gratis as it is with most voluntary board roles (and, of course, persons in those other roles are also extremely valuable contributors), a treasurer with solid, trustworthy, insightful financial knowledge and experience is more than the keeper of "the treasure." Filling the position with a person with that particular skill level and background—real expertise—is an actual treasure unto itself for a library support group. Finding a second person to serve as an assistant treasurer who willingly waits in the wings to take on the full position after being trained to follow in the treasurer's footsteps is exceptionally fortunate.

The reality is, however, that some groups may only be able to find someone who has minimal qualifications, is equally generous, is still interested in serving in the position, and feels capable of acquiring new skills. The promising news is that there are many helpful resources available for that person and even for fellow board members who need to be in the loop to educate themselves with solid financial advice and information. Being able to put this essential financial knowledge into action is the backbone of any nonprofit fundraising group. In this section, I will be examining what budgeting and preparing financials entails as well as what an elected treasurer needs to do when becoming an officer on a board of directors. The topics that will be addressed can be useful for anyone learning the ropes and even to someone who wants to fortify an already sturdy financial knowledge base.

Installing a New Library Support Group Treasurer

The first duty of a new volunteer treasurer is to ensure that the new role is official and that all legalities have been observed. Even if it is not the treasurer's direct responsibility, the person elected to the post must make certain that this has been properly done within a reasonable timeframe. After all, this position requires accountability for a great deal of money and the related financial tasks, and therefore a person taking on the performance of treasurer duties needs secure, documented backing.

The first way to seek confirmation that the board of directors has filled the office of treasurer correctly is by checking the organizational bylaws. Well-constructed bylaws for a compliant nonprofit need to include proper procedures and precedents regarding the adding and removing of any and all board members, particularly treasurers; confirmation that official power is granted to a treasurer in order to carry out the job legally and suitably; and precise stipulations about how the money earned by the organization is to be utilized. If the bylaws do not address these issues, for self and board protection, the treasurer needs to consult with the group's president, other officers, and/or other board members about reviewing the bylaw governance regarding amendments and propose that relevant changes and/or additions be made. Once an amendment is in place which revises and updates the document to cover the induction of all new board members appropriately and legitimately, the treasurer can potentially focus on the duties inherent in filling the office.[22]

I say "potentially focus" because other steps may be required if a board so chooses, and not all boards do. For ones that decide to take additional steps, it is because a library support organization operates independently, and the board wants the extra security that comes with certified protective actions. These would primarily include the conduction and passing of background checks and/or bonding for all board members who would be handling and be responsible for money in any way. Another reason these may be required is to cover anyone who would be privy to private or sensitive financial or donor information or data (and, as an aside, sometimes background checks might also be put into place for board or other group members interacting with youth).

There are pros and cons to having these prerequisites met before someone embarks into group service. On one hand, securing these further certifications is not free, and their costs would probably dip into money that is needed to fund the core mission of supporting the library. Plus, a treasurer or anyone else on the board may feel that they are looked upon as untrustworthy for being asked to submit to the requirements. However, the certifications do offer insurance against anything going wrong, and having them in place may be assuring for stakeholders, donors to the library cause, and the organization itself.[23] These are issues that a board needs to address when devising bylaws or special group rules, or when amending them. When doing so, it would be prudent to have whatever legal counsel the board depends upon to be an objective sounding board for getting advice about the possible incorporation of these rules and how to proceed with reputable agencies. The library itself may also be able to offer leads for these services if they have similar requirements for their employees.

Once these initial matters are addressed and once the treasurer is officially and legally installed and ready to go, there are quite a few more things for the board and the person who will hold the position to tackle for the job to commence. These include to:

- Learn about all the essential services the library support group deals with and collect current contact information. This involves such details as obtaining all bank records; arranging to have access to all accounts; obtaining the right to use checkbooks; getting credit card authorization; and getting access to software and training tools fundamental to completing treasurer tasks.
- Arrange for a smooth transition between the incoming and the outgoing treasurers. If a meeting could be set up to discuss all the topics that need consideration, that would be ideal. These topics would most likely cover financial policies and procedures, including preparation of the monthly and annual financial statements; what tax and registration forms need completion and when; learning about financial protocols and security precautions to keep data and information safe; tax rules and regulations that apply to the nonprofit; budget history to aid in producing future budgets; handling outstanding and upcoming payments due; discussing the need for audits and how to arrange for getting them done; obtaining MOUs should the nonprofit act as fiscal agent for its library beneficiary; and securing any advice on how the job might be improved by altering procedures or updating tools.
- Become familiar with nonprofit accounting regulations and management procedures. At times, volunteer treasurers have come from a for-profit background, and knowing the differences between that kind of setting and a nonprofit one is essential. These differences include tax-exempt status, budgeting needs, terminology, and reporting procedures. Nonprofits typically perform fund accounting, which is a means of identifying revenue sources and making transactions transparent to assure legitimacy. The basic idea behind fund accounting is that it monitors and documents assets that are donated by outside parties and makes sure that all available raised funds are used most efficiently to maximize the potential benefit of each dollar.[24]

If it fits into the organizational model for the library support group, build a finance/investment team or committee. Such a team can provide creativity in performing tasks, offer accountability, improve productivity, and enhance transparency. However, watchfulness in safeguarding sensitive records and being certain that those on the committee are honest and well-informed are important aspects to consider if you create such a team. If the organizational bylaws have incorporated bonding and/or background checks for everyone as a whole, including those in such a group, it would make the team's work more effective, secure, and less worrisome.[25]

Budgeting

It is evident that treasurers or financial officers of library support groups are indispensable because they are the lead persons in recording, monitoring, and reporting an organization's financial information. In that role, as mentioned, there are essential financial documents where their responsibility lies that comprise budgets, financial statements, and tax forms. I will start first with a simple definition of a budget.

In essence, a *budget* is an organization's strategy expressed in dollars. When a strategic and collaborative budget process is in place between a library support group and the library being served, it ensures that resources are being used most effectively to meet the missions and strategic plans of both and that stakeholders can readily see that a group is functioning in a sustainable and accountable manner.[26] There are quite a few different kinds of budgets, which can get somewhat complicated. Hence the need for someone who really knows the differences and knows how to manage finances—or is willing and able to learn.

Excel software skills are essential. If skills are lacking or limited, libraries often provide classes for learning Excel, or they might have self-paced, online training resources in the reference/research area of the library website. They will also most likely carry books in the library collection on Excel. In addition, there are plenty of tutorials on YouTube for personal instruction.

It is important to remember that the person serving as a board's financial manager is not operating solo, and that the bottom line to financial stability is the commitment of the entire board to continually participate in the administration of funds, which includes keeping tabs on income and expenses through timely reviews of financial reports and advance planning through budgeting.

The library that is the funding recipient can take part in this pre-planning process by committing to submit a request for costs to the library support group(s) that will be supplying financial aid a few months ahead of the final budget submission and approval. One technique that really works is for the library to decide on the programs, activities, events, and material additions for which it hopes that costs can be covered and to arrange them in a three-tiered, priority-ordered "wish list."

Tier one would list top-priority items that are urgently needed for imminent funding consideration. Tier two would include very important things that would make a strong impact, but the library could make do without them, if necessary, until a later time. Tier three would list desired additions that are not extremely vital at present but would be greatly appreciated to enhance and round out the library's offerings. The inclusions on each tier could be briefly but carefully annotated so that as the board considers the library's needs and what it can afford to donate, it possesses the details that are essential to making wise monetary decisions. Of course, an additional benefit to the decision-making process would be for a library representative(s) to come to a library support group board meeting(s) to more fully explain the library's requests and how granting the "wishes" could make a difference. Once the board reviews and decides which items it can fund, the costs can be given to the treasurer to include in a new fiscal year proposed budget.

The library requests that are chosen to be funded become an intrinsic part of each year's fiscal budget and payments are made as required. Once that is done, each well-run library support group board meeting includes a current treasurer's budget report reflecting what has already been paid for approved library needs; the library support group's own expenses; any other essential monetary considerations such as income earned and additional expenditures; an opportunity for attendees to ask questions, get answers, and make suggestions; and final approval of all financial reports.

Although a current annual budget update is usually an ongoing focal point, other budget reports can range through a wide variety of types depending on what else the board is addressing and reviewing. This might be reports finalizing the budgetary results of a fundraising program that the group has just hosted; an end-of-summer cost analysis of that year's library summer reading challenge; or a breakdown of the final invoices paid after funding the addition of a new library entryway. Other issues such as making a decision to change banking institutions to get a higher investment rate; precisely counting the money earned from a fundraiser, reporting the total, and safely depositing the profits into the organizational bank account; documenting the potential effects of replacing an income source that is suddenly no longer available; or receiving and monitoring the funds received through a grant to cover a special project can all fall under the responsibility umbrella of the treasurer, with input and approval from the rest of the board and assistance from the board as necessary. When thinking about all the aspects of financial management required, it is easy to understand the reasons why it can be challenging to find an astute financial expert to serve as a volunteer treasurer! Yet, as mentioned previously, there is help available for someone willing to learn how to take the reins.

One thing a good treasurer must be able to apply to financial management is flexibility. Because budgets are a guide to plan for the future and an assessment tool to gauge financial health, such flexibility is key due to the potential for the group's financial picture to be shifting at some point.[27] This could be as simple as adjusting to losing a previously reliable donor or as complex as when serious worldwide economic downturns occur, requiring drastic changes. In general, though, a central budgetary concern each year is preparing a basic annual budget while keeping flexibility at hand.

For basic annual budget preparation, which usually begins at least three months before the start of a new fiscal year, a suggested timeline would almost certainly follow as such:

- Determine the timing needed for scheduling discussion and board approval, then convene a budget committee to participate in putting these steps together if the organization desires one.
- Incorporate all agreed-upon financial goals.
- Review and understand all current income and expenses, then forecast to the end of the coming fiscal year.
- Be informed about roles and responsibilities for all budget aspects, then weigh and be able to explain any uncertainties.
- Create a draft expense budget to include anticipated costs for programs, organizational needs, and strategic plan goals.
- Create a draft income budget based on current fundraising and revenue information and projections along with anticipated needs and activities.
- Review the entire budget carefully, discuss any uncertainties as needed, make any adjustments, and review the final draft to ensure that it supports all goals and objectives.

- Turn in the final draft to the board and anyone else who needs to peruse it and be prepared to answer any questions before final approval.
- If not done already, generate a spreadsheet and systematize files reflecting the budget as approved.
- Implement, monitor, manage, and report upon the approved budget throughout the new fiscal year.[28]

Library Support Group Financial Statements

When addressing the topic of financial statements, first of all, understand that there are two accounting methods that library support group nonprofits employ depending on size and type of organization. These are cash-basis accounting and accrual accounting. The main difference between these methods is when financial transactions are recorded.

In cash accounting systems, the treasurer or financial officer records and recognizes revenue when money is received and records and recognizes expenses when funds are spent or when bills are paid. This accounting method is the more straightforward option since it follows cash in and out of the checking account in similar fashion to managing a personal checkbook. Most smaller-scaled library support nonprofits such as Friends of the Library groups use the cash basis because it is more understandable and requires less accounting experience.

Accrual accounting requires the recording of revenues when they are earned or pledged, and expenses are recorded and recognized when they are incurred. This accounting method is concerned with when services are rendered or when commitments are made instead of when cash is received or spent. It is the more accurate method because it matches revenues with expenses in the same period in which they took place rather than when funds change hands; it allows for a more accurate organizational financial picture; and aids side-by-side comparisons the financial statements of other organizations like yours. This can be important when seeking grants because many large grant makers want to see accrual-based financials to award funds. Bigger library support nonprofits, often foundations, trusts, and large Friends Foundations, will generally use this method, and as smaller groups might merge or grow, they usually switch to this system. If you are uncertain about which method is best for your group, check with a financial advisor or with the Internal Revenue Service which requires using the accrual basis rather than cash for certain very high gross receipts.[29]

As noted in the previous segment, a responsibility of a library support group treasurer or financial officer and board is to keep track of, complete, and turn in annual financial statements for nonprofits as required by federal, state, and local governments, which can be affected by which accounting method is used. Each nonprofit must find out which reports are necessary for their particular situation and location, plus the Internal Revenue Service (IRS) dictates that Form 990, called Return of Organization Exempt from Income Tax,[30] be completed and submitted electronically by every U.S. nonprofit group each year.

If an organization does not file its return, or files late, the IRS may assess penalties. Furthermore, if an organization fails to file as obliged for three consecutive years, it automatically loses its tax-exempt status.[31] It is evident that filing properly and on time is a crucial step for every library support group to take. The 990 form is rather complex and if a library support group treasurer is not up to taking on the task solo, it is important to get assistance from a qualified accountant or other tax specialist. As a matter of fact, if possible, it would be best to have even a savvy treasurer or manager engage in consultation with a qualified financial advisor to be sure everything has been completed properly before submitting.

In general, there are four financial statements a treasurer needs to complete. They include a balance sheet, a statement of activity, a statement of cash flows, and a statement of functional expenses. Three of the statements are the same kinds that for-profit companies must complete, but the functional expenses statement is unique to nonprofits only.

The nonprofit balance sheet is also known as a "statement of financial position" or a "statement of financial condition." These statements are generally not used by cash-basis nonprofits, but they are appropriate for accrual-based accounting. The accounting formula used for putting together the balance sheet is "assets = liabilities + net assets." For-profit companies use owners' equity rather than net assets, but otherwise the formula is the same. The purpose and value of the balance sheet is that it gives the best overall picture of a nonprofit's stability, supplying that information for anyone who needs to know how steady the organization is financially, and especially revealing that it is not beset by liabilities.

The "statement of activity" is the preferred term to "income statement" (which is associated with for-profit companies and reflects earnings), and it applies the formula "revenues – expenses = change in net assets." It is recommended that the revenue and expenses be separated to the level of line items needed for Form 990 reporting and then subtotaled for statement of activity presentation.[32] For nonprofits like library support groups, it explains the differences between funds coming into the organization versus operational costs which reflect specific service and mission support costs. The statement content for cash versus accrual accounting is somewhat dissimilar and each presents a variation of financial perspective, so the preparer must know which kind of form must be completed.[33] For either format, the key point is that nonprofits need to show positive changes in net assets over time in order to sustain stability in managing their programs and activities, rather than to confirm earnings as for-profits do.

The "statement of cash flows" is also similar to what is used by for-profit companies. This document's breakdowns in categories show operating, investing, and financing activity which explain where cash is coming from and how it is going out. Nonprofits need to track variations in cash flow to be cognizant of their ability to have an adequate supply of incoming money for funding library support and organizational program needs.

Finally, regarding financial statements, there is the statement of functional expenses. This is the document that is unique to nonprofits (and not completed by for-profit companies, which use a "statement of owners' equity" instead). The statement's purpose is to monitor nonprofit expenditures required to function, breaking down the expenditures into sensible and common categories such as programs, management expenses, direct mail campaigns, salaries (if this applies), and any other costs.[34]

You may find that the article published by the nonprofit support company, Springly, "Understanding the 4 Essential Nonprofit Statements," is a helpful online resource with simple, easy-to-follow information and advice about the purposes of all four financial statements while offering tips on what nonprofits need to incorporate into each one.[35]

Nonprofit Tax Forms

Besides the financial statements, treasurers or other financial managers of charitable organizations such as library Friends, foundations, and trusts must also complete and distribute nonprofit tax Form 1099-NEC when necessary. This is done after paying for services by vendors, independent contractors, individual persons, and subcontractors that are needed by the library support group to sustain their work during the tax year. There are four conditions that must be met that necessitate the use of this form:

- The organization made payment to someone who is not an employee of the nonprofit.
- The payment was for services conducted in the course of nonprofit organizational activity.
- The payment was to an individual, partnership, or vendor, collectively considered independent contractors (and not to an LLC or a corporation).
- The payment was to the payee in an amount of at least six hundred dollars during the tax year.[36]

Each independent contractor must submit a form W-9[37] to the nonprofit organization. In addition to the information on the W-9, the financial officer or treasurer must keep track of:

- Each category of payment
- The contractor's taxpayer identification number
- Tax-withholding information (although typically there is no tax withholding for independent contractors since that is complicated, well beyond most unpaid volunteer treasurer's capabilities, and conditions for it are outside the realm of most library support nonprofits—but check with a tax or legal advisor if you are unsure)[38]
- Total annual payment

TEXTBOX 4.6

**USEFUL RESOURCES FOR LEARNING ABOUT
AND CREATING BUDGETS AND FINANCIALS**

Candid Learning's "Where Can I Find Examples of Nonprofit Budgets?"[1]

This page on the Candid Learning website offers free online training; lists free, staff-recommended links to relevant topics and templates related to various aspects of nonprofit budgeting; and shares staff-recommended books, including ones that are free to download as ebooks.

Donorbox Blog's "Nonprofit Financial Statements: Guide and Examples"[2]

Nonprofits, including library support groups, must file four financial statements with the Internal Revenue Service to comply with nonprofit regulations. These financials are also beneficial to document your stability, ensure transparency, and build trust with donors. This guide covers each of the essential financial statements and gives examples for clarification.

(continued)

Smartsheet's Free Nonprofit Budget Templates[3]

Here you will find a wide selection of free downloadable budget templates in Microsoft Excel and Google Sheets formats for a general operating budget, a nonprofit grant proposal budget, a startup budget, a program-based budget, and several others, along with guidelines for using each.

Wallace Foundation's StrongNonprofits Toolkit[4]

This foundation is well-known for its support of youth endeavors (including in libraries), education, the arts, and other avenues that help communities to prosper. The StrongNonprofits Toolkit is a resource available to strengthen nonprofit financial management. In it, you will find downloadable information and templates, a Five-Step Guide to Budget Development provided on YouTube, a budgeting timeline, and links to other budgeting resources.

Notes

1. Candid Learning. 2023. "Where Can I Find Examples of Nonprofit Budgets?," https://learning.candid.org/resources/knowledge-base/budget-examples/.
2. Kristine Endor. October 28, 2022. "Nonprofit Financial Statements: Guide + Examples." Donorbox Blog, https://donorbox.org/nonprofit-blog/nonprofit-financial-statements.
3. Andy Marker. August 19, 2021. "Free Nonprofit Budget Templates." Smartsheet, https://www.smartsheet.com/content/nonprofit-budget-templates.
4. Wallace Foundation. [n.d.].

Notes

1. Community Sector Council. 2010. "Job Descriptions for Board Members," http://communitysector.nl.ca/board-development/job-descriptions-board-members.
2. National Council of Nonprofits. 2023. "Board Roles and Responsibilities," https://www.councilofnonprofits.org/tools-resources/board-roles-and-responsibilities.
3. Instrumentl. September 6, 2022. "What Does a Nonprofit Executive Director Do?" Instrumental Blog, https://www.instrumentl.com/blog/what-nonprofit-executive-directors-do#:~:text=A%20nonprofit%20Executive%20Director%20is,tools%20to%20implement%20programs%20effectively.
4. Community Sector Council. 2010.
5. Content taken from D. Macnaughton (2010). A little help from your Friends. Presentation at Ontario Library Service North Conference, Sudbury, ON; and L. Magahay, V. Marshall, and S. Durand (2008). What does it take to sustain a Friends group? Presentations at OLA Super Conference, Toronto, ON, https://accessola.com/wp-content/uploads/2020/09/21.Friends-Compilation.pdf.
6. Community Sector Council. 2010.
7. Nick Price. November 12, 2018. "How Ex Officio Board Members Can Impact Board Decisions for Your Nonprofit." BoardEffect, https://www.boardeffect.com/blog/ex-officio-board-members-impact-board-decisions-nonprofit/.
8. Sun Prairie Public Library. 2023. "Friends of the Sun Prairie Public Library," https://www.sunprairiepubliclibrary.org/friends-sun-prairie-public-library.
9. Wyoming State Library. 2022. "Effective Board Recruitment for Trustees and Friends." Reprinted from United for Libraries, https://library.wyo.gov/effective-board-recruitment-for-trustees-and-friends/.
10. Freechild Institute for Youth Engagement. 2022. "Why Youth Engagement?" https://freechild.org/about/why-should-youth-change-the-world/.
11. Sun Prairie Library. [n.d.] "Friends of the Sun Prairie Public Library," https://www.sunprairiepubliclibrary.org/friends-sun-prairie-public-library.

12. Terry Larson. Email message to author. January 18, 2023.

13. Funding for Good. January 23, 2023. "Nonprofit Strategic Planning—A Complete Guide," https://fundingforgood.org/nonprofit-strategic-planning-guide/.

14. Jay Love. 2023. "Nonprofit Strategic Planning: The Ultimate Guide + Examples." Bloomerang, https://bloomerang.co/blog/nonprofit-strategic-planning/.

15. The Team at Instrumentl. December 8, 2022. "How to Write a Nonprofit Strategic Plan: Ultimate 2023 Guide." Instrumentl Blog, https://www.instrumentl.com/blog/nonprofit-strategic-plans.

16. Library Strategies. 2021. "Strategic Planning for the Folks Who Raise the Money," https://www.librarystrategiesconsulting.org/2017/10/strategic-planning-for-the-folks-who-raise-the-money/.

17. Manoj Basnyat. March 18, 2020. "The Difference between Development Planning and Strategic Planning," https://manojbasnyat7.medium.com/the-difference-between-development-planning-and-strategic-planning-c45e4cd32791.

18. Bloomerang. [n.d.] "Nonprofit Glossary: Strategic Plan," https://kindful.com/nonprofit-glossary/strategic-plan/.

19. Bloomerang. [n.d.]

20. Bloomerang. [n.d.]

21. Dennis Walsh. February 13, 2010. "Treasurers of All-Volunteer Organizations: Eight Key Responsibilities." Blue Avocado, https://blueavocado.org/finance/treasurers-of-all-volunteer-organizations-eight-key-responsibilities/.

22. Jeanne at Springly. [n.d.] "Everything You Need to Do After Electing a New Nonprofit Treasurer." Springly, https://www.springly.org/en-us/blog/nonprofit-treasurer/.

23. Dan at Springly. [n.d.] "Is Bonding a Nonprofit Treasurer Really Necessary?" Springly, https://www.springly.org/en-us/blog/bonding-nonprofit-treasurer/.

24. AccountingEdu.org. February 6, 2023. "Fund Accountancy," https://www.accountingedu.org/fund-accountancy/#:~:text=Fund%20accounting%20refers%20to%20the,are%20donated%20by%20outside%20parties.

25. Jeanne at Springly.

26. Wallace Foundation. [n.d] "StrongNonprofits Toolkit," https://www.wallacefoundation.org/knowledge-center/resources-for-financial-management/pages/budgeting.aspx.

27. National Council of Nonprofits. 2023. "Budgeting for Nonprofits," https://www.councilofnonprofits.org/tools-resources/budgeting-nonprofits.

28. Propel Nonprofits. [n.d.] "Budgeting: A 10-Step Checklist," https://www.propelnonprofits.org/resources/10-step-budgeting-checklist/.

29. The Charity CFO. April 5, 2022. "Do Nonprofits Use Cash or Accrual Accounting?," https://thecharitycfo.com/do-nonprofits-use-cash-or-accrual-accounting/.

30. Internal Revenue Service. [Annual form] "Return of Organization Exempt from Income Tax," https://www.irs.gov/pub/irs-pdf/f990.pdf.

31. Internal Revenue Service. June 16, 2022. "Annual Filing and Forms," https://www.irs.gov/charities-non-profits/annual-filing-and-forms.

32. Barbara Walton. Email message to author, April 22, 2023.

33. Gianforte Family Foundation. [n.d.] "Learn to Read Your Statement of Activities," https://gianfortefoundation.org/wp-content/uploads/LEARN-TO-READ-YOUR-STATEMENT-OF-ACTIVITIES.pdf.

34. Chron Contributor. September 15, 2020. "Which Financial Statements Are Most Pertinent to a Nonprofit Organization?" Chron, https://smallbusiness.chron.com/financial-statements-pertinent-nonprofit-organization-14406.html.

35. Briana at Springly. [n.d.] "Understanding the 4 Essential Nonprofit Financial Statements." Springly, https://www.springly.org/en-us/blog/essential-nonprofit-financial-statements/.

36. Jitasa. December 7, 2022. "Form 1099 for Nonprofits: How and Why to Issue One," https://www.jitasagroup.com/jitasa_nonprofit_blog/1099-for-nonprofits/.

37. Internal Revenue Service. 2023. "About Form W-9: Request for Taxpayer Identification Number and Certification," https://www.irs.gov/forms-pubs/about-form-w-9.

38. Side Project, Inc. 2017 "Nonprofit Organizations and Independent Contractors," https://www.dosomeorganizing.org/single-post/2016/07/11/nonprofit-organizations-and-independent-contractors.

CHAPTER 5

Righting Things That Go Wrong with and in Library Support Groups

SEVERAL SITUATIONS AND SCENARIOS CAN OCCUR with and in library support groups that inhibit them from progress and sometimes threaten their continuance. In this section, using some real-life examples, I will highlight several things that might take place and how they have been or could be solved.

A Formerly Active Library Support Group Is Falling Short and May Disband

When new library support groups are founded, there is usually a great deal of enthusiasm and energy that spurs the members and the board into positive action. However, as time goes by, the optimistic condition of the board might fade. This is often caused by the initial group aging out, burning out, or moving on elsewhere, leaving a less than vibrant organization sorely needing direction and leadership. Other causes might be poor leadership, lack of promotion and recruitment, inept management, or a combination of negative factors. Whatever the reasons, when a library notices that one of their anchor sources for funding and volunteer contributions is diminishing, what can be done to remedy the condition?

As an example, here is a real-life situation that seriously needed attention. At the Brooks Library at Central Washington University, a medium-sized, public, regional comprehensive university in Ellensburg, Washington, they found that their once-active Friends of the Library's efforts had ebbed into inactivity. The diverse group had been formed in 1962, comprised of students, faculty, trustees, alumni, and local citizens. By the 1990s, the group was heightening community awareness, running book sales, and establishing an endowment. However, in the early 2000s, the Friends entered a period of decline due to poor leadership and management, lack of good communication, and limited collaboration with the library. By 2016, two years after the board chair had abruptly resigned, the library dean had to decide between two choices—recommending the disbanding of the group or helping the group to revitalize. Revitalization was chosen, and to meet this goal, several steps were taken that offer a good example other groups might follow.

- To identify the parties that needed to take action, the first step was research that revealed an intrinsic connection between the Friends group, the library itself, and the university's development office. In a public library setting, this might parallel a joint effort between the Friends or other support group, the library, and a community relations expert.
- The next step was for these parties to design and implement a marketing and membership promotional campaign that included detailed information about the regeneration efforts. A buy-in by local radio and television stations and other news sources to help the cause was sought along with recruiting a few key community members who genuinely cared about the library. Encouraging additional local business participation and community organization involvement was also part of the arrangements.
- Another step forward was having the existing Friends board partnering with the library's board of trustees to meet, discuss ideas, collaborate, and plan. Also, having a library staff member attending the Friends meetings proved helpful in sharing perspectives.
- Including a column contributed by the Friends of the Library for the library's newsletter was a further positive step. Even better, the Friends of the Library instituted a new logo, created a new membership brochure, and launched a more user-friendly, contemporary website. The new website was and now is useful for posting their newsletter, which is also available in print, to tell the overall community about what they were and are working on and hope to accomplish along with using it to encourage others to join the group.
- Reaching out to other libraries that have active Friends, foundations, or trusts was another important step toward discovering and applying useful advice. The Brooks Library reached out through a thirty-nine-university-library consortium to which they belong to connect with other Friends groups in institutions of similar size. In comparable fashion, public libraries could assist their library support groups to revamp by contacting other libraries or library consortiums to request guidance from their support organizations.
- Because there was no real leadership and the Friends group was on the brink of folding, the dean of libraries stepped in to help by planning a special reorganizational gathering for the existing group. Normally, the library itself does not control library support group activities, but the dean was acting as an ex officio leader in putting this event together. For it, current board members, Friends regular members still on the roster, and library advocates from the community were invited to attend. The result of the gathering was that two enthusiastic and progressive members were added to the board. Still, to maintain the newly rejuvenating momentum that was being created, it was clear that strategic planning was crucial.
- With the board now ready to move forward, an objective nonprofit professional consultant was hired to conduct a retreat to guide the development of a strategic plan. This vital step resulted in new ideas and initiatives, aligned positions and duties in a practical mode, allowed the development of new partnerships and promotionals, and increased the number of board positions from five to fifteen. Eventually, by 2018, the board reached capacity at fifteen very qualified members.

- As the library dean was serving, according to tradition, as an ex officio member of the board, the Student Engagement and Community Outreach Librarian took on temporary tasks, also in an ex officio capacity, to assist with management, communication, and clerical support. This later evolved into the librarian's redefined role as liaison between the library and the Friends. During this time, other library staff also temporarily assisted with the rebuilding of the Friends by attending meetings, firming up relationships between the two organizations, rebranding the Friends, enhancing communication options, encouraging more influential community figures to join the board, and more.
- All the hard work paid off, and once the Friends were back on their feet and beyond, they began to reinstitute and augment fundraising and community outreach efforts and once again become a stable enterprise.

As is evident, the rebuilding of this Friends of the Library group was a large undertaking, requiring time, effort, collaboration, and patience. By and large, this case study overview shows how an academic library Friends group was brought back to life through the combined efforts of the library administration and community's citizens who believed in the value and worth of the organization.[1]

Revitalization efforts can be applied and adapted to any struggling library support group, not just academic ones, through strategic planning by those willing and able to get the job done to build up membership and board participation. The investment of time and resources can result in monetary success; more library advocacy and support for initiatives; and strengthening library presence in the community. A case in point from the public library perspective comes from the Friends of the Blackstone Public Library in Blackstone, Massachusetts, a town with a population of 9,200. In this example, you will see that, at times, a library serving a smaller community may have less library support group volunteers available to help run an organization that benefits it.

The Friends of the Blackstone Library has existed since the 1980s and started as a kind of booster club for the library to purchase a much-needed, staff-requested Xerox machine by raising donated funds. At that time, the library was not only operating within a limited budget that did not allow money for the acquisition of the desired printing equipment, but it could not accommodate the funding for the higher level of programming that it wanted to offer. To help satisfy the library's needs, the Friends grew from their original roots into an active organization that was able to raise enough money for year-round activities; children's programs and performances; an annual summer reading program; prizes and a reception for an annual poetry contest; a Halloween party; and passes for a local museum that patrons could check out for discounts or free admission. The group had conducted ongoing and two larger annual book sales, had advocated for the library when budgets were being approved and, as a nonprofit organization, had gleaned grants and donations for the library. This Friends group evidently had done much to duly address its mission and had become a vital part of the community. However, they began to wonder if they would be able to keep the group afloat due to an increasing lack of new members.

Although the Friends group had developed a highly respected and appreciated presence, its president, a retired local schoolteacher, expressed concern that the group's membership had dwindled. In recent years, only four or five core members were taking on the responsibility for all Friends activities, and it was evident that without a push to get more members on board, the group may have had to disband. As demonstrated in the prior example, it is important for a group in this predicament to reassess their strategic outreach to enlist new members. In Blackstone, the remaining members have been recruiting new people to join at the Friends website with the upbeat messages saying, "Help out! Get involved! Have a great time!"

Along with the messages, there is information about the group's purpose and values, what they do to support the library, where they meet, and a textbox area to contact the group for more information on how to participate. There is also plenty of contact information given along with links to the group's Facebook and Instagram pages which have quite a few followers. In the spring of 2023, the group was accepting book donations and planning a book sale for May in addition to their ongoing Friends of the Blackstone Library limited edition mug fundraiser, and at this point they are still maintaining an active organization.[2]

Here is a list of additional pointers for getting new members to sign up for your library support group that might work if you need them:

- Create a strategic plan to diversify activities beyond book sales to add special events, unique fundraising efforts, and advocacy projects so you can increase exposure and provide additional public relations efforts in to community.
- Target "friend-raising" efforts for various age groups, including young people, at such places as coffee shops and brewpubs.
- On that note, move some library support group activities out in the community rather than at the library, especially in locations where you can connect with new people and share your message about potential involvement.
- Arrange for professional development training for your board so that members can learn more about outreach and coordinating vibrant, ongoing library support groups. Check with the director of the library for tips and leads for potential facilitators.
- Make marketing your group a priority and develop a strategic plan specifically to increase visibility.
- Think outside the box and consider designing a major fundraising event during which others can also learn about the group and be encouraged to join.
- Reach out to community leaders, prominent organizations, businesses, and educational institutions to ask for help in recruiting new regular members, board members, and volunteer aid in running fundraising programs and activities.
- Devise a challenge opportunity that will make a difference for the library and the community and promote it widely, perhaps to donate a book for an upcoming fundraising sale along with a can of food for a local food bank—a "read and feed" donation event.
- Be sure to make ongoing recruitment a priority in every annual strategic plan.
- Do regular evaluations of your board and previous strategic plans.[3]
- Personally invite people you know and meet who show interest in becoming part of the library support group and encourage other members to do likewise.
- Stay tuned for lots of ideas in upcoming chapters to bring these pointers to fruition.

When Library Support Group and Library Objectives Are in Conflict

There are distressing stories about library support groups that get out of sync with the mission of their libraries and neglect to follow their roles as volunteers, advocates, and funders. It might happen that a Friends group becomes cliquish and isolates itself from the library it is supposed to stand behind, perhaps being secretive about their financial or organizational status and determining how the money they have raised will be spent instead of allowing the library to have that choice. Group members might decide that they do not agree with decisions, goals, and policies of the library and withhold funds to express their disagreements. They may notice a community literacy program or other local organization that needs monetary support and tell the library that they are going to give their funds to it rather than the library, disregarding their library support mission. On the other hand, maybe the library itself expresses a desire to have some control over the group with which the group cannot comply. Any number of scenarios like these and more can take place, and when they do, the disbanding of the groups involved in such conflicts may potentially take place unless steps are taken for resolution.

Hearing about situations like these can cause some library directors to discourage the formation of nonprofit organizations to aid their own libraries, no matter how advantageous such additional monetary, volunteer, and advocacy support might be. Nonetheless, these kinds of unfortunate situations could be deflected before groups are dissolved or they could be completely avoided in the first place if handled carefully and directly. The bottom line is that by and large it well worth the effort to have library support groups and to strive to keep library partnerships with them healthy and effective.[4]

A principal way that libraries and library support groups can come into agreement about resolving negative conditions is through using a memorandum of understanding (MOU) and which was previously discussed. It can often be the first and most effective step taken to resolve issues and move forward instead of drawing out unpleasant circumstances without constructive resolutions. Without resolutions, unfortunately at times library support groups may have no other choice but to disperse.

In some cases, an issue causing conflict is when a Friends of the Library group is no longer able to access designated space needed for their fundraising efforts and/or the library itself wanting to exert more control over the operation of the organization. To illustrate, in California, the Friends of the Santa Maria Public Library found themselves in a challenging predicament. Organized as a nonprofit in 1983, they had been operating a bookstore from within the library building itself lease-free for ten years. When the city suddenly decided that the group must begin renting the bookstore space as an outside entity, concurrently, due to liabilities, the library wanted an MOU agreement that would give it managerial control for background checks of Friends group volunteers like its own library volunteers undergo. The Friends board wanted to be in charge of background checks themselves and did not wish to lease previously free library space for their fundraising efforts, but the MOU indicated that the group would have a responsibility to disband if it did not comply. Regrettably, an agreement could not be met.[5]

After a continuing, tenuous back-and-forth that still did not result in signing an agreement, the bookstore was closed. After fourteen months, in 2019, the Friends had not disbanded and had moved into a workable alternative bookstore space in a local mall to carry on and solely focus upon its fundraising mission.[6] This Friends group could in all likelihood have dissolved under these conditions, but they were dedicated to the task of supporting the library, and they found a solution for themselves and for the library. The work they do validates the group and provides a satisfying solution for both sides as they continue to provide library support, now as a truly separate and independent organization.

If a library support group is having conflicts about who is in primary control, perhaps it means that their close ties to the library are not practical. Severing the close ties and still supporting the library as a truly outside organization may very well supply a remedy. In this case, a revised MOU might be drawn up to clearly indicate the detached roles.

Another situation involving space issues occurred in Bend, Oregon. After forty years, the library there was likewise no longer able to offer a free area to the Friends of Bend Libraries group since the library itself needed to use the space. Although the library expressed great appreciation for the contributions the group had made to it, they needed the room more than they needed the Friends donations. A mutual decision was made to dissolve the Friends group with their remaining assets given to the library. At that point, the dedicated friends volunteers reassessed their mission and decided that continuing to support literacy efforts in their region was essential, with particular concentrations on early childhood literacy and reading proficiency programs for adults. They re-formed the group into a new nonprofit, the Supporters of Literacy in Deschutes County (SOLID) and have held and plan to keep on holding book sales to support their causes by using donated spaces.[7] In some cases like this one, library support groups may need to assess their missions, perhaps redirect and expand their nonprofit focus, and maybe still embrace the library they previously supported in a different manner.

Stepping on Toes and Duplicating Efforts When There Are Two Support Groups

There are only a few examples of fortunate organizations, agencies, educational centers, or service facilities that benefit from not just one but sometimes two nonprofits that are dedicated to helping them. As you have seen, some lucky libraries fit the bill as they are the recipients of the generous contributions of both a Friends of the Library group and a foundation or a trust. In many cases, those libraries are indeed blessed because the two support groups work well in tandem, each with their own unique mission to assist the library with which they productively partner. However, the relationships between two differing library support groups can suffer when they find themselves duplicating efforts, experiencing overlaps, getting in each other's way, or otherwise finding themselves in conflict. In these kinds of situations, how do the support groups—and the library itself—work together to iron out the disagreements?

First, let us think again about the common missions of these groups. A Friends of the Library nonprofit usually operates book sales, book shops, and fundraising efforts to monetarily aid their designated library with such causes as programming, special activities, staff development, and materials. Their core boards of directors are primarily comprised of community volunteers, although there are examples of Friends groups that occasionally have a paid position. Friends often run programs; provide a corps of volunteers; typically have membership drives to solicit new members; may ask for dues to enhance their coffers; create newsletters to inform members and the library public about their accomplishments, membership needs, and related activities; sometimes secure smaller-sized grants for particular purposes; and provide library advocacy. The money they provide is used for general library needs and not for capital projects.

Foundations and trusts vary in size depending on the range of their community populations and more regularly include some paid professionals on staff who manage their boards of directors as they focus on meeting their mission to help ensure that high-priced library projects are funded. Unpaid individuals are often well-regarded community members who have potential donor connections that make them influential fundraisers who can attain endowments and enlist continuous donors. The money they raise is earmarked for capital library projects and expensive programs that Friends of the Library groups would rarely be able to fund.

Considering their different focuses, it would appear that these two kinds of groups would be able to compatibly function successfully together, and usually they do. Even though the kinds of goals they address might fall into similar categories, they have notable differences. For example, while a Friends group might arrange a low-cost program featuring a local author, a foundation may cover an honorarium for a high-profile writer and perhaps even charge a fee for program attendance. A Friends group might fund prizes and tee shirts for a summer reading program, while a library trust may fund a bookmobile, an author award with a significant monetary prize, a library resource center, or a large-scale community literacy event. A Friends group often expects dues and runs fundraising projects to raise money, while a foundation might seek out large donations from prominent figures. Friends are great library advocates who might speak out about budgets and ballot issues, but members may not possess the connections to city officials and local corporations like foundation or trust members often do, so their combined influences can make advocacy stronger. When each organization stays within the parameters of its particular purpose, they can usually get along without issue and may even aid one another by having a representative serving on each other's boards as ex officio members. Troubles arise when overlaps cause concerns and conflicts.

When there are two groups seeking members for their boards of directors, they may be in competition to recruit the most outstanding representatives from their community. If a library director is expected to serve ex officio on the board for both groups, it may require too much time to do both and the one gleaning the most dollars wins out, which can cause hard feelings. Most of the time, a Friends group has existed a great deal longer than a foundation or trust, and when one of the latter organizations is formed in addition, the original group may experience negative reactions of "imposition." The list can go on and on about conflicts that might occur, but the important consideration is to work toward resolving any differences and getting the two groups to collaborate.

A chief concern is making sure that the creation of any new foundation or trust includes representation from a Friends group if there is one already active. If Friends are involved in the process, they will most likely understand that there is not a threat to their existence, understand and appreciate the complementary missions, and help to decide up front how the two groups can work effectively in tandem.

When two groups are already functioning, or the process of founding a new group is taking place, if conflicts or misunderstandings are happening, it may be helpful to draw up a MOU outlining the roles of each library support organization along with the roles of the library that is benefiting from their contributions. It can help to include a clause that ex officio representation will be made on each other's boards; a declaration that both boards will meet annually for a joint session; and that communications to the public and donors will clarify that there are two unique fundraising organizations supporting the library in complimentary ways. Once everyone agrees to the terms and signs on, it can make teamwork more effective on everyone's part.

If a Friends group and a foundation or trust feels that there is too much duplication of efforts and organizational operations, perhaps it could be time to begin conversing about merging the two groups. The concept of merging two library support groups was discussed in chapter 1 with three examples of combined groups and how they came about. You may want to revisit that section as a reminder of some good reasons for taking this step. If you are considering proposing this action, be sure that the Friends, the foundation or trust, and the library carefully discuss the pros and cons of that choice and that everyone buys in on decisions and planning. Every merger situation will be different and creating a progressive strategic plan to see it through is a must.

Once again, some of the benefits of merging include:

- Limiting confusion in the general public and with donors about the distinction between the two organizations.
- Allowing the opportunity to solicit members and other donors more than once a year for enhanced financial support.
- Building more effective advocacy through united activities and the ability to provide matching funds.
- Creating a vigorous, more prominent community organization for improved library support.[8]

What to Do about Board Resignations and Other Board Officer Woes

Because a library support group's board of directors is its organizational core and central to its legal status as a nonprofit, any disruption in retaining a complete board could cause upheaval and stress. There are several ways that a board might find itself in this predicament. In this section, I will cover ways to approach and resolve all of these resignation possibilities.

For whatever reason a vacancy might occur, it is essential to check the organizational bylaws and to follow whatever provisions that exist for accepting a resignation, forcing a dismissal, and lawfully replacing a board member. When bylaws are created, addressing what to do in case of vacancies must be taken into account. There may be legal issues surrounding the departure and replacement of a board member depending on individual states and types of library support groups, and it is important to be aware of any special procedures to follow. Consulting your legal expert might be an option to ensure that everything is squared away properly before installing a new officer.

One scenario that might take place is when an officer needs, for any number of reasons, to resign by giving advance notice, which can be challenging, especially if the vacated position is one that the executive director, president, secretary, or treasurer is holding. Alternatively, when a board loses any officer without notice due to sudden illness, death, or other emergency situation, it presents an immediate call to fill the vacancy, even if temporary.

Another way a board might lose someone is by forced dismissal. If an officer is not fulfilling duties, misusing trust, or causing conflicts, there may be a need to ask the person to resign or face dismissal. As you can imagine, it can be thorny to handle this kind of problem properly without bylaw directives to back up a dismissal, and those directives need to be based specifically on the documentation of negative behavior and/or performance issues.

The first situation—when a board member resigns with notice—is usually the easiest to manage, although that does not necessarily indicate an absence of difficulty. Before accepting a resignation, the actual reason for the notice of departure needs to be considered. According to *Robert's Rules of Order*, if the person's position and active input is imperative to the board, it would be prudent to encourage the person to stay. For instance, if the person is having complications in keeping up with the time demands of the office and an assistant could be appointed to provide aid, it could encourage the person to remain on the board. If the person is experiencing conflicts with meeting schedules, one accommodation that is acceptable to everyone might provide a resolution to the quandary. It is always worthwhile to investigate further when there is a chance that the resignation of an essential officer might be deflected.

The same thing holds true when the cause of a potential resignation is due to problems within the organization itself. A tactful, frank, intelligent, and kind discussion about any communication issues, disagreements, or conflicts, perhaps led by an impartial facilitator, may draw out solutions that are agreeable to a majority of the board members while protecting and respecting the rights of any minority. In other cases, if a distressed officer presents a verbal resignation, which is not considered official, it may take a simple, honest conversation with all the officers to resolve the problem. In these sets of circumstances, an officer may ultimately choose to remain on the board.

If, however, the officer truly plans to resign for personal reasons and there is no other recourse, then the proper protocol is for a formal resignation letter to be addressed and given to the board secretary, unless the secretary is the one who is leaving. Then, the letter would go to the president. The letter needs to include the date, the name of the addressee, the reason(s) for the resignation, and the departing officer's signature. The letter can be mailed, emailed (if signed and scanned), or delivered in person to the secretary. Once the secretary receives it, the letter can be given to the rest of the board for reading, consideration, and a vote for acceptance. However, unless there is a rule prohibiting it, if the person planning to leave decides to withdraw the resignation, this can be done prior to a vote. As soon as the resignation is accepted, the position is legally considered vacated. It then needs to be filled again as soon as possible according to the procedures in most organizational bylaws.[9] If it is not there already, a board may want to consider adding a potentially helpful clause in its bylaws stipulating that a resigning officer in good standing will be permitted to assist the board in finding a replacement prior to the effective date of the person's departure.

If the person who is leaving follows the accepted business and organizational protocol and gives ample notice in the proper format, it makes the vacancy less complicated than if the officer leaves without warning. However, sometimes the office holder does not have a choice. When a person must suddenly move to care for a sick parent, passes away, gets seriously ill, or experiences any other life-altering event or circumstance, leaving the board is not, in most cases, preplanned. Still, if possible, it is important for the board to receive official notice of the position vacancy as soon as reasonable and possible. It would be beneficial for any nonprofit bylaws to include instructions regarding board actions for addressing occurrences of unexpected vacancies and to make sure officers are aware of them.

While keeping all these points in mind, it is a good idea to follow these general steps when a board member resigns:

- Prepare in advance for unexpected vacancies. Whenever a vacancy occurs, it may impact the normal course of group operations. That is the reason it is crucial to have a succession plan ready and waiting to facilitate a smooth transition to an interim or incoming board member. To aid the process, it is a wise idea for governing documents to include resignation guidelines. This helps to ensure that resignations of any kind are properly and consistently handled.
- Review governing documents each year to make sure that the procedures outlined are up to date and the succession plan is still accurate. Part of this should include

checking that local, state, and federal laws are met to make sure that your documents remain legally compliant. You may want to consult your group's attorney to ensure that everything is correct.
- Keep a list of confidential documents and other materials, such as organizational handbooks that are routinely given to board members, so that there is an awareness of what any resigning board member has stored. Make arrangements to retrieve any documents or materials that will no longer be in the care of the resigning member.
- Be sure to have the board member's signed resignation letter with the departure date added to the agenda of the next board meeting for formal acceptance. Once accepted, the letter should be added to the records and minutes of the meeting.
- Set up an exit interview with the board member who is leaving. Regardless of the reason for departure, a respectful exit interview can provide valuable feedback to improve the board. It can also spark ideas for additional questions to add to the list for future exit interviews. Some questions you might want to consider for your initial list are:
  - What did you like best and least about your position on the board?
  - Did you feel well-equipped to succeed in your position?
  - Did you feel valued as a member of the board?
  - What suggestions can you offer to help the board improve?
  - Are there other issues you would like to address or comments you would like to make?
- On the effective date of resignation, make sure the resigning member's passwords, access to internal documents, and email accounts are deleted. Also, update any online resources, documents, or newsletters to eliminate the resigning person's name and contact information. Collect any vital materials still in the possession of the resigning member.
- Let any appropriate persons in the library or elsewhere know about the finalized vacancy, and if an interim board member or replacement has been appointed, include an announcement.
- Finally, formally fill the vacated seat on the board as soon as possible according to the bylaws and the availability of a qualified replacement.[10]

The third situation—asking a board member to resign or face dismissal—is the stickiest of all. However, since a board is expected to operate as seamlessly as possible as a team to reach its mission, when a member causes any kind of disruption or conflict, proves untrustworthy, or neglects the duties required, it may be time to encourage that person to resign or be released from the board. In any case, a president or other leader or leaders needs to carefully document the reasons for supporting a requested resignation or outright dismissal. Then there is objective evidence giving credibility to their actions that need to be put into motion as quickly as possible. The sooner these issues are addressed, the better for the sake of the board and the library it serves.

Some board member behaviors that may be the source these predicaments could be:

- Regular absence from meetings
- Declining to aid in fundraising efforts
- Following a personal agenda that does not mesh with the library or the library support group's missions

- Failing to deal with confidential information securely according to board requirements
- Begging off or avoiding tasks required of their position or leaving tasks incomplete
- Never participating in board discussions
- Monopolizing the floor during meetings
- Demonstrating mistrust in financial matters
- Behaving with disrespect toward officers and fellow board members

If the issues being addressed involve serious circumstances such as problematic financial errors or disclosing private information, in many cases it may call for immediate removal. For less urgent matters that may potentially be solved more easily without yet taking that step, start with a review of code of conduct requirements with the entire board. If you do not have such requirements, then by all means, proactively create them as soon as possible, present them to the board for approval, and make them official so that they are available in the future. By reviewing the requirements with the whole board, the problematic individual will not be singled out and will hopefully get the message about behavior from the review. Another benefit of a group review is that everyone gets a refresher about requirements and duties, which keeps the board on track.

In the unfortunate case that the concerning behavior continues, the board member causing the conflict will need to have a private conversation with the chair or the president of the board, which is one of the duties of those offices. The conversation needs to include three parts, which include:

- A clear explanation of how the exhibited behavior does not meet board member requirements according to objective documentation and observation
- A discussion regarding how the disruptive behavior affects the organizational image and the group's effective decision-making
- A disciplinary plan of action to which both parties agree, which will be put into effect if the behavior does not change

If the plan is not followed and improvement shown, then the problematic individual would be aware up front through the wording of the plan that removal would be imminent.

If and when the situation reaches that final point of noncompliance, the only choice, for the health of the organization, is removal of the individual who is causing the behavior. The person could be asked to resign, which is the simplest solution, but if that is not effective, then the issue would need to come before the board for a vote according to whatever rules are included in the bylaws. Before a vote takes place, the chair or president would present the behavioral reasons for the dismissal request; what cautionary steps preceded coming to this decision; and the exhausted disciplinary plan of action.

Board vacancies are usually never easy, and as you can see, they can be simple or quite complex to handle. A key element to preventing the difficult kinds of encounters described here is assuring that a board is run with carefully planned bylaws and rules along with an open dialogue and respectful interactions. When challenging behavior does arise, early intervention made with respect and dignity is usually the best recourse. However, it is best to have a plan in place and to be willing to take drastic, more effective action as necessary to keep the organization running smoothly.[11]

Finally, this is a good opportunity to insert a special note to follow the same three disciplinary steps to relieve a non-board essential volunteer from service when that person is causing problems or is having issues being compatible with others. The issue can likewise be addressed by documenting, objectively conversing, setting up a disciplinary action plan, and removal if there is no other recourse. It is wise to have job descriptions and backup plans for interim procedures that are prepared in advance to fill any indispensable volunteer roles that are suddenly vacated.

Volunteers in Charge of Essential Functions Suddenly Resign

When resignations occur by persons in essential volunteer positions leading a team or chairing a committee, it can have serious impacts similar to when volunteers are let go. Consider these situations:

- For many years, two married volunteers have been leading and effectively running the entire materials donation process and its distribution to branches and other locations for fundraising sales. They know all the key points about sorting, pricing, what sells best where, and which items are valuable enough to pass on to the online sales or special sales team. They are considered indispensable, and everyone on the board and within the group membership highly values their contributions and management. However, when their daughter moves to another state and they miss their grandchildren, they decide to move. At that time, they resign from their positions as Friends materials coordinators and leave the group for which they have been dedicated and dependable volunteers for a very long time.
- There is a volunteer who has been in charge of coordinating other volunteers for every library support group book sale and its book shop desk schedule for as long as anyone can remember. That person is coming up in years and is beginning to think about retiring from his longtime volunteer service. He is reluctant to take his leave because he enjoys his work, values the group, and knows that everyone depends upon him and his wonderful coordinating and scheduling abilities. However, he discovers he has a heart issue, and the doctor recommends that he finally slow down. Sadly, he gives a notice of resignation from the beloved volunteer duties, which he will sorely miss.
- A young and now early middle-aged woman has been dedicated to successfully arranging and organizing an annual author-centered fundraising program for two decades. She has great connections allowing her "an in" with publishers and can get top authors to come and speak at a nominal charge for special fundraising events. The library support group she belongs to depends on her to do this every year. Now she is getting divorced, and she is moving out of state to live closer to her sisters. She turns in her resignation as the chair of the author events committee and looks forward to offering the same services to the Friends Foundation in her new community.
- Two volunteers who have effectively partnered for almost five years to plan and organize the huge annual membership drive have a falling-out and each one leaves the group—and their volunteer responsibilities—in a huff. Because they have been handling the drive productively and the central tasks have been left to both for several years, there is no one else available who truly understands the process and procedures they have developed and put into place.

From library support group board and other leadership viewpoints, these scenarios probably instill a reaction of: "Now what happens?"

While you are reading these, you may wonder the same thing—*now what happens?* It may bring to mind some similar circumstances your group has experienced or that it has heard about that resulted in similar sudden vacancies, along with the outcomes. You might be thinking about the possibilities of needing to address any abruptly open positions like these in your group that could occur. Maybe you recall a past time when several volunteers engaged in bickering about something trivial or perchance very important, and all of them left suddenly and for good without a board member referee to get things under control. Whatever the reason in these types of scenarios, the question remains: "Now what happens?"

These are not unusual or especially creative examples, but ones that are shaped from real situations I have come across through the years. I have learned that there can be solutions to these problems that are similar to the ones already presented, and that can be honed down to the maxim: "Be prepared."

As with the admonition for library support nonprofit boards to have replacement plans in place to deal with potential unexpected vacancies, the same holds true for volunteer special committee and assignment leaders serving under board auspices. If a board has long-standing members who are running the show for specific critical organizational functions, leaving them to independently keep doing it indefinitely without backups is risky. On the spur of the moment, the board could, without warning, be faced with critical vacancies without having anyone who knows the ropes ready and able to take on the necessary tasks. This is why it is vital to:

- Create and have a plan at hand to fill or intervene for all vacancies as they might occur in important leadership areas beyond the board positions.
- Whenever possible, ask committee and activity leaders to partner with other members who can serve as second-in-charge and can learn firsthand from them what position assignments entail.
- Keep in close touch with those who are expert at their volunteer leadership posts so that you can show them appreciation, learn readily of any upsets or controversies, deal with those issues tactfully and directly, and keep tabs on potential unanticipated departures on the horizon.
- Have a detailed plan and flowchart with instructions for each leadership assignment and be sure the people assisting the leaders in those management and directional roles know how to assist and stand in occasionally.
- Make sure that the board of directors has a handbook section with lists of organizational tasks, duties, and procedures to guide them as they fill open chair and other positions of heightened responsibility and instruct new volunteers about each leadership role.
- Explain to leaders and those serving under them which board member(s) to contact privately with questions and concerns about uncomfortable circumstances before problems get out of control behind the scenes.
- Again, tackle issues of concern in a timely manner. Ensure that all parties involved or needing to be informed are plainly aware of situations surrounding the causes of disharmony. Avoid letting problems fester.
- Finally, always keep the aphorism, "Be prepared," in readiness.

Notes

1. Maureen Rust, and Julia Stringfellow. "Why Can't We Be Friends? Examining the Benefits and Challenges of Maintaining Your Friends of the Library." Collaborative Librarianship 10, no. 3 (2018): 202+. Gale Academic OneFile (accessed January 18, 2023). https://link.gale.com/apps/doc/A568118837/AONE?u=googlescholar&sid=bookmark-AONE&xid=2ad00286.
2. Lauren Clem. January 8, 2020. "Friends of the Blackstone Library May Disband, Impacting Programs." *Valley Breeze*, https://www.valleybreeze.com/news/friends-of-blackstone-library-may-disband-impacting-programs/article_7fd815a6-21f0-542f-a41d-c0b28e0abca3.html.
3. Library Strategies. 2021. "10 Quick Tips for Growing Your Friends & Foundation," https://www.librarystrategiesconsulting.org/2017/12/10-quick-tips-for-growing-your-friends-foundation/.
4. Association of Library Trustees, Advocates, Friends, and Foundations. [n.d.] "Fact Sheet #28 for Friends and Foundations: When Friends Aren't Friendly," https://www.njstatelib.org/wp-content/uploads/lss_files/When%20Friends%20Aren't%20Friendly_0.pdf.
5. Razi Sayed. September 6, 2019. "Friends of the Library Bookstore to Close Tuesday: Patrons, Volunteers Lament Loss." *Santa Maria Times*, https://santamariatimes.com/santamaria/friends-of-the-library-bookstore-to-close-tuesday-patrons-volunteers/article_cc6f72cb-d6c2-5c9e-8ca9-77405207e72f.html.
6. Razi Sayed. September 6, 2019. "Friends of the Santa Maria Public Library to Reopen Bookstore Months after Dispute Closed Doors." *Santa Maria Times*, https://santamariatimes.com/news/local/friends-of-the-santa-maria-public-library-to-reopen-bookstore-months-after-dispute-closed-doors/article_170a9cbd-264a-50f3-a4ab-37c802ca1bd9.html.
7. Rhea Panela. January 28, 2020. "Friends of Bend Libraries Disbands, Forms New Nonprofit." *News Channel 21*, https://ktvz.com/news/2020/01/28/friends-of-bend-libraries-disbands-forms-new-nonprofit/.
8. Library Strategies. March 22, 2016. "Why Can't We All Just Get Along?" Library Strategies Consulting Group, https://www.librarystrategiesconsulting.org/2016/03/why-cant-we-all-just-get-along/.
9. KidLink. [n.d.] "Membership, Officers" in *Robert's Rules of Order*, https://www.kidlink.org/docs/RobertRules/chap11.html.
10. Associa. 2022. "How to Handle a Board Member's Resignation," https://hub.associaonline.com/blog/how-to-handle-a-board-member-s-resignation.
11. DeLeon and Stang. 2023. "Tips for Handling Toxic Board Members," https://deleonandstang.com/insights/tips-for-handling-toxic-board-members?rq=toxic%20board%20member.

CHAPTER 6

Virtual and Other Promotional Outreach for Library Support Groups

EVERY SUCCESSFUL NONPROFIT GROUP aiding their local, school, academic, or special library or library system, whether it is a Friends of the Library, foundation, trust, or a combination of these, needs to develop a sturdy base of allies. These include an enduring assembly of volunteers; sources of individual, family, business, organizational, and/or other means of continual and new funding; camaraderie with the staff of the library to which it is dedicated; and a following by other local backers who appreciate, stand up for, and stand behind its mission.

Without this combined support, a group may find itself faltering. It is essential for any library support group to incorporate several ways to draw such varied contributors to the cause and to encourage them to participate however they might be willing and able. Using present-day technology to engage this combined support is one of the best ways to progress.

In this chapter, I will give ideas for devising and employing several useful methods to achieve this electronic outreach objective such as creating a meaningful logo; designing attractive membership and informational brochures that can be placed online in addition to otherwise-available print formats; developing a significant, attractive, user-friendly website and social media presence; and adding donor-friendly virtual spaces for monetary contributions and fundraising purchases.

To start off, I would like to address the importance of catchy, recognizable, and memorable logos.

A Little Logo Is a Big Deal

A logo might seem like a small thing, but when carefully formulated it is the opposite. This is true because it can express everything important without saying a word as it conveys feelings of respect, confidence, pride, distinction, and integrity. A well-designed logo with inherent meaning can be a catalyst for easy organizational identification; a means of developing cohesiveness and continued engagement among members, the community, and the library receiving support; a vehicle for drawing in new members; a promotional tool for a group to gain partnerships; a talking point for reaching out to and connecting with donors; and more.

The design of just the right logo requires the expertise of a professional designer, which may be costly, but even on a limited or nonexistent budget there are still ways to create the perfect logo. Perhaps the library receiving your support has someone who can help. Maybe a local college or high school graphic design class might take on the challenge of assisting with designing your logo. There may be someone within your membership ranks or on your board who has a lead to a graphic design artist who can create a fine logo or who may even possess the needed skills and volunteer their own time. Ask around and see what kind of help you can enlist if you cannot afford to pay a professional, or perhaps find a professional who will aid the library support group by designing a logo gratis or at a much reduced cost. Instead of these options, you may want to explore using the online creative resource Canva,[1] which you can use for free (or at a charge for advanced tools) to generate basic logos, other sorts of designs, and in various formats.

No matter who is helping you to approach the initial design, there are a few pointers to keep in mind:

- Explore other library support group websites and make note of their logos to gather ideas you might emulate.
- Choose a shape and color for your logo that makes it memorable.
- Start with the familiar, perhaps revamping a previous logo, and consider symbolic ways to update your logo and make it stand out.
- Beware of creating a logo that is too cryptic, difficult to decipher, too artsy, or that does not actually reflect the purpose of your group.
- Before finalizing a logo, ask library, community, board, and fellow group members for their honest opinions about the design and if they understand the message.[2]

Once you have your new logo in its final form, announce its release to the organizational membership, the library, and the community. Let people know that they will be seeing a new logo, the reason it was created or redesigned, and what it symbolizes. Start using the new logo in all your library support group communications, on your publicity, at events you host; on promotional T-shirts; and especially on all social media and your website.

TEXTBOX 6.1

A NOTEWORTHY LOGO AND WEBSITE REDESIGN EXAMPLE

In the spring of 2023, the Friends of the Knox County Public Library released their redesigned logo, created with the help of Robin Easter Design. Easter said her firm designed the new logo:

> to re-energize the brand and attract fresh faces, while also staying familiar to the many members that have made the organization a valuable piece of the community. The new design references the kinds of library stamps used in libraries for centuries, toeing the line between familiar and new by embracing a clean modern look. The logo carries over the same book used in the previous logo. This time instead of a solitary face, the book is accompanied by a heart, representing the love spread by Friends and the love for reading shared by its members.

The project was spearheaded by Bailey Foster, board president at the time of the redesign project, and communications committee chair Natalie Smith. Coinciding with the logo redesign was a refresh of the group's ten-year-old website, which now incorporates new fonts and an updated, bright yellow color; features more recent and larger photos; and shares the group's Instagram feed.[1]

Figure 6.1. The Friends of the Knox County Public Library's 2023 logo. For variety, there are also other versions: a dark blue, a lighter blue, and an outline version. *Courtesy of the Friends of the Knox County Public Library. Credit Robin Easter of Robin Easter Design.*

Note

1. Knox County Public Library. April 2023. "A New Look for Friends." Email newsletter, https://mailchi.mp/knox-friends.org/friends-kcpl-april-2766563?e=4b001489e0.

The Importance of Websites and Social Media

With thoughts in mind about website redesign and thinking back to the birth of the internet (if you are old enough to remember), you might recall that libraries at that time quickly learned that they could use websites and social media to greatly and effectively expand the reach of their resources and services. During my long librarian career, the use of technology became indispensible at each library and made our jobs more streamlined and much more productive. As time went by, I often did in-house explanations for customers about what was available for them on the library websites, which they were delighted to discover. I also frequently visited middle and high school classrooms and taught students about the library websites and how to use them to find books and do research. I always enjoyed referring to the websites as "additional" library branches—virtual ones—and I still do today when letting people who are unfamiliar know about these resources, which have evolved in so many positive ways with ever-expanding technological advances and improvements.

In the same manner, library support groups have been able to employ well-crafted websites and social media connections to introduce board members to the public; present their mission statements and share other documents of public interest; explain how people can get involved with the group; tout group achievements and honors; announce opportunities to donate and volunteer through the group; and much more. Although you have gotten a taste for these uses in previous chapters where there was some discussion about the importance of websites, connecting with the library community electronically, and using hi-tech means to manage group needs, here you will learn how to go about actually developing an accessible and pleasing virtual presence.

Creating a Social Media Presence

When considering the topic of social media presences, you may be thinking: "We only need a basic website, and that should be sufficient. Is the development of a more complex social media presence really that important?" The answer is that you need engaging and accessible digital platforms that reach a wide range of people—ones that are equally accessible for older adult audiences, middle-aged folks, "new" adults, and younger users.[3]

This is true because in today's world of technological advances and the widespread use of social media, library support groups need to rely on various communication methods well beyond the old standbys of simple websites, paper membership applications, flyers, posters, and other print mediums. There are so many additional ways that Friends, foundations, and trusts can reach out to the public that supports them as well as permitting them to reach out to new members, volunteers, and donors who may not know of their existence. Along with the old standbys, attractively designed, more comprehensive, user-friendly websites and social media platforms allow people to not only learn about the missions of library support groups, these new mediums offer places to spotlight news about upcoming events and notable accomplishments, and to set a path for attracting new members to the fold.

Although these are all spot-on reasons, not all library support groups may have the tools and/or the abilities to put effective website and social media resources to good use. Despite those challenges, there are means available to aid those who want to take advantage of offering useful online descriptions and details about their groups. Those resources can help groups put their best foot forward online via the creation of highly functional websites. Here are some ideas to mull over:

- Find out if anyone in your organization is experienced at web design and can step up to the task or if someone knows an experienced person who might help for no charge or a small fee. If you have youth involved in your support group, you may be surprised at their savvy computer knowledge and expertise and their willingness to help. You could also contact a local computer science teacher or a college computer science instructor to see if that person would be able to assist. Sometimes, teachers have students with the skills to create websites and who are anxious to do so for class credit or community service. It could also be a way to entice younger people to join your group as they work on website design projects. Additionally, your partner library may be able to offer assistance and/or guidelines. Trying out one of these options or a combination of them might be a straightforward and cost-effective way to get the job done right.
- Post volunteer job announcements on your website in a volunteer recruitment area or other available space. It can be brief as long as it is to-the-point. For instance, at the Friends of the Boca Raton Public Library in Florida, they posted ads like this, which read, "We are looking for a volunteer social media strategist to increase our organization's social media presence and engagement on LinkedIn, YouTube, Face-

book, Twitter, and Instagram," and "We are looking for a [volunteer] blogger to write content for our website that includes information and stories about our bookstore, our volunteers, our events, and sponsored library programming and events."[4]

- If using someone with limited experience is the only choice, or a small novice team gets together to take it on, they might start out by exploring the websites of other Friends, foundations, or trusts to peruse examples that stand out. Although the quality of layouts and content will vary greatly, it will soon be apparent which ones are the most user-friendly and informative. Check the library support group webliography at the end of this book to find links to some good examples of carefully designed and accessible websites.
- If you decide to take a look at those examples or others that you find, contact the groups that you feel have the best substance and presentation that are similar to your online goals, contact them, and ask if they can give your group any advice about how they developed such impressive pages. Many active groups have a notation on their website giving a phone number, or they encourage those who want to reach out to them to use either email or a "contact us" text message box that they post.
- There are a number of useful books and other resources available about creating new websites and employing social media for library marketing and promotion. Library support groups can apply the information in them to help develop meaningful virtual presences. You will find some of them included in this book's bibliography/webliography and your local librarian can also help you to access the most current and useful books, ebooks, and virtual resources on all aspects of this topic.
- Explore and use the many places online where you can find readily available, free advice and tutorials on creating websites and using social media. A selection of these can be found in the next textbox, which might be a good place to begin.

Remember, if you have someone in your library support group who is computer-savvy and knows how to design websites, you may be one step ahead of the game. Ask if that person might be available to work on starting a website for you or updating the one you already have. Keep in mind, though, that taking on this responsibility can impact the work schedule of someone who is donating time, and such volunteer web design experts usually need you to patiently allow them leeway to complete your project. If an extensive timeline for a website to be created is an issue, you may need to consider some of the other options that were listed.

However it comes about, making your website easy to use, attractive, and informative is an essential goal for most library service organizations in today's communication and marketing climate. Even if you have no other choice but to hire someone to do it (once more, see if you can get a deal since you are a nonprofit helping the library), it can be very much worth the investment.

No matter how you get your website designed or revamped, a huge factor in keeping the public engaged with your site is to promote it well and, most importantly, to keep it as current as possible. There is nothing more discouraging to a person trying to access your website for information, to make a donation, or to register to become a member than to find postings and details that are old and outdated. Since keeping your website updated is a topmost priority, be sure you have someone assigned to manage the task. The secretary of a group's board might be skilled at doing this or a volunteer from the board or from

TEXTBOX 6.2

BUILDING WEBSITES AND USING SOCIAL MEDIA

These websites will aid you in developing a virtual presence for your library support group, from website creation to choosing and using a variety of social media platforms.

Infopeople[1]

You can find lots of helpful advice on this website to learn about using social media in relation to library support group promotion. Go to the website, create a free online account, and in the search box, enter "social media." Several webinars and other information sources covering social media will be found. By the way, there is also plenty of other useful guidance for library support groups besides using social media when you search the site.

Techboomers[2]

This website will give you information about employing a variety of social media sites as well as connecting you to resources for building a website.

Techsoup[3]

Billed online as "technology for nonprofits, charities, and libraries," Techsoup is a free virtual resource with tutorials for nonprofits to find technology information, solutions, and skills to effectively provide a virtual presence, whether it is for digital marketing, building a website, or other reasons.

YouTube[4]

If you want to find instructional videos on designing websites, securing email lists, creating a blog, using Facebook to promote events, Instagram marketing, Search Engine Optimization (SEO), and just about anything else related to virtual resources, you will find them at this site.

Notes

1. Infopeople, https://infopeople.org/.
2. Techboomers, https://techboomers.com/.
3. TechSoup, https://www.techsoup.org/.
4. YouTube, https://www.youtube.com/.

the regular membership pool could be an option. When you are doing the recruiting for your group, consider making the management of the website a specific job to include on a brochure/application list of choices for volunteer opportunities.

Lastly, make sure that the person in charge of monitoring and maintaining your website is familiar with Search Engine Optimization or "SEO," a method/process for making sure your website receives as many hits as possible. If guidance is needed about this topic, as indicated in the prior textbox, there are helpful videos that can be found on YouTube by making a subject search using the term "Search Engine Optimization."

TEXTBOX 6.3

HELPFUL ADVICE FROM A LIBRARY SUPPORT GROUP WEBSITE MANAGER

Managing any website is an inexhaustible task, but also a valuable one. A well-maintained library support group website amplifies the organization's activities, reach, and even impact. From a promotional standpoint, you want your community to find accessible and up-to-date information about what you're doing and how they can participate, whether it's putting the next book sale on their calendar or being aware of a donation event so they can give in time. It is also a good way to maintain credibility as people will know they can rely on your online presence for accurate information. The more awareness people have of what you're doing, the more successful your activities can be.

Luckily, a regularly updated website feeds into that goal because Google and other search engines consistently prioritize the most current content. Every time you update a page, it helps search engines recognize that your website is still alive, and they will push it higher in search results. When people search up "used book sales" or "local reading events," your website will be more likely to pop up on the first page.

However, website maintenance and Search Engine Optimization (SEO) is a mouth in need of constant feeding. I help maintain and update the Poudre River Friends of the Library website, and it's not always easy keeping it as cutting-edge or organized as one would like. Especially since I work a full-time job, it's been important for me to develop routines I can move through consistently and with ease to help ensure a presentable website.

The first major element of this was making sure the website itself was organized. After joining my local Friends and being elected to the board, I did a moderate content overhaul to both optimize SEO and make the site easier to maintain. I wanted to set pages that were reasonably static (and thus rarely in need of updates) and have only a few dynamic pages where people could reliably check for current new content. Those dynamic pages ended up being the home page, the board information page, and the book sales page.

By concentrating the number of places that needed regular updates, it has been easier to make changes in a consistent fashion, where it's always easy to see what is now old and where to apply new information across the site. After that, it became routine to update the site with new events and meeting documents, which themselves have a regular release pattern. It's still easy to fall behind, but with today's easy-to-use web platforms, the updates are never too time-consuming. With that in mind, my best advice is to take the two minutes to make an update as soon as new information enters your email inbox.

Samantha Ye
Poudre River Friends of the Library Board of Directors/Website Manager
Fort Collins, Colorado

Friends of the Library Applications and Dues (or No Dues)

One item that is usually included on a Friends of the Library or Friends Foundation website is an online form to join the group, pay dues, volunteer, and/or make another kind of donation. In most cases, the online option is in addition to supplying print application forms, not instead of, to reach more potential members. As a rule, library foundations and trusts do not have these membership applications, but they do typically have an online place to donate money on their organizational websites. Friends Foundations have similar online donation spots on their websites and sometimes people can use the website to sign up as a library volunteer. All this will vary depending on purpose and how individual groups are set up to function. For this section of the book, I will focus on the general "Friends" issue of membership applications and why requiring, suggesting, or eliminating dues payments can be reasonable choices depending on the philosophy and format of particular groups.

With that in mind, in general today's Friends of the Library and Friends Foundation groups still require some sort of designated dues to become a member. Traditionally, Friends of the Library groups have functioned through the annual contributions of dues-paying members, many of whom are also ready and willing to volunteer. For most groups, annual dues payments provide a boost to the year's fundraising efforts. Even in times of emergency when fundraising might not take place as usual, dues might still be collected to help to keep the organization afloat.

On the other hand, requiring dues has, in some circles, become controversial. This is because there are adults who love their library and want to help it by joining the Friends, but they may not be able to afford the dues despite how small the requested amount might be. They may, however, be able to offer volunteer talent and/or time to assist with fundraising activities and other group functions. Likewise, young people might be drawn to becoming a library Friend, especially if a junior-level status is provided, so that they can donate time to help a community facility they care about, but paying the dues might be inhibiting. In these cases, Friends are most likely missing out on loyal volunteers to aid in a number of fundraising activities merely because the volunteers are not able to pay the dues.

In some Friends of the Library groups, this has changed owing to some very simple solutions. For instance, at the Friends of the Ada Public Library in Boise, Idaho, they have an application form that a person can use saying, "Yes! I want to be a member of the Friends Group!" Following that, the person has two choices of boxes to check. One, or the other, or both, can be checked and any choice or combination holds equal weight. One says, "I want to contribute financially $_____," and the applicant can fill in an amount if desired. The other box says, "I want to contribute my time (volunteer)."[5]

With an application designed like this, someone who is interested in volunteering, but who doesn't have enough money for dues, or someone who is only able to offer a dollar, can feel just as valuable and important as a person who chooses to give a large donation and applies to volunteer—or decides to skip volunteering at all. It is completely up to each individual whether money, volunteer time, or both are given. After all, time and effort hold value just like money, and this is a considerate way for a Friends group to handle the question of requiring dues.

Similarly, at the Friends of the Salado Public Library in Texas, dues or donations are not mentioned on their application at all. As a matter of fact, their policy is that organizational membership is simply open to anyone in the community; they state outright that there are no dues; and that all that is required is an application to join, on which any volunteering interests can be expressed.[6]

Those systems can be workable for some groups, but for those Friends who want and/or need to have dues, they may need to decide what amount of dues are fair but impactful as fundraising tools. Decisions will depend on each organization's location; its community's socio-economic composition; what feasible fundraising alternatives might be undertaken; and other factors deemed important by the board. As you have seen, even though some groups have eliminated requiring dues or have never had dues from the start, their successful resolution may have been to request volunteer fundraising service instead. Then again, other groups may have managed the dues dilemma effectively for their area by allowing applicants to choose their own individual dues donation amounts with volunteering optional.

Dues rates can vary greatly depending on each library community and often special dues levels are provided. For example, when considering children or senior citizens, library support groups may decide to have lower dues amounts, perhaps a dollar or two, for youngsters up to a certain age, for tweens and teens, or for elders above an allocated age. In many other cases, dues payments for adults might range from ten to twenty dollars with an option for a family membership that is slightly higher and a student membership that is lower.

One word of caution, though: If you choose to offer discounted rates for youth and seniors, that option may be commendable, but you need to be sure that there are appropriate benefits, volunteer opportunities, and honors bestowed upon them as you would with any other level of membership. If you do not, it can mean that, while some of those members are drawn in by potential chances to experience library support volunteerism and there are no times or opportunities available for them to take part, you may discover the following year that they choose to refrain from renewing their dues and let their memberships lapse.[7]

Friends board members should bear in mind that dues requirements already in existence are changeable and can be revisited annually if it appears that adjustments are necessitated. However, it would almost certainly be best for a group that has already operated without dues to keep from suddenly adding them since members and volunteers most likely value the no-dues system with which they are familiar. They may react to such a change as an imposition unless you demonstrated that adding dues has become a financial necessity. In that case, the dues design and roll out would need to be carefully planned and marketed as a positive funding move.

Membership Applications and Promotional Brochures

No matter what sort of dues arrangement a Friends of the Library group has, it is still important to have an application form for membership. A well-designed form, usually a brochure, allows applicants to enroll as members, find instructions for payment (if dues are required), convey a desire to be a volunteer or serve on the board of directors, and tell about any special interests or abilities they are able to add to help the cause. Such a brochure/form is also a method of telling the community about the existence of the Friends, explaining what Friends do to support the library, and maybe even touting some of the group's accomplishments.

Brochures/forms can be printed on paper and displayed at the library and around town. They can be given to people when they sign up for a new library card or given out at special events. They can also be designed as online fill-in applications along with a method to pay dues and donations electronically. Another approach would be to offer a PDF that prospective members or those renewing can download and print out or send in via email. It also helps to have a mail-in or drop-off choice for submitting paper applications. Multi-choice options are the most effective so that applicants can select whichever virtual or paper format is most appealing.

Whatever formats and content are chosen, it is imperative to have a carefully designed, attractive brochure/application. It is well worth the effort and cost to get the most striking and informative layout possible. If your group has a member who knows how to design such brochures and is willing to volunteer time to do the job for you that is a plus. You might also ask the library that you serve to direct you to a library staff member or someone else who may be able to help you complete the task. Your application brochure is one of your central promotional materials. Make sure it is the best quality that it can be.

You can peruse three good examples of Friends of the Library membership brochures in the appendixes. These are from the Friends of the State Library and Archives of Florida (courtesy of the Division of Library and Information Services); the Junior Friends of the Groton Public Library in Connecticut; and the Friends of the Saint Clair Shores Public Library in Michigan. Notice the concise, carefully worded content and the differences in the kinds of information given on them based on the purposes of each organization. When you create or revise your brochure, these examples can aid you in choosing design and content.

Once people actually apply, no matter what format they choose, it is imperative to send a message in a very timely fashion acknowledging that their application was received and is appreciated. Be sure all applicants are added to appropriate group mailing lists and email lists and that they are kept readily informed about the ways they can contribute.

Reaching Out to Individual Donors through Websites and Other Means

The missions of all Friends of the Library groups, library foundations and trusts, and Friends Foundations call for ongoing efforts to seek further income through supplementary contributions beyond dues, fundraising activities, and grants. I will be covering fundraising, grants, endowments, and other aspects of giving in depth within upcoming chapters, but for now I would like to focus on the regular "donorship" aspects of individual contributors. This information is aimed both at those organizations like trusts and foundations without "dues memberships" but that rely on "donor memberships" to raise funds, and at Friends groups that list auxiliary donor options outside of standard dues.

For some Friends and Friends Foundation groups that have yearly dues memberships, generally scheduled by calendar year, their dues membership drive materials and membership renewal reminders may be accompanied by a tiered list of further donation options. Regarding foundations and trusts, when those groups make appeals to people of means who become "members," they ask them when they enroll to consider giving from a range of amounts. For these donors and for many dues-paying members of Friends who choose to provide supplementary large donations to their dues, it is common for them to renew those donations each year. Because a large number of these donors continuously give the same amount, encouraging this reliable donor base to continue their support is a wise objective along with reaching out to new donors. This is imperative, because the facts are that though soliciting funds from business, corporate, or foundational donors are, of course, positive moves and ones not to be ignored, the reality is that of the approximately $350 billion given annually to charities in the United States, about 84 percent of the money comes from individuals. Since library support nonprofits represent a measure of this overall charitable combination, it makes reaching out primarily to individuals a smart approach.

One of the most effective ways to seek membership donations and further gifts beyond dues is by establishing a variety of suggested contribution levels from which donors can choose. In this way, it allows you to provide each donor with a selection of giving opportunities that can offer both a suitable match to donors' personal financial situations and their depth of dedication to your mission.

You may be wondering how an organization determines donation levels. A good method might be to chart the donorship contributions your group already receives. Then estimate the donor capacity of the current, ongoing givers and the anticipated, viable prospects. You want to make your suggestions for potential donors flexible but in the overall ballpark of what people in your community might be agreeable to and capable of giving.

On the other hand, you want to make sure that anyone wishing to give more or less than the amount you have suggested feels comfortable choosing a different amount than what is listed in your suggestions. One good way to do this is to design a list of possible amounts and to allow anyone wishing to donate to choose from it. Some library support groups assign names to the various levels and add special perks for donors at each level. For groups that add perks for donors, make sure that the benefits are not so valuable that they offset any tax benefits the donors might receive. You can check with your legal advisor to make sure that what donors might receive will not be too extravagant or minimally affect their ability to claim a write-off.[8] If this sounds confusing, the information in the next textbox will help you to envision how to do this.

TEXTBOX 6.4

DESIGN IDEAS FOR SETTING UP A LIBRARY SUPPORT GROUP DONATION PAGE

As an example, the Tulsa Library Trust posts the following message on its website with suggested gift amounts and buttons to click for donor choices:

> Please help us make a difference. The Tulsa Library Trust depends on financial gifts to pay for valuable programs today and build the endowment fund for the future. With your financial support we can make a difference. Your donation to the Tulsa Library Trust is tax-deductible.
>
> - $50
> - $100
> - $250
> - $500
> - $1,000
> - Other: $_____

(continued)

In addition to the list, the Trust posts a dropdown box for donors to select where their money will go. The box says, "WHERE MOST NEEDED," and donors can choose between dropdowns reading, "SUMMER READING PROGRAM" or "LITERACY."

Following the directions for actually making the donation, the Trust mentions that donors are also welcome to give a special gift in someone's memory or in honor of someone admired. In the case of honoring someone, they send personal notes to honorees letting them know about the gifts. Finally, the Trust explains that donors can "ensure lifelong learning for generations to come" by including the Trust in their wills and estate plans.[1]

As another example, an option is to design a list of choices like the one given on the Denver Public Library Friends Foundation (DPLFF) website. It gives donor ranges, names for each, and what perks donors receive. The introduction to the membership page says:

> When you join or renew your membership, you do a lot more than just keep the library free for everyone. You help thousands of people learn and grow every day. DPLFF members provide sustainable organizational and financial support for library collections and services that are not available through other funding sources.

Next, the membership levels and benefits are listed:

Friend of Learning: $20–$49

- "I'm a Friend" library card and sticker for first-time members only
- Magnetic bookmark
- E-subscription to the DPLFF quarterly newsletter

Friend of Knowledge: $50–$99

- 10 percent discount on the Red Chair Surprise Book Boxes (specially selected box of books by genre/age)
- One free book at any used book sale with a purchase

Friend of Experiences: $100–$249

- 10 percent discount on Denver Public Library and DPLFF merchandise

Friend of Opportunity: $250-$499

- Invitation to the annual invitation-only Holiday Lighting Party

Friend of Community: $500–$999

- Copy of *The Library Book* by Susan Orlean for first-time members only
- 10 percent discount on the Booklovers Ball tickets

Friend of Curiosity: $1,000–up

- Personalized behind-the-scenes tour of the Western History and Genealogy Department

Finally, it states: "Memberships are valid for one year. All memberships include benefits listed under previous levels. All contributions to the DPLFF are tax-deductible to the extent provided by law."[2]

Notes

1. Tulsa Library Trust. 2017. "Donate," https://tulsalibrarytrust.org/donate/.
2. Denver Public Library Friends Foundation. 2023. "Membership," https://www.dplfriends.org/how-to-help/become-a-member/.

Setting Up Methods of Payment

Whether for one-time or recurring donations, dues applications or renewals, charging at book sales or book shops, or selling online, to set up payment services for accepting credit cards, you could consult with your library support group's banking institution, although it may not be the most effective course. As Robin Gard, a former president of and now the vice president at the Friends of the Poudre River Friends of the Library in Colorado, told me, "We tried a small, semi-portable credit card machine from a bank and it turned out to be a nightmare and more expensive than we wanted."[9] From that point, the group moved on to other credit card processing services. This took place about ten years ago, so perhaps banks have improved the way they offer this kind of service, and some banks may do it better than others. Still, chances are it would probably be a more expensive choice. You might start out by seeing what your bank can provide and comparison shop with online purchasing services.

There is an abundance of these services available that library support nonprofits can use to set up credit card charging for various types of donations and purchases by community supporters. However, selecting the one or ones that will work best for your library support group requires research and perhaps even some trial and error. Even longstanding library support organizations may want to employ some of the advice I am giving in this chapter to switch from payment services that are not as cost-effective, efficient, or useful as they had hoped.

A good beginning is to list all the ways that your group may wish to collect money virtually and assess how much you can afford in service fees for each. Another helpful step is to find out what already established groups of your size with similar online payment needs are using and the reasons they recommend or discourage particular platforms. A third step might be to make a chart of the pros and cons of each processor you investigate that could be discussed at board meetings to make final decisions. Your treasurer might be the right person assigned to take this on, either solo or along with a small sub-committee of regular members or board members who have appropriate financial backgrounds. If they are accessible, you might even consider asking representatives from the payment services that are in the running for your business to do in-person or virtual presentations at your board meetings to explain what they can offer you and to answer questions about how their service operates. Based on your group's needs, you might want to deal with different services for varying purposes, for instance one for book sales and another for donations.

Robin Gard explained the reasons their Friends group has been doing just that by using three different services. She said that ten years ago, when they began taking online membership applications and dues, PayPal was the easiest service for online charging, and so far they still use it for that purpose today. However, they are considering possible options due to present costs. It is wise for all library support organizations to do the same—be aware of costs and make the effort to change services when and if justified.

Next, they wanted to begin taking credit cards at book sales, and Square was recommended to them. They liked it because they could use its app at any location with Wi-Fi for a nominal charge, that no hardware was required, and only a cell phone or tablet was needed. Since sales are held at library locations that have library Wi-Fi, the library tech staff checked the library's security protocols and Square became and still is the service of choice at sales in addition to cash and checks.

Finally, the group wanted to start taking credit cards at the Friends used book shop and also for "honor system" self-service customer payment at used book centers called "Book Nooks," located at two of the library branches. Because Square is not accommodating for self-service charging, the group discovered Clover, which fits the bill and which they now successfully use for this purpose.[10] By the way, for people wishing to pay with cash or check instead of charging with Clover, their payments can be dropped into a nearby secure lock box.

Ultimately, besides the ones mentioned already, there are myriad payment processing options from which you can choose. If you have a treasurer who is savvy about online charging, your library has a financial manager who is able to advise you, or you have a board or regular group member who is familiar with financial issues, see if you can get some guidance. Otherwise, you can find a host of advice and comparisons by doing an online search using the key words "best online payment processors for nonprofits" or, once again, find some useful video recommendations on YouTube. Your local librarian who is at the ready to lend a hand can also help to provide information to help make selections.

When you are investigating the choices, you will want to consider both well-known products as well as ones that are not as recognizable. Be patient and thorough in your research. In the meantime, there are some potential services to think about for a start. One, as mentioned in chapter 3, is Candid's Seal of Transparency program for attaining a basic Bronze Seal, which allows nonprofit access to Apply Pay for online donations.[11] In addition to that option, there are PayPal,[12] Square,[13] and Clover,[14] which were mentioned earlier. Then again, a few other notable examples of online payment services are Stripe,[15] Zeffy,[16] and Venmo,[17] and there are many more you will discover during your searches and through your comparisons.

Which service you choose depends on how you plan to utilize it and how it fits into your budget, and, as the Friends group in Colorado has done, you may decide to use more than one platform for different purposes. You may also decide at any time, as the Colorado group has done, to reevaluate for cost and efficiency and decide to take another online payment direction instead of the one or ones you may be currently using.

Notes

1. Canva. 2023. https://www.canva.com/.

2. Alexander Westgarth. November 30, 2018. "The Importance of Having the Right Logo." *Forbes*, https://www.forbes.com/sites/theyec/2018/11/30/the-importance-of-having-the-right-logo/?sh=38f78d8b1ccb.

3. Michal Halperin, and Ben Zvi. July 18, 2023. "Designing Age-Inclusive Products: Guidelines and Best Practices." *Smashing* magazine, https://www.smashingmagazine.com/2023/07/designing-age-inclusive-products-guidelines-best-practices/.

4. Friends of the Boca Raton Public Library. 2023. "Volunteer," https://www.bocalibraryfriends.org/volunteer.

5. Friends of the Ada Public Library. [n.d.] "Membership Information," http://www.adalib.org/star/sites/default/files/Friends%20Brochure%208-5x11.pdf.

6. Friends of the Salado Public Library. 2022. "Friends of the Library," https://www.saladolibrary.org/about-us/friends-of-the-library.

7. Joyce Braun Poderis. [n.d.] "Membership Campaigns: The How-To." Raise Funds, https://www.raise-funds.com/membership-campaigns-the-how-to/.

8. Joyce Braun Poderis. [n.d.] "Membership Campaigns: The How-To," https://www.raise-funds.com/membership-campaigns-the-how-to/.

9. Robin Gard. Email message to author, April 17, 2023.

10. Gard.
11. Wayne Chan. January 20, 2023. "Introducing 2023 Candid Seals of Transparency." Candid, https://blog.candid.org/post/introducing-2023-candid-seals-of-transparency/.
12. PayPal. 2023. "Boost Your Online Fundraising with Tools for Nonprofits of Every Size," https://www.paypal.com/us/non-profit/fundraising/fundraising-online.
13. Square. 2023. "Use Square as a Nonprofit Organization," https://squareup.com/help/us/en/article/6397-use-square-as-a-nonprofit.
14. Clover. 2023. "Credit Card Processing for Nonprofits," https://blog.clover.com/credit-card-processing-for-nonprofits/.
15. Stripe. https://support.stripe.com/questions/fee-discount-for-nonprofit-organizations.
16. Zeffy. https://www.zeffy.com/.
17. Venmo. https://help.venmo.com/hc/en-us.

CHAPTER 7

Successful Member, Volunteer, and Donor Recruitment and Retention

OF COURSE, THE REASON you are doing all the things covered in the previous chapter—creating and monitoring logos, brochures, online resources, and establishing social media sites—is to raise money, promote your group and your cause, and gain new members. As you know, in this book I have frequently brought up a variety of virtual methods to encourage prospective library support group members to sign up, participate, and reach out to donors. These can be teamed up with continuous in-library and further outreach efforts, some through passive advertising and some through in-person communication, to expand the message even more to let people know that the organization needs a constant stream of new and continuing donors, members, volunteers, board members, and any others who can fill the roles required to satisfy its mission goals.

These complementary endeavors can widely range from efforts like setting up an information booth at local events for organizational publicity; finding ways to recruit young participants to the group, or thinking outside the box to imagine unique approaches to engage the community. They can also provide opportunities to thank current members, showcase the accomplishments of the group, and allow them realize that their contributions are worthwhile.

On those notes, I would like to focus next on extended paths that library support groups can utilize to institute these additional ventures. As a start, I would like to address subjects near and dear to my heart—youth engagement and getting youth involved in making a difference for you and their libraries.

Seeking and Retaining Youthful Members, Volunteers, and Board Officers

Although I have previously touched upon the engagement of minors with and in library support groups by having them serve alongside adults, here I would like to insert additional explanations as to why youth can enhance nonprofits and their boards beyond working directly in sync with their older counterparts. They can do this either by being direct members of the group, or by operating as separate youth library support entities while working in tandem with the library and their Friends or Friends Foundations. Keeping with these concepts, I will present some real-life examples of youth library support groups that are actively taking part and truly serving independently as friends to their libraries and communities.

Later, I will proceed to an older crowd and discuss how to include those over the age of eighteen to middle age who are still among the more youthful span of individuals. These represent the younger adults who are often willing and able to fill roles in library support groups but may not feel welcome due to various factors in organizational operations that inadvertently leave them out.

A good kickoff point to focus on the younger set is addressing the potential roles of those under the age of eighteen in and with library support groups. I will do this by giving further details about the Freechild Institute for Youth Engagement, which I mentioned in chapter 4.

Freechild is a private, nonprofit association that contracts with government organizations, community organizations, and schools to foster youth engagement. They offer training, tools, programs, consulting and other services, plus in addition, their no-cost, user-friendly website is a readily available tool for adult leaders as well as youth to learn how and why young people can be engaged in our changing world. Their guidance is available to all adult leaders, but for those who are struggling against racism, economic discrimination, educational inequities, and other social injustice issues, their website can be an instructional lifeline in teaching how to effectively and positively reach out to and connect with children and youth from all backgrounds in your community.

The Freechild Institute has an overarching belief that the basis for nurturing constructive life outlooks among youth centers upon finding places that permit youth voices to be respected and heard while giving young people opportunities to take on active roles alongside adults in our society. By engaging youth within our world, children, tweens, and teens can feel ownership in their life choices and play a significant, more giving role in their communities. Youth can be encouraged to connect with any roles they are passionate about to help change and boost up society in uplifting, powerful ways. When books, reading, and libraries are a focal point for their interest, what better ways to do that than by providing avenues for them to take part in meaningful activities for contributing to their libraries?[1]

By establishing library support group opportunities for youth, whether through creating youth-oriented sub-groups, developing completely separate groups that function independently amid an adult library support group partnership, or having youth enrolled as an essential part of an all-ages library support group where they are able to lead and share noteworthy roles, you can aid youth in having fulfilling experiences that make a difference. Also, when you give youth a chance to participate in their libraries and communities in this manner, you are promoting positive youth development and hardwiring their brains for constructive growth as they reach toward and finally navigate adulthood. In addition, you help to create lifelong readers, library users, and library supporters throughout their lifetimes and, in turn, provide a foundation for their offspring to follow in their footsteps.

With those thoughts in mind, you will need to figure out where and how your library support group and your beneficiary library can partner to get youth engaged and involved. Please recall that when I talk about "youth," I mean young people under the age of eighteen or those who have not yet reached the age of majority. Once young people are no longer minors, it is an easier but not necessarily an easy process to incorporate their library support group membership and involvement into adult-level participation, a topic coming up after the discussion of youth involvement for those who are minors concludes.

As far as minors go, an essential guideline to which you will want to refer when interacting with children, tweens, and teens as they support your library is Hart's Ladder of Children's Participation. This scale of the levels of youth participation within and with adult organizations can help you to design a plan for adding youth elements to your library support group's organization and mission in an affirmative manner. It comes from a rather notable article, "Children's Participation: From Tokenism to Citizenship," published by the International Child Development Centre of the United Nations Children's Fund in 1992. In the article, Professor Roger Hart, a celebrated children's rights advocate, presented a schema for adults working with youth in various community groups and institutions to use as a tool for engaging youth in the most respectful and meaningful ways possible, giving them equal rights in solidarity with others as a fundamental democratic right.[2]

The Ladder of Children's Engagement is built on a scale of one-to-eight "rungs." The "ladder" rates the "levels of youth engagement" adults can make available to young people in descending order with the peak of it situated at the highest rung of eight. Here are the "rungs":

8. Youth-initiated and co-decision-making with adults. Because they are older and usually more responsible and mature, it is primarily teenagers who are engaged at this level, and they share decision-making authority, management, and/or power with adult partners and allies.
7. Youth-initiated and directed by adults. Youth design and create complex projects by working together with other youth, and while adults are there to observe and assist them as needed, they refrain from interfering with the process or from playing a directive or managerial role.
6. Youth participation is adult-initiated and decisions are shared with youth. Although adults initiate the projects for which youth are involved, the youth share decision-making authority and project management with the adults.
5. Youth are consulted and informed. Participants are carefully consulted and informed by adults, and though the organizational operations and projects are ultimately planned by their elders, those occur with youth input, young people understand their roles, and young people know that their opinions have been taken seriously.
4. Youth are assigned but informed. Young people fully understand the adult intentions for what they are expected to do, they know who made the decisions, and they grasp the reasons for their involvement. As they comprehend their roles, they realize their contributions will hold meaning, and, with this knowledge at hand, they willingly volunteer to participate.
3. Tokenism. Youth are seemingly given a voice regarding matters of importance to adults but their opinions and ideas are not followed or appreciated.
2. Decoration. Youth images and in-person appearances are used to promote events or activities without giving them any clues about the background reasons for their participation.
1. Manipulation. Youth are asked to participate in a project or activity without any understanding about what is behind their participation.[3]

When adults in library support groups use these guidelines to plan for and design youth involvement, it can help to ensure that the top levels of youth engagement are correctly assessed, addressed, and targeted. The goal for such engagement at its best should be to place the occasions for youth involvement on the "participatory" five upper levels of four to eight, avoiding the lower three levels of one to three. You can incorporate these levels in your strategic planning for involving youth as partners with and within your organization.

With the youth participation gauge at the forefront, it is important to remember that when youth are invited to sign up as members and/or volunteers for a library support group, you need to assure them that they will be offered opportunities that reflect spots on one or more of the top five levels. This prevents them from being placed on the lower three levels that are considered non-participatory and that lack real purpose. In those cases, where non-participatory youth members may pay dues and simply be added to rosters, they are not given or barely given useful roles, they remain uninformed, and they are not actively steered in a constructive direction, adult leadership should not be surprised when volunteering interest wanes and youth memberships lapse. This holds true for any youth-oriented organization. Considering those points, I will view the positive side by presenting ideas to keep youth firmly on the top five rungs.

First of all, to engage youth, library support group boards of directors need to buy in to the concept of having youth in active roles and perhaps, as included in chapter 4, even serving on adult boards in some capacity. It is essential for the board members themselves to advocate for this kind of participation. Once there is acceptance and everyone agrees about the benefits of having youth readily involved, groups can move forward to begin or expand their youth-based participation.

Because there might not be qualified or willing adults in a library support group to take on this kind of planning and engagement, that is the reason it may very well be appropriate to work in partnership with children's, teen, or general youth specialists from the beneficiary libraries to get youth participation underway and to keep it going. It is helpful for boards to consult with the administrators of their targeted libraries about the possibilities of engaging youth to develop meaningful courses of action. Also, it is very worth the effort to request input and feedback from any potential youth who are enthusiastic about getting involved in the discussion and plans for youth taking on library support roles.

The bottom line is that what adults accomplish by providing these planning and participatory opportunities for youth is that they are contributing to positive youth development. The United States government has an excellent website, Youth.gov, which provides a wealth of information, guidelines, and resources about this topic and the real values in engaging youth. In the introduction to the section on positive youth development on the website, it essentially recaps the points I have just shared:

> Youth involvement can benefit organizations and their programs as well as the youth themselves. Programs that are developed in partnership with youth are more likely to be effective at engaging the population and, therefore, to have a greater impact. Involving youth as partners in making decisions that affect them increases the likelihood that the decisions will be accepted, adopted, and become part of their everyday lives. In addition, empowering youth to identify and respond to community needs helps them become empathetic, reflective individuals, setting them on a course to potentially continue this important work in their future. Meaningful youth engagement views youth as equal partners with adults in the decision-making process. Programs and activities

Figure 7.1. The Strategies for Youth Engagement graphic shows the various ways that youth involvement and leadership can make a difference. *Credit: Adam Fletcher and the Freechild Institute for Youth Engagement. Used with permission.*

are developed *with* youth, rather than *for* youth. In this kind of equal partnership, both adults and young people need to be fully engaged, open to change in how things are done, and share a unified vision for the partnership.[4]

Overall, the Youth.gov website is an excellent reserve of advice for further investigation into engaging youth with and in your library support group. It is filled with facts about youth; gives leads for funding sources to aid youth endeavors; provides assessment tools; and offers further guidance. This site, along with the Freechild one, can help you to develop a philosophical base for determining how to set up and where to direct your group's youth involvement strategies.

Junior Friends of the Library

With that informational background in tow, I want to move forward and describe some pointers for establishing actual youth library support organizations in partnership with the adult factions. One of the methods for engaging youth in library support activities is by establishing a Junior Friends of the Library group, whether it is for youngsters, tweens, or teenagers. It may seem like a challenge to establish such a group, and honestly, it can be without careful planning and research. Despite the challenges, the time and effort to do it right can be extremely worth it. Remember once again that incorporating strategic planning methods to find direction is always a good choice and can certainly be applied to the development of youth participatory engagement.

To guide the involvement of youth in and with a library support group, there must be an adult leader to take on the responsibility along with any other adults who may be eager and available to lend assistance. However, an adult library support group board may be concerned about liabilities in taking on youth as a sub-group of or as a separate faction of their adult one. This is because an actual "youth group" differs from simply including youth at "student" or "junior" membership levels where they can be invited to fill roles as volunteers alongside adults. Giving youth various opportunities in those official capacities as volunteers in adult groups are fine and worthy goals, and they do keep youth playing effective parts on the acceptable middle rungs of the youth participation ladder. Here though, I am referring to youth operating autonomously with adult guidance, in addition to adult group functions, or in conjunction with adults. That means with the youth planning their own fundraisers; deciding how they will target their aid to the library and community; contributing to the adult support group causes as partners when practical; evaluating themselves; and creating their own strategic plans.

Having youth library support groups like these might seem like a pie-in-the-sky idea, but remember the Freechild philosophy that our job as adults is to make sure that our youth are given opportunities to become the leaders and readers of the future. What better approach than to give them chances to help their libraries and communities through their own, youth-led support groups? There are ways to make these happen effectively, and though they are few and far between, there are exemplary pockets of youth library support groups that have already been formed to serve as models for other communities that wish to likewise engage youth in this manner. I will be highlighting them in this section.

One thing to remember is that although adult nonprofit library support groups must exist as completely separate entities from their library beneficiaries, youth groups may be able to be formed under the auspices of the recipient library and its children's, teen, or youth services librarian's guidance, and sometimes, especially with the youngest set of participants, when parents buy in and also assist as needed. It depends on the legalities of the library, community, and state in which the junior group would be formed, so a first step would be to consult with library administrators and legal counsel to see if establishing a youth-only fundraising and volunteer group that partners with an adult group but operates as an independent organization might be feasible. If it is deemed a worthy and doable venture, then, as already mentioned, you can work with library administrators and staff and/or your library support group board to put the wheels in motion.

An outstanding example of such a youth Friends group comes from the Groton Public Library in Connecticut. There they established a Junior Friends of the Library group for children age twelve and younger in 2013, which has grown and flourished through the years since. Their model can serve as an example for other libraries and library support groups to emulate.

Figure 7.2. Bumpers & Books, a literary trunk-or-treat created by the Junior Friends of the Groton Library, hosts over 500 people annually to see book-/author-themed cars. Here are a grandma and grandson, a Friend and Junior Friend, receiving the state award for Best Project from the Friends of Connecticut Libraries. *Credit: Onostasha Parfitt.*

TEXTBOX 7.1

JUNIOR FRIENDS OF THE GROTON PUBLIC LIBRARY

Adults looking for volunteer opportunities usually have a world of options. But what if you wanted to teach your five-year-old how to give back to the community? Where could your nine-year-old donate their time and money? The Groton Public Library has found the answer in the creation of their Junior Friends group. The group was founded as a way for children to actively support the Library and the community through volunteering, fundraising, and sponsoring events that involve and inspire young people.

Established in November 2013, the Junior Friends of the Groton Public Library has almost seventy members from communities including Groton, Pawcatuck, Mystic, Stonington, New London, and Norwich. To join the Junior Friends, children ages twelve years old and younger must pay a one-dollar annual membership fee. In return, they receive a membership card, a "Library Helper" pin, and evites to all the Junior Friends' events.

The group generally has three events a month to accommodate families' varying schedules. They hold fundraisers such as bake sales and community dine-out nights, as well as Library Helper Days to work on projects that assist the staff like craft prep and cleaning. At a recent Library Helper Day, the children each "adopted" a shelf to keep alphabetized and tidy. They also host monthly "Crafting for a Cause" events in which they make crafts but are not allowed to keep them. The crafts instead are donated to nursing homes, veterans' groups, and homebound individuals.

One of the group's favorite projects was organizing a community-wide book drive. After the children collected gently used children's books, they purchased a bookshelf with money they earned, decoupaged it, and delivered it filled with the books to a low-income housing complex. They also held a pet food drive to benefit the Groton Pet Food Locker.

The Junior Friends meet twice a year for a Membership Drive and Social. It is at these meetings that the children vote on projects to undertake and what to purchase with the money they earn. They recently purchased a highway sign to direct people to the library because the Groton Public Library didn't have one. The children are particularly proud of that purchase because once the sign is installed, they will see a tangible result of their hard work whenever they drive by it.

In short, volunteerism needn't be reserved for the older generation. If you're looking for a way to bring young people into the library, give them an opportunity to voice their ideas about children's programs and services, encourage their charitable giving and volunteerism, then consider starting a Junior Friends group.[1]

Kimmerle Balentine
Librarian and Volunteer Coordinator
Groton Public Library, Connecticut

Note

1. Kimmerle Balentine. Email message to author. March 17, 2023.

Figure 7.3. The graphic from the Junior Friends of the Library Penny Drive. *Credit: Sheila A. Sullivan.*

Figure 7.4. Two members of the Junior Friends of the Groton Public Library, Sabine Balentine (left) and Katie Houghton (right), wrap pennies donated during their Penny Drive fundraiser. *Credit: Kimmerle Balentine.*

Another highly functioning Junior Friends group helps to support the Joseph H. Plumb Memorial Library in Rochester, Massachusetts. This group, for those between the ages of eight and thirteen, started in 2009, and it has evolved into a very well-known community service youth group. Its mission is to help the Plumb Library, assist the Plumb Library Friends Group, and aid Rochester community organizations while also developing programs for younger children and the members of their own group. Even though the upper membership age is thirteen, older teens who wish to participate in the group's service projects can express interest and take part in them, and/or they have an option to join the separate Teen Team of library service project volunteers.

The Junior Friends, who designed their own logo for their group T-shirt, assist the library staff and the Friends of the Library with programs and projects. They also help community groups by volunteering their time, energy, ideas, and talent. There are occasional planning meetings or get-togethers to brainstorm ideas; make projects that will help members of the community; hold discussions to plan Junior Friends–facilitated programs for fellow youth; and join in for special clubs or workshops developed for Junior Friends members.

These Junior Friends have had many accomplishments such as participating in the community's Plumb Corner Marketplace holiday events; creating centerpieces for the annual Veteran's Dinner at the Senior Center; assisting the Council on Aging's Outreach Coordinator by creating holiday cards for home-bound seniors; adding designs to the Lions Club Thanksgiving and Christmas Food Basket flyers; helping to fill shoeboxes at the First Congregational Church's Operation Christmas Child event; and painting "kindness rocks" for the Rochester Land Trust and Meals on Wheels recipients. In addition, at the library or community events, they have presented science lessons to younger children as the "Friendkensteins"; serenaded families with their instrumental skills at the Friends Holiday Fair and Tent Sale; and contributed baked items for the bake sale. They also manage a "Bake Sale at the Book Sale" annually with all proceeds from their bake sale donated to assorted charities, donated to purchase something for the library, or used for a group activity. In August 2018, the Junior Friends also created a book club for members and named it Book Buds, which sports a member-created a logo and has extended its reach to build three different book clubs for varying age groups.[5]

The last "junior" group I want to feature is one that operates for the Uniondale Public Library in Uniondale, New York. This tween and teen group is sponsored by the Friends of the Uniondale Public Library and is for youth in sixth to twelfth grades. Members contribute two dollars per year in dues to belong. The group is an award-winning organization made up of ambitious, positive youth who support their library and earn community service credits. One of the unique tasks they have undertaken is book reviewing for the library's teen blog. They meet once a month to voice their ideas, develop valuable leadership and organizational skills, and sponsor and promote library programs. You can find their informational application form in the appendixes.[6]

You might consider some elements of these illustrations of youth Friends groups as you investigate creating one in your own community. Notice that they can be founded under the auspices of a Friends of the Library or a Friends Foundation as a sub-group, but they can also be run under the guidance of a library staff member and work alongside the adult Friends as needed, depending upon your particular circumstances. You will also note that the age groups of these three examples spans children, tweens, and teenagers, which means that any junior group can center on the ages that suit its community youth the best. Additionally, think about how each group allows youth to easily

TEXTBOX 7.2

A JUNIOR FRIENDS OF THE LIBRARY ADVISOR—
AND JUNIOR FRIENDS—SPEAK OUT

A Junior Friends of the Library Advisor Speaks Out

I started the Plumb Library Junior Friends group in 2009 to provide children with a library-based youth group to help the library and the community while also providing a fun "club" for school-aged children. The group continues to flourish, grow, and develop well into our fifteenth year. We are well-known in the community, and we are consistently asked to be part of community events. We have worked together to create several offshoots, like Book Buds, a children's book club (now with four different age groups); the Volunteens/The Teen Team, for kids aged thirteen years old and up; the Friendkensteins (which focues on STEAM projects for children); and the bake sale at the Book Sale Team.

I am extremely proud of the achievements of the Junior Friends group and of each member individually. Many of these kids have stayed connected with the library even as they begin working or go to college. I have written many college or employment letters of recommendation.[1]

Lisa Fuller
Youth Services Librarian
Joseph H. Plumb Memorial Library
Rochester, Massachusetts

Junior Friends of the Library Members Speak Out

I joined Jr. Friends at my library after years of being someone who both came to the library for books but also to participate in the activities. I've been coming here since I could barely walk, and it's been a safe space to find friends, knowledge, and fun for years, which is why joining the Junior Friends was something I always wanted to do.

Emily D.

I like being a Jr. Friend because I like being part of my community and I get a badge.

Andrew Jacques

I like Jr. Friends because it helps me learn about raising money and it helps me build leadership skills.

Abby Jacques

Participating in the library Junior Friends means to help others and to do something that isn't just for you. Personally, I feel like participating is showing someone that you are interested in what they have to say or show. It makes you a better person and spreads a message of community and connection.

Maisie McLacklan-Post[2]

Notes

1. Lisa Fuller. June 28, 2023. Email message to author.
2. Lisa Fuller. June 29 and August 3, 2023. Email messages to author.

participate on the upper rungs of the Ladder of Children's Engagement where they have a voice, respect, and significant purpose as they contribute independently and also in conjunction with adults.

Essentially, in "upper ladder" youth Friends groups like the ones featured, young people are given opportunities to work beside adult group members at times, but they can also "do their own thing" and develop their own fundraising techniques, programs, and project ideas, as well as take charge of running their groups autonomously with adult library staff and/or Friends to assist as needed. They can earn service learning credits for school, outside clubs, churches, or other associations to which they belong, plus have a way to boost their community volunteer histories for job, college, and scholarship applications. Most of all, they are potentially preparing themselves to eagerly join and take bigger roles in their adult library support groups in the future.

Seeking Younger Adult and Middle-Aged Members

Now that we have considered the potential library support roles youth can assume, I will move on to the important subject of encouraging membership and participation for additional adults—younger adults—to take part. Your group might be concerned about the older ages of those serving in your group and on its board of directors, and express fears of your group "aging out." This can be a legitimate concern considering some previous scenarios from this book and possibly from the ranks of your current group if you already have one established. It will most likely be a long time before any of the "junior friends" are able to come forward as adults to take the places of those who have deeply engrained themselves in your organization and at some point, might be leaving you without backup persons in the wings. However, remember that, chances are, there are younger people in your community right now who might be wishing to find a place in your group, if only the organizational roles schedules, and conditions better suited their needs so they would be able.

The reality is that while most people would guess that the largest cohort of available volunteers in the United States comes from the sixty-five-and-older set, you will probably be astonished to find out that most potential volunteers are between the ages of thirty-five and fifty-four years old. Furthermore, a large number of the adults who are under the age of forty-five, in the lower end of this age spectrum, are often choosing to give their volunteer time to various youth-based organizations and educational endeavors because they have school-aged children. Since these people with children are specifically aiming for volunteer causes that focus on working with youngsters, perhaps they could be persuaded to start or join groups created to support their school libraries (refer back to chapter 3 for examples) or to take on leadership roles for junior library support groups.

Another point to consider is that the original library support nonprofit startups that were founded to serve libraries have, by now, been functioning in "traditional" ways for at least fifty to seventy-five years or so, sometimes simply collecting dues and holding book sales to raise money. As you can see in this book and in everyday life, the world has changed in many ways, and groups that want to draw in new and active members must look toward innovative horizons and adapt to those changes. More so, you might want to reflect on the facts that the makeup of many families has evolved to two-parent working environments with child care needs; that community demographics have become more diverse with organizations looking, to a greater extent, toward more multi-faceted representations in their ranks; that there are more blended families with increased home and job management time demands; that there are more grandparents raising their grandchildren; that some older people have stayed in or been forced to return to the workforce; plus other variations that were not common when "nuclear families" and "carefree retirees" were considered the predominant norm. Despite these changes, in many cases library support groups have continued to hold monthly and annual meetings at times that suit most present-day retirees but are not accommodating to the time schedules of many other adults or even the youth whom they want to attract.

Besides all those conditions, as you may have already noticed, are the huge changes resulting from the fast-paced developments in technology. Many library support group volunteers today prefer attending remote meetings and conducting electronic correspondence. There are also many tech-oriented folks who would like to be more involved in volunteering to help with websites, social media platforms, date entry needs, membership database management, and other tasks that library support groups must now utilize if they are to keep up with the times.

By now, you are probably wondering precisely how you might need to adjust your group dynamics to attract a good selection of these multi-faceted people from your community to join and participate. It may seem like a daunting endeavor. However, you have already been given some good advice already in this book, and there is more to come. As far as gaining new, younger, and more varied members, these are the top changes you can make to get new, active adult participants:

- As is done with the various roles for a fundraising book sale, break essential tasks for projects, activities, outreach efforts, or donation campaigns into simple, uncomplicated parts that busy people can manage and that are flexible in their execution.
- Engage more volunteers to participate in smaller segments of meeting tasks rather than having just a few people addressing everything. You might be surprised at the positive responses you get when you avoid asking busy people to do too much and permit them to be meaningful contributors in ways they can manage.
- Encourage more members to volunteer using the professional skills they possess to satisfy needs. People love to be able to share what they know and what they are able to do well to help a good cause!
- Be sure to explain to each volunteer how important each task they are undertaking is and how their contribution will make a difference to your group in completing its mission.
- Never forget to thank volunteers, praise them for jobs well done, and honor them in any ways possible for their dedication. Always remember that even the smallest task completed thoroughly and carefully is important!
- Keep in mind that meeting attendance can be difficult for many people, so be sure to provide alternative means for potential dedicated volunteers who are concerned about this issue. Figure out how to incorporate meetings and other tasks remotely.
- Remember to learn about and reach out to people of various backgrounds and skill sets in your community to promote more well-rounded community representation in your membership and on your board. Let the community know up front that you need help by including statements to that extent on your website. For instance, while seeking donors, the Poudre River Library Trust in Colorado adds one, with contact information, that says, "The Trust Board is always in need of fresh ideas and extra hands to pull off our efforts to make the Library District a success. Put

your talents and passions to work by helping us plan and coordinate fundraising and donor events, writing grants, or doing administrative work."[7]
- Be sure to keep a database of everyone who agrees to make a time and task commitment along with their accurate contact information. If they have agreed to help once and have had a positive experience, they most likely will say yes again.[8]

As a final point in this section, United for Libraries has put together an "action planner" called *All Ages Welcome: Recruiting and Retaining Younger Generations for Library Boards, Friends Groups, and Foundations*. It provides an in-depth philosophical base for efforts to include younger, more diverse library supporters within the fold and adds "workbook" elements of fill-in-the-blanks and checklist sections to use during learning and training sessions for library support group boards. Although the print version of the action planner is a bit pricy for its size, by contacting United for Libraries you can arrange to purchase cost-effective, downloadable, and print-ready PDFs for meetings and trainings.[9]

Membership Drives and Other Ways to Promote Library Support Groups

To get new members of all kinds for library support groups, some of the best ways to spread the word widely are through membership drives and activities that highlight the existence of the organizations. There can be many angles to these efforts, which, as a whole, can help to encourage prospective members to join, sign up for various volunteer roles, and even be considered as board candidates.

Although membership drives or promotional activities can take place at any time of the year and most likely at several times and places a year, a particularly notable occasion to zero in on bringing library support groups to light in your community and getting new members to sign up is during National Friends of Libraries Week, celebrated the third full week of each October. This dedicated time gives library support groups of all kinds chances for special recognition and celebration in their communities and libraries; opportunities to increase awareness about their existence and purposes; and forums to enlighten people from the community about how they can get involved.

To help out with the promotion, United for Libraries provides an array of ideas and resources for commemorating this week of appreciation and targeted attention including a helpful webinar; a National Friends of Libraries Week Awards program; press release, marketing, and social media publicity materials; and recommendations for ways libraries can thank and honor their "friends."[10] You will want to be sure that your beneficiary library staff remembers this important week and that they are familiar with what United for Libraries has to offer for planning.

There are many other avenues for dedicated library support organizations to shine and be recognized by their libraries, communities, and among their own boards and members, which can in turn encourage more people to become part of the group. The following are some examples of additional recognition ideas that work:

- Well-earned honors can be received publicly from libraries and local mayors, state governors, or other dignitaries when those figures are inspired to create proclamations of appreciation for their library support groups. Samples of downloadable content for these kinds of proclamations and a design example can be found at the United for Libraries website.[11] Libraries that have been the recipients of support group service can be instrumental in recommending the bestowing of these honors to their local leaders in addition to offering their own appreciation.

- In cases when such proclamations are issued, Friends can post the documents in visible places in libraries, share them in newsletters, add them to group websites and social media, and append photos of members holding the proclamation with invitations and instructions for joining the group.
- Local newspapers and other media can be contacted with press releases that encourage them to bring to light information about your group and its accomplishments in support of libraries. When doing this, remember to include essential background details, including programs sponsored, money raised and donated for particular causes, volunteer hours given, and any additional notations about contributions and roles.[12] You might want to append a copy of your most current annual report as well.
- You might also offer to arrange interviews for a feature article or a video segment about your group, especially if the library being served is willing to take part. As with proclamations, be sure to include links to published articles and post videos that have been released on your website and in social media.

Ideas for Getting and Retaining Members

If you have participated or are preparing to participate in a National Friends of Libraries celebration, you have set the stage for an actual membership drive. Even if you have not, it may be time to plan it—or them, if you intend to hold more than one drive during the upcoming year. As you are embarking on your membership drive(s), consider making the retention of current group members a central part of the mix.

A place to start before creating a target membership goal might be to put ideas for recruiting new members as a topic on the agenda for a membership or a board of directors meeting. Make sure attendees get advanced notice about this inclusion so they know to be thinking about suggestions.

To that end, you may wish to share the ideas given next with current members ahead of time. Before your meeting discussion gets underway, have a white board and markers or similar recording materials handy to use for brainstorming and honing the list of ideas. Once you have your list of potential ideas, the goal and budget planning committee work that needs to follow will have guidelines. To begin, peruse this list and see which ones might fit your plans:

- For annual membership meetings, encourage those attending to bring a friend or family member who may choose to become a member. Create an attractive invitation that members can use to specially invite guests. Inform regular members that you need them to take part in enlisting potential members and to be especially encouraging to their guests. Put together a "welcome packet" for the guests consisting of the mission statement, a recent calendar, the latest annual report, contact information, and specifics on how to join. If you collect contact information from guests, follow up with an email, postcard, or phone call thanking them for attending and reminding them how to sign up.

- Reach out to former members or those who have not renewed their membership yet because some of them may appreciate the reminder and be ready to continue or come back. Let them know about special areas in which they might consider becoming involved.
- If you have a newsletter, ask members to encourage others to read it as an informational device to instill enthusiasm, especially when the members are included in it to segue to an enrollment invitation, and invite receptive readers to join.
- Encourage board members and regular members alike to create an "elevator speech" to explain the purpose and benefits of joining the group. Writing and practicing the speech might be a fun activity at an annual or other group meeting or gathering.
- Consider alternative meeting times and places that might be appealing to people who cannot attend the currently scheduled meetings, perhaps including options for virtual attendance. You might even try hosting your annual meetings in more than one location, especially if you are in an area with a large, multi-library system. Input and votes could be put together and tabulated after all the meetings are done. Likewise, you might consider holding your annual meetings in locations off-site from a library meeting room, for instance at a local coffeehouse large enough to facilitate a group or the meeting hall of a local service group like the Lions or Elks.
- Get group members to volunteer together for a special community event where they can tout the purpose and benefits of the group and perhaps entice new people to join, such as a local fair, park cleanup project, or a holiday parade.
- Remind board and regular members to include their membership and participation on their resumes, applications, and work biographies. What members do for and with your group is worthy experience to note. Those reading about their participation may discover that their business, organization, or school might be a good partner for your group and its endeavors.
- For junior members, make sure they know that they can apply their membership and participation to service learning credits, other extracurricular credits, on job applications, and as they apply to colleges. Ask them to discuss their experience during interviews when appropriate and to encourage others to join the group if there is an opportunity to do so.
- Create buttons, bumper stickers, imprinted canvas book bags, and other publicity that members can use to let their friends and the public know about your group and to encourage inquiries that might result in new memberships. When members volunteer for special projects and roles, give them a T-shirt specially designed with the group's name, logo, and website added.
- Arrange for new and renewing members to receive perks such as book store discounts, gift certificates, or even coveted parking spaces as incentives to join and stick with the group.
- Create a promotional video that you can share on social media and that members can share with others. Consider including testimonials from members and the library being served to enhance the points. This could be a fun volunteer project for some skillful members to take on.
- Consider creating a LinkedIn profile for your group and using it for promotion. The person responsible for your social media and website might be the right person to get this started, but it would be a good place for other board and group members to be involved as well.

- To keep reenlistment high, be very sure to plan special events to thank the current members and to highlight especially outstanding service. Gratitude can be expressed on videos, on social media, or in the group and/or library newsletter. A celebratory event might take place at a restaurant, a library meeting room with caterers, at a picnic, or via a pool party. Much more on the topic of expressing appreciation can be found later in the chapter.
- Make a list of each year's great group achievements and monetary contributions, such as paying for educational opportunities, helping to run successful library events, supplying funding for updated library building configurations, and providing beneficial services that may have resulted from your fundraising, donations, and volunteerism. Share and link the information about these in as many places as possible—through local media, on your website and in social media, in your annual report, in newsletters, in appreciation letters to members, and in email campaigns. Ask the library being served to share in spreading the news.
- Consider creating a position for a board or regular member to serve as your "recruitment specialist."
- If you have the means, launch a direct mail or phone campaign for getting new members. Also, follow up with any potential members who expressed interest but who have yet to join.
- Be sure to add a "join us!" link on your website and make online registration as easy and streamlined and possible.
- Have members volunteer to give talks at local organizations, agencies, churches, and other places where they can tell others about the group and encourage recruitment and participation.
- Host a special guest author or other speaker who can draw a crowd and who can promote the benefits of group membership as part of their talk.
- For special programs or events that cost money, give members a perk of a discount or freebee. If you are hosting an after-hours gala that requires tickets, have a members-only rate. If you are holding a book sale to raise funds, give volunteers who are running it a free book of their choice or a discount on any book purchased.
- Help to sponsor a local event with funding and by supplying volunteers. Ask to have your group name and logo appear in the list of sponsors.
- To raise money, host a charitable event like a cycling challenge or a fun run/walk. When people sign up and donate the cost to participate, you might also offer a discount such as 50 percent on a new organizational membership or renewal for registrants. You would gain donations for your cause, have a chance to advertise your group, and gain some new members. You might even want to have special T-shirts for each participant made with your group's logo, website address, and the name of the event to reflect their event participation and further promote your group. Make your event as diverse as possible—maybe, in the instance of a fun run, by offering divisions for various ability levels, ages, and family groups with strollers.
- Ask the library staff to share stories about how your Friends, foundation, or trust helped them. You could print testimonials in a newsletter, in a blog, or even make videos with library staff members touting the importance of your contributions. For example, if expensive but meaningful new puppets conveying diversity were purchased for the storytime room with your group's donated money, a librarian who runs the program could describe the need that was filled, why adding the new puppets was essential, and how the puppets are effectively being used for storytime

programs. The video could be posted in various social media spots, and the library support group's need for new members could be mentioned.
- If your community has a "newcomers club," ask if you can put your promotional brochure in the packet that new residents receive. Likewise, check with businesses and other organizations to see if you can put your brochures in areas for their customers or members to take them. You can also make flyers and posters that can be posted in local bookstores, coffee shops, on community bulletin boards, and at the library you serve along with your brochures. A "take one" holder on a poster to hold brochures can do double duty.
- To that end, keep going! Think of as many other places in the community that you might connect with people new to the area or unfamiliar with your library and its support group(s). For example, reach out to local realtors to see if any of them would be willing to share brochures about the library and your organization(s) with their clients.[13] Other good places to reach out might be a community website or neighborhood connection resource such as Next Door.[14]
- If your city or town has a community directory, be sure that your library support group is included in it. In addition, if there is a volunteer clearinghouse, ask if your group can be added. Also, see if your group's events and activities can be placed on community calendars, in newsletters, and in newspapers.[15]
- For Junior Friends groups, have special members-only events such as a screening of a popular movie with popcorn and drinks; give T-shirts with a Junior Friends logo (possibly designed by an artistic member) to each youth serving a set period of time or a certain number of hours; hold bring-a-friend activities where guests can be invited to join the group; offer fun opportunities to decorate a library float, march in a parade and hand out information about the library, or decorate cookies or ornaments for a special event. By honoring young members, inviting their buddies to join, and giving them enjoyable yet meaningful work to do, you can keep current members engaged and gain new ones.
- Devise a challenge through which the group's volunteers and board members receive a tokens of appreciation for certain levels of donated time plus have book plates with names and volunteer hour milestones placed in new library books that each honoree chooses.[16] Be sure to announce the ability to attain these awards when writing group publicity.

Planning Your Membership Drive

Many organizations start with a simply stated goal: "hold a membership drive." However, to have a successful one, you need to gather your board together or convene a membership committee to thoughtfully devise a strategic plan based on the SMART goals method described in chapter 4. It could be a goal such as "get fifty new members by such-and-so date." This basic goal is specific (S), measurable (M), attainable (A), relevant (R), and time-bound (T) and could be developed into a true plan. The recognition ideas that are listed above would, as a side result of employing them in the plan, possibly help you to garner new members.

After you know what the goal is and what is needed to put your plans into action to make it happen, you will want to consider the monetary requirements. Aim for a suitable membership drive that will attract new members while retaining the members already on board. To do this, you will first need to figure out the overall expenditures it would take and what your group can actually afford.[17] It would be very helpful to have your treasurer involved in this process to assist in determining potential outlay costs versus how much money would most likely be gained from new memberships and donations.

As you are in the process of doing your strategic and budget planning for your drive, be sure your website and social media platforms are squared away, current, and all set to heighten your efforts. Likewise, make sure that you have funded an eye-catching, updated, comprehensive membership brochure to have on hand for all aspects of your drive. Make a point of adding in the cost of producing posters, flyers, or other publicity to compliment and accompany your membership brochure.

Whether you are having a single membership drive or several spaced out at different times during the year, you will also want to make a list of duties that need to be taken on as the plan unfolds. This might work best as a strategic plan unto itself. The backbone to the plan might be to appoint a person to lead as membership drive chair and to form a membership drive team that would oversee planning, supervise seeing plans through, and keep good records of results. The team would recruit current regular and board members to fill needed roles in plenty of time and ensure that each person would be aware of their responsibilities.

The upshot is that, through your plans, you may be able to find new, younger, and diverse members and volunteers in all sorts of places. Begin by having everyone already enrolled in your organization ask their own friends and family members to consider enlisting while reminding them that it is okay for time commitments to vary. They can tell potential recruits that each dollar and hour given is appreciated and helps to support your wonderful library.

Another avenue is to contact area schools—most likely the principals and/or career or guidance counselors—and let them know that joining your group and volunteering can help students to satisfy school community volunteerism requirements. Additionally, reach out to local civic organizations such as Rotary, Lions, or Soroptimist clubs, which exist to support and give back to their communities, and offer to have someone give talks to their members about your group. You might even be able to make announcements in local church bulletins. Keep in mind the list of ideas given in the previous section. Use your imagination; as mentioned, perhaps hold a board brainstorming session to collect ideas; and discover that the opportunities for recruitment can be endless.[18]

Evaluating Your Membership Drive

Once you set your membership drive(s) in motion by following the strategies you have laid out, the drive chair or assigned team members would need to keep careful records of results. From those records, once plans were completed, the compiled results could be placed into a format to be presented to the board at a meeting or meetings and then discussed.

It would be important for the board to consider whether or not the membership drive or each individual drive (in the case of multiple ones) met its/their goals; what money may have been earned from new memberships compared to the cost of running the drives; how many volunteers were needed to run the drives; what obstacles were faced and how they were addressed; whether strategic plans were on target; what could be learned from the results to make improvements; and what was successful enough to continue doing. With the evaluation of the drive or drives at hand, the board would have useful information for planning the following round of membership recruitment endeavors.

TEXTBOX 7.3

WELCOME LETTER AND MATERIALS FOR NEW OR RENEWING MEMBERS

When I first joined a Friends of the Library group and renewed my membership in three different places through the years, I always received a letter of welcome and thanks. When you create a welcome letter, it could be accompanied by a detachable membership card, discount coupon for a bookstore, bookmark, informational brochure, or whatever additional materials the group would like new registrants to receive.

A letter to enrollees can be general, short, to the point, and enthusiastic using a template and composed on attractive letterhead that gives group contact information and its web address. A group coordinator, board secretary, other board member, or a regular member volunteer could be appointed for letter responsibility. Here is an example adapted from the Friends of the Knox County Public Library in Tennessee, demonstrating what such a letter might say:

(Date)
(Name/address of member or members)
(Dear _____)

Thank you for (joining, renewing)! Your membership and generous donation of (if dues and/or a monetary gift was given) shows that you support the (library support group name)'s mission of fostering a love for libraries, books, and reading in our community. We are glad to have you as a member.

The (name of library receiving aid) depends on public funding, but to thrive and to have a continuing impact on future generations, we are thankful to have your donation and participation. Because of your support, the (library support group name) can keep moving forward to fulfill its mission as we:

(List and bullet a handful of the group's contributions/programs/volunteer roles.)

Libraries are a fundamental resource for the citizens of (town/city/county/region) and provide transformational and life-enhancing services. We will keep you informed about opportunities you will have to help work with us to fundraise and volunteer.

Together, we can continue to make a difference.

Thank you,
(Name of group secretary or other representative/title)

[Please note—You may wish to consult with your legal authority to decide if you must add the following notation to the end of your letter and how it should read:

The Internal Revenue Service requires (name of library support group), a 501(c)(3) public charity, to inform donors of benefits received as a result of their monetary gifts. As you received no goods or services in consideration for your gift, over which (name of library support group) has exclusive legal control, the entire amount of your contribution may be considered a gift for tax purposes. Please retain this letter for your files. EIN (Employer Identification Number) (group number).[1]]

If you have started or partnered with a Junior Friends of the Library group, you will likewise want to create a letter specific to welcoming new youth members. Here is a sample of such a letter from the Junior Friends of the Groton Public Library in Connecticut:

(continued)

(Date)
(Name of youth)
Address
City, state, zip code
Dear (name of youth),

Thank you for joining the Junior Friends of the Groton Public Library! Your membership card is enclosed.

The Junior Friends of the Groton Public Library are committed to supporting the Library and the community through volunteering, fundraising, and sponsoring special events that motivate and inspire young people.

We will keep in touch with you regarding upcoming Junior Friends meetings and events. Please spread the word—joining the Junior Friends of the Groton Public Library is a great way to meet new people and support a cause you believe in!

Thanks again.

Sincerely yours,
(Library staff or library support group advisor name, signature, title)[2]

Notes

1. Friends of the Knox County Public Library. 2023. Membership renewal welcome letter.
2. Kimmerle, Balentine. Email message to author. March 17, 2023.

Partnering with Volunteers from the Community

At times, you may need even more volunteers than your membership roster and/or a sub-group of junior friends can accommodate. You can encourage volunteers of this ilk to officially join your group or to collaborate with you to see special events and activities through. However you approach these partnerships, be sure everyone signing on to help is insured along with your group or is covered through their own organization in case of liability issues.

You may be wondering from where these additional helping hands might come. Here is a list of ideas you may want to pursue:

- Find out if the library you support has an active teen or tween advisory group, teen council, teen leadership team, or similar group functioning through the teen or youth services department. Connect with the library staff member supervising the group and ask if the youth would be willing and able to help out. If they are, that staff member can recruit qualified youth to assist your cause.
- If you have a college or university in your community with fraternities and sororities, contact them to see if they may be able to provide assistance. For example, at my former library in Colorado, they have enlisted fraternity members from Colorado State University, who swiftly handle the setup and takedown at Friends book sales.

- Scouting groups are always on the lookout for worthy causes to assist. Contact your local Scouting or similar organization to engage youth for helping you out. If the youth are using their times of service to earn badges or other honors, you may be asked to verify their participation, a small price to pay.
- The same holds true for partnering with church, synagogue, or other faith-oriented organizations that ask youth congregants to offer community service. Connect with your own faith community and others in your city or town to see if volunteers are available.
- These days, many businesses and agencies require their employees to give time and donations to the community. Find out if any workplaces near you have this rule and let them know you would appreciate some help.
- Once again, inform local school principals and/or guidance counselors that your organization is a place where students can earn service learning or community service credits for classes, graduation requirements, or extracurricular clubs. They can promote your cause as a potential student selection for volunteering and help you to find the right students to meet your needs. Remember that you will probably be asked to sign off on tasks completed and perhaps give evaluations on student performance.
- Consider connecting with volunteer recruitment organizations that will pair community volunteers with your particular needs. These include such agencies as Volunteers of America,[19] AmeriCorps,[20] and VolunteerMatch.[21] I worked alongside or supervised several such volunteers through the years as a librarian and Friends board member, and they were positive experiences. You may want to contact these agencies and let them know your needs.

When you reach out to any potential community partners for recruiting volunteers, be sure to submit job titles needed, job descriptions, and a general overview of your organizational mission so those can be included in postings along with your organization's full contact information and directions for applying.

Managing Members and Volunteers

For any library support group, an essential component, top priority, and endgame to recruiting and maintaining members, volunteers, and donors (whom I view as volunteer givers) is extending gratitude and providing tributes for participation at all levels in a timely fashion. The more kinds of recognition and thanks you are able to give, the better. Put simply, volunteer and donor appreciations are acts of thanking those who generously give their time and money while recognizing their contributions to your organization, the library being supported, and the community being served. It means that, beyond just saying thanks, which in itself is always important, these appreciations are sets of ongoing, planned activities that buoy your overall volunteer and/or donor management strategies. To fulfill these strategies, and to accomplish all the additional means needed to get there, it helps to have a designated volunteer and/or donor appreciation manager or coordinator. In the rest of this section on volunteers, I'll be specifically focusing on volunteer management; however, actual donor management will be covered in chapter 10 on donors. For now, the point is that all volunteers deserve the highest thanks.

If you incorporate volunteers from your membership ranks along with those willing to partner with your organization as volunteers, you might want to think about assigning a board member(s) to the task of serving in such a management leadership role. If you offer several different programs and activities as part of your group's mission, you might consider choosing individual volunteer coordinators for each one. If you are one of the few library support groups that are able to afford a paid volunteer coordinator or your beneficiary library is able to provide a staff member to double-duty or partner in this role for you, you are very fortunate. No matter who is given these roles, they will play a fundamental part in making these volunteer management endeavors run smoothly.

For any of these approaches, the duties of a volunteer manager would include recruiting, scheduling, supervising, engaging, and retaining volunteers. They would also include tracking volunteer time, acknowledging volunteer contributions, developing ways to improve volunteer efforts and opportunities, and figuring out and staying within an appreciation budget.[22]

Figuring out a budget is key, because providing gifts, honors, and perks for library support group volunteers will have a cost and naturally, the amount allocated for this purpose must fit within your financial limits. The person(s) in charge of volunteer appreciation will need to make the efforts as cost-effective yet as meaningful as possible, planning carefully in advance for what is hoped to be accomplished so that there is certainty that the estimates will be workable.

Because taking on volunteer management is a big yet rewarding job, it would behoove anyone taking charge for a library support group to access and use the free resource, "Volunteer Management: The Complete Guide," provided online by Galaxy Digital, a company that creates volunteer management software.[23] Although it is not specific to library support groups, the information is all-encompassing for anyone taking on the role of a nonprofit volunteer manager. The book, *Library Volunteers: A Practical Guide for Librarians* by Allison Renner, which is included in this book's bibliography, would also be beneficial to nonprofit library support group volunteer managers in addition to library staff members.

Showing Appreciation for and Honoring Volunteers

You have already read about National Friends of Libraries Library Week earlier in this chapter with some suggestions for honoring library support groups during it. National Volunteer Week, National Library Week, and others special weeks or days you feel would fit your recognition efforts can also be focused upon to provide more opportunities for acknowledgment and gratitude. Even a seemingly simple thing like providing volunteer name badges can make volunteers feel valued and important during meetings and activities. When you incorporate meaningful, ongoing appreciation in as many ways possible, you will discover that volunteers feel a greater sense of satisfaction and belonging, plus it minimizes turnover.

Bear in mind that in addition to special celebratory weeks or events, it is important to offer appreciation quickly, as soon as volunteer service has taken place. The following five best practices for thanking volunteers will be easy to remember and put into action:

- Be timely. "The sooner, the better" for extending thanks is a good motto. A general guideline is to send a thank-you note no more than two to four business days af-

ter tasks or services are performed. It helps to always keep a supply of note cards, envelopes, and stamps handy.
- Be consistent. Make sure all volunteers are thanked within the same time frame; that anyone who is responsible for extending appreciation is aware of it; and that the post-service timeline of sending messages in no more than four days, tops, is adhered to.
- Be personal and genuine. Instead of recycling pre-written messages, always personalize each one; rather than "dear friend," use each volunteer's name; and specifically address the volunteer actions just completed.
- Be mission-focused. Because volunteers give time to organizations with undertakings they know and care about, acknowledge and show the connections between the tasks completed and how they help to fulfill the library support group's mission.
- Be creative. When it seems like repeatedly sending thank-you notes and cards is redundant, try some of the alternative ideas given next.[24]

Whether you are facing those special weeklong celebration times, local library or community celebrations, or "just because," here are some more ideas for you to mull over, some tried and true go-tos with variations, and some new and creative options you may have never even thought about:

- "Virtual" gratitude is unique and can be strongly expressed by the library staff, individuals, and families your group's volunteers have served and supported. You might capture a short video message in which people express how much a contribution personally impacted them and send it via email to an individual volunteer with a message of appreciation from your organization.
- Similarly, publicly recognize volunteers with a short story about a contribution or accomplishment on your social media and website that is created by friends, family, library staff, and group colleagues—and that is another easy an inexpensive way to make volunteers feel special and valued.
- If your volunteer is using out of the ordinary work skills and talents to advance your mission, consider sending a message to their employer to let them know how the volunteer's expertise is making a difference for your group, your library, and your community.
- Surprise a dedicated volunteer with a gift card, note, or flowers for no other reason than your wish to give them thanks for a job well done or for keeping an ongoing commitment.
- Instead of giving a volunteer another plaque or paper certificate, think about selecting something meaningful to display in their home or office such as a piece of art made by a grateful individual being served. A personal message on the back of the piece or attached to it adds significance.[25]
- Ask local businesses if they will offer discounts to volunteers from your organization. Be sure your volunteers are notified of these discounts and are aware of how to request them.
- Whenever possible, have snacks and drinks ready for volunteers to enjoy while doing their work, on breaks, or at meetings. Refreshments can be simple as long as there is some variety and enough for everyone participating.
- Have special T-shirts made for all volunteers in general and/or for pinpointed volunteer activities such as book sales, donor drives, or children's events. Ask for

T-shirt sizes on member/volunteer applications but make it optional—or use your observation skills to estimate the right ones. Volunteers will be proud and enjoy wearing the shirts and your group gets some more publicity. Ask local T-shirt shops to possibly give you good deals since your nonprofit is benefitting the library.[26]

- Give volunteers small, branded gifts. Do some research and try to find items that volunteers would like. Maybe a water bottle, an outdoor kit with mini bug repellant, sunscreen, and lip balm? How about a sticker for their car, a magnet for their fridge, a rubber jar opener, or a special bookmark? Ask around to get other ideas and find ways to get the items inexpensively. Focus on items that will actually be useful and appreciated and will not be regarded as junk for the landfill. Think about "keeper" gifts that you have received. I, for one, am still in possession of several useful gifts like this from my years of library work and library support participation!
- Small gift cards in denominations of five or ten dollars are surprisingly appreciated. Who would not like to get a card for a special coffee shop treat, ice cream cone, or movie theater admission? Again, look around and be creative about what kind of gift cards you choose. Pay attention to what volunteers like and would enjoy. Ask if you might get a discount if you buy some cards in quantity. If your budget is tight, consider giving volunteers a five-dollar gift card to use at an upcoming book sale or library support group used book shop.
- Take photos of volunteers in action or posed at volunteer events and activities. Select the perfect shots, have prints made, and place them in inexpensive frames. Get crafty and paint the frames, then write the dates, events, and personal messages on the backs of the photos before presenting them to each volunteer.[27]
- Hosting a volunteer-appreciation event is a wonderful way to show your gratitude. There are many ways you might plan to do this. If it can be arranged and fits your budget, you might take volunteers out for a meal or for coffee and snacks at a restaurant. Then again, you could have a taco bar or ice cream social in a library meeting room, or hold any number of events that can range in expense depending on what you are able to do. The essential elements are making your volunteers the focal point, showing them that they are special and valued, and giving them a chance to get to know each other better.
- Ask each board member to call volunteers to say thanks and to let them know how much they are appreciated. Perhaps each board member could take some names so that each one could express their gratefulness while the time spent making calls could be divided. To make the calls extra-special, sharing small or large details beforehand about each volunteer's particular contributions that could be mentioned by the board members increases the value of the calls and lets the volunteers know that their work has been noticed.
- Even though a handwritten letter or notecard may seem like a small gift, in this digitally focused world, it can be a nice surprise and much appreciated. A thoughtful, handwritten message can be a source of warmth and meaning to the recipient, and it is often something they will keep as a reminder of how much they are appreciated by your organization.[28]

TEXTBOX 7.4

VOLUNTEER THANK-YOU TEMPLATE FOR A LIBRARY SUPPORT GROUP

This basic thank-you template can be expanded and personalized as needed:

[Organization's logo & letterhead]
[Organization's address]
[Date]
Dear [volunteer name],

    Thank you so much for volunteering for [volunteer activity or event]. Your willingness to give your time and service [through or for] the [organization name] is greatly appreciated. Your contribution allows us to continue to fulfill our mission to foster the [library name] and make it a better resource for all.

    Again, thank you so much for your willingness to donate your time and talents. Your efforts play a big part in our success. We look forward to your continued involvement with [organization name].

Best wishes,
[Your name], [Your title]

Remember, when you effectively show appreciation for any and all volunteers—and this includes board members!—you will hopefully have a whole positive-minded crew working in tandem to support your group's mission. Besides that, there are many other reasons to show thanks. Volunteers who feel valued will talk about your group to others because they are part of a team accomplishing important goals for the library, and so they will encourage others to join the cause. They also may be inspired to give their own money to the cause because they see firsthand the meaningful results of library support group donations in action. Plus, good volunteers who demonstrated interest, skills, and knowledge that can benefit the board of directors may prove to be worthy and willing nominees and candidates for board election or committee appointments in the future.[29]

Notes

1. Freechild Institute for Youth Engagement. 2023. "About Freechild," https://freechild.org/about/.
2. Organizing Engagement. 2023. "Ladder of Children's Participation," https://organizingengagement.org/models/ladder-of-childrens-participation/.
3. Organizing Engagement. 2023.
4. Youth.gov. 2023. "Involving Youth in Positive Youth Development," https://youth.gov/youth-topics/involving-youth-positive-youth-development.
5. Joseph H. Plumb Memorial Library. [n.d.] "Join the Junior Friends," https://www.plumblibrary.com/just-for-kids/junior-friends/.
6. Uniondale Public Library. 2023. "Junior Friends," https://www.uniondalelibrary.org/teens/junior-friends/.

7. Poudre Libraries. 2023. "Poudre River Library Trust," https://www.poudrelibraries.org/trust/.
8. Library Strategies. November 5, 2018. "How to Make New Friends," https://www.librarystrategiesconsulting.org/2018/11/how-to-make-new-friends/.
9. American Library Association. [n.d.] "All Ages Welcome: Recruiting and Retaining Younger Generations for Library Boards, Friends Groups, and Foundations." ALA Store, https://www.alastore.ala.org/content/all-ages-welcome-recruiting-and-retaining-younger-generations-library-boards-friends-groups.
10. United for Libraries. 2023. "National Friends of Libraries Week." American Library Association, https://www.ala.org/united/events_conferences/folweek.
11. United for Libraries. 2023. "Promotion and Celebration Ideas for Friends Groups." American Library Association, https://www.ala.org/united/events_conferences/folweek/friends.
12. United for Libraries. 2023. "Promotion and Celebration Ideas for Friends Groups."
13. United for Libraries. November 8, 2023. "Get Ready, Stay Ready: Supporting Proactive Community Advocacy for Library Professionals." Webinar. (get url when posted on UL)
14. Nextdoor. 2023. "Discover Your Neighborhood," https://nextdoor.com/.
15. Tatiana Morand. August 9, 2019. "101 Ways to Get New Members for Your Organization." Wild Apricot, https://www.wildapricot.com/blog/ways-to-get-new-members.
16. Winnefox Library System. January 31, 2011. "Great Ideas to Promote Friends Memberships." Library Sparks, https://sparks.winnefox.org/2011/01/31/great-ideas-to-promote-friends-memberships.
17. Bisma Hanif. April 8, 2022. "A Step-by-Step Guide to a Successful Membership Drive." GlueUp, https://www.glueup.com/blog/membership-drive-ideas.
18. Library Strategies. November 5, 2018.
19. Volunteers of America. 2023. "VOA," https://www.voa.org/.
20. AmeriCorps. 2023. "Bringing out the Best of America," https://www.americorps.gov/.
21. VolunteerMatch. 2023. "Remarkable Outcomes," https://www.volunteermatch.org/.
22. Eli Samuels. April 12, 2023. "What Is Volunteer Appreciation?" Galaxy Digital, https://www.galaxydigital.com/blog/volunteer-appreciation.
23. Addison Waters. April 4, 2023. "Volunteer Management: The Complete Guide." Galaxy Digital, https://www.galaxydigital.com/blog/volunteer-management.
24. Instrumentl. April 11, 2023. "How to Write a Thank You to Nonprofit Volunteers," https://www.instrumentl.com/blog/how-to-write-thank-yous-to-nonprofit-volunteers.
25. Nonprofit Leadership Center. 2023. "Five Creative Volunteer Recognition Ideas," https://nlctb.org/resources/five-creative-volunteer-recognition-ideas/?gclid=CjwKCAjwrdmhBhBBEiwA4Hx5g49x-xA2Vu7SGauan1lJOWB4APLaGn-xqfB3EEJbxVezja6hij-ohBoCU14QAvD_BwE.
26. Eric Burger. 2023. "How to Thank Volunteers in 2021." VolunteerHub, https://www.volunteerhub.com/blog/thank-volunteers-2021/.
27. Sandy Rees. March 12, 2023. "18 Ways of Thanking Volunteers So They'll Feel Appreciated and Stick Around Forever." Get Fully Funded, https://getfullyfunded.com/18-ways-of-thanking-volunteers/.
28. KM Clark Consulting Group. 2021. "Our Favorite Ways to Thank Nonprofit Volunteers," https://kmclarkcg.com/our-favorite-ways-to-thank-nonprofit-volunteers/.
29. Rees.

CHAPTER 8

Fundraising for Library Support

FUNDRAISING IN ITS MYRIAD FORMATS AND TYPES is the heart and soul of most library support groups. After all, the bottom line reasons that Friends, foundations, and trusts exist is to provide funding and resources for the libraries that are their beneficiaries. Supplying this funding and helping to plan programs and activities, making volunteers available when able, aiding in the design of capital projects, or being advocates for library needs and causes are all important roles that group members can play through their monetary and personnel contributions. Frequently, as we have seen, the reason filling those roles is essential is because adequate funding is lacking. That means library support groups must be attuned to the libraries' requirements that are not being met and figure out ways to get the money for the unfunded needs as well as for the important wants whenever possible. In general, that is the mission of all library support nonprofits.

I have served on two previous boards of directors of Friends of the Library groups and a question that surfaced every year when planning for the next year was always, "How will we raise more money?" Of course, book sales of various kinds—in-person large sales, book shops or book nooks, and online book sales were the basis of our fundraising in addition to grants, membership drives, and donor campaigns. We tried a few other kinds of fundraising projects, but sales were the foundational blocks of our money-raising activities. At the second library where I served on the board, we also worked closely in collaboration with the library trust, which raises funds from donors, corporations, bequests, non-cash assets, and other sources, and encouraged each other as we worked to fulfill our missions.

Now that I am serving on my third board, this time for the Friends of the Knox County Public Library, I find that the members here employ the fundamental book sale philosophies for traditional fundraising with which I am familiar along with other unique methods to raise funds. For example, with the help of additional sponsors, the annual Stay Home and Read a Book Ball raised $5,800 in 2023 to fund the Storybook Trails program. In 2022, the event earned $8,900 for author events, and in 2021, $17,000 was raised to buy more e-format books and audiobooks.[1] Plus, the library foundation raises additional dollars to support further endeavors that require financing to make the library stronger and more vibrant for the community.

In researching for and writing this book, I discovered so many more distinctive, creative, and interesting programs that library support groups are doing and that you might want to consider trying. In this chapter, I will be giving a wide variety of illustrations of programs you might consider choosing to adapt along with some resources you can use to ponder further potential choices.

The first step to embarking the path to raising money is to create a fundraising plan. By carefully putting together a nonprofit strategic plan as part of your overall annual strategic plan (refer back to chapters 3 and 4) to pinpoint your next year's goals, objectives, and outcomes for making money to aid your library, you will be in a great position to find success. Remember, strategic plans serve as blueprints for organizational achievements in fundraising as they do with all other elements of conducting your nonprofit business in a positive manner. Here are some essential steps for developing the fundraising piece of your strategic plan:

- If your organization was operational last year, reflect on that year's fundraising accomplishments by using the data your board has collected. Ask yourselves important questions. How much money did you raise? How many people were involved? Were there enough volunteers? Did partnering and co-sponsoring factor into your previous events, and were those positive collaborations? What were the winning endeavors your group was most proud of and what were the obstacles and challenges? How can you build on your successes and overcome the difficulties?

- If yours is a newly formed library support nonprofit, choose your start-up fundraising activities carefully and keep them simple. Avoid overwhelming your group the first year. Reflect the second year and afterward, then revamp and build on the previous years' results.

- Brainstorm ideas for the coming year using previous data and/or the resources given in this chapter. Hone the ideas into a final list that will serve as the basis of your new plan. Task regular and/or board members to research how each idea can be accomplished and when. Depending on how large your group is, you might want to have sub-committees to take on these researching duties. Create goals and targeted outcomes for each desired event or activity.

- Take an inventory of your current resources of finances, people power, and supportive technology. Be realistic about availability and constraints. If you are starting out fresh and lacking resources, find out if your beneficiary library can help you to fill any gaps to get you started. For instance, see if there is a computer available for your group to access for planning, recordkeeping, and contacting members or donors. Perhaps you can get permission to use one of the library's meeting rooms for an event or for storing materials. Or, maybe a librarian can solicit teen volunteers to help with a book sale.

- With your list of ideas and resources at hand, create a timeline for events to be prepared and take place. Be sure to avoid conflicts among your event dates and other important group dates such as meetings! Also, check local schools and community administrative offices as well as media to ensure there are no local, national, or other events taking place when you want to hold yours. For example, proms, big televised football games, or graduations can keep people from participating in any fundraising activities you have arranged concurrently. Place all elements required for your events on a master calendar—preparation activities, deadlines, setup and takedown times, publicity needs, actual event dates, and any other essential information.

- Keep careful notes and data for follow-up event or activity evaluations. Review these with the board of directors at a subsequent meeting and use them when you plan the next year's events and activities.

TEXTBOX 8.1

SELECTED RESOURCES TO DISCOVER NEW FUNDRAISING IDEAS

This textbox includes some helpful resources that you might want to peruse to find a variety of moneymaking ideas—new and exciting, easy-to-do, more complex but with big profits, and other kinds of fundraising possibilities. Originators of these websites offer packages to subscribe to for supplementary assistance at designated costs, but you can search through the free ideas given in these sites without payments of any kind.

Best Fundraising Ideas[1]

An especially useful website with a great number of ideas, Best Fundraising Ideas gives you all sorts of choices for searching potential fundraisers. The opening page has links to several targeted categories. These include "Events," "Holidays," "Creative and Unique," "Virtual," and "Quick and Easy." There are also links to "Matching Gifts" and advice for seeking corporate philanthropic contributions. A search box for specific terms and limiting filters are provided, along with links to the site's tried-and-true favorite ideas. Users are encouraged to "grow the fundraising idea bank" by contributing their own inventive ideas. Free links to further resources are included for such topics as "Fundraising Online: The True Beginner's Guide." This is a website you do not want to miss when you are out to raise money!

10 Charity Event Ideas That Could Change Your Fundraising[2]

Do not let the name of this webpage fool you! There are, indeed, ten interesting charity event ideas given here, but within the page are links to additional ideas that expand its reach beyond ten and that also give additional resources with helpful information. For example, the charity event planning basics section leads to a charity event planning guide, and the seasonal events idea section expands into further events for fall, winter, and spring. If you are hoping to host a gala event, you will find descriptions of successful ones like those that are covered elsewhere in the following chapter, which can illustrate the points made about galas.

77 Fundraising Event Ideas for Nonprofits and Charities[3]

Here are potential ideas for a wide range of original in-person, online, or hybrid events. They include events for schools and colleges, simple events, events requiring little initial costs, virtual events, and many kinds of seasonal events. Their best fundraising ideas to raise large sums include galas, murder mysteries, fashion shows, and more.

130+ Awesome Fundraising Ideas: Contests, Challenges, Raffles, & More!

The focus of this webpage from Wild Apricot is creating profitable, competitive, challenging, and luck-of-the-draw events that are fun, exciting, and engaging for members of your community. You will find plenty of guidance and helpful recommendations here so that your group can wisely select events that are relevant and doable for your city, town, and/or library setting. For each entry, you will see potential costs and expected returns rated using a scale of "$ to $$$$," and probable complexity

(continued)

factors rated from one to four, with one being "quick and easy" and four requiring lots of coordination and buy-in from stakeholders.[4]

215+ Amazing Fundraising Ideas for Your Organization[5]

With a philosophy that essentially says, "Carrying out the same fundraising campaign over and over gets old," you will be encouraged to engage supporters through fresh and exciting ideas to draw them in for your cause. The collection of ideas given will provide a brainstorming session kickoff boost and might be the catalyst for raising more money. Entries are broken down by the top fundraising recommendations, family-friendly ideas, holiday-oriented ideas, top virtual events, and so on.

Notes

1. Best Fundraising Ideas. 2022. "Discover the Best Fundraising Ideas to Raise More Money!" NXUnite, https://bestfundraisingideas.com/.
2. Maria Walda. [n.d.] "10 Charity Event Ideas That Could Change Your Fundraising." Social Tables, https://www.socialtables.com/blog/event-planning/charity-fundraising-ideas/.
3. Hannah Durbin. March 9, 2023. "77 Fundraising Event Ideas for Nonprofits and Charities." Classy Blog, https://www.classy.org/blog/fundraising-event-ideas-raise-money-cause/.
4. Tatiana Morand. June 6, 2023. "130+ Awesome Fundraising Ideas: Contests, Raffles, Challenges, & More!" https://www.wildapricot.com/blog/fundraising-ideas.
5. Double the Donation. 2023. "215+ Amazing Fundraising Ideas for Your Organization," https://doublethedonation.com/fundraising-ideas/.

Traditional, "Old Reliable," In-Person Book Sales

Most library Friends, foundations, and trusts depend on donations of money, but the legendary library support book sales are still alive and well and fruitful. Big sales are a staple with all sizes of library support organizations although these days there are usually other items besides books for customers to buy, and the ways the sales are planned and conducted often fluctuate. Some groups have small sales throughout the year and one or two large sales in addition; others have regular sales, but they supplement them with book shops or other continuous ways to shop; and still others tie in their big sales with additional activities to draw in more crowds. For some groups, vendor purchases are a difficulty and they do not encourage them, some permit vendors but limit access, while others allow anyone to come and buy books at any time during a sale for any reason. Each library support organization must figure out what formats and plans work best for their members and allow them to most effectively gain profits for their beneficiary library.

In this section, I am including a few examples of productive book sales in the traditional vein as well as those including supplementary formats. You can find some interesting ideas here that you might choose to integrate or adapt as you are reassessing the planning and desired outcomes of your own organization's sales. Examples from groups serving populations that range from large cities to small towns are included to show how book sales can work for any size of library support nonprofit.

Following the descriptions of more traditional and continuous auxiliary sales, you will find further information about exceptional kinds of book sales that your group might want to investigate and try out:

- Denver Public Library Friends Foundation, Colorado: As an example of a large city library support group fundraising effort, in 2023, the Denver Public Library Friends Foundation held its first major used book sale in three years with over eighteen thousand books available for purchase, with proceeds to benefit the Denver Public Library. The event was held at the Historic Elitch Gardens Theater, a renovated 1891 facility devoted to production and study of performing arts, for a three-day weekend in August.

    The unique aspects of the sale were the special activities for children on Saturday afternoon and the "fill a bag with books for $12" event on Sunday afternoon. The Friends Foundation's large sales are in addition to smaller sales offered periodically at local branches and at a local brewery (more about arranging brewery sales coming up soon).

- Poudre River Friends of the Library, Colorado: As with many library support organizations that depend on book sales as their focal point for revenue, the money this Friends group makes at their sales is earmarked to fund library programs in their medium-sized city. The yearly goal is to run Friday-Sunday quarterly book and media sales with a large corps of volunteers behind them. Between the big sales events, the Friends encourage library visitors to take notice of smaller, ongoing alternatives. Those consist of a Friends Bookshop at the Harmony Library Branch and Book Nook self-service sales areas at both Harmony and the Old Town Library locations (more about continuous sales also coming up soon).

    Prices for used books range from fifty cents to four dollars, books are color-coded according to price, and all sales are final. Teachers always get a 50 percent discount if they are purchasing books for their classrooms. Book resellers must show proof of their tax exempt status. Local laws mandate a City sales tax of 3.85 percent, and customers are forewarned that the Friends must impose this requirement. Purchases can be made with cash, credit cards, debit cards, or checks with printed name(s), addresses, and telephone numbers on them. When accepting checks, there is a stipulation that a twenty-five-dollar surcharge will be added to the face value of any returned checks.[2]

    A donation jar is also placed near all cashier stations. People are very generous and often give their change to the cause and sometimes donate larger amounts of money. It is a valuable way to make additional profits at the sales and many customers are more than glad to contribute. Another aspect that adds value, which most other groups do at big sales, continuous sales, and special kinds of sales is to have membership brochures handy on site so buyers may be encouraged to join and participate.

- Friends of the Dover Public Library, New Hampshire: Do not be discouraged if you are starting or continuing a group in a small community. Even Friends in communities with lower populations can hold profitable book sales to support their libraries. There may be fewer books to sell, and fewer customers, but positive profit results are usually proportionate and often go above and beyond due to strong local appreciation for the library that the group serves. One example of many is the Friends of the Dover Public Library's sale, which, like the larger groups mentioned, also runs for a long weekend in the spring in the Library Lecture Hall. The library serves a community of thirty-four thousand. At the sale, hundreds of books and other items are sold, and on the Monday following the sale, all leftovers are given away for free.

Prices range from fifty cents to three dollars, with all proceeds benefitting the Dover Public Library in many ways. The Friends organization pays for library programs all year long, supports the Summer Reading Program, purchases a selection of museum passes, which are available for library customers to check out, and much more.[3]

- Friends of Weathersfield Proctor Library and the Library Fundraising Committee, Weathersfield, Vermont: Another example of a sale that is held in an even smaller community of 2,800 in Vermont comes from this community's dual library support groups. Library support here stems from these two active groups working both independently and in tandem (you will see them featured again later in this chapter). For their annual Book, Bake, and Yard Sale, they collaborate to hold the event.

  The actual event is usually held outdoors on the library grounds because the library is too small to sort out thousands of books. The sorting takes place weeks before in local barn space during which books are placed in labeled boxes according to genres. Early on the event day, the books are transported to the library and set up on labeled tables outside, and yard sale items are displayed on the lawn. If the weather is not good, the books remain in the barn and customers drive over to the relocated "rainy day" sale, homemade edible goods that are donated by group members are kept and sold in the library to avoid getting them wet, and yard sale items find shelter under a variety of tents and canopies that are set up. Funds raised by the groups are used to purchase library equipment, pay for speakers, help with building maintenance, cover additions to the children's area, and more.[4]

TEXTBOX 8.2

PLANNING AND PUBLICITY ADVICE FROM A SMALL COMMUNITY

We have planning sheets that are very detailed. Certain people are responsible for particular categories. For instance, "refreshments" may have just a few names listed. Those people, in turn, would ask others to bake something, supply paper goods and eating utensils, help with serving, or whatever else is needed.

Public-relations efforts are crucial. If no one in the group can design a poster, some printing places will help with that. Postcards with the same or similar design as the poster can also be made up to mail as reminders about an event date and to relay that friends or neighbors are welcome. Local newspapers, radio and television stations, and the town website are also good for advertising.

To save money for repeated events, banners and large signs can be made with the option of using them again if they are designed so that a new date can be put over the previous information.[1]

Friends of Weathersfield Proctor Library and Library Fundraising Committee
Weathersfield, Vermont

Note

1. Friends of Weathersfield Proctor Library. November 28, 2022. "Weathersfield Proctor Library Fundraising Review." Email message to author.

Remember, although your library support group may benefit a tiny or smaller-sized city or town library, people will come through with books and other items to donate for your sales if you publicize carefully. The dimensions of your sale will fit the size of your community, and you will still glean enough profits to help your library with special extras. I like to think of groups benefitting libraries in less populated communities as "small but mighty," and if your organization's members have this philosophy as well, you will be able to hold successful sales just as the bigger library support groups do.

By now, if you are feeling overwhelmed by the idea of holding a big book sale or you hope to improve the planning for upcoming sales that are repeated yearly, you can find a document in this book's appendixes that might help you to prepare. The Poudre River Friends of the Library generously gave permission for me to include their most current book sale guidelines document that you can read through and adapt if you wish. Although the example is specific to their own book sales, you will get a good idea of the things you may want to incorporate and address when you are doing your own.

Unique Varieties of Book Sales

Even though library support organizations have traditionally held the standard kinds of familiar book sales, some have tried to inject enticing twists to make the sales more inviting. Ideas like selling special items besides books, promoting library and support group merchandise, offering half price days, or having sales of specialized types like cookbook sales or children's book sales, are all ways that Friends and other groups aim to entice the community to take part. In addition, the health emergency that libraries and support groups dealt with in the early years of the 2020s actually helped to formulate several new kinds of fundraising book sales. The positive result of this "forced" creation of alternative ways to make money is that many of the redesigned options often proved to be keepers.

I remember when the Friends board of directors to which I belonged in Colorado met on Zoom to find methods for fundraising during that difficult time. I was tasked with figuring out a way we could still have a safe and profitable experience that would engage the community. After doing quite a bit of research, I connected with other library support groups that were managing to raise money despite the challenges. I got details, and narrowed them down to a workable recommendation for an outdoor, drive-through, cash-only (in a big jar) "grab bag" sale, held with permission in one of our library's parking lots. To prepare, the Friends board and other members met outside our book warehouse wearing masks to sort books on tables, fill the grab bags, which were then stapled shut ("No peeking allowed!"), and labeled the bags by genre and age level. The bags were placed according to category in the trunks of volunteers' cars, which were opened in the parking lot during the sale for quick distribution to drive-in customers.

We had heavily advertised the event and, lo and behold, we needed to end the scheduled three-hour sale in one hour because we sold out quickly. Because of the success of this greatly welcomed grab bag sale, we did two more that also proved profitable. Likewise during this time, other library support nonprofits were catching on to this helpful idea. When the health emergency abated, the "grab bag" idea continued to flourish because it had proved to be a good one.

Another successful enterprise occurred several years earlier when some libraries tried a new technique to get customers to check out more books. They invented the concept of "book bundles," which proved to be popular. The idea was that library staff would select groups of titles that fit certain genres and interest levels and bundle them together for checking out as a package deal to take home and read. To this day, offering book bundles has become a more widespread part of library reader advisory and customer service.

A number of library support groups noticed the success of this model and incorporated "book bundles" into their book sale offerings. In many ways, book bundles and grab bags are similar as complimentary ways to uniquely fundraise by selling used books. For instance, grab bags typically might include genre books that are a "surprise," while book bundles and other grab bags may be seen, or selected together by request, prior to purchase.

TEXTBOX 8.3

RECEIVING BOOKS AND OTHER DONATED ITEMS FOR SALES

To have the most effective system for securing donated materials for fundraising sales, every library support group needs to explain to its public what their book donation policies are. It is usually expected that the creation and maintenance of the policy will be done collaboratively with the beneficiary library because often the library will be involved in the collection process in various ways. Here are some helpful guidelines to bear in mind when planning book donation policies and procedures:

- The leaders of the library support group board need to meet with the library staff and administrators who will be involved in managing the materials donation processes. Both parties need to give input and final approval before the policies and procedures are established and put into place.
- Both library staff and library support group members alike need to be aware of all the policies and procedures that everyone needs to follow to keep the process effective and on track.
- Flexibility is the name of the game. If the policies and procedures for book and material donations are no longer working sufficiently, reevaluation and revamping is a must. Revised information must be relayed to all volunteers, library staff, and stakeholders in a timely fashion.
- Members of the library community being served need to be given straightforward and direct information about the reasons materials are being solicited; who is involved in collecting materials; what materials will be accepted; what materials are unacceptable; where to drop off donated materials; and what time(s) they may bring them to be donated.
- The details about the donation policies and procedures need to be shared on the group websites, library websites, social media, and in printed matter.

To get a clear picture of how this information might be conveyed, the following examples from library Friends groups that have such policies and procedures posted on their websites will give you a place to start or revise your own:

- Friends of Johnson County Library in Kansas: "Do you have gently used books to donate to the Friends (for sales)? We hold Drive-up Donation Events every Saturday (except during inclement weather). Volunteers will be available to accept your donations on Saturdays from 9:00 a.m. to 11:00 a.m. at Friends Headquarters (address). Small quantity donations (one bag, small box, or armful) are now accepted during library business hours at most library branches including (branches are listed by names). Donation bins are coming soon to (name of park)."

    This information is followed by a list of desired items with a "Yes, please!" notation beside those that will be accepted—gently used adult and kids' books of all types; cookbooks; textbooks; repair manuals; DVDs; music CDs; audiobooks on CD; LPs; and complete puzzles. This is followed by a "No, thank you!" list of various materials that comprise ones that are in bad or unusable condition; magazines; board games; encyclopedia sets over ten years old; VHS and music cassettes; and Readers Digest Condensed Books.[1]

- Friends of the Knox County Public Library in Tennessee: "Friends sells donated items at our used bookstore, our semiannual and branch book sales, and our online store. We also distribute books and audiovisual materials through our Books in the Community program. The money raised by book sales supports programming, purchases equipment not included in the library's budget, and maintains the Friends office. If you itemize deductions, your donation of materials may be tax-deductible. At your request, Friends will provide you with a receipt for tax purposes. It will be up to you to determine the value of your donation. Please do not place donated materials in book returns or leave them outside library doors. Many thrift stores accept books and other materials as donations that do not meet our criteria. Please consider (names of other organizations)."

  The web page also adds details about what is and is not acceptable as donations. This includes gently used books; magazines; sheet music; and audiovisual materials except VHS or cassette formats. Encyclopedias or textbooks are considered after contacting the Friends office. Donors are also asked to please contact the Friends office or the donors' library branch first if there are more than three boxes or large sets of books or magazines because space fluctuates at each branch, and Friends want to make sure there is room for each donation. Otherwise, up to three bags or boxes can be taken to the circulation desk at any library branch or to the Friends bookstore at the downtown library during bookstore hours.[2]

- Friends of the St. Charles City-County Library in Missouri: "Clean out your closets and empty your bookshelves! Donate your gently used books to the Friends. Most library branches can accept up to four medium-sized boxes. Large book and material donations are accepted at the Friends' Warehouse (location and hours given). We are unable to pick up materials at individual homes. Support the Friends of the Library as they support the Library. Only with the help of the Friends can the library offer (lists funded programs, activities, and materials)."

  The introduction is then followed by contact information and details about what is accepted and what is not. Items include new and used books in good condition; textbooks published in the last five years; CDs, DVDs, and Blu-rays; sheet music; jigsaw puzzles; computer games; and video games. A final notation says that sadly, they are not able to accept magazines; encyclopedia sets; records; VHS tapes; or auto repair manuals.[3]

As you can see from these examples, the requisites for accepting donated materials and what will be accepted will vary depending on each library and each library support organization. Your group will want to tailor its material donation policies and procedures according to your individual organizational needs.

As a final point, it would be a great help to create a flowchart of the donation processes and procedures that lead to whatever selling systems are in place. If you were to craft such a handy tool and keep it updated, all volunteers who assist and work with each element of book/material donation gathering, sorting, and distributing will have guidelines to handle each step needed to eventually sell the used items and raise funds. As a matter of fact, designing flowcharts for any and all essential organizational fundraising activities would be a plus.

(continued)

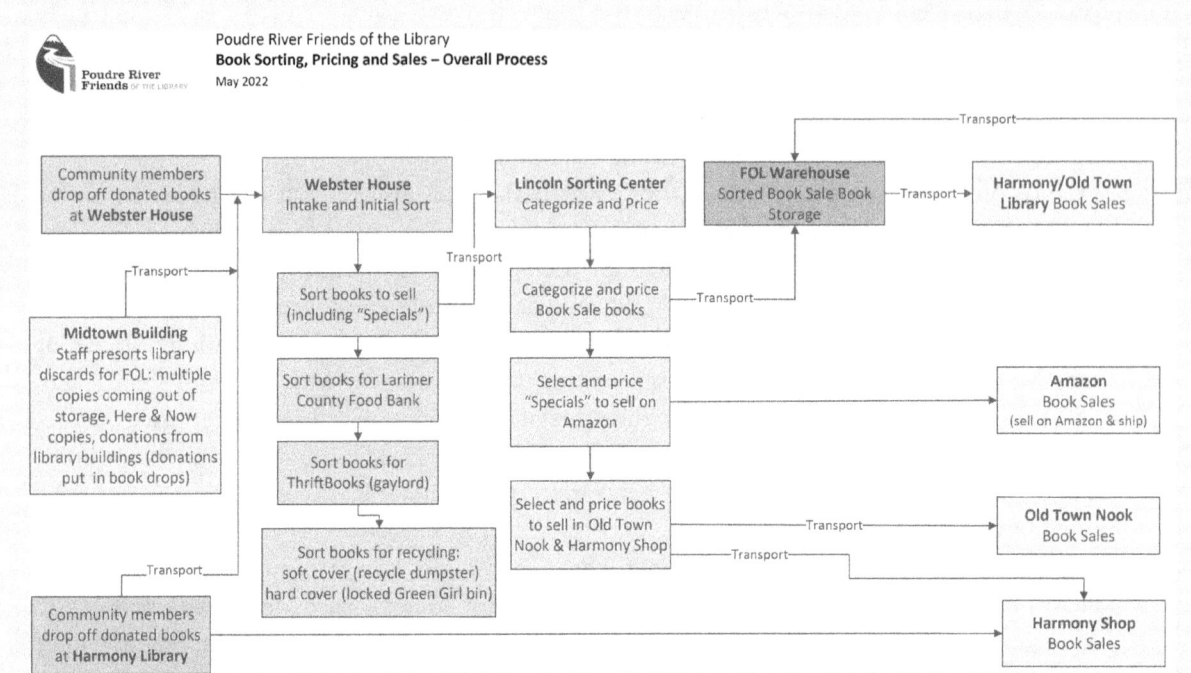

Figure 8.1. The Poudre River Friends of the Library in Colorado created a flowchart of their sorting and distribution process. Such a resource can be a valuable aid for those working with a library support organization's donation, sorting, and selling procedures. *Credit: Maggie McDonald.*

Notes

1. Friends of Johnson County Library. 2023. "Donate to the Friends," https://www.friendsofjcl.org/page/donate.
2. Friends of the Knox County Public Library. 2023. "Donate Books," https://www.knoxfriends.org/donate-books/.
3. Friends of the St. Charles City-County Library. 2023. "Donate Your Gently Used Books to the Friends," https://www.stchlibrary.org/friends-donations.

Continuous Sales: Grab Bags, Book Bundles, Gift Cards, Book Shops, Book Nooks, and Online Sales

In the next sections, I will give examples of Friends and other groups that are augmenting their book and material fundraising sales by using novel techniques that allow them to make even more money. The following organizations have incorporated these types of sales in inventive and practical ways that work for them. Take a look and perhaps your group will find a feasible idea or two that you can adapt and add to your book-selling repertoire:

- The Friends of the Library, Montgomery County, Maryland, have a book bundle selection and shipping service through their bookstore. For a flat fee of thirty dollars, customers can order and be invoiced for a book bundle of six to eight hardcover and paperback books to be shipped to any location in the United States. There is also an option to pick up the book bundles at their Rockville Bookstore. Customers can order online by completing a form, which includes contact information, shipping address, whether the bundle is for the customer, a loved one, or as a donation for the Friends to provide for someone in need. Buyers can choose from a wide range of genres and types, including children's, award-winning, Pride month, science fiction/fantasy, history, biography, women authors, authors of color, a small press poetry variety pack, and a variety pack of music CDs to listen to while reading for ten dollars. For a children's or custom book bundle, there is a text box for noting each receiver's age, grade, reading level, and other pertinent information. Special requests including condition, though welcome, are not guaranteed as noted on their website. They also have online book sales at Amazon, on eBay, and at their own online bookstore, plus customers can purchase gift cards for the bookstore and receive special offer discounts as they are advertised.[5]

Setting up book sales of all kinds on Amazon takes a bit of research, but it is one of the best-known sources for resale book purchases and may be worth the effort. They have several selling plans and referral fee categories, and costs depend on a number of factors, such as whether Amazon ships the books for you or you do your own customer mailings. Luckily, Amazon provides an extensive, comprehensive online guide that will tell you everything you need to know if you are exploring this option.[6] eBay also provides a multifaceted seller center online that will give you similar details and thorough directions.[7]

- The Friends of the Knox County Public Library in Tennessee have an online grab bag book option. For ten dollars, customers can request a grab bag of titles in large print, fiction, for children and middle-graders, in the mystery/thriller genre, audiobooks on CD, or DVDs. Grab bags of books contain eight to ten titles and audiovisuals contain five to eight, which are selected according to any specifications indicated, such as the age/reading level of a child or other particular preferences. The selection and preparation of grab bags takes a week, and the bags can be picked up at the Lawson McGhee Library in the downtown area, although DVDs can be retrieved at one of three other library branches.[8]
- At the Friends of Chapel Hill Public Library in North Carolina, they hold three major book sales a year with Friday open for a Friends-member-only sale and Sunday offering a fill-a-bag sale. In addition, they have an online bookstore through which customers can buy an adult grab bag of four to six books for five dollars in genres ranging from fiction, mysteries and thrillers, world or United States history, and biographies and memoirs. A children's grab bag is also available for five dollars and contains seven to eleven books that can be easy readers, picture books, fiction, nonfiction, or young adult. After email notifications, customers can pick up their grab bags at a designated location and during certain times with reserved parking available. In addition, customers can order digital gift cards that have redemption codes, purchased in denominations from ten to fifty dollars, that are good for one year from the purchase date for any regular book selections from the online store, grab bags, or special items for sale.[9]
- Making good use of ongoing book sales, the Friends of Johnson County Public Library, who, since 2016, are part of the Johnson County Public Library Foundation, created what they lovingly call "Booktiques" at two of the library system's branches in tribute to two special Friends members. One honors Philomena Ross, a founding member of the Friends, and the other is in memory of Amy Kitchen, their longtime, talented graphic designer who created the Booktique signs and the Friends logo. Presently, the Booktique movement has expanded to all branches of the library. Any book or other item for sale is two dollars, which can be paid for via cash, checks, or credit/debit cards. In addition to the Booktiques, the Friends

hold regular large book sales to provide resources, programming, special events, and materials for the library, and they serve as its advocates.[10]

- The Chattanooga Public Library Foundation in Tennessee sells book online by using two different online sales services, Abe Books and Alibris.[11] At Abe Books, an organization can sign up to start selling by using the information provided on their website. Monthly fees start at twenty-five dollars after creating an account. Sellers describe, store, and ship the items themselves, set up their own shipping records and speeds, and have the items on their page listed in six international websites.[12]

  At Alibris, there are two plans a seller can choose. One is the basic plan for nineteen dollars a year to list up to one thousand non-digital books, movies, and music, with access to pricing and inventory management tools and being listed on the Alibris and its partner networks. The gold plan offers the same listing and tool services, plus the ability to list unlimited items, be part of special "seller store" and reward programs, and gain access to live chat support for a nineteen-dollar setup fee and a low monthly fee based on inventory level.[13]

- Really large library support groups often have quite impressive shops for raising funds. The Library Foundation of Los Angeles has an amazing array of products customers can buy in person or online in addition to books. Pickup is in person within ten days of purchase and the store is usually open six days a week. At the store, the Foundation carries T-shirts and unique clothing items, totes, stationery items, coasters, mugs, pens and pencils, prints, totes, and much more. A great deal of the merchandise is designed in-house and inventory is sourced from a variety of vendors and small businesses including local artists and cause-related organizations.

  Customers can also purchase digital gift cards that are emailed to the recipient or physical gift cards, which are available at the shop in denominations ranging from ten to one hundred dollars. A purchase of two hundred dollars or more bestows free Foundation membership and all members of the Foundation receive discounts at the store.[14]

- Medium-sized library communities can also have active book shops, and this one, with a local population of 130,000, is quite inspiring. The Friends of the Ferguson Library in Stamford, Connecticut, formed in 1979, operates the only independent book shop in the city with two locations, one at the Main Library and one at the Harry Bennett Branch Library. In them, they sell quality books donated by the community that are usually priced at five dollars or less, and they also offer an online book shop. Customers are able to contact the Friends to request special items with volunteers checking the inventory for availability. Friends of the Library members automatically receive a 10 percent discount on their purchases. After selecting their books from the comfort of home, online shoppers can retrieve their choices at a book shop and pay for their purchase when they arrive. To supplement their overall Friends mission statement, this group provides an additional mission statement specifically for the book shops: "We sell quality used books at reasonable prices to benefit the Ferguson Library's numerous community outreach and enrichment programs." Training for its one hundred book shop volunteers covers customer services, sales, and merchandising.

  The $250,000 that is raised each year from the book shops and other fundraising means goes to pay for the summer reading program, book discussions, film programs, cultural events, staff development, and scholarships. The Friends also sponsor special events such as its annual Literary Competition, Author Series, Pub Crawl, and Mini-Golf family event. Their Books for Babies program supplies a free first book to every baby born at the Stamford Hospital, and they purchased a bus for the library's Purple Bus Program to bring schoolchildren without libraries to the public library for field trips. A short video on their website demonstrates some of what this enthusiastic Friends group has accomplished.[15]

- Even a small library community might have an active book shop. The Friends of the Campbell Library in East Grand Forks, Minnesota, with a local population of about nine thousand, has a used book shop located in the library. In it, they sell other items besides books, including movies, snacks, postcards, and gifts. They also have a heavy-duty, stylish, zippered book bag customers can buy for seven dollars. With the money they raise from the book shop, semi-annual book sales, membership dues, lifetime memberships, and any additional support, these Friends are able to fund summer programming for children; special library programming such as cultural events, author presentations, and contests; and scholarships for high school seniors. They also engage volunteers to enhance the library's services and maintain the Campbell Library Literacy Endowment.[16] When I have referred to "small but mighty" library support organizations, they are another prime example, especially for other groups that are similarly located in less highly populated areas.

- State library support groups can likewise play an important role in supporting libraries through book sales. The Friends of the Library of Hawai'i is a nonprofit that exists to help maintain the fifty-one free public libraries in the state; to promote the extension of library services statewide; and to expand the facilities of the public library system beyond the limitations of regular library budgets. They also encourage and accept monetary donations through bequests and gifts; accept book and manuscript donations; and appreciate receiving any other suitable materials that can be used to enrich the cultural opportunities in the state.

To that end, the Friends operate a physical bookstore in Honolulu called Village Books & Music, plus a large online bookstore, with over twenty thousand materials for sale. Online purchases may be picked up after three days at the in-person location or customers can make arrangements with the Friends to ship their selections at personal expense.

Besides online sales, these state Friends have run a huge annual sale since 1947, which boasts over 125,000 items for purchasing. The book sale is much more than books, and also features audio-visual CDs and DVDs; comic books and manga; other specialty items that are hard to find; lithographs, sculpture, and prints from local artists; and the ever-popular, very eclectic selection of donated modern art.

The sale has several business, corporation, and foundational sponsors and runs for eleven days. There is a preview day (and free rare book evaluation) for Friends members, and the main sponsor, Hawai'i State Federal Credit Union (which Friends members can join), is also invited to attend. The sale has free parking; includes three days that offer a 10 percent purchase discount for teachers, librarians, military, and seniors over the age of sixty-five; and a second-to-the-last-day "everything is 50 percent off" sale. On the very last day, all remaining items are only fifty cents.[17] Obviously, this is an immense endeavor, but with a state library Friends group like this one at the helm, there can be incredible results to benefit libraries throughout the entire state.

TEXTBOX 8.4

SOME ADVICE FOR ONLINE SELLING

Online sales can be very profitable. I volunteered at the Mesa Library in Arizona doing online sales for sixteen years. I don't have the actual figures, but during many years the profits were well over one hundred thousand dollars. We had a large operation, but certainly it can be done on a smaller scale.

No matter how large or small the online sales operation is, here are several important aspects to making it work:

- There needs to be someone to coordinate the operation who understands selling in general and is committed to making online sales work.
- Volunteers are needed to do the bulk of the actual work involved.
- An area needs to be set aside for the volunteers to work; for items such as shelving and carts to be stored; and for shipping to be completed.
- The library can help to solicit donations since many donations are needed in addition to the discarded items removed from the library's collection.
- Computers and printers must be available for the volunteers to use for online sales.
- Sellers need a general knowledge of books and book publishing. They need to be computer literate with knowledge of the selling sites like Amazon and eBay.
- There needs to be a person who deals with any returns and can answer questions about the sales.
- It is important to create an online sales training manual to be used for training new volunteers.
- Finally, a lot has changed in the world, as we all know, and Amazon has changed, too. Check first to find out if any changes they have made are ones you can deal with. As of this writing, eBay is still very user-friendly for resellers.

Nancy Mumpton[1]

Note

1. Email message to author, September 30, 2023.

Beer or Coffee Brewery Book Sales

As craft brewing has become a popular enterprise nationwide, one unfolding trend in book selling is to partner with local beer brewing establishments to help raise library support funds at their places of business. A number of Friends and other organizations are taking advantage of these partnerships as another place to successfully reach book sale customers.

One illustration of this lucrative collaboration is from the Friends of the Knox County Public Library. Throughout the year, the Friends have books sales that rotate

Figure 8.2. One of the Friends of the Knox County Public Library book sales is held at Hi-Wire Brewing. *Credit: Natalie Smith.*

between most of the county library branches and other locations. In 2022, they added another book sale site at the Hi-Wire Taproom in Knoxville. Between their other special events such as trivia nights and Ping-Pong tournaments, Hi-Wire promotes a "book fair" for the Friends for six days on the honor payment system during both the summer and fall. Customers of the taproom can peruse two-dollar paperback used books and select titles for purchase while visiting the establishment.[18]

In comparable fashion, the Denver Public Library Friends Foundation rotates ongoing small "pop-up" book sales in various Denver Library branches, but it also holds periodic one-day pop-up sales in collaboration with the aptly named Fiction Beer Company. Adult fiction, nonfiction, and art books are available for purchase at bargain prices there during the sales. Proceeds are earmarked to support the Library's free literacy programs, lifelong learning, workforce development, equitable access to resources, and more for all ages of Denver's citizens.[19]

Keep in mind that it is not just beer brewing establishments that might help to support your off-site book sale efforts. Some coffee shops and roasters may also be willing to help out by providing a space to facilitate extra book sale profits. For instance, at the Friends of the Longview Public Library in Washington State, they have a regularly stocked book sale shelf near the Library's lower entrance, but they also have book sale stations at local coffee businesses, the Monticello Coffee House and the Keebler Coffee Roasters.[20]

If your community has a popular brewery establishment of any type or perhaps one with a different focus (maybe tea?), your library support group may wish to contact them and see what kind of aid they might be willing to extend. Believe it or not, there are also breweries that are providing additional kinds of library support organization fundraising events that I will examine next. If your interest is piqued, it could be highly worth the effort to inquire about what those in your own community would be willing and able to do for you.

Beer and Coffee–Related Fundraising Events

Besides book sales taking place at breweries, some library support groups have found that special fundraising events with a "brew" focus are profitable. The following are some instances of library support groups successfully raising money through inventive and enjoyable events with a brewery slant:

- Books & Brews: Since 2015, this has been the largest fundraiser for the Friends Foundation of Worthington Libraries in Ohio, open to those twenty-one and over. Attendees can enjoy popular craft beers from Ohio breweries, wine, food, and music. It is held in the Old Worthington Library, and money is raised from ticket sales, sponsorships from area businesses, and silent auction proceeds.

    In 2023, six area breweries were featured along with catered appetizers from a local notable restaurant, Bosc & Brie; music by locally renowned jazz pianist and music teacher Tony Hagood; enticing silent auction packages; and a trivia contest. Tickets cost fifty dollars for members of the Friends Foundation and sixty dollars for nonmembers. Advance registration was strongly recommended for prospective attendees to avoid a sold-out event as that had happened in previous years.

    The proceeds from this fundraiser, along with memberships and donations, support the annual Library Grant Fund, which provides ongoing programs and enrichment activities at the library and also recognition and development programs for library staff.[21]

- The Friends Coffee Shop: In 2023, the Friends of the Saratoga Springs Public Library celebrated the opening of their new coffee shop on the first floor of the library building with a raffle and other giveaways. The initial hours for the coffee shop have been 10:00 a.m. to 1:00 p.m., Monday through Friday, but subject to change. During the hours they are open, the coffee shop sells a variety of hot and cold beverages and snacks. Baked goods are available from the Bread Basket, a local shop that donates its profits to charities fighting food insecurity and hunger. The new retail establishment allows the Friends to expand how library patrons and staff are served, in addition to offering financial aid for the library's programs and services.[22]

- Pint Night Fundraiser and Angel Wings Program: To help support their new Spokane Valley Library, which had its grand opening in June 2023, the Library Foundation of Spokane County held two fundraisers in partnership with the YaYa Brewing Company in Spokane Valley, Washington State.

    Its Pint Night Fundraiser provided a portion of the event sales to the Foundation for the new library. During the event, those who donated additional money received a "blind date with a book," which meant that they were given a "surprise" title to take home and try. Whether they liked the book or not, it was all in good fun, and their contribution helped enhance the total proceeds from the event.

    After that, the brewery further assisted the Foundation through their Angel Wings Program. During the period from October through December, whenever customers purchased the brewery's flagship Angel IPA (named in honor of the owners' late sister, who was greatly involved in community service), a portion of the sale was donated to the new library cause. As an aside, this generous brewery is an exemplary business helping its community, because, since its founding in 2019, it continues to rotate donations of sale percentages quarterly to new, worthy, nonprofit recipients through the Angel Wings Program.[23] You never know, unless you ask around, whether programs like this might exist through businesses in your area, too.
- Coffee Fundraiser: The Friends of the Beacon Falls Library in Connecticut did a coffee fundraiser that ran for a month in partnership with a local business, Great Minds Coffee Roasters. Customers were able to select from four different types of coffee, including one decaf kind. After people ordered coffee during the allotted time, a sales percentage was donated to the Friends. Orders were taken online, and purchases were picked up at the library following the ordering period.[24]
- Group-Run Coffee and Tea Fundraising Sales: If your library support group is looking to increase profits through selling additional items beyond book sales and such, you may be interested in pursuing the idea of general coffee- and tea-oriented fundraisers. You may be familiar with these endeavors taking place at churches or schools to raise money, and library support organizations can benefit from them, as well. The positive thing about these kinds of fundraisers is that they can be done as a special event, through a book shop, or in conjunction with a big book sale. There are companies that can help you to plan and organize these kinds of sales to supplement your other fundraising choices. Here are a few samples of specialized companies that help charitable organizations to set up these kinds of sales:

    ◦ Dean's Beans—This business offers organic, fair trade, and kosher products for organizations to sell for their essential fundraising needs at high profit margins. They provide coffee, specialty treats, and tote bags for groups to incorporate for selling.[25]

    ◦ The Giving Bean—With their easy-to-start and coordinate coffee fundraising program, they guide clubs, organizations, and other nonprofits through the process of raising funds with high-quality products, no startup costs, simple guided methods, free custom labels with a group's name and logo, and a combination of online and order form sales. Fundraisers can select an order form system accepting cash or checks only or from online choices that allow cash, checks, or credit payments. Profits vary from 25 to 40 percent of sales depend-

ing on the plan that is chosen. They profess an environmentally friendly and all-natural commitment.[26]
- Java Joe's Fundraising—A women-owned-and-operated business, they specialize in helping important causes to raise much-needed dollars. Organizations can order a free coffee sample and for fundraising, choose from freshly roasted coffee; packages of specialty beverages; cookie, brownie, and cupcake mixes; and fudge. Nonprofits earn 40 percent in proceeds.[27]

If you and your organization find the possibilities intriguing for coffee, tea, and more fundraising, you may wish to explore these selected companies, or go further by doing an online search for "coffee and tea nonprofit fundraisers" to research other potential matches for your organization.

- Brew & Bee Adult Spelling Bee: Billed as the "buzziest event in town," the Huntsville-Madison County Library Foundation in Alabama held this special evening of wordplay and friendly competition at the Straight to Ale Speakeasy so that participants could test their spelling skills, have fun, and offer financial support for the Foundation, which has a mission to advocate and acquire enhanced resources for the library. Competitors formed teams of up to five people and could join in by signing up online with an entry fee of one hundred dollars. Plus, if they wished, they could pay an additional thirty dollars to buy a last-chance mulligan if they were about to lose. At no extra charge, spectators were welcome to cheer on the participants and share in the good time. You can find a flyer with the rules used for the contest in this book's appendixes.[28]

TEXTBOX 8.5

HOW TO PLAN AN ADULT SPELLING BEE FOR FUN AND PROFIT

Adult spelling bee fundraisers involve teams, and the hallmark of a good event is the element of competition and friendly rivalry between the teams. The teasing and banter that can result is enjoyable for both the contestants and the spectators, and it can be a worthwhile way to raise money. If your library support organization likes this idea and wants to hold a spelling bee to raise funds, the following details offer guidelines for you to plan your own event:

- Form a team or committee to research and design the spelling bee using the recommendations that are given here. Create a strategic plan for the event, which would include reflecting the cost to hold it and the expected profits.
- Find out what sponsor or sponsors are willing to aid your cause by offering a spot where you can hold your contest and/or by providing funds so they would be added to your publicity. Figure out how many volunteers you will need and their roles, then put out a call for those interested in helping. Be sure to publicize the volunteer call and the event itself far and wide through all available channels, including at the library you are supporting.
- It is a good idea to have both online and paper form team registrations where competitors pay their fees, and you may limit the number of teams if you feel it is necessary based on the size of your event site.
- Rules for adult events tend to vary from the familiar competitions for children, and they can be organized with a team approach. As each word it given, it is normal for the teams trying

to spell them to consult each other quietly and then write the word on a whiteboard with a marker or on a blackboard with chalk. You would need to provide these writing materials, but they are easily purchased online or in local stores. Your beneficiary library might also have some you can borrow.

- All teams try to spell the same word at once and hold up the boards with their responses on a command or when a bell or buzzer sounds. Usually, rules limit the teams' attempts to thirty seconds for each word, by which time the teams must hold up their answers. If any of them are not able to do so, it counts as a misspelling.
- You can devise the scoring system in different ways. You might choose to have "rounds" of ten words each, where designated points are given to teams for each word that is submitted on time and spelled correctly. Each round is totaled for each team, and you can finish with final rounds. Or, you might decide to have an "eliminator" competition, where two words spelled incorrectly in a row leads to elimination. The best formula is up to the event planners and the number of teams they have included. Unless there are lots of teams, it is best to have as many competitors for as long as possible before subsequent rounds whittle down the teams for the final rounds.
- Have a confident master of ceremonies (MC) with a sense of humor who can run the event from up front, keep spectators engaged, clearly explain the rules, and conduct the progress of the competition. If there is a local celebrity willing to take on the task gratis or for a minimal fee, that would be a plus; however, there may be some excellent event MC talent among your group's members. You may be able to locate an MC who can host as well as announce the words, or you may decide to have another person working in tandem with the MC as the word caller.
- Ahead of time, give the person who will be calling the words a plentiful list of the ones to use, in sentences for context, along with definitions. Ensure that the caller will carefully practice all the pronunciations, definitions, and sentences. On the night of the event, have a backup list of the words handy.
- Whether the MC or a partner presents the words, the caller needs to:
  - Say each word, pronouncing it clearly and correctly.
  - Give a definition for each word.
  - Use the word in a sentence.
  - Repeat the word.
- Figure out what words to use in advance and double-check spellings. You can use the many online websites available to choose words, or you might try using the official dictionary of the Scripps National Spelling Bee, the *Merriam-Webster Unabridged Dictionary* (there are many editions—check your local library to borrow one or for help downloading a free online version).
- Choose what entry fees you wish to charge teams. You might decide on a per-team fee and limit team size to four or five for one hundred dollars, or you might decide to charge a per-person fee of, say, five dollars, and create some on-the-spot teams of individuals who show up to participate on the fly. You can also choose to allow eliminated teams to buy their ways back for a second chance if they wish, maybe by contributing an additional thirty dollars for the opportunity.
- You also would need to decide if spectators can attend for free or if you want to charge admission. If you charge admission, make it small and reasonable, perhaps five dollars per person, with tickets for door-prize drawings. If the event is being held in a brewery or tea/coffee establishment, it is probably wise to admit spectators at no charge and have the establishment agree to give you

(continued)

a percentage of sales. If the event is being held in a regular library or other free venue meeting room, you may be able to sell refreshments if desired, but be sure to ask beforehand.
- Even if you are holding your spelling bee event in an establishment where your group would miss getting a percentage of sales, you may wish to include door prizes, a raffle, a silent auction, or a combination for the attendees to try their luck and earn more money for your library.[1] Your MC would need to tout these bonus competitive options if they are chosen and your event location approves.
- Toward the end of the event, tally up scores and have the MC present the prizes to the winning teams. You would, of course, need to have selected prizes that would attract entrants instead of ones that are ho-hum. These could be cash, gift cards, trips, shopping sprees, movie theater tickets—use your imagination and choose wisely. You may even be able to get desirable prize(s) donated by businesses serving as co-sponsors. If you have held special additional contests like a silent auction or a guessing game, the MC would also announce the results for those at the end, perhaps while the spelling bee scores are being tallied.

Note

1. Better Fundraising Ideas. 2023. "Spelling Bee Fundraiser," https://www.better-fundraising-ideas.com/spelling-bee-fundraiser.html.

There you have it—a helpful selection of useful fundraising suggestions that you may want to try to support your library. But wait—there's more! Stay tuned for the next chapter, in which you will discover further interesting ideas and advice for adding ways to raise money.

Notes

1. Friends of the Knox County Public Library. 2023. "Stay Home and Read a Book Ball," https://www.knoxfriends.org/stay-home-and-read-a-book-ball/.
2. Poudre River Friends of the Library. 2023. "Book Sales," https://www.prfol.org/booksales/.
3. City of Dover. 2023. "Friends of the Dover Public Library Book Sale This Weekend," https://www.dover.nh.gov/services/online-services/news-events/news-2023/friends-of-the-dover-public-library-may-book-sale.html.
4. Friends of Weathersfield Proctor Library. November 28, 2022. "Weathersfield Proctor Library Fundraising Review." Email message to author.
5. Friends of the Library, Montgomery County, MD. 2021. "Bookstores," https://www.folmc.org/bookstores/online-store/.
6. Amazon. 2023. "How to Sell Books Online in 2023: Step-by-Step Guide," https://sell.amazon.com/learn/how-to-sell-books.
7. eBay. 2023. "Welcome to the eBay Seller Center," https://www.ebay.com/sellercenter.
8. Friends of the Knox County Public Library. 2020. "Grab Bags," https://knoxfriends.square.site/shop/grab-bags/2?page=1&limit=60&sort_by=category_order&sort_order=asc.
9. Friends of Chapel Hill Public Library. [n.d.] "Welcome to the Friends Online Bookstore," https://friendschpl.org/online-book-store.
10. Johnson County Public Library Foundation. 2023. "Friends of JCPL," https://www.jcplf.org/friends.
11. Chattanooga Public Library Foundation. [n.d.] "Book Sales Links," https://www.thechattanoogapubliclibraryfoundation.org/.

12. Abe Books. 2023. "FOLCHATT," https://www.abebooks.com/servlet/SearchResults?sortby=0&vci=82535226.

13. Alibris. 2023. "Chattanooga Public Library Foundation," https://www.alibris.com/stores/chattlib?slr_ref=chattlib.

14. The Library Store. 2023. "Supporting the Los Angeles Public Library," https://shop.lfla.org/.

15. Ferguson Library. 2023. "Friends Book Shop," https://www.fergusonlibrary.org/friends/book-shop.

16. Campbell Library. 2023. "Love Your Library: Become a Friend," https://www.eastgrandforks.us/203/Friends-Membership.

17. Friends of the Library of Hawai'i. 2023. "Friends of the Library of Hawai'i," https://friendsofthelibraryofhawaii.org/.

18. Hi-Wire Brewing. 2023. "Events/Knoxville," https://hiwirebrewing.com/events/category/knoxville/list/.

19. Denver Public Library Friends Foundation. 2023. "Red Chair Books," https://www.dplfriends.org/news-events/blog/fun-new-pop-up-book-sales-in-2023/.

20. Longview Public Library. 2023. "Friends of the Longview Public Library, Book Sales and Fundraisers," http://www.longviewlibrary.org/support.php.

21. Friends Foundation of Worthington Libraries. 2023. "Books & Brews," https://worthingtonlibrariesfriends.org/books-and-brews/.

22. Hannah Campbell. June 30, 2023. "New Coffee Shop Opens at Saratoga Springs Public Library." *Times Union*, https://www.timesunion.com/business/article/saratoga-springs-public-library-announces-coffee-18179169.php.

23. Library Foundation of Spokane County. 2023. "Fundraisers with YaYa Brewing for New Spokane Valley Library," https://www.supportscld.org/ways-to-give/fundraisers-with-yaya-brewing-for-new-spokane-valley-library/.

24. Cheddar Up. 2023. "Friends of the Beacon Hall Library Coffee Fundraiser," https://my.cheddarup.com/c/friends-of-the-beacon-falls-library-coffee-fundraiser?cart=a26993bc-ee24-4554-9cf4-3e44ec32aace%21%2158746985.

25. Dean's Beans. 2023. "Organic, Fair Trade Fundraising," https://deansbeans.com/pages/fundraising.

26. Giving Bean. 2016. "The Giving Bean Fundraising Is Simple and Sustainable," https://www.givingbean.com/coffee-fundraising-program/.

27. Java Joe's Fundraising. [n.d.] "The #1 Coffee Fundraiser!" https://javajoesfundraising.com/.

28. Huntsville-Madison County Public Library. 2023. "Brew & Bee," https://hmcpl.org/foundation/brewandbee.

CHAPTER 9

Additional Fundraising Ideas That Work!

YOU HAVE ALREADY DISCOVERED quite a few unique, interesting, and productive fundraising ideas that work in the previous chapter. However, there are more good ideas ahead to consider. The upcoming mix of ideas will provide more food for thought and potential fundraising choices. Read on to discover more proven ways to make money for library support. Remember, as always, you can zero in on one of the ideas and if it appeals to your organization, adopt or adapt it as you wish.

Flockin' Flamingos Fundraiser
Friends of the Austin Public Library, Austin, Minnesota

To raise funds for the library, these Friends held an event during which members stealthily placed plastic flamingos in the designated yards of donors' friends or whomever they chose. People paid the Friends for the opportunity and the flamingos stayed on the lawns for twenty-four hours. Those who had been "flocked" got an opportunity to pay a donation and flock another "victim." However, people who would rather not have had flamingos installed on their lawns could pay for "anti-flocking insurance." Customers' flocking choices came in three sizes and prices: small (twelve for twelve dollars); medium (twenty-four for twenty-four dollars); and large (thirty-six for thirty-six dollars). A ten-dollar contribution provided "anti-flocking insurance" for anyone who wanted to prevent being flocked in the first place.

The Friends invested in eighty plastic flamingos, enough for three "flocks" and extras for incidentals, plus three yard signs, one for each flock. They also recommended extra legs for the flamingos as they were surprised at how unexpectedly they could go missing. You can buy the flamingos and additional items at the Pink Flamingo Site,[1] which provides pricing and sometimes has discounts, but you can also get the plastic pink birds from other places—check online. Additionally, for publicity, the Friends purchased a 650-sheet pack of pink paper for sixteen dollars.

Figure 9.1. Plastic flamingos grace the lawn of a Flockin' Flamingos "victim" during the special fundraising event held by the Friends of the Austin Public Library in Minnesota.
Credit: Elizabeth Carlton.

The publicity consisted of posts on the Friends' Facebook page and library website posts; flyers stuffed in bags at the local grocery store checkouts; flyers posted around town and in the library; and emails sent to the Friends members about the event with encouragement to spread the word.

After creating an order form for donors, they used several methods to reach out to everyone who may have wanted to order. They used a Google Pay form; a PayPal donation button/link; printable forms emailed to those on their email list or those who called with inquiries; paper forms sent in the regular mail; and paper forms made available at the library. Since the first year of the event, the Friends were overwhelmed by orders and had to cut them off at certain points, so after that they decided to limit the timing from two months to six weeks.

There were fifteen volunteers who did the flocking for the event periods. They picked up the already-installed flamingos from lawns at the end of each day in the early evenings (remembering to bring along the extra legs!); drove to the next houses to be flocked to re-place the flamingos and drop off information sheets; and completed the tasks at each house by taking photos of the yards for delivery confirmation.

The Friends reported that this fundraiser had a large financial impact and gleaned much positive feedback, especially expressions of enjoyment at seeing the flocks about town. The group was happy to conduct a fundraising event that brought a lot of attention to their organization along with some pleasure for the public.[2]

TEXTBOX 9.1

FLOCKIN' FLAMINGOS FUNDRAISER INFORMATION SHEET

Providing informational sheets explaining the fundraiser's purpose and procedures was essential so that people would understand what was going on. To exemplify how to word or adapt the information in an upbeat, friendly, and positive manner, here is the letter that was used by the Austin Friends. It said:

> Don't despair!
> This is a fundraiser by the Austin Friends of the Library. A friend of yours paid us to place these pink darlings in your yard. This flocking is done in good spirits and is not meant to be mean. These flamingos will roost on your lawn until this evening, when they will mysteriously migrate to another friend's (victim's) lawn.
> Unfortunately, we are no longer accepting new flocking orders, but if you want to donate to the Friends of the Library, we would greatly appreciate your donation. (Directions for online or mailed giving added here.)
> Of course, the removal of these flamingos will be done at no charge, so please don't hurt our pink feathered friends.
> Thanks for your sense of humor and your support.

Handcrafted Greeting Cards
Friends of the Boynton Beach City Library, Florida

Friends of the Library members run and manage their Friends of the Library Bookstore, which is open year-round and located by the library's main entrance. They sell books, DVDs, and other items at bargain prices.[3] Some of the specialty items they offer are handcrafted greeting cards. The cards are a big hit with buyers. Initially, the cards had been made by program participants at the Library's Custom Card Crafting Club who chose to donate their creations to the cause. After that, "crafty" Friends members who also enjoyed the undertaking of making the unique cards for purchase were enlisted to contribute their talents as well.

This all began with the makerspace librarian's discovery that a library staff member had outstanding custom-made cardmaking skills. As a result, the library's Crafting Club was born. Soon though, an idea shared at a Florida Library Association Breakfast urging Friends to make sellable cards for fundraising motivated adding another dimension to the idea. That inspiration prompted the Friends to offer card-crafting workshops for interested members, and volunteers drawn to producing the cards for sale at the bookstore were able to use Friends funds for maker supplies. Those volunteers could also take materials home to continue their cardmaking there, if desired. Simultaneously, those who were making cards at the Card Club, with supplies paid for by the library's programming budget, were offered the option to contribute some of their handmade creations for sale at the shop to support the Friends. By blending these two sources of cards, the bookstore now had a well-stocked card inventory.

For the Friends cardmaking workshops, they enrolled eight members for two separate workshops, four members in each one. They used A2 standard greeting card sizing made from 100-pound 8½-×-11 heavyweight cardstock for the card bases and made pre-cuts on the Cricut cutting machine[4] so they would be maker-ready. They also used a Sizzix Big Shot[5] die-cut machine with a selection of dies and slide paper cutters. Other supplies were pairs of scissors; stamps; colored and patterned paper of any weight; quality liquid glue and precision craft glue; and crafting foam squares.

If your group likes this idea and the library you support has a makerspace, you may be able to partner with them to make use of it and their instructional skills. However, if a craft instructor is unavailable to you and you would like further access to information about custom card crafting, there are numerous instructions and videos online, or you can check your local library for a variety of practical guidebooks.

As far as fundraising goes, are some recommendations for selling the cards:

- Sell the handmade cards at your book shop if you have one as well as at book sales.
- Buy envelopes in the proper sizes to fit the cards you are selling and buy plastic sleeves that you can place the cards and envelope in for purchase. You can buy these online and it is worth the investment.
- Be careful to charge enough for the cards! People are willing to pay more for a handcrafted card and envelope in a plastic sleeve. Charging fifty cents each is too little, and you should consider a price of at least one dollar, depending on your community. It is perfectly acceptable to charge up to four dollars per card.
- Consider adding beautiful and creative handmade bookmarks to your instructional workshops and use them to increase your sales inventory, perhaps charging two dollars apiece.[6]

Snuggle Up with a Book Ball
Johnson County Public Library Foundation, Indiana

To help this Foundation continue bringing award-winning authors to their community for their Authors at JCPL series, they held their fourth annual Snuggle Up with a Book Ball on a Saturday in 2023, promoting it as "the event you don't attend." The idea has been that since February weather in Indiana can be iffy, a perfect alternative to venturing out during that month to come to a fundraiser would be holding one that could be done right from people's homes or at neighboring locations on the appointed date. Participants selected their donation levels and how they wished to take part. They could snuggle up with a book anywhere, anytime, with anyone, or even by themselves.

There were two ways for community members to "not attend" on event day. They could donate any amount, stay at home, snuggle up, and read anytime, for as long as desired. Or they had the option of being part of a joint effort, either by becoming a team captain or joining a team that had been created. Either way, team captains received a commemorative gift while the team members who donated the highest amount and an individual who singly contributed the most money all won a private event with one of the future authors coming for the visiting authors series. In addition, beginning at noon on the day of the reading event, hourly door prizes were awarded to a person who was registered. Notices of donors and winners were posted on the Foundation's Facebook page unless any contributors had chosen to remain anonymous.

Even though individuals could take part solo, those who desired to be placed on a team could complete a request form to be matched with open teams being created. On the other hand, those who enjoyed leading social interactions and wanted to be team captains could volunteer to do it by completing a registration form. Their jobs were to plan get-togethers for their team members in any way they devised. For example, they could invite their book club members to come over for a reading party; host reading parties in loungewear with their families; have a coffee or tea gathering at home or at a coffeehouse; read with the team in reserved library meeting rooms; organize a virtual party and check in on reading progress and reactions online; or simply coordinate a team all taking part as individuals reading alone at home. The choices were completely up to the teams or solo readers, and everyone could read, eat, drink, and wear whatever they wanted. No matter what approaches were chosen, participants were encouraged to share their reading event experiences on Zoom, Facebook Live, or via any other electronic mediums.

Most importantly, participants could register online where they authorized their donation amounts. They could contribute from a selection of literary-oriented donation suggestion amounts similar to choices listed on library support group donor pages (see chapter 6):

- Potter's Pals = less than $50
- Alcott's Ambassadors = $50–$149
- Shakespeare's Scholars = $150–$249
- Austen's Angels = $250+

About ninety people registered to take part in 2023 using amounts representing all four levels, making this fundraiser a rousing success.[7]

Historical Notecard Fundraiser
Friends of the Longview Public Library, Longview, Washington

These Friends have an ongoing sale of beautiful black-and-white notecards they have had made using historical images of their distinctive small community archived in the library's extensive Longview Room historical collection.

Cards are 5"x7" with a matte finish and come with envelopes. A single card is two dollars, a set of ten is eighteen dollars, and a set of twelve Christmas/winter cards is twenty-two dollars. Orders can be placed online through the Friends' website via the GiveButter[8] platform and picked up in the library's drive-through.[9] If the library you support has a history room, consider transforming some quality historic photos into note card, postcard, or calendar reproductions as a fundraiser.

If you are drawn to trying this idea, the American Library Association's Copyright Advisory Network, comprised of "librarians, copyright scholars, and policy wonks," may be able to advise you about any copyright restrictions on reproducing historic photos into items for sale. Prior to creating any such items using old photographs, you will want to investigate whether there are any restrictions or if the photographs are in the public domain. The Network has a "Resources" section with helpful tools to self-evaluate fair use of materials and a forum through which they knowledgeably respond to questions if you are uncertain.[10]

A Button Machine for Profits
Friends of the Library, Montgomery County, Maryland

To increase profits, the Friends of the Library in Montgomery County invested in a button-making machine to make unique buttons for sale. These Friends repurpose discarded books from the library or from unusable donations to make the buttons. It is a great project for Friends volunteers and teens needing community service hours, which can produce excellent profits. The buttons can be sold at book sales, in the library, at special events, or online—whichever way or ways are most effective for your group.

The Friends who do this project try to choose catchy, funny, meaningful, and high-interest images and words to use on the buttons. This results in every button being distinctive, often making just the right connections with the right buyers drawn to their particular topics and focuses. The buttons are priced at a reasonable one dollar per button, which, in their locale that requires nonprofits to pay sales tax, accounts for a price of ninety-four cents plus tax, rounded up to one dollar for ease of change-making. However, your group could decide what seems most logical for your community and price the buttons accordingly.

You may be wondering about copyrights on the words and images from the books that are used for the buttons, and I did too. I learned that as long as the materials are owned by individuals or organizations, not copied, and the materials that are taken from the actual books owned are used to make the buttons, it is not prohibited. After all, the used books can be resold at library support group sales without penalty. These Friends checked with their lawyer who said this repurposing was permissible, but you could always check on this yourself with your group's own law professionals[11] or by using the Copyright Advisory Network mentioned in the previous example. In the meantime, to assure you, here is the law:

> The first sale doctrine, codified at 17 U.S.C. § 109, provides that an individual who knowingly purchases a copy of a copyrighted work from the copyright holder receives the right to sell, display or otherwise dispose of that particular copy, notwithstanding the interests of the copyright owner.[12]

If you want to pursue the idea of button-sales fundraising, take into account that the initial costs for a button machine and any necessary supplies vary greatly, so doing a thorough search online to find the best choices for your library support group is the way to go. You can also confer with your library's makerspace specialist if there is one on staff for advice both on what to buy and how to generate the buttons. If an informed person is unavailable for this, you can find a good selection of online YouTube tutorials on purchasing a button maker and how to make buttons with it.

Another idea that you might want to consider for making useful and attractive products to sell is to have Friends and other volunteers make glass refrigerator magnets. You would need the clear-glass pebbles, strong neodymium magnets, and E6000 adhesive. These materials are available online or in a craft store. You could repurpose discarded books or old magazines for the images that would reflect through the glass. Instructions for making these refrigerator magnets are online and YouTube has tutorials for them as well. You may need to charge a bit more for the magnets—perhaps two or three dollars—to see a profit.

Weathersfield Town Challenge
Library Fundraising Committee of the Weathersfield Proctor Library, Weathersfield, Vermont

When a small town with a very involved community that includes a library with two active library support groups working well together—the Friends of the Library plus the Library Fundraising Committee—great things can happen. That is true of Weathersfield, Vermont, population 2,800, where the two groups have big ideas to support the library with the funding it needs. Sometimes events are in partnership, and at other times they are sponsored individually, an arrangement that works well.

One of the events they hold to raise money, sponsored by the Library Fundraising Committee, is their trivia Town Challenge for which community members donate money to support various teams each March. Prior to the event, to encourage donations for their favorite teams, friends, family members, and local businesses are asked to contribute. Additional donations are also collected at the door on the event night and that money is added to the donation pool. The team getting the most donations receives some type of special recognition. There are also door prizes and refreshments for the attendees.

Town committees, boards, the junior high student body, and teachers recruit volunteers to represent them for the competition. Three representatives are required for each team, and an alternate can take someone's place at halftime if desired. The limit for the competition is usually ten teams.

Five large tables are set up along a meeting room wall, with a team of three stationed at each end of a table. Placards designating team names and players are placed in front of competitors. There are ten rounds to the Challenge with teams alternating the answering of questions about town history, current events, geography, spelling, "name that tune," and sports. A square box, with categories written on all the sides, is tossed into the air and lands on the floor to determine from which face-up category each subsequent question will be taken. A point is earned for each correct answer and the two highest-scoring teams have a runoff round.

A trophy is awarded to the winning team, and it is displayed in the town office each year. The winners all get prizes such as hats or T-shirts.[13]

Seeking Special Guest Authors for Fundraising Events

At some library support group fundraisers, top authors are the stars of the show. By selling tickets to attend these featured-author speaking events, library nonprofits can often earn respectable sums to aid their beneficiary libraries.

Before describing a few outstanding author fundraising events as examples, I would like to share some hints for getting these high-caliber authors to come to your library or other meeting spot in the first place. Remember that you will most likely need to invest money to get big-draw authors to come to your events, so, before you contract with any of them, you will need to estimate your outlay and income expectations to see if those particular authors would be viable financially. Also, trying several avenues and possible choices to secure top authors is your best bet because success in contracting the most popular for an event can be hit or miss. Here are some tips that might help:

- Because people who are drawn and dedicated to libraries are usually book lovers, consider that some of them may have connections to local and national authors' agents or publicists who may offer good leads to suitable available speakers. Ask around! Furthermore, additional connections within your library and library support group networks might be catalysts for getting discounted speaker fees.
- Even though they might not have a widely known reputation nationally, consider investigating the availability of local authors who may be popular in your region. This can be a very cost-effective and well-received pick for your event.
- Contact publishers' speakers bureaus and other speaker agencies. There are several big-name speakers bureaus you may want to check out, including Penguin Random House Speakers Bureau,[14] Simon & Schuster Speakers Bureau,[15] and Hachette Speakers Bureau.[16] You can try these for mainstream fiction and nonfiction authors, but they are especially helpful to find an author you are targeting from another field, such as an athlete, an academic, or a journalist who is getting buzz for a notable autobiography or other work. In addition, you might consider trying other national speaker agencies because they may coordinate speaking engagements for authors who also use outside agencies that are unaffiliated with their publishers.
- Peruse author websites to more directly see if they are promoting visits and giving information on how to arrange them. If there is a booking agent and a publicist named, contact the publicist first to see if the author has a national tour or local engagements that you can tie into.
- Keep up-and-coming authors in mind who have yet to be asked to do an author talk. Also, remember midlist authors who have target subjects they write about that might have particular high interest for your area, such as an author who has written a notable book about skiing adventures and is available to speak at a Colorado library.
- Partner with your local bookstore. Depending on what kind of author event you are hoping to hold and how many people you expect to attend, partnering with your local, independent bookstore can often be a positive choice. Booksellers are frequently the first to know about new book releases and author book tours so you can get a heads-up on what authors might be available for your event by partnering with them. They are also sometimes familiar with author presentation skills and their willingness to speak, so you can be assured ahead of time that you have a dynamic author/presenter on board. To wrap up, whether you are planning an author event as a special fundraiser or you are simply hosting a free event at your library and still hope to make a modest profit, having a willing bookseller on hand to facilitate book sales and offer you a cut would be beneficial for you while being highly appreciated by attendees as well as by authors and their publicists.[17]

Author-involved events can be great fun and a productive way to enhance the profits to support your local library. By following the suggestions just given, your group may find itself planning and hosting well-planned and winning author events. These could be simple, single-author presentation events with signings at the end for a small attendance fee, or a major program endeavor. To inspire you, the following section describes some successful, more elaborate events held by library support groups that you might be drawn to emulate.

Galas, Major Author Events, and Other Grand Affairs

The unique and creative large-scale events featured in this section of the chapter are ones that have required advanced planning and preparation to raise a large amount of money at once to support the beneficiary libraries. Some of them might include an author speaker or speakers; however, the author is only one facet of the enjoyment and entertainment.

Estimated populations of the cities and towns are given to demonstrate that all sizes of communities can create such exciting and productive events as long as there are dedicated library support group members conducting them. If your group is considering a major event like these ones, you will find ideas and themes here that you can ponder and possibly adjust to fit your needs.

A Taste for Wine and Murder

Austin, Minnesota (Population 26,000)
Friends of the Austin Public Library

The fourth annual murder mystery affair, called A Taste of Wine and Murder, was planned by the Friends in 2023 to raise funds for an Austin Public Library construction project.

Participants (limited to seventy-five) were invited to come to the event to test their detective skills and attempt to solve a murder mystery from 6:00 to 9:00 p.m. The forty-dollar ticket price included hearty appetizers provided by the culinary team from the Home. Also, during the evening, an optional wine tasting was held for an additional fifteen-dollar ticket.

Each attendee attempted to solve a mystery surrounding the discovery of the body of a local vineyard owner, missing for six years, during a California wine tasting festival. With the discovery, several new clues came to light. After "interviewing" suspects and searching for new clues, accusations against the murderer could be made by participants, and those guessing correctly received a mystery book as a reward.[18]

The event was held at the Hormel Historic Home in January. This former home of the George A. and Lillian Hormel family is now a museum and community resource that not only preserves the home but also honors the family's legacy by providing a community site for meaningful programming and outreach.[19] It was an ideal location for this event.

Wine & Words

Brainerd, Minnesota (Population 15,000)
Friends of the Brainerd Public Library

Books, books, books . . . and authors, authors, authors! This is the essence of Wine & Words, which has been taking place since 2013. In 2023, these Friends were still doing something very much right because again, the entire three-day event was sold out. How did they do it? By not only providing outstanding authors to hobnob with attendees up close and personal, but also by having a helpful corps of sponsors that enabled the event to succeed through various levels of enjoyment and participation.

Both Wednesday and Thursday, the first and second days, they had a social time and silent auction at 5:30 p.m. This was followed by Book Booths for an hour, dinner, author presentations, and finally, book signings. On Friday, almost the same schedule took place except as a brunch event starting at 10:30 a.m. For each of the three days, individual tickets sold online were fifty dollars, and a table of eight was four hundred dollars. Premium tables for eight were five hundred dollars, with two bottles of wine provided and a guest author seated at the table. Six local sponsors donated the grand venue for the event; guest author accommodations; wine; books; printing the tickets and event booklets; logo design; and event funding. Local individuals, book clubs, and businesses donated the items for the silent auction.

This annual event is truly a meaningful collaboration of the library-and-literature-appreciation community in Brainerd to support its library.[20]

Wine & BBQ

Lawrence, Kansas (Population 96,000)
Lawrence Public Library Friends & Foundation

In August 2023, this Friends & Foundation held a special fundraiser to help fund the Library's programs for older adults. In particular, this event aimed to add support for the library's two-year Retirement Boot Camp pilot program to help seniors transitioning to retirement in a positive manner, and it was initially funded by a local savings bank grant.[21]

The event centered on three specially selected wines and barbecued meats for participants to enjoy. The presenter from the City Wine Market took them on an informational journey through the winemaking process, customs, and regions of each wine and paired them off with foods from a local renowned restaurant. Tickets to the sold-out event, held in the Library auditorium, were fifty dollars and were limited to fifty registrants who were automatically entered in a drawing to win a free bottle of one of the featured wines.[22]

Spring Author Fundraising Event

Lancaster County, Pennsylvania (Population 557,000)
Council of Friends of Public Libraries

The Spring Author Event that is held by this Friends group is a fundraiser for all seventeen libraries in the Library System of Lancaster County. The group has organized and run this event featuring best-selling authors for twenty-two years and has been able to provide $140,000 for the library system. In 2023, they initiated a partnership with Midtown Scholar Books, located in Harrisburg, Pennsylvania, when they hosted author Robert Dugoni. Tickets for the event were fifty dollars, and attendees got to hear the author speak; received a trade paperback copy of the author's book, *Her Deadly Game*; could access the author's backlist titles to purchase; and had a "meet & greet" and book signing time with the author. A local church provided the facility for the event.[23]

Vive le Livre—Long Live the Book

Madison County, Alabama (Population 404,000)
Huntsville-Madison County Library Foundation

For over thirty-seven years, this library foundation has held a gala event featuring a cocktail reception, a seated dinner, and a top-selling author keynote speaker as they celebrate books, authors, and all things library-oriented. Benefits from the events are used to support all ten branches of the Huntsville-Madison County Library System. The event is held at the Jackson Center, the area's world-class conference center. Individuals can purchase tickets for the event, but sponsorships are accepted first in tiered donation amounts ranging from five hundred to five thousand dollars. Depending on the donation, sponsors receive several perks including event reservations, an autographed book, and their name and/or company listed in the event program.[24]

Party in the Stacks

Milford, Connecticut (Population 51,000)
Friends of the Milford Public Library

This fun, after-hours, annual event is hosted by the Friends in the library itself to raise funds. Each event has a special focus. For instance, in 2022, it was "Where Dreams Come True," featuring a storybook theme. The adults-only event includes delicious theme-related appetizers, specialty drinks, and adult beverages from local establishments, music and dancing, a raffle and auction, and a trivia contest. Costumes to fit the theme are optional but encouraged. Tickets are fifty-five dollars per person, and for those who wish to support the Friends but cannot attend, there is a "donate" button they can access if desired. Items offered for the auction and raffle can be previewed in advance online, and during the event itself, paper bid sheets and raffle tickets are available.[25]

Figure 9.2. At Party in the Stacks, one group posed in storybook princesses–inspired costumes. *Credit: Melissa Carroll.*

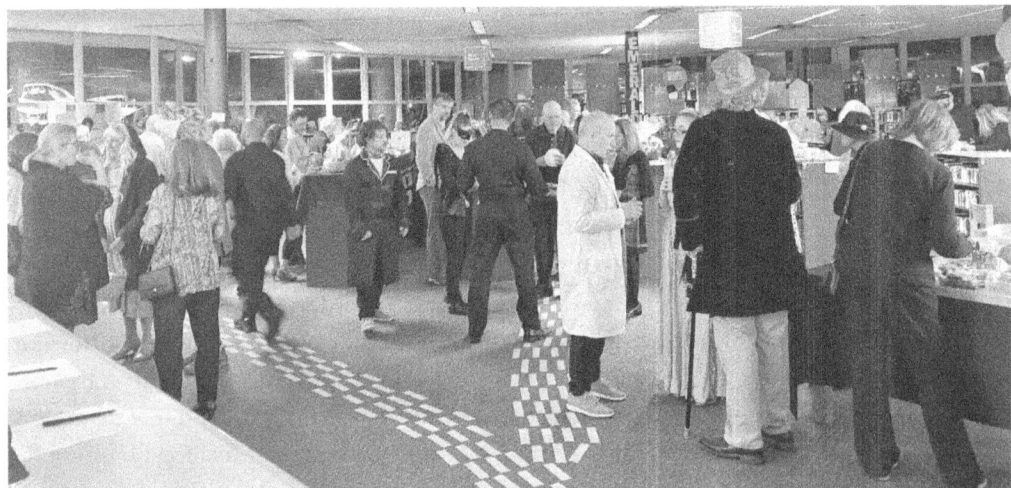

Figure 9.3. Party guests mingle and enjoy food at Party in the Stacks 2022. The *Wizard of Oz* yellow brick road leads guests to the Emerald City décor. *Credit: Jennifer Burgess.*

A Novel Occasion

Millis, Massachusetts (Population 8,800)
Friends of the Millis Public Library

Even a small library community can have an event that makes a difference in a big way. Since 2021, the Friends have offered a special, annual two-and-a-half-hour-long virtual author gathering on Zoom during which ten best-selling authors met online with attendees to talk about their books and answer questions. Several local sponsors aided the Friends in hosting this event. Individuals could buy per-person tickets online for the early bird rate of sixty dollars, pay seventy-five dollars after the discounted deadline, and offer an additional donation to help the Friends if they so wished. Donors received a swag bag delivered to their homes and a book by their favorite author who served as a speaker; could "sit" at two intimate author roundtables; and had chances at winning multiple prizes during the event. Participants were encouraged to register early so they could be scheduled in their two preferred author "roundtable" breakout rooms, each with a moderator to keep the conversations flowing and capped at fifteen attendees. A technology production team was available during the entire event to assist with logins and troubleshooting.

This well-attended event shows that even when having an in-person affair proves unaffordable or difficult, offering a carefully planned and promoted virtual option can also be a productive alternative.[26] This could be particularly true for a regional library that covers a wide-spanned service area.

Novel Tea

Olathe, Kansas (population 143,000)
Friends of the Olathe Public Library

For over ten years, this library support group has hosted its annual Novel Tea fundraiser, which includes an author serving as a guest speaker. The afternoon event sports a different theme each year. For instance, in 2023, the theme was "Back to the 70s." While having tea and light refreshments, guests enjoy the giveaways and imaginative table settings. Tickets go on sale a month in advance of the tea.

Julie Clark, the finance administrator at the Olathe Public Library who partners with the Friends on the Novel Tea event and book sales, said, "The Friends Novel Tea has become a popular social event in Olathe each spring. We have community organizations pay $10 for the opportunity to set a table according to that year's tea theme and they provide a creative and fun element. We choose a local author to speak, and the topic of their talk helps determine the theme. We have a buffet of 'tea' type foods and a tea station set up for attendees to help themselves. We sell tickets for $20 each and make about $10 per ticket. The money raised is used to fund scholarships for library teen volunteers. Tea Sponsor forms and pictures are sent out to local organizations that may be potentially interested in setting a table."[27]

Figure 9.4. Novel Tea flyer. *Credit: Katy O'Neill.*

Figure 9.5. At the Novel Tea, community organizations pay to set tables according to that year's tea theme, a creative and fun element. *Credit: Julie Clark.*

Books & Brunch

St. Charles, Illinois (Population 33,000)
St. Charles Public Library Foundation

For several years since 2014, this Foundation has held its Books & Brunch fundraising event among its other events to financially support the St. Charles Public Library. Through all those events, they have provided the Library with enhanced programming and services; speaker and concert series; building upgrades; landscaping projects; and further projects beyond the Library's regular operating budget.

The 2023 brunch event was held on a Sunday in October from 12:00 to 3:00 p.m. at a local country club and featured a lecture and book signing with bestselling author of legal suspense thrillers Scott Turow. For a sixty-five-dollar ticket, brunch attendees were treated to good food, community building, a wonderful guest author presentation, and above all, the knowledge that they had contributed to supporting their beloved Library. In addition to book giveaways, guests were able to bid on themed raffle baskets that included restaurant gift cards, spa packages, theater and sporting event tickets, and additional desirable baskets. Prize sponsors ranged from the Chicago Zoological Society/Brookfield Zoo to the Paramount Theater to the Turf Room Restaurant, and more. The main financial sponsor was CIBC Private Wealth Management. Tickets for the event could be purchased online or in person at the Library.[28]

Summer Evening with Friends and Neighbors

Library Fundraising Committee
Weathersfield, Vermont

Once again, if your library support group is funding a library in a small or small-ish community like Weathersfield, Vermont, you can still provide a wonderful major event that will help you raise money. It simply takes that "small but mighty" attitude that has been mentioned previously. If you remember from other examples about this town, there are dual library support groups there. The Library Fundraising Committee often works in partnership with the Friends of the Library, but the event featured here is sponsored solely by the former.

The Summer Evening event is always held in July from 6:00 to 9:00 p.m. at the Weathersfield Meeting House and Church, high up in the hills of their town. There are only a few older homes there along with a small green with a Civil War monument. The town's Historical Society museum is located directly across the road in what is known as the Dan Foster House, which was built for a long-ago church pastor. I was told that this information is important because the location of the event adds much to its ambiance and its several components.

With an admission fee of fifteen dollars, each person receives a token for a free glass of wine, beer, or soda, and there is charge of four dollars for additional purchases of beverages. Coffee, tea, and iced-tea punch are available for free. There is also an array of delectable appetizers that serve very much like a meal, and during the entertainment break, delicious desserts are set out.

Besides food and drink, there is entertainment. Music from a well-known jazz, folk, country, or big band–style group is provided, and a space is allotted for dancing.

During the evening, guests are encouraged to place bids on about thirty different silent auction items that were donated by local businesses or event patrons. Each item has a bidding sheet for name, phone number, and an offer in a rounded-dollar amount. Bids on the items close at the end of the entertainment break. Attendees must find out if theirs was the winning bid pre-departure, and payment is expected at that time.[29]

If your library support group is hoping to create a unique ticketed event to raise money like the organizations in these examples, it may seem like a daunting task. As with other special library programs and events described in this book, the key is to form a committee to devise a strategic plan built around a theme to make it happen. Other important elements are to contact potential sponsors to see if they might be willing to partner and to send out publicity encouraging local businesses, service clubs, government agencies, and other places to see if they are able to contribute money, resources, or volunteer time to get the event off the ground. However, for your first endeavor, remember to keep it on the smaller size instead of planning a grandiose event. If the event is successful and you wish to make it an annual affair, build on what you learn from the initial try to make it more deluxe the next go-round and beyond.

Notes

1. The Pink Flamingo Site. 2023. https://thepinkflamingosite.com/.
2. ALA eLearning. October 19, 2022. "Friendraising & Fundraising Ideas for Friends Groups and Libraries of All Sizes." United for Libraries webinar, https://elearning.ala.org/course/view.php?id=862&pageid=3869.
3. City of Boynton Beach. 2022. "Friends of the Boynton Beach City Library," https://www.boynton-beach.org/library/friends-of-library.
4. Cricut. 2023. https://cricut.com/en-us/.
5. Sizzix. 2023. https://www.sizzix.com/sizzix-big-shot-overview.
6. ALA eLearning. October 19, 2022.
7. JCPL Foundation. 2023. "4th Annual Snuggle up with a Book Ball," https://www.jcplf.org/snuggle.
8. GiveButter. 2023. https://givebutter.com/.
9. Longview Public Library. 2023. "Friends of the Longview Library Book Sales and Fundraisers," http://www.longviewlibrary.org/support.php.
10. Copyright Advisory Network. 2015. "Copyright Advisory Network: A Community of Librarians, Copyright Scholars, Policy Wonks. Join Us." American Library Association Office for Information Technology Policy, https://librarycopyright.net/.
11. ALA eLearning. October 19, 2022.
12. United States Department of Justice Archives. 1854. "Copyright Infringement—First Sale Doctrine," https://www.justice.gov/archives/jm/criminal-resource-manual-1854-copyright-infringement-first-sale-doctrine#:~:text=The%20first%20sale%20doctrine%2C%20codified,interests%20of%20the%20copyright%20owner.
13. Friends of Weathersfield Proctor Library. November 28, 2022. Email message to author.
14. Penguin Random House Publishers. 2023. "Penguin Random House Speakers Bureau," https://www.prhspeakers.com/.
15. Simon & Schuster Publishers. 2023. "Simon & Schuster Speakers Bureau," https://www.simonspeakers.com/.
16. Hachette Publishers. 2023. "Hachette Speakers Bureau," https://www.hachettespeakersbureau.com/.
17. Library Strategies. April 6, 2016. "Securing Authors to Headline Your Fundraiser or Special Event," https://www.librarystrategiesconsulting.org/2016/04/securing-authors-to-headline-your-fundraiser-or-special-event/.

18. Austin Public Library. 2023. "Friends of the Library," https://www.aplmn.org/friends-of-the-library.
19. Hormel Historic Home. 2022. "Hormel Historic Home," https://www.hormelhistorichome.org/.
20. Friends of the Brainerd Public Library. 2023. "Wine & Words!" https://www.wineandwordsandfriends.com/wineandwords.
21. Lawrence Public Library. 2023. "Retirement Boot Camp," https://lplks.org/retirement/.
22. Lawrence Public Library. 2023. "Wine & BBQ Pairing Fundraising Event," https://lawrence.bibliocommons.com/events/6493597864c37d34008a9dd0.
23. Library System of Lancaster County. February 14, 2023. "Bestselling Author, Robert Dugoni, to Appear at the Spring Author Event!" https://lancasterlibraries.org/author-events/.
24. Huntsville-Madison County Public Library. 2023. "Vive le Livre," https://hmcpl.org/foundation/vive.
25. Friends of the Milford Library. 2022. "Friends of the Milford Library—Party in the Stacks," https://www.biddingowl.com/Auction/home.cfm?auctionID=15627&CFID=56316933&CFTOKEN=8d49df7d64735eee-8324FAF4-CF7B-8B25-25AD942D5950DA42.
26. Millis Growing with the Library. 2023. "A Novel Occasion," https://www.anoveloccasion.com/.
27. Clark, Julie. Email message to author, February 22, 2023.
28. St. Charles Public Library. 2023. "Fundraising Events," https://www.scpld.org/about/foundation/books-and-brunch/.
29. Friends of the Weathersfield Proctor Library. November 28, 2022.

CHAPTER 10

Donors
The Heart of Fundraising

THE CONCEPT THAT DONORS are at the heart of library support group fundraising, whether by paying annual dues, giving extra money at book sales, contributing on designated special "giving" days, remembering your organization in their wills, gifting steady annual sums, or providing grants is a fundamental element to which all nonprofits adhere. Even if singular fundraising events requiring tickets or purchases are held as well, they are usually tied in to this idea by sponsorships and additional giving options related to the events. In this section, I will explore how the notion of donor-centered fundraising is more effective than traditional fundraising. It may take more time and effort, but it can be worth it for the results.

You might be thinking, what is the difference? According to Penelope Burk, a fundraising expert with over forty years' experience with nonprofit fundraising:

> Donor-centered fundraising is an integrated and collaborative approach to raising money that inspires donors to remain loyal longer, to make more generous gifts, and to shift their giving from modest to generous sooner. The concept is easy to understand. It focuses on the things that make fundraising more profitable and it comes from the donors themselves.[1]

Traditional donorship responses from organizations to donors are more impersonal, and there can be a rather high percentage of those giving money once and then discontinuing their gifts in the future. In comparison, donor-centered fundraising responses set the groundwork for encouraging enduring gifts. That is because, according to Burk, all donors want essentially the same three things that donor centered fundraising provides. This is true whether donors are renewing their dues, sending in a monetary gift, awarding a major grant, or any other kind of contributing:

- Timely, meaningful, and sincere acknowledgment whenever a gift is given.
- Affirmation that any gift, large or small, will be targeted for a particular program, event, project, or initiative that plays an essential role in meeting the library support group's mission as a whole.

- Feedback via messages or reports that provide measurable results of how the money was positively used to enhance the beneficiary library before the donor receives requests for further contributions.[2]

You can accomplish these three things by taking a few important steps. The most crucial is to ensure that your donor gift acknowledgment correspondence is a regular priority of your organization. Coming up next, to that end, I have added useful recommendations on how to accomplish this undertaking.

Donor-Centric Thank-You Letters Fashioned with Care

Frequently, to save time and money, nonprofits resort to sending out mass thank-you letters to donors who have given financial support. This encompasses the valuable contributions of new donors, regular donors, and donors contributing both large and modest amounts. In essence, mass mailings to all contributors are a self-defeating method of sending acknowledgments and appreciations. This is because donors want to feel like they are more than just numbers in your system or that the contributions they have made have been pre-judged. When your library support organization sends out these kinds of thank-you letters, it can present a less-than-caring impression, so you want to make sure your donors receive that all-important personal touch in your messages.

With those thoughts in mind, here are some recommendations for thanking donors to convey that you really mean what you say in you expression of thanks:

- Take the time to go to the library that your group is assisting and observe the results of donor gifts firsthand. Take notes about what you see and hear from appreciative library staff and customers. Include to-the-point observations and testimonials in your thank-you letters as they effectively fit.
- Be sure to send letters that appear to have been created singly for each donor by personally addressing each person in the letter heading using donors' full names and addresses. It tells donors that you are both conscious of their gifts as well as of them, the individuals who made the contributions. You can accomplish this by merging your donor file with your letters.
- Go one step further by eliminating "Dear Donor," "Dear Supporter," or "Dear Friend" salutations and using the donors' actual names instead. Choose the most considerate ways to address your particular donors, whether by first names or by using courtesy titles with last names following. In very special circumstances, you may wish to send a personal note in handwriting.
- Make your letters concise and of one or two short paragraphs. The main purposes of your letters are to clearly let donors know that you received their gifts and that the gifts are appreciated. Later on, you can report to donors about qualitative and quantitative results once their gifts have actually been used to achieve them. At the same time, avoid using your thank-you letters as a sales pitch for future donations.
- Focus on the persons who have given the donations rather than the money they have given. Instead of giving the amounts of the donations sent as statements (which should already be solved for donors by IRS statements), explain in what ways the generous gifts "will make it possible" for your organization to fulfill its mission in supporting the library. If your records show that someone has been an

ongoing giver through the years, you will want to succinctly mention appreciation for their loyalty to the cause.

- Start your letter with a sincere and original opening line. Instead of "thank you for your gift," perhaps say, "Our accomplishments in helping [name] Library begins with you." Another choice might be, "You are an important part of our success story in providing essential aid for [name] Library." Make brief reference(s) to the intended use of the funds without detailing plans.
- Write and mail your thank-you letters in a very timely fashion. Prompt acknowledgments of monetary donations can be directly related to donors' decisions to continue their support in the future. Whether one person or more is in charge of completing this task, have reminders on calendars or via messages to meet an objective of getting thank-you letters into the hands of donors within a two-week timespan from donation receipt. If, for some unfortunate and unexpected reason, you or other letter writers are delayed, refrain from including apologies in your letters, as that transmits a perception of guilt on your part. Instead, keep on topic and stay to the point.
- Use good quality paper that reflects your gratitude. Carefully check spelling, grammar, and message content to prevent errors or confusion. If someone is available and there is time, ask for critiques of your letters before sending.
- Compose new letters for each giving cycle and refrain from reusing the wording of previous letters. Each letter should be fresh and distinctive.
- Be sure to set up a quality electronic donor relationship database and use it to keep tabs on contributions and letters that have been sent.[3] It will be a very worthwhile investment.

Because donor acknowledgment and appreciation is so crucial, it would behoove your board of directors, your board secretary, a library support group coordinator, a specially designated volunteer, or perhaps even a library staff liaison to be in charge of getting these messages thoughtfully written and sent out on time or directing others who are taking on the task. Bear in mind that this task is just one facet of donor relationship management, an essential component of any nonprofit that wishes to retain its steady contributors and reach out to new ones.

Whether one or more people take on the duties of donation relationship management, your board can incorporate whatever responsibilities are associated with it as part of your annual strategic plans and evaluations to make sure your communications and donor outreach efforts are as effective as they can be.

Donor Relationship Management

Donor relationship management is an ongoing process of attentively and positively nurturing relationships with fresh donors while showing sincere appreciation for current and continuing donors to foster donor retention and engagement. Through this process, clear goals and action plans emerge to provide definitive direction for how contacts and interactions will accomplish desired funding results.[4]

If yours is a large library support organization, you would most likely want to procure a donor manager who would have a few other individuals appointed to supplement the duties needed for donor-related needs. For a medium or small organization, you may choose to have one person in charge of managing donors with assistance from others as required. In either case, a person serving as a donor manager would need to organize donor information, track interactions, take charge of strategic planning, ensure that thanks are expressed readily, and maintain relationships between donors and your organization.[5]

Electronic Giving: The Value of Online Donation Pages and Text Donations

Some of the most effective tools for nonprofits to acquire donations are through donation pages on organizational websites and through texting-to-give options. Back in chapter 6, when I discussed websites and how to make them accessible to users and beneficial for fundraising, I included examples and information about online options to promote and receive donations. You may wish to revisit that chapter as I add further recommendations here about making optimal use of virtual giving.

To begin with, you will want to make it easy for donors to support the work of your library support group by having a secure and current donation page on your website that reflects your purpose and financial needs. As indicated in chapter 6, the page should be as simple, straightforward, and understandable as possible. The following are best practices for boosting results from a website donation page:

- Make sure the donation page is easy to locate on your organizational website. Be sure the page is attractive and is customized using your group's logo, colors, and any other identifiable elements.
- If you decide to have a "membership" incentive for donating, there are benefits to doing this for your group and for the donors. It provides a predictable revenue base and helps to develop a loyal supporter base for your organization as you provide perks for those who become members. Decide what members will receive, such as exclusive access to newsletters, members-only events such as author-visit previews, gala discounts, or special invitations to affairs that make them feel connected to your mission.
- Include a recurring or sustaining giving option to make monthly or annual giving effortless and offer a pre-selected range of giving amounts. You may wish to add appreciative titles to the "levels" of giving that donors select as indicated in chapter 6. Or you may allow donors to choose the targeted areas or projects toward which their money will go.
- Include social media sharing options on the page so that donors who support your cause can spread the word to others whom they know may also want to contribute.
- Be sure to test your page on mobile devices as well as on computers. Mobile-responsive designs can help nonprofits increase donations tremendously, but they can only be useful if they work effectively.
- Decide if you want to add a convenient text-giving option which allows people to make a donation to your cause, if they wish to do so, by sending text message donation invitations to their mobile phones. However, you will want to use text-to-give campaigns sparingly and selectively to avoid overwhelming your donors. To set up a text-giving option, there are many services that can help your organization to add it. If you do an online search, using "text to give platforms for nonprofits," it will connect you to a number of services that might work for your group.

- Consider a direct mail campaign to solicit donors in addition to your virtual options. Promote donors' ability to access virtual options within the mailings so that they know they can choose the most appropriate way to personally give, whether by returning a card or paper form or heading to a computer or phone to donate electronically.
- As always, be sure to thank virtual donors in a timely manner, carefully keep track of all virtual donors and their giving, and remember to continually express appreciation for sustaining donors who give automatically as they may easily be overlooked.[6]

TEXTBOX 10.1

RESOURCES FOR DONOR MANAGEMENT ASSISTANCE

In addition to the second edition of Penelope Burk's book, *Donor Centered Fundraising*, the resources in this textbox can be useful if you wish to pursue the concepts and procedures of donor management more fully. They include first-rate advice and links that can be helpful, no matter the number and variety of donors you may have and the magnitude and scope of your organization.

Donor Management from Bloomerang + Kindful

This extremely informative, free-to access webpage is from two merged businesses that specialize in fundraising assistance and donor management software. They aim to help nonprofits thrive, a mission that is reflected on this helpful page. Besides plenty of written guidance, a free planning template and an ebook are offered, plus links to two webinars and two videos that can help direct your donor management efforts successfully.[1]

Hiring Directors of Donor Relations from LinkedIn Talent Solutions

If you are seeking a volunteer, appointing a board member, or hiring someone, and whether yours is a small, medium, or large library support organization, you can use the information given at this site to justify having a person assigned as a donor relations manager. You can also use it to decide upon required and preferred skills and abilities; use the template provided to adapt and craft a job description; and use the suggestions given to design the right set of interview questions for your group's particular needs.[2]

The Ultimate Guide to Donor Management for Nonprofits from Keela

Keela is a Canadian business that focuses on accessible, inclusive, and supportive fundraising and donor communications tools to aid nonprofits of all sizes and types. Their guide gives details on the subject matters that nonprofits need to understand to effectively manage donors. It has links to related articles and webinars that expand information on targeted topics.[3]

Notes

1. Bloomerang + Kindful. [n.d.] "Donor Management," https://kindful.com/nonprofit-glossary/donor-management/#:~:text=with%20your%20donors-,What%20is%20donor%20management%3F,should%20be%20a%20central%20focus.

2. LinkedIn. 2023. "Hiring Directors of Donor Relations." LinkedIn Talent Solutions, https://business.linkedin.com/talent-solutions/resources/how-to-hire-guides/director-of-donor-relations.

3. Keela. May 9, 2021. "The Ultimate Guide to Donor Management for Nonprofits," https://www.keela.co/blog/nonprofit-resources/ultimate-guide-to-donor-management.

Capital Funds Campaigns

Capital campaigns are comprehensive endeavors by library Friends, foundations, or trusts to raise enough money through donations to meet specially targeted, essential financial goals to benefit the libraries which they serve. These campaigns could be for any number of major needs not provided in libraries' budgets, such as new equipment for computer labs; a new bookmobile; revitalizing an old library or providing needed items for a newly constructed one; renovations of children's rooms and storytime areas; new seating areas and landscaping outside library buildings; or whatever highly desired large projects are on libraries' immediate wish lists or annual ongoing needs for materials and supplies outside of regular budget coverage. These could also be additions that are proposed by the support groups which libraries welcome as assets for their collections, services, and facilities, such as sculptures for a library outside seating area and garden.

These campaigns aim to fulfill particular objectives, and they have limited, designated timeframes for completion beyond the regular donation and fundraising efforts planned for extended periods. Often, they include seeking grants in addition to other types of fundraising. In many cases, campaigns run from about six to twelve months, but they can be shorter or longer depending on library needs and group variables.

When library needs require it and donors are receptive, some short-term campaigns are repeated annually, such as the Love Your Library campaign that is run every year by the Huntsville-Madison County Library Foundation in Alabama. In 2023, on the library's website space that gives information about events and fundraising for their Foundation, they stated:

> The Library Foundation exceeded its fundraising goal in this year's Love Your Library campaign by raising $16,527 during the month of February. These proceeds will be used to support Madison County children and families through the purchase of children's books and resources and to provide critical programs that help prepare children for school. Because libraries have always served children years before they start in a formal school setting, the Huntsville-Madison County Public Library staff naturally fosters early literacy and social skill development.
>
> Thank you to our generous donors for supporting this year's Love Your Library campaign! Your donations are providing quality educational experiences for our youngest library patrons.[7]

In like fashion, another popular one-day opportunity for receiving donations is Library Giving Day. This designated fundraising day began as an idea generated by the Seattle Public Library Foundation. The intention was to hold a national day of giving targeting public libraries that the public would readily support. From its successful roots in Seattle, Library Giving Day has evolved into a national event during National Library Week in April, and it has also left its legacy of a Library Giving Day website that offers campaign tools that any library support group can access. At the website, fundraisers are encouraged to share their post-event Library Giving Day success stories, which can potentially inspire new partakers in the project.[8]

As many library support groups around the country participate in Library Giving Day, they promote the occasion with special events and activities; they provide online and other opportunities for giving; they make sure to tell donors where their money goes; and they extend sincere thanks. Here are some tips for how it is most effectively done:

- Devise a marketing approach comprised of consistent messaging paired with a seamless donor experience facilitated by a strong campaign page and publicity materials. Figure out a fundraising goal and use the Library Giving Day toolkit to plan.
- Spotlight the range of services your beneficiary library offers for the community and those that your library support group helps to provide so that people realize there is so much more available to them than lending books. This shows potential donors the place where their dollars are going and how they can make a difference for it.
- Be sure to employ your organizational branding in all campaign materials to provide a sense of legitimacy to the effort. This includes all campaign emails and social media posts; your website fundraising page; and printed campaign materials.
- Prepare your board and other members to be on the same page as they endorse the campaign. Develop a Library Giving Day promotional pitch and help your organizational team to know it and encourage them to share it. Ask everyone who is part of the group to spread the word, which is one of the most effective ways to advance a campaign.
- Consider including a goal thermometer on your website. You can visually measure and display progress toward a specific fundraising goal with the gauge, accompanied by a written passage about why the money raised through the campaign is essential. For those accessing the image and information, this would enhance the sense of urgency about supplying the needed costs for the project within the designated timeframe.
- Extend heartfelt thanks online and in written communications as fits your particular campaign and organization.[9]

By the way, another helpful method of extending the success of giving day drives is to locate donors who promise to provide matching funds. Funding matches are usually very productive avenues to encouraging positive community responses to donation drives. After all, with matches, every dollar given is essentially doubled. To illustrate, in 2023, the Madison Public Library Foundation received a thirty-thousand-dollar match from a dedicated group of donors. The Foundation used an announcement of this match in its publicity for the campaign to motivate additional givers. In this way, they helped to secure the necessary funds beyond public dollars alone to aid the library in developing new, inventive programs and resources to benefit the community with creative outlets and increased ways for connection.[10]

Unlike the short annual Love Your Library campaign targeting children's school readiness and the Library Giving Day campaign for programs and resources, larger campaigns that are designed to raise even more significant funds for things like new library wings or bookmobiles require longer completion times and extra intensive efforts. In those cases, sometimes larger nonprofits even hire consultants to manage them. For smaller-scale library support groups, the work these efforts entail is usually left to the board and membership. If boards have qualified members who are willing and able to take leading roles in seeing campaigns through, that is a plus. Otherwise, you may have members who are enthusiastic to learn how to plan a capital campaign and make it a success. The information given in this chapter aims to help.

Before moving on to planning guidelines, I would like to consider some further reasons that capital campaigns make sense for your library support group besides aiding your beneficiary library:

- If you already have a consistent supporter base, asking them to join in and support your campaign mission with details about why it is significant will renew their enthusiasm for helping the library.
- Running a capital campaign increases the likelihood that new major donors will buy in to your cause, perhaps to even provide matching funds.
- Capital campaigns can inspire already established donors to give again.
- A campaign can engage local media and provide publicity which builds your library support organization's public profile and may garner new members.

Now that you know some worthwhile rationales for creating capital campaigns, and once you or other persons in charge have the go-ahead to put a plan into action, it is time to begin preparing. What follows here is a step-by-step outline for designing a successful capital campaign and seeing it through:

- Decide who will lead the campaign and help to devise a strategic plan to see it through. It can be a board member, an appointed team, a committee working together, or even a hired consultant.
- When you are proposing projects to benefit the library, you will want to ensure interest, get approval, and seek counsel from them. If they are the ones instigating campaigns to fund any major projects by asking for your monetary aid, your organization will need to decide if it is able to handle the request. In either event, they may want to appoint administrators or staff members to serve as liaisons for the projects who can offer valuable perspectives for timelines and logistics. You will want to confer with them early on regarding what input and feedback is required from both parties and to regularly keep each other in the loop.
- Once the party or parties responsible for the campaigns convene, objectives must be written; the amount needed must be calculated; a budget must be made; and a timeline for fundraising completion must be set.
- Necessary resources need to be determined such as assuring that your donor database is updated and organized, deciding what kinds of physical advertising and acknowledgment materials are needed, and settling on any other particular items that must be addressed.
- Once the basic blueprint for a campaign is decided, specific duties can be assigned to committee members, team members, or volunteers with target dates for completion and necessary resources then determined.
- On your timelines, you will need to import pertinent dates to kickoff your campaigns. Make sure publicity from all angles is planned and addressed by the allotted deadlines, including "donate here" buttons or tabs on your website and social media pages; plans for direct mail appeals; arrangements to email your supporter base; and plans for contacting local public media.
- Reach out to stakeholders, supporters, and previous donors to spark your campaign roll-outs. Nonprofit experts say that up to 75 percent of ultimate goals may be reached at the onset of campaigns through these initial contacts, although it depends on the size and scale of an organization and library, the action plans for the projects being funded, and the scope of campaign financial goals.

- Regularly schedule check-in meetings for those involved and make adjustments to your strategy and tactics as needed.
- Evaluate all aspects of your campaign at its conclusion, especially whether or not you reached your financial goal. Meet with those involved in creating and running the campaign and ask some important questions: Are we able to complete the designated project with the money we have raised? What can we do in the future to ensure our fundraising efforts are successful? What might we choose to repeat next time, do differently, or eliminate?
- As a final point, as always, make thanking every single donor for supporting your campaign a priority as contributions are received and keep donors updated later on project results.[11]

Crowdsourcing for Donations

Another avenue that library support groups may quickly and efficiently use to raise funds is through crowdsourcing. Using crowdsourcing—a method of fundraising that employs social media and networking to explain a need, seek donations, and provide a means for giving donations—could be done on its own or in conjunction with a fundraising campaign.

There are many crowdsourcing platforms, and, if you explore them online, you will discover that some are probably better fits for your organization than others. However, I would like to point out two in particular that are beneficial for library support groups.

Fund Libraries has a crowdsourcing website that permits library Friends, foundations, trusts, any combination of those, and even individual library boosters to build a campaign and solicit donations from supporters. Public and school library support groups, libraries themselves, Little Free Library stewards, special libraries, and even overseas libraries can all use the site to raise money.

The service utilizes the "power of the crowd" to support your fundraising campaign by advertising your project to a national audience of nearly half a million library lovers on Facebook. You can, at the same time, promote your cause and lead potential donors to your Fund Libraries listing through your own publicity.[12]

The same is true in many ways for another crowdfunding platform, DonorsChoose, which appeals to individuals wishing to make a direct impact with their donations to individual teachers seeking much-needed classroom resources. If you support the students and media specialist or teacher/librarian at a school in your community as a Friends or other library support organization (see chapter 2), you might want to add this option to your fundraising repertoire. It has a very successful track record in raising funds for schools and it experienced its most prolific year yet in 2023 by reaching ten million dollars overall in donations during Teacher Appreciation Week in May. It even brought in a two-million-dollar donor-matching contribution from the Bill and Melinda Gates Foundation in August.[13]

If these two supplementary fundraising options or other crowdsourcing choices are of interest to your group and library, it may prove worthwhile to explore them further. There are several YouTube videos online that can be of help. To access them, do a search at YouTube under the keywords "nonprofit crowdfunding."[14]

TEXTBOX 10.2

HELPFUL RESOURCES TO PLAN AND RUN CAPITAL CAMPAIGNS

For more in-depth details about capital campaigns, the following guides can be of assistance:

Capital Campaigns 101: The Ultimate Guide for Beginners[1]

Capital Campaign Pro is a support system for nonprofit leaders and their teams. Their women-owned business offers expert consulting, as well as a free online research library to aid nonprofit organizations in planning and completing successful fundraising campaigns. In this "ultimate guide," you will find step-by-step details on all aspects of campaigns, and you will be able to link into further information from the "Capital Campaign Knowledge Directory." One of the owners, Andrea Kihlstedt, also has a book you might find useful called *Capital Campaigns: Strategies That Work*, now in a fourth edition (see bibliography).

Capital Campaigns: A Crash Course for Your Nonprofit Team[2]

The information given in this resource gives a plethora of advice for nonprofit organizations large, medium, and small to devise strategic plans for fundraising campaigns by using SMART (specific/measurable/attainable/relevant/time-bound) goals, building a capital campaign team, and much more.

Capital Campaigns: The Ultimate Guide to Capital Fundraising Campaigns[3]

This resource pinpoints specific information you need to know to develop a fruitful fundraising campaign with your board, volunteers, and perhaps even an outside consultant. It explains exactly what is needed to do a campaign right by providing details and plenty of links on everything from best practices to evaluations.

YouTube[4]

The old standby, YouTube, provides useful video resources, this time ones that explore and examine capital campaigns. You will find an array of helpful recent videos by doing a search at the YouTube website using the keywords "nonprofit capital campaign." There are videos covering feasibility studies, phases of campaigns, the roles of board members in fundraising campaigns, and many additional applicable topics.

Notes

1. Andrea Kihlstedt. 2023. "Capital Campaigns 101," https://capitalcampaignpro.com/capital-campaigns-ultimate-guide/.
2. Donorly. December 2, 2021. "Capital Campaigns: A Crash Course for Your Nonprofit Team," https://donorly.com/thedonorlyblog/capital-campaign-guide.
3. Kristine Ensor. August 4, 2023. "Capital Campaigns: The Ultimate Guide to Capital Fundraising Campaigns." Donorbox Blog, https://donorbox.org/nonprofit-blog/capital-campaign.
4. YouTube. 2023. "Nonprofit Capital Campaign," https://www.youtube.com/results?search_query=nonprofit+capital+campaign+.

Setting Up Donation Web Pages

Whether you are setting up a donation page on your website for ongoing donations, for a special giving day, for a capital campaign, or for crowdfunding, there are, as already pointed out, many options from which to choose. You may want to refer to chapter 6 that covers designing websites and social media pages to refresh your memory about adding donation pages or buttons. As recommended in that chapter, you would want to consult with the person(s) who are creating or have created your library support group website to figure out where and how to insert your online donation tab onto it. How do you want it to appear? Maybe you would like it on a separate page just for donations, or as a button on the main page? Perhaps you want it placed in several locations so that potential donors will not miss it.

Be certain to research, discuss, and plan what donation payment platform you want to use (again, see chapter 6) and how it will reside on your website and on social media sites. You may want to revisit YouTube as a resource since they offer an abundance of current videos about donation platforms and setting up donation pages. Simply do a search using the keywords "how to create donation page."[15]

Also remember to provide alternative formats for giving. That means you will want to have online printable forms, as well as printed paper forms, available for donors who are uncomfortable using computers for monetary transactions and want to send a mailed-in or dropped-off check. Always make sure that all potential donation methods are squared away and at the ready so you can welcome and accommodate everyone who wishes to contribute.

Revisiting a suggestion from the capital campaigns section, you may find it beneficial to add a donation gauge or a giving thermometer for your annual donation goals. Remember that a fundraising thermometer helps to motivate fundraisers; track fundraising goals; and encourage supporters. You might also want to add a cardboard display version in a strategic location—perhaps in the library you serve—or use one printed on informational flyers and newsletters.[16]

Including Library Support Groups in Estate Planning and Endowments

Another avenue for raising money is to encourage people to consider your nonprofit for estate planning and endowments. All library support nonprofits can reach out to the most loyal donors along with people who may not realize that there is such a choice by tactfully promoting options to leave legacy gifts. Legacy gifts permit donors to make enduring organizational mission impacts for your group by arranging for major gifts to be imparted to your group after they have passed away. Gifts like these can be an elemental source of funding while generating a meaningful path toward personal fulfillment for those who make such caring contributions. At the same time, surviving family members and others may receive benefits of considerable estate tax breaks.[17]

Many library support organizations do promote legacy opportunities on their websites and in printed group publicity, but others have not yet taken advantage of addressing this positive way to eventually secure funding even if it does usually take time to receive it. Still other groups have promoted it to a certain extent, but perhaps not as widely as they might have been doing. It is worth taking the time to create an informational page online for donors who want to take advantage of these alternative giving choices and to include the options in printed materials.

In this section, I will discuss how legacy gifts can be publicized and give some examples of library support groups that are effectively letting their communities know about these consequential and highly appreciated choices to provide aid for their beloved libraries.

Kinds of Legacy Gifts

There are several ways that donors can employ planned giving to help the library support groups that serve the libraries they use and value. Organizational leaders should check with their legal advisors about these options and others that might be appropriate as well as how to proceed. With guidance, library support organizations can determine what gifts of these kinds they wish and are able to accept. Meanwhile, what follows here are the most common choices for legacy or planned giving:

- Bequests: These are the most popular and basic kinds of legacy giving. For these gifts, donors name whatever they wish to leave to a library support organization. This could be a certain amount of money, stocks, valuable art works, a percentage of their estate, or a combination of these.
- Life insurance: If a donor has such a policy, they are able to specify a nonprofit cause as one of their beneficiaries upon their passing or, if they choose to discontinue the policy, they might choose to donate its accumulated value.
- Individual Retirement Accounts: When a donor sets up a tax-deferred retirement plan, they may decide to name an organization as a beneficiary or as a recipient of a percentage of the proceeds.
- Charitable gift annuities: In the case of very large library Friends, foundations, or trusts, charitable annuities may be an option that can be set up for donors. This works by having the donors make large contributions during their lifetimes and in turn the library support nonprofit makes a fixed income available for the rest of donors' lives. When the donors pass away, the remaining funds are left to the organization.
- Retained life estates: There are other non-monetary alternatives for legacy giving. Donors might choose to give library support groups some property they own while retaining the right to make use of it during their lifetimes until they pass away. At that time, organizations can keep the properties, sell them, or perhaps, if circumstances are warranted, even donate them to the libraries they sustain for new building projects.[18]

As an example of how a library support organization might reach out to donors, the Friends of the San Francisco Public Library have a legacy giving program through their Mary Louise Strong Society, named after the dedicated co-founder of the Friends in 1961. Through it, donors can include the Friends in their estate planning and they become members in the Society. They provide full information on what kinds of gifts are welcome, including what is bequeathed through wills and trusts in the forms of cash, real estate, publicly traded securities, personal property, retirement funds, life insurance, and even books. They have a small chart showing how a donor might want to set this up and contact information for inquiries.[19]

TEXTBOX 10.3

USEFUL RESOURCES FOR UNDERSTANDING AND PROMOTING PLANNED GIVING

The following online resources will provide you with valuable information as you discuss how your library support group might put a planned giving program into effect.

A Complete Guide to Planned Gifts for Nonprofits

After explaining what planned giving is and why it matters, DonorSearch thoroughly describes the different types of giving; explains the tax breaks for donors; tells how to launch a planned giving program, which includes branding it and creating marketing materials; and gives advice on effectively communicating with donors about such gifts, especially acknowledging them.[1]

How Your Nonprofit Can Start a Legacy Giving Program

In this free webinar for nonprofits of all sizes and kinds, which was recorded and made available on YouTube, you will get an overview of what legacy (or planned) giving is and what it is not. It is especially pertinent for board members and other library support group leaders of small to midsized nonprofits ready to explore this option for raising money and to delve into it.[2]

How to Launch a Planned Giving Program: 21 Steps and Resources

This page is about starting and building a sustainable planned giving program, though it goes far beyond simply defining the kinds of giving and describing the steps to creating a program. There are ample links, tools, and downloadables you can access for additional information and assistance as you are researching and putting your particular planned giving program into action. The plentiful information on this page is free, but there are some linked resources that nonprofits can subscribe to for a cost if they wish to dig deeper.[3]

Planned Giving: A Complete Guide to Legacy Giving Programs

This guide from Freewill, which offers self-help solutions for common estate planning needs and related educational content for nonprofits, explains what planned giving is; the impact planned giving can make for nonprofit organizations; how donors can benefit from choosing planned giving; the types of planned giving; strategic planning to put the option into place; and setting up a legacy society. It also provides a library of further resources on pertinent topics.[4]

Notes

1. DonorSearch. 2023. "A Complete Guide to Planned Giving for Nonprofits," https://www.donorsearch.net/planned-gifts-complete-guide/.
2. National Council of Nonprofits. April 21, 2021. Webinar. "How Your Nonprofit Can Start a Legacy Giving Program." YouTube, https://www.youtube.com/watch?v=_3k7RXQXlR4.
3. PlannedGiving.Com. 2023. "How to Launch a Planned Giving Program: 21 Steps and Resources," https://www.plannedgiving.com/resources/how-to-launch-a-planned-giving-program/.
4. Freewill. December 9, 2022. "Planned Giving: A Complete Guide to Legacy Programs," https://resources.freewill.com/planned-giving-guide.

As another example, the New Rochelle Public Library Foundation in New York has a legacy giving page that describes the kinds of bequests library devotees can put in their will. These are specific bequests of a set amount; residuary bequests, which are the remainder of an estate once everything is settled; and contingent bequests, which name the Foundation if named beneficiaries pass away before the donor does. Another option can be to leave part of an IRA or pension fund to the Foundation. They also mention how such financial resources are used to keep the library strong and offer a question and answer section along with a form that can be used to contact the Foundation for more information. Finally, they provide the wording that donors may choose to include in their wills along with a notation that gifts to the Foundation are not subject to estate tax. I have altered the format so that you could adapt the wording to your organization:

> I hereby bequeath to the [name of library support group], a 501©3 charitable entity located at [address of library support group] [Federal Tax ID#(add number)] the sum of [add dollar amount] or, as an alternative [the percentage of residuary estate].[20]

Endowment Gifts

Contrary to some beliefs, you may be surprised to learn that nonprofit library support group endowment gifts can be uncomplicated. To begin, I want to define endowments in relation to library support needs. An *endowment* is a dedicated source of long-term funding comprised of voluntary donated gifts that provide financial backing for the work that fulfills the mission of a philanthropic library organization. Once established, each year an endowment is paid out as an annual distribution to fund facets of the general work of the library support group to aid its beneficiary library. Any appreciation in excess of this annual distribution is retained in the endowment so that the money can grow and continue to provide funding.

At times, smaller endowment fund amounts may be given that are earmarked for such reasons as library staff educational training opportunities; special ongoing library programs or events; and various kinds of scholarships. When your library support organization is reaching out to the community to consider planned giving for financial assistance to the library, you may want to encourage endowments as an alternative option for certain people who still want to make a difference with their wealth.

In your invitation to take part, use your mission and vision statements and relevant data, along with details about how an endowment could be used and appreciated by your organization as it supports the library. You might suggest targeted needs that endowments would address such as yearly book festivals or scholarships for high school students who have been exemplary library volunteers and offer to name the endowments in honor of the donors.[21]

If your library support group chooses to go the path of incorporating endowments into its options for planned giving, there are several types of endowments. Seek the expertise of your legal and/or financial advisor about the best way to set up endowments for your particular organization. You may also want to explore some of the video resources on YouTube in which experts cover pertinent information about endowment topics. Also, you might want to explore some of the library support group web pages that promote planned giving and endowments. Here are a few helpful examples:

- The Lake Forest Library Foundation in Illinois has an easy-to-navigate page called "Ways to Give." Each way is clearly described with details on how to proceed. They include endowments; named funds in memory or honor of someone; planned giving; general donations; and book donations through the Friends of the Library group. Links lead donors to a page with the Foundation's investment policy and to the Lake Forest Library gift acceptance policy to which the Foundation adheres.[22]
- The Library Endowment Trust, which was established in 1986 by the Friends of the Metropolitan Library System in Oklahoma, exists as a channel for donors to give for library needs now and in the future. Funds are also raised annually by hosting a major fundraising dinner, Literary Voices. On their website, they explain several ways that the Trust funds library programs, materials, and scholarships for library staff, and that donors may give via cash, check, or credit card. They also state that corporate sponsorships and planned estate gifts are welcome. A giving gauge is posted on their webpage so donors can see the community impact of donorship and the profits from the Literary Voices event.[23]
- At the Cary Memorial Library Foundation in Lexington, Massachusetts, they have a page that covers "ways to give" that briefly explains what endowments are. Each method of giving has a link of its own so that interested parties can click the ones they want to know more about. Endowment gifts are one of the choices, and they explain that donors can establish a Named Endowment Fund, either for unrestricted or designated purposes, with a gift of five thousand dollars or more. In addition, donors may choose to add further contributions of any amount to an existing endowment fund by sending a check with the name of the fund. Contact information is included for the executive director.[24]

As you can see from the featured endowment examples, there are many ways to approach the promotion of endowments. If your organization wants to consider adding endowment choices for donors, or if you already offer them and your publicity needs some sprucing up, these illustrations might help.

Fundraising from the Sidelines

There are other ways to build your library support group coffers besides out-and-out donor solicitations. I will cover two of them in the next few sections of this book. One is to sign up for and take advantage of neighborhood grocery store programs through which portions of their sales are donated to various worthy nonprofit causes. The other is to tie in to and benefit from potential volunteer fundraising efforts of local youth who participate in organized groups and clubs at their schools and public libraries.

Local Groceries Donating Sales Percentages

Another way that library support organizations can gain donations is by offering grocery store sale percentage options when they are available. These are uncomplicated means to raise money when you get a grocery to include your group among their giving designations and continuously advertise it. Once people sign on to have the donations given to your cause, the grocery automatically contributes their percentage to you on a regular basis. Here are some examples of stores that offer these donation programs:

Kroger Community Rewards

As they announce on their website, the Kroger Family of Companies has made a commitment to participating in community engagement, fostering positive social impact, and providing charitable giving at both the local and national levels. There are a variety of stores with different names in this "family," and there may be one near you. To meet these goals, which transfer to their grocery establishments across the board, they offer their Kroger Community Awards program. Through it, customers who have digital accounts can enroll, select their preferences from the list of nonprofits that have joined the program, link their accounts to whatever organization they choose, and have the money automatically contributed annually to their targeted cause. Complete instructions for both organizations enrolling and customers signing up are on their website.[25]

You will want to be sure to include promotional notices on your organization's website, in social media, and any other spot that's appropriate. For example, at the Friends of Johnson County Public Library, part of the Johnson County Public Library Foundation, prominently feature a picture of the Kroger shopper's card along with this message:

> Link your Kroger Plus card to the Friends of the JCPL in Kroger Community Rewards in your Plus card account. The rewards translate to CASH to support the Friends. You'll still receive your Kroger discounts and points. When linking your card, type "Friends of the Johnson County Public Library CY705" in the search box. If you do not have a Kroger Plus card, they are available at the service desk in-store.[26]

Walmart Spark Good

Walmart has a simple process to donate money to library support groups through its Spark Good program. Spark Good is a digital giving platform that allows customers to donate to nonprofits they care about and for nonprofits to register to access their philanthropic resources. Once a charity is enrolled and customers sign up, they can donate by rounding up their purchases or donate items from the charity's registry and have the items shipped directly to the charity. Thorough information and instructions on participating for both nonprofits and customers is provided on the Spark Good page of the Walmart website.[27]

The Charlotte Mecklenburg Library Foundation in North Carolina has the Spark Good option included on its donation choices page under a section called "Maximize Your Philanthropy." They say, "Support your Library every time you shop. Donate spare change by automatically rounding up your orders to the nearest dollar at checkout when you enroll in Walmart Spark Good." Further, a box is added to click and take potential donors to the page where they can sign up to participate and to select the Foundation as their donation recipient.[28]

Check with your local grocery retailers to see if they may also be promoting programs to support library fundraising efforts. Depending on where your library is located, you might find a way to get community funding dollars from such grocery businesses as Publix (for schools),[29] Shop Smart Foods[30] stores (with varying names), Kennie's Marketplace,[31] or other local grocer establishments.

Teen Service Groups Raising Money to Donate

If teen service organizations or clubs know that your library support group needs a financial boost, they may be enthusiastic about taking on a fundraiser to help the cause. As a matter of fact, I remember that a few years ago at the last library where I worked, a high school service club was looking for a place to support in the community. They decided upon the public library and held a penny drive. The drive managed to raise two thousand dollars, which they donated to help fund teen library programs. If more schools in communities were informed about funding needs for their school and public libraries, the students might be available to do similar profitable activities to help raise money for library programs, materials, and services. As an objective, library support groups could aim for reaching out to school clubs or organizations like Scouting and enlist youth for fundraising projects and activities.

As you have seen in earlier chapters, youth of all ages can participate in efforts to raise money for their library support groups through Junior Friends of the Library organizations. If your library lacks having Junior Friends but has a teen advisory board or leadership council, you may wish to see if they may be interested in participating in fundraising for the library support group causes, as well.

One example of this comes from the Lied Scottsbluff Public Library in Scottsbluff, Nebraska. The Teen Advisory Council members there hosted an Escape Room fundraiser for three consecutive days in the summer to help support teen events at their library. The escape room had teams of up to six members who paid ten dollars each for adults and five dollars each for children or teen registrants of the summer reading program for the opportunity to try and solve the "Mystery of the Missing Podcaster." Each team had a one-hour timeslot (with arrivals requested ten minutes prior to the allotted times) scheduled at some point between 1:00 and 7:00 p.m. on Thursday or Friday or 10 a.m. and 6:00 p.m. on Saturday during which they could attempt finding a solution to the mystery and beat the escape room. Reservations could be made in advance at or by telephoning the library, and payment was collected when each group arrived for their timeslot.[32]

Escape rooms (or puzzle rooms) are innovative ways to get participants working together in teams to consider clues, solve problems, and employ creativity to discover a solution that will allow them to "escape" the room. They are popular with both adults and youth.

Sure, it might seem evident that library support groups can arrange escape room fundraisers on their own, but teenagers enjoy doing this and can be drawn in and counted upon to not only earn money by admissions—they can devise unique escape rooms of their own making. This is important because, even though there are services available that can be hired to set up an escape room event, there is a cost for them that you might find prohibitive. Having teens design and prepare the program themselves engages them in your fundraising process, gives them a sense of ownership in it, provides them with a feeling of success and commitment, and saves dollars.

As I have mentioned, through my years of working with youth in libraries, I engaged members of our teen advisory group to volunteer with fundraising and library advocacy efforts with our Friends of the Library. The youth truly enjoyed the events they helped with and felt a real sense of belonging and commitment as they participated. Beyond these personal experiences, in researching other middle school and high school-aged library fundraising involvement, I encountered quite a few similar great examples similar in both school and public libraries. I learned about tween and teen fundraisers who designed their own events with adult guidance and supervision that included car washes; Valentine-themed bake sales; holiday gift wrap services; used book sales; and Parents' Morning Out child care services. In addition to raising money, teens have also assisted their libraries' advocacy and promotional efforts by taking part in local parades, speaking out about library issues, and serving as attendants for summer reading challenge programs.[33]

Even if your library support group does not sponsor or partner with an officially organized Junior Friends of the Library, as discussed in chapter 7, you can still engage teens to actively raise funds and donate to your cause as members of a library teen advisory council, board, or group. Contact your local school or youth services librarian, find out if a youth group like this exists, and see if perhaps the members might want to aid your fundraising, volunteering, and advocacy efforts as partners. You could also contact your local schools to see if any of the youth service clubs might want to be of assistance.

As one who has seen firsthand how this really does work and keeps youth involved in their libraries into adulthood, I highly recommend adding this dimension, especially if you have adults in your organization willing and able to interact effectively with this age group and the library staff members who supervise them.

Annual Reports and Other Informational Feedback

As a final point, whether through letters, newsletter updates, or other mediums (or a combination), it is important to give feedback on the programs, events, projects, and initiatives that donors have funded, and volunteers have supported once they are completed. Add photographs, pie charts, or other illustrative details to make the reports come alive for the donors. Name and thank any donors in particular who were instrumental in seeing the activities through by making their financial contributions, and include their logos when available and appropriate. Likewise, highlight volunteer time and service given and express gratitude for those contributions as well.

Design attractive, thorough, and detailed annual reports that can be printed out on paper for distribution in your library, at the Chamber of Commerce, and in other tactical locations. Also, electronically post the reports on your group's website, on the library's website, and on social media. Make certain that all members of your organization receive copies, as well, which promotes continued membership support.

These annual reports need to include your organization's name, address, city, state, phone number, email address, website address, mission statement, and goals. You will also need to add summaries of activities and financial information for each fiscal year that has just ended, plus a list of board members, officers, and any staff members. Explain the reasons that your organization is needed, tell how many members there are, and how many volunteers gave hours to the cause.[34] Use photos, illustrations, quotes, and any other additions that will boost interest.

Remember, that by tooting your group's own horn, you are also accentuating and praising your library and those who have given their money, time, expertise, and other aid to help make it the best it can be. By following these recommendations, most donors and volunteers cannot help but want to start or continue assisting such a worthwhile endeavor as your library support group.

Notes

1. Cygnus Applied Research, Inc. 2020. "What Is Donor-Centered Fundraising?" https://cygresearch.com/donor-centered-philosophy/.
2. Penelope Burk. *Donor Centered Fundraising*. Second edition. Chicago: Cygnus Applied Research, 2018, 12.
3. Burk, pp. 45–62.
4. Bridgespan Group. January 15, 2016. "Donor Relationship Management," https://www.bridgespan.org/insights/donor-relationship-management.
5. Kindful. [n.d.] "Donor Management," https://kindful.com/nonprofit-glossary/donor-management/#:~:text=with%20your%20donors-,What%20is%20donor%20management%3F,should%20be%20a%20central%20focus.
6. Raj. June 2, 2023. "11 Simple Ways to Raise Money for a Nonprofit." Donorbox Blog, https://donorbox.org/nonprofit-blog/ways-to-raise-money-for-nonprofit.
7. Huntsville-Madison County Public Library. 2023. "Love Your Library," https://hmcpl.org/foundation/lyl.
8. Library Giving Day. 2023. "What Is Library Giving Day?" https://librarygivingday.org/.
9. The Engage Blog. March 8, 2023. "How to Make This Your Most Successful Library Giving Day." Blackbaud, https://blog.blackbaud.com/how-to-make-this-your-most-successful-library-giving-day/.
10. Madison Public Library Foundation. 2023. "Support Our Annual Fund," https://mplfoundation.org/give/things-we-fund/annual-appeal/.
11. Bloomerang + Kindful. [n.d.] "Capital Campaign," https://kindful.com/nonprofit-glossary/capital-campaign/#:~:text=A%20capital%20campaign%20is%20a%20multi%2Dfaceted%20effort%20to%20reach,equipment%2C%20or%20a%20relocation%20fund.
12. Fund Libraries. 2023. "Fund Libraries," https://www.fundlibraries.org/.
13. BoardSource. August 21, 2023. "DonorsChoose Breaks Donation Record." BoardSource SmartBrief, https://www.smartbrief.com/servlet/encodeServlet?issueid=FAA82711-6A6E-45E1-AD89-50A4F62039C0&sid=4a527a3f-1847-4460-91a4-d5d28276065c.
14. YouTube. 2023. "Nonprofit Crowdfunding," https://www.youtube.com/results?search_query=nonprofit+crowdfunding.
15. YouTube. 2023. "How to Create Donation Page," https://www.youtube.com/results?search_query=how+to+create+donation+page.
16. Ibrisevic, Ilma. August 3. 2023. "How to Use a Fundraising Thermometer—for Nonprofits." Donorbox, https://donorbox.org/nonprofit-blog/fundraising-thermometer-for-nonprofits.
17. DonorSearch Team. May 22, 2023. "Legacy Gifts: Taking Your Org's Strategy to New Heights." DonorSearch, https://www.donorsearch.net/resources/legacy-gift/.
18. Network for Good. 2023. "What Is Legacy Giving and How to Get Started with It," https://www.networkforgood.com/resource/what-is-legacy-giving/.
19. Friends of the San Francisco Public Library. 2021. "Mary Louise Strong Society," https://www.friendssfpl.org/stong.html.
20. New Rochelle Public Library Foundation. 2023. "How to Create Your Library Legacy," https://nrplfoundation.org/legacy/.
21. Karen Houghton. April 15, 2022. "Endowment Gifts for Nonprofits: Legacies of Giving and Sustainability." Nonprofit Hub, https://nonprofithub.org/endowments-gifts-for-nonprofits-legacies-of-giving-and-sustainability/.
22. Lake Forest Library Foundation. 2022. "Ways to Give," https://lflibraryfoundation.org/support/.
23. Library Endowment Trust. 2022. "Welcome to the Library Endowment Trust." Metropolitan Library System, https://supportmls.org/let/.
24. Cary Memorial Library Foundation. [n.d.] "Endowment Funds," https://www.carylibraryfoundation.org/endowment-gifts.
25. Kroger. 2023. "Kroger Community Rewards," https://www.kroger.com/i/community/community-rewards.
26. Johnson County Public Library Foundation. 2023. "Friends of JCPL," https://www.jcplf.org/friends.
27. Walmart. 2023. "Spark Good," https://www.walmart.com/sparkgood.

28. Charlotte Mecklenburg Library Foundation. 2023. "Ways to Give," https://foundation.cmlibrary.org/ways-to-give/fundraise/.

29. Publix. 2023. https://www.publix.com/.

30. Smart Shop Foods. 2023. https://www.shopsmartfoods.com/custom_retailer/Community/.

31. Kennie's Marketplace. 2023. https://www.kenniesmarket.com/rewards-and-programs/community-rewards/.

32. NBC Nebraska Scottsbluff. June 21, 2023. "Scottsbluff Public Library Set to Host Escape Room Fundraiser," https://www.nbcnebraskascottsbluff.com/2023/06/21/scottsbluff-public-library-set-host-escape-room-fundraiser/.

33. Diane P. Tuccillo. June 1, 2018. "Teens at the Helm: Library Fundraisers." Voice of Youth Advocates, https://www.thefreelibrary.com/Teens+at+the+Helm%3A+Library+Fundraisers.-a0545022854.

34. Friends of Tennessee Libraries. [n.d.] "Annual Reports," https://www.friendstnlibraries.org/wp-content/uploads/Annual-Report-Resources.pdf.

CHAPTER 11

Library Support Groups Making Community Connections

MOST LIBRARIES ARE HUGE PROPONENTS of partnering to engage in community efforts. Because this is so, it stands to reason that library support groups would be on board to back or even instigate those efforts whenever possible. This is done through both assisting with funding as well as with providing volunteers. The breadth of these joint efforts can range from participation in parades to reading and literacy promotional programs to providing scholarships for locals embarking on studies to becoming part of the library world, and on and on. There is no telling how far-reaching community connections can go when a determined library support group and its beneficiary library puts their unified mind to it.

In this chapter, I will be exploring several ways that library support organizations of various kinds have collaborated with their libraries and communities to expand library outreach, promote the library, foster literacy, and get locals involved with their causes. You will find lots of thoughtful examples you can emulate and that can inspire you to develop new and innovative library-community connections of your own.

Donating Books in the Community

One way library support groups can aid the promotion of reading at libraries, schools, and in communities is by donating books for worthy causes that help meet their and the libraries' missions. These activities might include planting and shoring up Little Free Libraries in areas that need them; participating in various book giveaways projects for children; promoting and supporting "one book" programs through schools and libraries; aiding regional disaster victim evacuees; and so on. In this section, I will share details exemplifying these kinds of activities and projects and how library support groups are making a difference through them. Your group may want to consider some of these ideas or think up unique ones that suit your mission for your particular community. We will begin with Little Free Libraries.

Support for and with Little Free Libraries

By now, most people are familiar with Little Free Libraries, the small house-shaped boxes with glass fronts that hold donated books for members of the surrounding community to "put and take" on the honor system to extend the joy of reading beyond the walls of official neighborhood libraries. You might not know that the Little Free Library nonprofit organization and its movement began in 2012, and it has grown to be the catalyst for over 150,000 little libraries in all fifty states and around the world. It has a wonderful website filled with helpful information.[1]

Those community members who wish to start and maintain a Little Free Library are called volunteer "stewards," and there are various ways for stewards to make a new little library official with all the benefits that come with it. A steward can purchase a kit to build a little library and install it on a chosen site, which could be the corner of a steward's own front lawn, or in a spot in a selected park, greenway, church property, school campus, or other location with pre-approval of the site owners or other responsible parties.

Kits can be pricey, over two hundred to more than four hundred dollars, but each comes with an official charter. A steward who personally builds a little library instead of purchasing a prefabricated kit is still expected to purchase a charter for about forty dollars. However, the Little Free Library website provides building blueprints; repurposing and material advice and ideas for construction; and installation instructions for free.[2] Both methods permit stewards to reap the benefits of holding an official charter.

The benefits of holding a charter include creating a steward account that gives the option to add the new library to the official world map of Little Free Library locations via the steward portal or official app; tips for being a steward; a Steward Card; bookmark; access to a private steward Facebook page for sharing ideas; and a helpful e-newsletter. The Little Free Library website offers additional useful tips and aids for stewards.[3]

With all this in mind, how can library support groups connect with and benefit Little Free Libraries in their communities? Here are some ways:

- Grants for indigenous communities. Little Free Libraries provides Indigenous Library Program grants with the guidance of tribal leaders for organizations that work with or serve people on tribal lands and indigenous communities in the United States and Canada, in places where books are needed most to improve literacy. A library support group in or near one of these areas could apply to receive a little library, installation materials, and a starter set of books.[4]
- Grants through the Little Free Library's Impact Library Program. Through this program, grants are given to provide no-cost little libraries in rural communities or urban neighborhoods where books are scarce, the variety and quantity of books is poor, and the need to promote literacy is great. If your library support group is in such a location and has the means to maintain the little library, consider applying for the grant. Grant recipients are expected to fill the library with books for at least a year; hold one or more community activities or events in the first year; submit a photo and story of the impact of the library installation; and respond to communications from Little Free Library and local media as requested.[5]
- Fund and maintain a Little Free Library with library support group proceeds. Decide to participate with your organization and develop a plan to effectively partner and work with your library, schools, and/or other community agencies to build a little library and keep it stocked. Luckily, Friends of the Library groups have access

to donated materials which provides a ready source of books to keep a little library filled and volunteers who can pitch in to help. There are even informational Ask This Old House videos you can access on YouTube. One gives instructions for building an elementary class–designed Little Free Library shaped like a school bus,[6] and another shows how to install a little library, complete with the aid of student helpers, at an elementary school where a library was being placed.[7]

- Take over the maintenance of library-established Little Free Libraries. As an example of a "takeover" by a library support group, in Chico, California, the library instituted twelve Little Free Libraries around Butte County with funding from the Chico Friends of the Library, but library administrators decided that maintaining the little libraries and supporting their liabilities was unsustainable. At that point, the Friends stepped up and took over the entire responsibility, keeping the little libraries stocked and maintained.[8] Any library support group that finds their library in this predicament could consider embracing the task to keep one or more little libraries afloat.
- Take the Read in Color Pledge. To go a step further than supporting a little library in some way, take the Read in Color pledge that Little Free Library offers and promotes. Read in Color encourages the inclusion of diverse books and distributes books that provide perspectives on racism and social justice; celebrates BIPOC, LGBTQ+, and other marginalized voices; and incorporates perspectives from all identities for all readers. Those who take the pledge receive access to bookmarks, stickers, social media badges, and even a Read in Color sign that can be added to a little library door.[9]
- Provide books for free in difficult times. During times when stewards might find it complicated to get more books to refill a depleted little library, a library support group may be able to intercede. As a for instance, when the pandemic emergency occurred, the Friends group in Colorado where I served on the board of directors obtained a list of the local stewards. This was achieved after contacting the Little Free Library nonprofit via their website; explaining what we wanted to do; contacting the stewards to let them know we could provide free books to restock; and asking them to let us know if we could assist. About half of the stewards responded to receive aid, so we sorted, packed, and delivered bags of books to their porches. In other times of emergency, Friends groups like the one I belonged to may want to consider providing books for little libraries as a community service.
- Offer a discount at book sales for stewards. At Friends of the Library book sales, discounts are often provided for those who work in schools or community needs facilities. Consider adding another discount for little library stewards who present their Steward Card at your sale so that they can use the books they purchase for restocking. Be sure to advertise the discount in your publicity.

Beyond aiding little libraries in any number of ways, what follows next are more illustrations of situations where library support groups can lend a hand.

Aiding Special Needs Organizations and Agencies in the Community

Another of the generous and kind acts that Friends of the Libraries perform is offering ongoing free books and other materials as giveaways for special needs organizations and agencies in communities, or by simply providing such giveaways for everyday folks who need a hand to get items that may otherwise be unaffordable. This section will highlight some Friends groups that include such services as part of their mission. After all, Friends receive their stock of books and supplementary materials from community donations, therefore after the sales at which they raise library support money with those donations, adding the action of offering overstock without charge as needed further demonstrates to the community that they care.

The first group I would like to mention is the Friends of the Palo Alto Library. Palo Alto is a community of about sixty-three thousand in California. Each month on the second Saturday and Sunday, these Friends hold a large sale of an impressive array of around fifty thousand gently used and sometimes new materials to support the library with funding. These materials include books, audio-visuals, puzzles, games, and software. A few are former library books, but 95 percent of the donated items for sale at reasonable prices are given by individuals, estates, and community businesses.

On Sunday afternoons following each sale, teachers and nonprofits can come and select paperbacks and hardcover books in a wide variety of genres for children, teens, and adults at no cost. The Friends do not stop there either. They additionally offer an opportunity for anyone from the community to come in the Monday evening after a sale to select as many books and audiovisuals that they may want and need without a nonprofit affiliation. The only stipulation is that those picking up free materials come equipped with bags and boxes for the items they choose.[10]

Here is another example. The Friends of the Wichita Falls Public Library in Texas was formed to uphold and support the Wichita Falls Public Library and especially focuses upon promoting juvenile literacy through providing books and other means to foster the joy and rewards of reading. However, in addition to filling twenty-three Little Free Libraries and with plans to expand that reach, they also target the causes of providing free books to the homeless; the under-employed or unemployed; shut-ins; and the blind. Likewise, no-cost books are available for teachers; home-schoolers; pastors and church libraries; various nonprofits; social service organizations; medical facilities; jails and prisons; and governmental agencies. The Friends keep going with their community support by setting up giveaway tables with books, magazines, and audio-visuals outside their book warehouse, weather permitting, whenever the facility is open.[11]

This Wichita Falls Friends group was organized in 1991 to help fund a new library facility, and they now boast about one hundred volunteers who help to run their large, seven-thousand-square-foot warehouse facility that stocks one hundred thousand books given by various sources in the community,[12] especially the local school district and Midwestern State University.[13] Even though their population is a modest 104,000 people, this is a city that pulls together for the purpose of supporting their library and Friends group, and aiding other members of their community.

As a last example, the Friends of the Knox County Public Library organization in Tennessee has a Books in the Community program. The program provides books and other items to organizations servicing marginalized communities in Knox County which is a metro area of about 784,000. Although Friends book sales take place regularly throughout the year to raise funds for the library system, the group also focuses on community needs, and special emphasis is made to purchase and place diverse books. These are often written by and about people of color, allowing young readers to see themselves reflected in the books that they read. Friends volunteers work with the organizations that request aid to select appropriate books and arrange either for delivery to their facility or for pickup at the Friends book sale shop at the downtown Lawson McGhee Library. In 2022, the Friends distributed 11,364 books and other materials to thirty-nine community partners and to sixteen Little Free Libraries.[14]

If your Friends or Friends Foundation is looking to expand its reach further into the community by offering free books and materials to those in need, it can be a wonderful good will effort that will help other people while encouraging still others to contribute to your cause. Keep in mind that the examples given in this section range in community population size, showing that even library support groups in smaller communities can offer free services like this when able.

Providing Aid in Emergencies

Besides the above-mentioned help given to little library stewards during the pandemic emergency, there are bigger ways that library support groups can make a difference in community assistance during challenging times. One way is by helping out with the American Library Association (ALA)'s Disaster Relief Fund, which can accept donations for libraries experiencing emergency conditions. In addition to library support groups contributing through ALA, they can also give through any number of more localized relief services that offer aid during urgent situations. The website for the ALA fund includes donation information along with details about individual areas with libraries that are experiencing crisis.[15] For urgent needs that require immediate assistance, library support groups can make a direct localized impact. The following shows ways some have done this.

The first illustration also comes from California's Chico Friends of the Library, a group mentioned in the Little Free Libraries segment. When the horrific Camp Fire disaster hit the area in late 2018, two of their libraries were seriously affected. These Friends once again stepped up, providing two-hundred-dollar Visa gift cards each for nine library staff members personally impacted by the wildfire.[16] Friends members, notably one Nancy Leek, also supported the community sheltered at the Disaster Recovery Center by providing donated books that were replenished twice a week.[17]

In 2021, the Caldor Fire forced the evacuation of thousands from the South Lake Tahoe, Nevada, area. Volunteers from the Friends of the Carson City Library brought donated books to the shelters as well as giving vouchers to evacuees for free books at their Friends bookstore so that people had access to reading material while they were cut off from their homes.[18]

When Hurricane Harvey hit Houston, Texas, in 2017, local libraries provided shelter and aid, but so did many people around the country who donated money to help. This included library support groups. For example, the Friends of the Library in Tualatin, Oregon, donated all their used book sale shelf proceeds during the emergency time period to the Houston Library's cause through the Texas Library Association's Disaster Relief Fund, along with other organizations from around the country.[19]

When terrible tragedies strike a community, whether it be fire, flood, storm, earthquake, or pandemic—the library is often there to help along with its library support group(s) when it can. In such an event, maybe the library itself could be in need. It might be a worthwhile idea to create a potential plan of action for your group in the case that it finds itself in a similar emergency aid situation. That could include creating a process for a telephone tree or a "what if" list of potential items that the organization might be able to provide. An ultimate rule of thumb is that it is better to have a general plan that can be adapted for specific situations and not be needed, than to need a plan and not have it.

Imagination Library Participation

Another great way for libraries and their library support groups to aid their communities is through Dolly Parton's Imagination Library program, which fosters literacy among youngsters via the nonprofit Dollywood Foundation. The program began in 1995, when Parton took her father's frustration about his inability to read and write as the motivation for creating a new program to develop a love of reading for the preschool children of her home county of Sevier in East Tennessee. She did this by providing them with an ongoing gift of specially selected books up through the year they are age four.

Now the program has grown tremendously, spanning the United States, Canada, the United Kingdom, Australia, and the Republic of Ireland. As a result, over two million free books selected by literacy experts are distributed to children in these countries monthly.[20] If you are curious to learn about the incredible process of preparing and mailing out these books in the United States through Penguin Random House Publishers, you can find an excellent video on YouTube that explains it carefully.[21] YouTube also lists a number of other videos that share further details and inspiring messages about the Imagination Library program.

A library support group can be a perfect means for providing an Imagination Library program in partnership with the library being aided. For instance, at the Cedar Rapids Public Library in Iowa, there is an Imagination Library program that was started in 2018 and is funded by the Cedar Rapids Public Library Foundation using community donations (a "donate" tab appears on the program information page in the event that someone wishes to support their efforts; however, giving money is not a requirement).

Adults who wish to register children under age five who are residents of Cedar Rapids can do so online or by completing and submitting a paper form. There are two adult responsibilities for those registering their children. Those are are promising to notify the library of a change of address and agreeing that they will read to their child or children.[22]

Another successful idea to fund this program comes from the Friends of the Knox County Public Library in Tennessee. They hold a Seeds of Imagination Luncheon annually to raise money for the Dolly Parton's Imagination Library of Knox County cause, as well as to specially honor local individuals and organizations that have made an impact on early childhood literacy in East Tennessee. Several community partners help to sponsor this event, held at a local country club, with donations on a tiered scale ranging from five hundred to ten thousand dollars, including luncheon seating and recognition benefits. Plus, there are individual tickets available for $125 or a table for eight that costs one thousand dollars. For the literacy awards, people from the community are invited to submit nominations.[23]

If the Imagination Library program does not exist in your community and your library support organization would like to work with your library to initiate one, there is plenty of information on how to do so on the Imagination Library website. The best way to move forward would be to confer with your library administrators along with a representative from the children's department, and, if you get the go-ahead, to contact the Imagination Library program via the website's How to Start a Program page.[24]

If you introduced the low-cost, turnkey Imagination Library program at your library, it could help children in your area to develop a love of books and reading that can last a lifetime, which is a goal that fits the missions of most library support groups, most likely including yours. To meet that goal, your funding organization would be responsible for paying $2.10 per child toward the cost of books and mailings; for promoting the program and building awareness; for arranging with your library to set up a registration process for children; and for entering information into the book ordering system. The Dollywood Foundation would cover all administrative costs and overhead expenses; provide Book Order System database access and support; coordinate the book selection committee; and synchronize the monthly book orders and fulfillment processes.[25]

Becoming part of the Imagination Library program can be an affordable, win-win program for your organization, your library, your community, and especially its children.

Supporting Literature, Music, Art, and Writing Community Programs and Festivals

Library support groups can play a significant role in helping to fund special community programs that connect their beneficiary libraries and the people they serve by expanding opportunities to learn about literature, music, art, and writing beyond the library walls. This kind of programming is best created through a great deal of partnering and teamwork.

As you have seen in the previous chapter, sometimes library support groups may fund major guest author talks to sustain their libraries' regular programming agendas, possibly in partnership with well-known local independent bookstores. They may also participate in the funding and the planning of events that encompass several authors, writing activities, and informational lessons about literature as major community-wide events. Often, group members serve as volunteers to help see the programs and events through.

In some circumstances, support groups can be the actual catalysts for planning and running special literary events instead of serving as background players who provide the money and volunteers to allow the library to do all the preparations and facilitating. Either approach can be valid and important depending on the programs. Overall, there are myriad ways that fundraising groups can and do aid their libraries and communities in offering such literature-focused programs and activities. In the following section, you will find examples of notable events or programs that you may wish to adapt or pursue in ways that suit your group and your library community. Events range from single-day to multi-day schedules of programs and activities for a variety of targeted audiences.

Creators in Residence, Los Angeles, California

The Los Angeles Public Library Creators in Residence program was established in 2022 to provide a forum for creative locals from diverse backgrounds to produce new and innovative work that would have been influenced and motivated by the Library's collection and services. Besides being inspirational for the creators, the program emphasizes the impact of the library as a focal point for resourcefulness and inventiveness. It is funded by the Library Foundation of Los Angeles along with an endowment by the Lenore S. and Bernard A. Greenberg Fund.

The program is open to creators of all kinds. Applicants may be artists, photographers, filmmakers, designers, architects, writers, storytellers, poets, illustrators, cartographers, composers, podcasters, or anyone working with creative media. Two creators are chosen based on the strength, uniqueness, and significance of their previous creations and how well their proposals contribute to the Library's mission to offer free and easy access to information, ideas, and technology for the community. They must also arouse enthusiasm, interest, and interpretation of the fundamental perspectives and stories from the Library's collection and its users.

The successful candidates each receive a twenty-thousand-dollar award to honor the time, research, travel, creation, and presentation needs of their appointed work. They collaborate closely with the Library and Foundation staff; survey and use the Library's collections and facilities; participate in relevant programs; and develop and carry out their creative endeavors as appointed.

The first two Creators in Residence were Kwasi Boyd-Bouldin, a photographer, and River Garza, an interdisciplinary visual artist. The first-rate projects they developed were thoughtful, serious, and meaningful reflections of the Library system and community identities that remained on display at the Central Library through the summer of 2023.

New applicants are encouraged to apply until a July deadline for the subsequent programs. They must be at least eighteen years old and reside in Los Angeles County. They must commit to attending occasional meetings at the downtown Central Library. Most importantly, they must propose and develop an appropriate and original project in a physical or digital format that meets the project criteria, that becomes part of the library's permanent collection, and to which the public can readily connect.[26]

Although this is a very large and highly funded program at a major library system, its example serves to show that even a smaller city or town library might be able to develop a comparable kind of program with backing from its library support organization. I recall several such programs we offered at libraries at which I worked through the years that were funded by our Friends groups. For instance, one of them provided a puppeteer-in-residence for children and teenagers during one spring break, and another offered a series of summer art classes for teenagers.

Fort Collins Book Fest, Fort Collins, Colorado

The Fort Collins Book Fest has evolved successfully for several years as a popular, informative, imaginative, and enlightening offering. It began in 2016 as a one-day event, continued as a free in-person, multi-day annual event until 2020, when instead of in-person it was offered virtually. In 2021, it was transformed into an in-person or virtual hybrid event, and it was revamped again in 2023 as a monthlong series of free in-person events for all ages during February, which is National Library Lovers Month and I Love to Read Month.

The Fest was conceived by librarians, writers, book lovers, and community members who had an aspiration to combine the city's unique cultural heritage and its passion for the literary arts into celebrations of literature, literacy, and social conversation. The events were coordinated by the Poudre River Public Library District, however, you can imagine that such an undertaking would require much additional teamwork, volunteerism, and funding, and this event could never have taken place and continue without the contributions of corporate and academic sponsors, foundations, individuals, and the library's two support groups, the Poudre River Library Trust and the Poudre River Friends of the Library.

The inaugural Fort Collins Book Fest sported the theme Brewin' Up Books, which highlighted the regional social and economic influence of craft beer, artisan coffee, and tea. Through the years, the themes varied to focus upon music, science, food, social connections, a historical look-back at the themes for the first five years, and the love of reading.[27]

Fort Collins is a medium-sized city of 169,000 with a vibrant library district, a prominent university, and dedicated community members who see the value of creating and holding such ongoing, literary-oriented events. Whether your community is small, medium, or large, this type of theme-oriented festival might just be a good fit for your library, community, and library support group(s) to design and sponsor.

Children's Book Festival, Atlanta, Georgia

The inaugural Children's Book Festival in Atlanta, held in May 2022, featured prominent children's book authors, book signings, storytimes, music, activities to engage youth from infancy through the teen years, and more. As Gayle E. Holloman, the executive director of the library, announced as the festival date approached, "The need for live, in-person and engaging events for youth that are focused on literacy has never been greater. After nearly two years of remote learning, increased screen time, and virtual programs for children of all ages, we're ready to bring our young people together for this special day."

To meet this goal, the daylong festival, which is now an annual event, was held in collaboration between the Atlanta-Fulton Public Library Foundation and the Fulton County Library System along with other community partners at the recently renovated Central Library in downtown Atlanta. In addition to the author presentations and signings for youngsters, there were an author discussion panel with teens; activities relating to the Mayor's Summer Reading Program; musical and dramatic performances from the Atlanta Opera, Alliance Theater, and the Atlanta Symphony; and a puppet workshop by the Center for Puppetry Arts.[28]

Of course, like Los Angeles, Atlanta is a major metropolitan area, and if you are a much smaller library support organization and assist a medium or small library, you may wonder if you can fund and help to arrange such a large, impressive event. Try to think outside the box and remember that your community might also have local music and drama organizations willing to participate, local authors willing to take the stage for little or no cost, talented library staff and volunteers to help with storytime events and creating events for associated reading programs; and/or an independent bookstore to provide theme-related book sales (or perhaps have a used book sale with Friends of the Library donations). With the possibilities of some or all of that collaboration at hand, refrain from allowing the smaller size of your city or town to dissuade you.

Figure 11.1. The Children's Book Festival poster promoting the event sponsored by the Atlanta-Fulton Public Library Foundation in Georgia is appealing and inviting. *Credit: Ariana Thomas of Flylight Creative.*

Children's Festival of Reading, Knoxville, Tennessee

As a second example of a festival that celebrates children, books, and reading, the Friends of the Knox County Public Library, along with several media-related sponsors and a host of others such as the Tennessee Arts Commission, United Way, and Members of the Knoxville City Council, fund the annual Children's Festival of Reading from 10:00 a.m. until 3:00 p.m. in the downtown World's Fair Park each May. Admission is free for the one-day event and so is parking in several lots and garages thanks to the University of Tennessee. Booths and stages under tents and other areas with covered space like the Amphitheater provide shelter for festivalgoers, rain or shine. There are also vendors available for the purchase of food or merchandise.

Activities and performances are provided by the Knox County Public Library and its community partners. The celebration kicks off with a Parade of Books led by the city mayor and attendees are invited to join the parade which leaves from the famous Sunsphere in the park. Another kickoff is provided by the Library at a special tent where children, teens, and adults can sign up for the Summer Reading Club. Costumed characters are present to give children a chance for photos with their favorites. The Music and Storytelling Tents feature a variety of performances and activities, including those incorporating poetry, singing, yoga, dance, theater, science, and even live animals. The Author/Illustrator Tent and Signing Tent give all ages a chance to hear guest authors speak and get books signed.[29] Concurrently, the Friends of the Library members provide a special, affordable used book sale.

Planning and organizing an event like this one takes monetary support, teamwork, and lots of volunteers, but the results are definitely worth it. A nice thing about holding an annual festival like this is that once you do it, you have a plan of action to follow in subsequent years.

West Virginia Book Festival, Charleston, West Virginia

The annual West Virginia Book Festival is another free, annual, one-day event geared toward book lovers of all ages, promoted by the county library support groups. It offers programs by both local and international bestselling book authors. It also provides a Marketplace, where attendees can find book sellers, publishers, individual authors, and other literary-oriented vendors featuring a wide range of books and related items including books signed by Festival authors.

In another organizational twist, as a "committee" of the Library Foundation of Kanawha County, the Friends of the Library also offers a used book sale during the event for festival-goers get books inexpensively. The Foundation is one of the organizations serving as charter presenters for the festival along with the Kanawha County Public Library, the Charleston Gazette-Mail, and the West Virginia Humanities Council. There are also sponsors such as the Marshall University Foundation, the West Virginia Library Commission, and even the Tri-State Roofing and Sheet Metal Company. However, many additional organizations and sponsors work in tandem to bring the annual festival to life.[30]

Wisconsin Book Festival, Madison, Wisconsin

In 2021, the Wisconsin Humanities Council founded the Wisconsin Book Festival, and in 2013, the Madison Public Library, in partnership with the Madison Public Library Foundation, took over. The lively festival has brought thousands of local and internationally acclaimed authors to downtown Madison and offers myriad opportunities to celebrate literacy, dialogue, and creativity. The format is unique in that it offers free, year-round events, both in-person and virtual, led by all genres of authors culminating in a four-day-long weekend celebration in the fall. Events are held at the Central Library or other downtown venues with about fifteen thousand people attending each year.[31]

As you can imagine, the budget for such a major festival is steep, about $250,000. In a metro area of over half a million, the Foundation is able to glean almost half of the needed funds through membership donations. To become a "member," a person can give one hundred dollars or more and get special benefits. This includes two reserved seats for ten to twelve select author events; priority email messages with news and updates; and an invitation to a festival launch party in the fall. For donors at the "benefactor" membership level, someone can give one thousand dollars or more and receive the regular member perks, plus be recognized on the festival website. The last category is "corporate" sponsorship, for which donors receive member benefits and recognition not only on the festival website but also onscreen before and after live-streamed festival programs. There are numerous corporate sponsors, one being the Friends of the University of Wisconsin-Madison Libraries.[32]

Contribution solicitations for manpower also take place from there as it takes many volunteer hours to run such a complex and ambitious festival. The Foundation puts out a call for volunteers to enlist for various roles as booksellers, direction givers, book signing coordinators, author event hosts, or whatever other tasks are required.[33]

Putting on a festival of this magnitude requires many kinds of community participants, but the Foundation does an admirable job working alongside the library to plan for, recruit for, and fund it. If your library support group has the inspiration to develop a plan for a similar undertaking, the Madison Public Library Foundation provides an exciting model.

These are but a sampling of the kinds of festivals that library support groups can plan and run, partner to do, and/or aid financially. If your organization wishes to follow suit and plan a similar endeavor, especially if you are aiming to make it ongoing, it is best to start small and evolve the events as time goes by. Devise a meaningful and interesting festival or celebration to begin, and give your group a chance to assess before moving forward to expand it. Also, it can help to contact organizations that have already planned and run such events to get advice and informational materials to help with strategic planning.

TEXTBOX 11.1

HOW TO PUT ON A LITERATURE FESTIVAL

The following two resources offer helpful guidance and step-by-step instruction for creating and holding a literature festival:

20 Bedford Way[1]

The United Kingdom is famous for putting on literature festivals. The advice and instructions on this web page from 20 Bedford Way, a central London events venue, will give you a place to start, a pathway for devising precisely how your particular literature festival will unfold, and ways to promote it effectively.

Book Festival Organizers Toolkit[2]

From the Empire State Center for the Book, which promotes literature, literacy, and libraries in New York State,[3] this PDF toolkit was produced with funding from the New York Council for the Humanities. Though it is promoted by the New York Library Association and centers on holding such events in New York, the information can be adapted for anyone wishing to develop their own literature festival.

Notes

1. 20 Bedford Way. [n.d.] "How to Put on a Literature Festival," https://20bedfordway.com/news/how-to-put-on-a-literature-festival/.
2. Empire State Center for the Book. [n.d.] "Book Festival Organizers Toolkit," https://www.nyla.org/userfiles/Center%20for%20the%20Book%20Documents/Book%20Festival%20Organizers%20Toolkit.pdf.
3. Empire State Center for the Book. 2023. https://www.nyla.org/4DCGI/CFTB.html?MenuKey=CFTB.

Fostering Special Community Reading Programs

One of the best ways for Friends and other groups to connect whole communities or segments of communities with books and reading is by funding or co-funding "One Book" programs in partnership with their libraries or other community facilities or agencies. Sometimes, library support organizations not only provide funding but they also take the lead in organizing and running such programs. In this section, I will explain and explore the purpose of one book programs, the reasons why they are important and effective, and how to plan and run them.

First, I will share a bit of background. The One Book movement originated in 1998 when celebrated librarian and reading advisor Nancy Perl, then-executive director of the Washington Center for the Book at the Seattle Public Library, created a special program called, "If All Seattle Read the Same Book." Monetary backing was provided by the Lila Wallace Reader's Digest fund and a number of local sponsors.

The first book selected for concurrent community reading was *The Sweet Hereafter* by Russell Banks. As a culmination to the program, Banks was brought to Seattle for a three-day stint to facilitate discussion of his book in a series of free public programs.[34] After this kickoff reading event, the idea took off in other communities around the country, and libraries began to incorporate similar programs.

In a nutshell, One Book reading program projects like this are designed to unite community members with literature as they all read a designated book during a set period of time with book discussions that follow and, at times, with the authors of the books invited to present talks and/or to participate in the conversations. The programs have become increasingly popular everywhere and they are often organized and facilitated by libraries. However, since the programs require funding, that is where library support groups can come into play, either independently or as co-sponsors. Now, as time has gone by, more and more Friends and other groups have gotten involved in financing the programs and even in taking charge of them. The following information can help you for offering funding or taking charge, too.

TEXTBOX 11.2

STEPS FOR PLANNING AND EXECUTING A COMMUNITY READS PROGRAM

- Set your program goals. Designate your targeted audience; decide what you hope to accomplish, such as promoting reading and literacy and/or community dialogue; identify the needs and interests of your audience; and determine the outcomes you want to meet.
- Begin planning and organizing. Convene a planning committee of library support group members who want to play a role, plus librarians, community leaders, school representatives, or anyone else who might want to be involved; figure out funding needs and devise a budget; and develop a timeline at least six months in advance of the program, and longer if possible.
- Select a book. Decide on a book in a manner that fits your community, whether via a selection committee, a library recommendation, suggestions from the public, or other means. Choose a book that meets the program goal; is accessible in various formats; is targeted to a range of ages and interests; meets regional significance; focuses on particular themes; and/or is tied to a certain author you wish to include.
- Develop events and programs. Create partnerships with local bookstores, theaters, museums, universities, or other community organizations that can assist in enriching your program participants' experiences. Decide on whether you will be having events presented virtually, in-person, or as a hybrid of these. Choose locations and facilitators for any discussion events you are anticipating. Decide if author involvement is essential, whether to include a lecture or presentation of some type, if you want to design a related art or music program, or if you wish to add another kind of enhancing activity.
- Do you want to host an author? If you choose to host an author, you will need to consider author availability, budget, and what activities in which you wish the author to be involved. This could encompass such activities as a lecture or informal talk; a recorded interview; several school visits; a reception for an author meet-and-greet; and/or book signings. Return to chapter 9 for advice on securing authors for events.

(continued)

- Promote your community-wide reading program. Establish a promotional or communications committee, and heavily publicize all aspects of your One Book program on your website and perhaps even a specially created program website; on the library's website; in local media; on social media; with posters and flyers; through promotional materials; with paid, discounted, or free ads in newspapers and via other local media; and in whatever additional ways you are able. For the kickoff, plan a program launch party, invite local dignitaries to speak, and request local media to cover it.
- Secure books for your events. Work with your library to ensure the library purchases enough copies of the selected books for the collection in various formats. Order copies of the books that you wish to offer for sale at events or contact your local bookstore to see if they are willing and able to provide copies of designated books for sale and signings at your events.
- Evaluate and follow up after your program concludes. Document your events with photos and videos, and, with permission, share these with local media, on social media, and with the participating author and publisher. Send a final report to the publisher with details about the event success, including the audience sizes, book sales, and any supporting materials and information. Meet with your planning committee and community partners to evaluate outcomes and whether goals were met.[1]

Note

1. Common Reads. 2023. "Community Reads Resources." Penguin Random House, https://commonreads.com/community-reads-resources/.

In this next section, I will explore several communities of varying sizes and audiences where "one book" reading programs take or have taken place so you will have prime examples to consider and will perhaps decide to emulate based on the goals of the library that your organization serves. Some of these programs have been planned and run by and/or financially backed by the library support organizations for their particular libraries. The ones that have not been are taking place in schools without Friends backing, and I offer them here as examples so that you might consider potentially proposing them to your local educational institutions in case they could be interested yet are unaware of the one book options, and lack such support.

You might also think about creating your own kinds of one book programs to address different audiences of readers, maybe by choosing a single title for adults, one for teens, and one for children. Be creative! Find out if your public library, educational institutions, or community centers are interested in buying in to the concept and, if so, what approaches you and they might want to take. There can be lots of ways to design this kind of communal literary programming. Find out which one or ones might best suit you library's needs. In the meantime, here are some inspiring illustrations.

Two Towns–One Book, Friends of the Clifton Park-Halfmoon Public Library, Clifton, New York

"Two Towns–One Book: Clifton Park & Halfmoon Read!" (TTOB) is an annual program that began in 2011 and is sponsored by the Friends of the Clifton Park-Halfmoon

Public Library. This library serves two communities that are located in Saratoga County which have a combined population of about sixty-three thousand, and therefore the program is coined as "one book for two towns." The Friends' goal is to bring members of the community together via the shared reading and discussion of a common book. The group chooses titles that foster meaningful discussions and serve as catalysts for related events, and it posts discussion questions on its website. Adults and teenagers alike are encouraged to join in by reading the selected title.

In similar fashion, the program invites even younger members of the community to take part in tandem by encouraging them to read companion books and to be involved in related activities. This program for younger readers is called Our Kids Read, Too! For this portion of the program, a special committee chooses junior companion books for families to read together and to then participate in the youth-oriented discussions.

The leaders and volunteers for the TTOB program encourage everyone in the community to get involved in some way. They especially encourage people to secure copies of the selected titles from the library or elsewhere, in whatever format(s) that appeal to them, and signing up for email notices about and then attending related programs and events as they desire and are able. Those taking part can also nominate titles to be considered and potentially used, and they can also vote for the final choices.

Another way to participate is to spread the word about TTOB to friends, neighbors, co-workers, and family members, and especially to encourage book clubs from the surrounding areas to join in by completing a special registration form. Book clubs that are registered have singular events planned for their members and receive notification of upcoming program-related activities. In addition, anyone who wishes to serve as a volunteer can work on sub-committees and events. Sub-committee choices include Book Selection, Book Readers, and Our Kids Read, Too!

The Book Selection sub-committee completes its tasks from February through May. Anyone from the community may nominate books to be considered, even by naming multiple books to consider. Ballots are made available at the library, at Friends events, and online. Nominations are whittled down to the top five, and community residents vote from those five to select each year's targeted title. Events and discussions are designed to connect to the themes of the chosen book to compliment the reading experience. An archive of past books and events is kept that people can access online. A few of the previous community reads titles were *Becoming* by Michelle Obama, *Before We Were Yours* by Lisa Wingate, *The Book Thief* by Markus Zusak, and *The Lincoln Highway* by Amor Towles.[35]

The Friends reach out to any business or community organization that would like to provide financial or in-kind support for the program. Those who contribute are included in publicity and are given public thanks by having their business or organization specially noted on the TTOB webpage. Quite a few community partners provide help, such as the Town of Clifton, the local school system, the senior community center, the local YMCA, and others. One community business partner is the Stewart's Corporation, a company that runs convenience markets,[36] which has supported the successful TTOB programs with grants for over ten years.[37]

One Book, One Tulsa, Tulsa Library Trust, Tulsa, Oklahoma

Another annual community reads program, called "One Book, One Tulsa," is sponsored by the Tulsa Library Trust, sometimes co-sponsored by other community agencies and organizations depending on the themes being addressed, and it is hosted and run by the Tulsa City-County Library. In this case, the Trust is responsible for giving monetary support and partnering with other sources for additional funding as needed.

For this system-wide initiative, Tulsa County residents are encouraged to read the same book, and, as was shown in the previous example, the purpose of the program is to foster literacy within the community and to promote conversations about a meaningful book.

In 2023, the book that was chosen for everyone to read was *Crying in H Mart* by bestselling author Michelle Zauner, which is a powerful memoir about the author growing up Korean American, losing her mother, and figuring out her personal identity. After a book discussion at the Central Library to culminate the community read experience, the author gave a presentation, answered questions, and signed books.[38] Some other books that have been selected for community-wide reading are *The Soloist: A Lost Dream, an Unlikely Friendship, and the Redemptive Power of Music* by Steve Lopez, which focuses on the topics of mental illness and homelessness,[39] and Woodie Guthrie's *House of Earth*, which is about the Dustbowl years.[40] As with the 2023 title, discussion program funding has included either featuring the author of the book in-person or providing a related presentation or activity.

Community Reading Programs Especially for Youth

After the initial spark that lit the "one book" movement in cities and towns, schools and school districts began to be involved as well. Some programs for elementary students have been operated solely within a school, some have been district-wide, and some have been designated for particular grade levels. In high schools, a program might give all students a choice to pick one title from a small selection of books, or, as with other programs, they might ask the students to all read one designated book collectively. There can be any number of ways that "one book" programs can be arranged to take place in schools.

These kinds of schoolwide programs for community reading could be funded by a school-oriented library support group or maybe by a Friends or other organization associated with a local public library to encourage a school–public library partnership.

One Book, One City for Kids, Grand Rapids Public Library Foundation, Michigan

In Grand Rapids, Michigan, the Grand Rapids Public Library Foundation, the Michigan Arts & Culture Council, and the nonprofit Wege Foundation, a local family foundation targeting arts and culture, education, environmental issues, and community wellness,[41] jointly fund the One Book, One City for Kids program via the Grand Rapids Public Library and local schools. This is an annual reading program that invites all upper-elementary-school students to read and discuss the same book. Proponents say that the program helps to develop a lifelong love of reading among young people; it inspires readers to connect with the story themes in real life through discussion and creative activities; and it is a catalyst for collaboration between the public libraries, the school libraries, and the city schools.

For 2023, the book selected for all students to read was *Isaiah Dunn Is My Hero* by Kelly J. Baptist. This book is a thought-provoking read for children about a ten-year-old child who has taken on huge responsibilities to solve problems for his family that include poverty and housing insecurity when his father dies. Not only was this wonderful book made available for all the children to read, but an excellent teacher's guide was produced for background information, discussions, classroom activities, website links to get further information about the topics included in the book, and a list of read-alikes for students who want to find titles with similar themes.[42]

One Book Read City, Friends of the Knox County Public Library, Tennessee

One Book Read City began in 2022 and has become an annual community-wide program that offers kindergarten through fifth-grade students in Knox County elementary schools a chance to all enjoy reading the same book. The goals of the program are to promote reading at home, encourage unified dialogue, increase exposure to books and literacy, build strong community identity, and connect local businesses, nonprofits, and schools by way of activities and events that focus on the themes of each book selected.

Funding for the program is in partnership with Knox County, Knox County Schools, Knox Education Foundation, the Friends of the Knox County Public Library, and additional supporting community partners who provide further funds, make in-kind donations, enlist in community activities, and provide prizes. There are several sponsorship levels from which donors can choose. The program supplies books not only for all students but also for all school staff so that they can participate in the discussions too. That means thirty-three thousand books are needed to facilitate this program.

At this junction, the Friends of the Library has collaborated with the other partners by taking on funding for all the books at four elementary schools. However, everyone in the whole community must play roles to make the initiative successful including school principals, teachers, librarians, parents, parent-teacher organizations, and other community partners.

The program starts off with special announcements in all schools and promotion continues with two weeks of celebrity videos, classroom activities, and community events. Every school is encouraged to find their best approach to the program based on their school identity.[43]

One District, One Book, Oneida School District, New York

Here is a novel program idea that a school library Friends group may wish to support. At the Oneida School District in New York, they conduct a community reading experience called One District, One Book, which is based on reading the same book aloud. It may seem like an unusual approach, but in truth it is educationally sound. As a matter of fact, reading professionals recommend that the act of reading to young people from materials that are beyond children's own reading levels is very beneficial. This is because when they do, students become more readily able to connect to the literature they personally encounter. Due to this fact, it is a given that parents, teachers, and caregivers should continue the practice of reading chapter books even with older youth who are able to read on their own.

During several designated months during the school year, this school district chooses particular titles for shared reading that can be followed, comprehended, and enjoyed by younger students but that will still draw the attention of and be appreciated by older students. At special school assemblies, students each receive a copy of the book along with a tailored fifteen-minute nightly reading schedule that they can bring home to their families. To reward and enhance attentive at-home listening, daily trivia questions and related classroom activities take place at schools as follow-ups to the readings. Some of the books that have been used are *The World According to Humphrey* by Betty G. Birney, *Bunnicula* by James Howe, and *The Lemonade War* by Jacqueline Davies.

Reading aloud in this manner becomes a fun, meaningful family activity because not only does it prepare children to be effective readers themselves, but it allows all ages of family members to participate. Why, the school district does not even stop there in promoting their selected book—the expectation is that everyone who plays a role at the school takes part. This means that, as with the Knox County programs, students, teachers, parents, bus drivers, nurses, maintenance staff, and administration staff all join in and reap the many benefits of the reading program.[44] As a matter of fact, if a school library Friends group or groups decided to sponsor and fund such a program, the Friends members might be able to partner with the media specialist(s) to design ways to effectively promote it and perhaps even take on some read-aloud classroom visits or conduct library gatherings for reading activities.

TEXTBOX 11.3

SPONSORING AND SUPPORTING A SCHOOL-WIDE COMMUNITY READING PROGRAM FOR YOUTH

Do you want to aid your local, regional, or state school(s) through efforts to increase student interactions with books and to promote the joys of literacy in and through schools like the ones you are reading about in this section? If so, your school library support group or public library support group (in partnership with a school library) might decide to propose, fund, and even help run a One Book, One School program. Here are some guidelines and tips to get started:

- Remember that One School, One Book programs are created to build a reading community within a school or schools. They help students to develop a delight in reading and allow parents, teachers, and others to discuss literature with them. Programs need to be proposed and designed around this concept and promoted as such. With this in mind, when you feel ready to move forward with gaining school approval, develop a basic strategic plan for funding and conducting the program for the targeted school community.
- In your plan, include as appropriate within the school climate the intention to draw in students, teachers, library administrators, parents and caregivers, all school support staff members and supplemental employees, members of your organization, and any significant others to participate. Help to create a culture of reading at the school(s) by designing the program to be an enlightening social reading experience for everyone.

- You might want to consider perusing the Read to Them website to see if you can use their information and resources to help fund and set up a specialized reading program for young people, their families, and their schools in your town, city, region, or even state. The Read to Them nonprofit organization, which was founded in 2006, provides useful links to grant makers who may have available funds to set up these reading programs or, with the right program qualifications, schools may qualify for Title 1 funding from the Department of Education.[1] The organization offers a list of 150 titles for elementary- through middle-school students that may be desirable for "one book" programs. You can search for suitable titles by preferred themes, targeted audiences, and length of programs. Those actually conducting such programs are welcome to recommend additional titles to add to Read to Them's list of book choices. Guidance for running a summer reading "one book" program can also be accessed. A library support group that wants to propose a "one book" program of any kind for youth can find a wealth of resources through the Read to Them website, though there is a cost to having them provide the particular arrangements for a program that a Friends or other group may need to cover.[2]
- No matter if a program proposal is created with Read to Them aid or from scratch, the next step forward would be to contact the school librarian or media specialist at the school being supported by your organization and present the idea for the program. If potential is recognized and enthusiasm is shown, the librarian will intervene for you with the school principal and/or other administrator(s) who would need to give approval.
- One School, One Book programs usually run for a designated month, during which an entire school community follows a shared reading schedule for a specific book. They can take place once during a school year or multiple times with a different book for each targeted month. However, setting up another sort of timetable, perhaps as a summer reading program, could also work. Choose a timeline that works for you and the school(s).
- With input from the school librarian and other teaching staff, consider daily events that would reinforce the program and promote enthusiasm for the book. For example, the school might implement plays, dances, family nights, trivia, and contests related to the reading experiences. Plan to have families and other members of the community involved as a top priority. If there happens to be a local author, or even a non-local author, whose book has been chosen for community reading, see if that author might be available for an in-person or virtual school visit(s).
- Use designated profits from your library support group's fundraising efforts or from grants to purchase copies of the book for students and staff members as needed. Also think about acquiring downloadable copies in ebook format that can be accessed. In addition, be sure to contact your public library to let them know about your program so they may provide any aid they might wish to offer and purchase additional copies of the school "community reads" titles for people to borrow.[3]

Notes

1. United States Department of Education. [n.d.] "Parents/Prepare My Child for School," https://www2.ed.gov/parents/earlychild/ready/edpicks.jhtml.
2. Read to Them. 2022. "Programs," https://readtothem.org/our-programs/.
3. Sam Northern. March 25, 2019. "One School + One Book = A Love of Reading." Knowledge Quest, Journal of the American Association of School Librarians, https://knowledgequest.aasl.org/one-school-one-book-a-love-of-reading/.

One School, One Book, Simpson Elementary School, Franklin, Kentucky

The One School, One Book program, which originated at the Simpson Elementary School, has been coordinated to include three schools in the district, which means eight grade levels take part in it. Because of this, the selected book's audience must, as in previous examples, be appealing to a wide range of age interests. This schools district's experience is an especially pertinent illustration because the teacher who founded the program arranged for students to take vital roles in the planning and execution of it and its related activities.

The first One School, One Book program in the school district featured a title that is popular with an array of students from elementary school to high school, *The One and Only Ivan* by Katherine Applegate. Since the book includes themes relating to animal welfare issues, many applicable discussions and activities resulted from the community reading experiences. These included the creation of library book covers based on the book and learning to draw gorillas like Ivan, the book's main character. The school library brought in service dogs, and students were taught how to properly care for pet animals. Students even partnered with the local Family Resource Center and held an animal shelter supply drive.

The next One School, One Book selection prompted even more student participation. First of all, thirteen primary-grade students from the Student Leadership Technology Program read and evaluated book reviews and through this process they chose the title *Hooper Finds a Family* by Jane Paley, which features a dog who was lost during Hurricane Katrina. The students contacted the public library to ensure the book would be available in digital format via the library's Hoopla subscription, and they created a tutorial to help teachers utilize the Hoopla interface. They also petitioned the principal of the school to purchase multiple copies of the book. Plus, they decided to video-record teachers and administrators reading selected chapters and sent a message to the book's author, seeking permission to use her copyrighted material in this way. They received a positive reply along with some complimentary book-related materials, a personalized letter, and a signed copy of the book.

Among the student-designed and requested activities were having a STEM (science, technology, engineering, and mathematics) activity explaining tropical storms, which led to a student-created infographic on them; proposing and securing approval to launch a fundraising campaign for American Red Cross hurricane relief efforts; producing a student-created book trailer and classroom trivia contests based on the book; and participating in several visits to the school by a "reading dog" and its trainer.[45]

You can imagine how school library support groups might partner with enthusiastic teachers and school librarians to be catalysts for funding and helping to run programs similar to this one. Teachers are very busy, yet simultaneously many of them often envision the benefits of having a One School, One Book program for their students—if only they had enough time and money to do it. School library support groups could be the deciding factors in making such programs possible.

One Book, One School, Oswego High School, Illinois

You may be thinking, What about high school community reads programs? Are these kinds of programs viable options for teenagers, too? It is a legitimate question, because high school students are often more focused on personal choice in reading instead of communal reading. However, "one book" programs can be successful for high schoolers, too, with the right encouragement. At Oswego High School in Illinois, they have continued it for over seven years with their One Book, One School program.

First of all, they promote the program as a "school-wide book club." In their publicity for the club, they are upfront about their goal: "In partnership with our school community, we aim to develop engaged readers to enhance a love of learning through literacy."

As with the programs for younger readers already mentioned, they encourage everyone—students, teachers, administrators, school staff members, parents, and community members—to participate. The idea is to boost independent reading and critical thinking for all who take part. To augment this targeted outcome, throughout the academic year periodic events and educational opportunities are put forward to go along with the One Book, One School program. In addition, the older students have a sense of buy-in because the titles used for the program are selected using electronic ballots by staff, and also by students, who are thanked for their participation in the process.

Teen-oriented titles that have been used reflect current young adult concerns and interests. Some of them are *Dear Martin* by Nic Stone, which includes a theme of racial profiling; *The 57 Bus: A True Story of Two Teenagers and the Crime That Changed Their Lives* by Dashka Slater, which presents a challenging exposé about race, class, gender, crime, and punishment; and *Hey, Kiddo* by Jarrett J. Krosoczka, a graphic novel about grappling with family addiction. As you can see, the chosen titles offer age-appropriate appeal because the students themselves have a voice in the selection procedure.[46] To draw readers in, the page on the school website touting the program features a slideshow of students in action reading and holding up copies of the books.

If a Friends or other school library support group hoped to help their high school librarian to devise a "one book" program, doing so would require following the same approval and partnering paths already recommended for younger students. To help support a school "one book" program, copies of books could be supplied, materials could be provided for special activities and events, and volunteer aid could be offered.

The One Book Community Reading Concept in Academia

Bear in mind that, because some colleges and universities also have library support groups, perhaps worthy undertakings for those organizations would be to financially support "one book" programs on campuses through their academic libraries and provide volunteer assistance as required or requested. Programs in these settings, which could be designed with the help of various partners and co-sponsors, would use titles geared to college-level audiences and university missions as their focuses.

One Book, One U, University of Miami, Florida

Since 2017, the University of Miami has offered a One Book, One U program that encourages participants to explore interrelated issues of climate change, structural racism, inequality, and other social justice concerns through the joint reading of a selected text. The program is designed to engage the entire university community in meaningful conversations about the human experience. Invitations are sent to campus divisions so that students and others can submit suggestions for events relating to each selected book's themes.

For the spring semesters, program sponsors and campus partners put together schedules of events that are connected to the subject matter of the chosen books, which each include a signature event with the book's author. Free copies of the books that are being read are made available at select events and instructors are encouraged to incorporate the texts in their classrooms whenever feasible. All are invited—students, instructors, friends, and other academic community members—to take advantage of the reading program and dialogue.

The program originated when two professors received a grant to establish the first common reading program in partnership with the Office of Institutional Culture to promote the mission of diversity, equity, and inclusion. However, in 2020, the University of Miami Libraries decided to become the official home for the One Book, One U program because the Libraries have the unique position as a central entity to serve the entire university community. In that role, the Libraries are able to ensure continual significant impact of the program across the university campuses.[47] Besides, the Libraries have a Friends of the Library organization behind them to support programs, secure gifts, and conduct fundraising projects as needed.[48]

To illustrate how the One Book, One U program encourages understanding and brings awareness to essential action on a range of interrelated social justice issues, the title selected for 2022–2023 was *The Water Will Come* by Jeff Goodell, one of the world's foremost environmental journalists. His book addresses the global effects of climate change due to rising sea levels, and its concepts tie in perfectly within the university's commitment to environmental sustainability and the teaching, research, and service related to its new Climate Resilience Academy.[49]

One Book Villanova, Villanova, Pennsylvania

Another university program that features a single title that is read campus- and community-wide is the One Book Villanova program. As with the University of Miami program, its program takes place during an entire academic year and targets a title that is worthy of close reading, course adoption, and spurring dialog and discussion among everyone who is part of the campus population. As a truly community-wide activity, distribution of books and participation spans university offices, academic departments, support staff, facilities departments, and even local book clubs that have joined in and affiliated themselves with the program.[50]

Each year, an online nomination form on the program's website is available to all faculty, staff, students, parents, and alumni so that the community can play a part from the ground up. Using the list of nominated books, the One Book Villanova Committee, which is comprised of faculty, staff, and students from across the University, confers and makes a selection for the forthcoming program title. Books are chosen based on broad appeal; manageable length; exploration of and relevance to complex issues and themes with contemporary social and cultural significance; suitability for discussions, spurring imagination, and promoting critical thinking; and format availability.[51]

In 2023, the book used was *Dear America: Notes of an Undocumented Citizen* by Jose Antonio Vargas, which is the author's personal account of being an undocumented immigrant living in the United States. The author presented an in-person lecture as the one book program's culmination, which was followed by light refreshments and a book signing with limited copies of the book available for free.[52]

One Book, One Minnesota, Friends of the Saint Paul Public Library, Minnesota

Another way that large Friends or other library support groups might promote a common reading experience is by sponsoring a statewide program in partnership with other library and literature-related facilities, organizations, and agencies. A good example is the statewide book club called One Book One Minnesota, for which libraries and schools throughout the state connect their communities through stories chosen to bring Minnesotans closer together. Citizens of all ages read each seasonally selected title in programs called "chapters" and come together virtually to discuss the books, reflect, and interact with the authors.[53]

The program is presented by the Friends of the Saint Paul Public Library, which serves as the Minnesota Center for the Book, in partnership with State Library Services, a division of the Minnesota Department of Education.[54] Other program partners include the Council of Regional Public Library System Administrators[55]; MakinVIA (provides eBook and database resource management)[56]; Minitex (a state-funded library support organization)[57]; and the University of Minnesota Press.[58] The Friends are able to fund the program with legislative appropriations from the Arts and Cultural Heritage Fund.[59]

Although this is a huge, wide-reaching program, other states could possibly consider designing similar programs through the efforts of major library support groups in large cities in their own regions with the collaboration of various state organizations, agencies, and other appropriate partners. This would require a great deal of outreach and advocacy to set in motion, but the Friends group in Saint Paul demonstrates that it can be done successfully. A few other states such as Maryland, which gets funding by the Maryland Humanities Council,[60] and Iowa, which receives funding through the auspices of the state library,[61] are conducting similar programs, but for states that lack such support it is possible for a large library support group(s) with the right enthusiasm and clout to take the lead and set the wheels in motion in their own regions.

Resources to Find Prospective Titles for One Book Programs

Once you have decided that your library support group is going to sponsor, run, host, or otherwise be a catalyst to getting the ball rolling for a new "one book" program, you will probably need further resources to help select books and plan related events. Therefore, to conclude this section on "one book" programs, I would like to give you a few places where you can gather some ideas for book selections and other needs. These resources list books have been previously used successfully by other "one book" reading programs and they give further useful tips and links to help you in planning any "one book" programs that you are putting together.

The first resource is from the Vintage and Anchor imprints of Knopf Doubleday Book publishers. They offer a Reading Group Center website with a One Book, One Community guidance page. On the page, you will find a list of titles previously read for other community "one book" programs. They also provide a list of titles with regional appeal, broken down by Northeast & Mid-Atlantic, South, Midwest, and West & Southwest. Plus, the page has a "How We Can Help" section that explains that they can serve as an author information resource and liaison if the author who is chosen is one of theirs;

tells how they can provide related graphics for your program and book ordering information; shares details on getting available reading and discussion guides for participants; and has links to other useful online resources.[62]

Simon & Schuster publishers provide a lengthy list of titles that have been used throughout the country in schools, libraries, at universities, and more places. You can search through the list to see if you can find a good match to begin your own "one book" program. They also have a national map with regions outlined so that you can find books with regional interest; links to lists of titles broken down by various age groups; a catalog of suggested titles that they have published; and information about their author speakers bureau.[63]

The last resource from Goodreads focuses on potential "one book" selections for schools. It is a list of suggested titles with ratings by those who have read them and with further suggestions given by those who enjoyed those stories.[64]

Friends Promoting Literacy in Head Start Classes

There are some Friends of the Library groups that help to fund free books for children in special classrooms such as those in Head Start centers. One example is akin to the Imagination Library program, called the Give a Kid a Book program, run by the Friends of the L.E. Phillips Memorial Public Library in Eau Claire, Wisconsin, which donates more than four thousand children's books a year to many local agencies. This includes the school district and the Head Start program with the goal of giving every child a new book during the holiday season.[65] Similarly, through their Snuggle Up & Read program, the Friends of the Library serving the Alachua County Library District in Florida, along with some members of the library staff, visit all Head Start classrooms in the county annually to tell the children about the featured book for that year and to distribute copies for each child to take home and keep.[66]

These are certainly worthwhile ways to connect children and books. However, in addition to donating books and instilling a desire to read them, Friends of the Library groups can contribute to Head Start in another way that goes beyond book donations. Volunteers from libraries and library support groups can get in the mix by providing outreach reading/storytime sessions in Head Start classrooms. These storytime visits can include reading books to the children, finger plays, songs, and other educational contents that advance literacy and learning.

Head Start is a truly outstanding program that was established in 1965 after President Lyndon B. Johnson created it after his State of the Union address in 1964, in which he declared a "War on Poverty." Its aim was and is to foster school readiness for children from low-income families through educational, nutritional, health, social, and other services. Since the program began, millions of children from birth to age five and their families have been served. Congress authorizes the funding for Head Start each year, and the program is run under the auspices of the Administration for Children and Families within the Department of Human Services. Federal grants are awarded to public agencies, private nonprofit and for-profit organizations, tribal governments, and school systems for operating Head Start programs in local communities.[67]

An example of what can be done by Friends of the Library groups to aid in promoting reading and literacy through Head Start beyond donating books is illustrated by the collaborative program offered by the Friends of the Knox County Public Library in

Tennessee. Through a partnership between the University of Tennessee, Knox County Schools, Knox County Health Department, Tennessee Early Intervention System, Department of Human Services, Knoxville's Community Development Corporation, Knox County Public Library, Friends of the Knox County Public Library, Pellissippi State Community College, Child Care Resource and Referral, and the Kiwanis Club, Head Start centers receive aid and support beyond what the federal government provides.

The local Knox County Community Action Committee oversees the Head Start program as part of the targeted activities under its charge, which is to serve all people from infancy through those in the elderly age group. They meet the needs for food, shelter, transportation, education, advocacy, training, and case management, and they extend opportunities for volunteerism to those who wish to give back through outreach.[68] Community Action Committees can be found in many locations throughout our country with the purpose of bringing together a coalition of community leaders from local organizations, hospitals, universities, and more to make a difference in their communities.[69]

This is where the Friends of the Knox County Public Library came and comes into play. In 2010, member volunteers began reading visits for five weeks in April and May to eight Head Start classes at the Claxton West Head Start Center. These visits are like the storytimes held in a library—volunteers read several books on a theme and add songs and finger plays to match as appropriate. Children can join in as the readers encourage them to at particular times during the session. Sessions can last from twenty to thirty minutes, depending on the age of the children.

To get the program started, Knox County Library staff members contacted the Friends and asked for volunteers, developed plans for the storytimes, created lists of which books to use, and trained volunteers. The Friends supplied books and special book bags to contain them and any other needed materials.

In the beginning, the reading visits took place at every Head Start center through alternating years, and after an increased effort to gain volunteers, the program was able to accommodate each center annually. To cover all the centers, six of them have been visited for six weekly sessions in either the fall or the spring, and either in the morning or afternoon, by a corps of twelve volunteer readers (and six substitutes). The Knox County Public Library book collection, books donated to the Friends, including Imagination Library re-donated books, and books left over from the library's Storytimes-to-Go kits have been used to stock the Head Start reading visitors' book bags.

In time, it became evident that, with classes representing diverse populations, more books incorporating themes of diversity were essential to balance the topical themes designated for each weekly visit. The Friends allocated two hundred dollars per year to purchase ten to twenty appropriate titles. Also, the centers instigated a requirement that all volunteers turn in a signed Standard of Conduct form that expresses the school rules and expectations before volunteers visit the classrooms.[70]

The program continued successfully until late winter of 2020, when it was suspended due to the critical worldwide health emergency that continued for two more years. In the fall of 2022, the program resumed. By that time, this author had moved to the area and, as a new Friends member and because of my youth librarianship background, I signed on to become one of the volunteer readers. I can attest to the careful organization and planning of the program, how enjoyable and meaningful the visits are, and that this is a program I hope other Friends groups will consider proposing in communities that provide Head Start.

TEXTBOX 11.4

TIPS FOR STARTING A LIBRARY HEAD START PROGRAM IN YOUR COMMUNITY

If you are considering the creation of a Head Start reading program in partnership with your library's outreach services and/or children's services department(s), here are some helpful tips and some questions to answer to get started:

- Who would coordinate or co-coordinate the program for your Friends group?
- You would need to have a good feel for the Head Start program in your area. Find out how many centers exist and the average number of classes at each center.
- How often might you like to assign volunteer readers and for how many weeks? Once a week per assigned class can work well, and you can determine the frequency with the school.
- What time(s) of day to you propose to have readers visit? Does the school have preferences?
- Do you have the resources to be able to assign volunteer readers all year? Or do you need to read for a short period(s) of time during the school year?
- How many volunteers might be needed, and how many do you have available? How would volunteers be recruited and oriented?
- How would the books be supplied? Consider the following:
  - Would you check books out from your library?
  - Does your Friends group or library have non-circulating books that are available for outreach?
  - Does your Friends group have funds available to purchase special books for Head Start outreach?
  - Would the children's librarians from your library be available to help you select and prepare books?
  - Would volunteers be charged with finding their own books, or would the coordinator of your program select the books?
  - How would you coordinate the sharing of the books between all volunteers?

- Once you have these details ironed out, you can approach your local Community Action Committee with a proposal. Start small with one school and try to have a reading experience scheduled for each class. Once you feel secure in how the program is running, you can add additional centers if you have enough volunteers and books.

Natalie Smith[1]
Former Coordinator
Friends of the Knox County Public Library's Head Start Program

Note

1. Natalie Smith, email message to author, January 24, 2023.

Special Award Programs and Honors

Library support groups can be leading, key, or collaborating players in bestowing any number of special awards, scholarships, and other honors to members of the communities that their libraries serve. They can also honor workers at their libraries, contest winners, or selected authors. In this final section of chapter 11, I would like to bring some of these particular kinds of awards to your attention through several fine examples.

Perhaps your Friends, foundation, or trust would like to designate new or additional awards in your community to help increase the notoriety of authors from regional minority populations or for those who write for singular audiences such as young children. Or maybe your organization is considering putting your nonprofit money to good use by offering scholarships, service awards, or holding distinctive contests with desirable prizes. Then again, maybe you are hoping to create your own unique kinds of awards or honors. As with other illustrations throughout this book, you might consider adapting or emulating the ones you will read about here next, or simply put them to use for inspiration as you brainstorm.

Tulsa Library Trust, Tulsa, Oklahoma

Each year, the city and county of Tulsa, its library community, and the surrounding areas are beneficiaries of quite a few generous award programs. These program examples may provide food for thought in designing and developing your own kinds of award programs and events.

The first one I want to feature is the annual Anne V. Zarrow Award for Young Readers' Literature, named in honor of an Oklahoma philanthropist and established by the Tulsa Library Trust in 1991. The award process and adjoined programming is conducted by the Tulsa City-County Library and made possible by a grant from the Anne and Henry Zarrow Foundation to the Tulsa Library Trust.[71]

The purpose of the award is to give formal recognition, on behalf of the Tulsa County community, to a nationally acclaimed author who has made a significant contribution to the field of young adult literature. Each recipient of the award is presented with a seven-thousand-dollar cash prize and an engraved crystal book. After the special award presentations, esteemed authors speak about their lives, their writing, and their books in addition to helping to distribute prizes to young authors between the ages of ten and eighteen who are winners in the associated Young People's Creative Writing Contest, also provided by the Trust.[72]

In conjunction with the author awards and writing contests, there are also annual teacher educational opportunities that are hosted by the Library and entitled Mr. Henry's Books: Educators' Workshops, named in honor of Henry Zarrow. Each teacher who participates receives a copy of a selected book by that year's author award winner along with a curriculum plan that is focused on that winner's work. Teachers also receive lessons about the effective use of the library's online educational resources and youth-oriented library programs to further engage their students in literacy, learning, and library usage. Additionally, each teacher is entered into a drawing for the winning author to visit their classroom.[73]

The Tulsa Library Trust also gives an annual award called the Peggy V. Helmerich Distinguished Author Award, named in honor of a former Hollywood starlet who left that career for family life and became dedicated to charity work surrounding health care and libraries in Tulsa.[74] The purpose of the award is to bestow formal recognition on behalf of the Tulsa County community upon internationally acclaimed authors who have contributed a renowned body of work to the field of literature and letters. Honorees receive a forty-thousand-dollar cash prize and an engraved crystal book at a black-tie dinner in December at which each selected author speaks.

In addition to the prize award ceremonies in December, titles by the selected authors are donated to area classrooms and teachers devise curriculums to match them; students are given private author presentations; and the Central Library provides free public author presentations with time allocated for asking questions and book signings.[75]

Two other author awards are given by the Trust along with its partners. The biennial Sankofa Freedom Award, which began in 2005 by the African American Resource Center and the Tulsa Library Trust, honors a nationally notable author whose work positively features the intricacies of the cultural, economic, and political issues involving the African American community. Winners receive a ten-thousand-dollar prize and an engraved plaque, and they each give a public address on the awards presentation day.[76]

Finally, I come to the American Indian Festival of Words Writers Award, which was started in 2001 and is given during odd-numbered years. It is the first and so far only award given by a public library to honor American Indian writers for outstanding contributions as authors, poets, journalists, or scriptwriters and for which the winners receive a ten-thousand-dollar cash prize. The award is jointly sponsored by the Maxine and Jack Zarrow Family Foundation and the Tulsa Library Trust and presented in conjunction with the library's American Indian Festival of words, a series of enlightening programs about the history, culture, arts, and achievements of American Indians.[77]

Friends of the Clifton Park-Halfmoon Public Library, Clifton, New York

Another way library support groups can offer community outreach is through scholarship programs. Providing these opportunities is especially important for and appreciated by students today as college costs continue to rise. Offering scholarships is one more positive way that Friends or other library support organizations can provide community assistance, which is related to reading and learning.

Here are the details. At the Friends of the Clifton Park-Halfmoon Public Library in New York, the Friends of the Library organization awards one-thousand-dollar scholarships to two high school seniors each year through its Friends Community Scholarship Program covering college tuition and expenses. Application deadlines are in March and decisions are made by early May. For convenience, the multi-faceted application packet can be downloaded from the Friends website. Applicants must be high school seniors who will be attending accredited two-year or four-year colleges or universities. They must be graduating seniors from the local high school, residents of the library tax district but attending an outside public or private school, or locals being homeschooled.[78]

The Albert Wisner Public Library Foundation in Warwick, New York, has a different approach than requiring a completed packet of information to apply. They ask interested college-bound students from the library's service district to compete for two $2,500 scholarships through an essay contest. Each year, the essay prompts vary. For instance, in 2023, the topic was, "Tell us about a book that has affected you deeply and why." In an effort to be fair, in subsequent years prompts are completely different.[79] Any library support group interested in providing a scholarship competition must decide upon the most equitable way to design the application process in their community.

With all this in mind, most library support groups that provide scholarships offer funding that ranges from five-hundred-dollar awards up to two thousand dollars. Some choose to offer one scholarship, and others give them to the top three candidates. For instance, a Friends group might decide to give a student who places first in their assessment of qualifications a $1,500 award and those who place second and third five hundred dollars each. It greatly depends on how much funding the organization has at hand to allot to the cause and how it chooses to distribute the money.

If a group designs a scholarship award one way one year, it is fine to revamp the process for applying or the amounts given the next year, although some groups prefer to keep a yearly award consistent as they are able. It is best for a group to determine what is most effective for them and for the needs of the community. No matter what, good public information about the program, up-to-date advertising, and clear timelines are essential.

Notes

1. Little Free Library. 2023. https://littlefreelibrary.org/.
2. Little Free Library. 2023. "Build a Little Free Library," https://littlefreelibrary.org/start/build-a-little-free-library/.
3. Little Free Library. 2023. "Registration Process," https://littlefreelibrary.org/stewards/registration/.
4. Little Free Library. 2023. "Indigenous Library Program," https://littlefreelibrary.org/programs/indigenous-library-program/.
5. Little Free Library. 2023. "Impact Library Program," https://littlefreelibrary.org/programs/impact-library/.
6. This Old House. 2022. "How to Build a Little Free Library." YouTube, https://www.youtube.com/watch?v=NuNvSqGdurU.
7. This Old House. 2022. "How to Install a Little Free Library." YouTube, https://www.youtube.com/watch?v=dqbHnjWO0TE&t=195s.
8. Elizabeth Berghold. "Little Free Libraries." *Chico Carrel*, February 2019, http://www.chicolibrary.org/Carrel/2019%20Carrels/201902%20February%20Carrel.pdf.
9. Little Free Library. 2023. "Read in Color," https://littlefreelibrary.org/programs/read-in-color/.
10. Friends of the Palo Alto Library. 2023. "Book Sale Info," https://www.fopal.org/book-sale-info.
11. Candid Foundation Directory. 2023. "Friends of the Library Book Warehouse," https://fconline.foundationcenter.org/fdo-grantmaker-profile/?collection=grantmakers&activity=result&key=FRI1411.
12. Alignable. 2023. "Friends of the Wichita Falls Public Library," https://www.alignable.com/wichita-falls-tx/friends-of-the-wichita-falls-public-library.
13. Michael Grace. March 24, 2021. "Friends of the WF Public Library Giving Away 30,000 Books for Free." News Channel 3, https://www.newschannel6now.com/2021/03/24/friends-wf-public-library-giving-away-books-free/.
14. Friends of the Knox County Public Library. 2023. "Community Outreach," https://www.knoxfriends.org/community-outreach/.
15. American Library Association. 2023. "ALA Disaster Relief Fund," https://www.ala.org/aboutala/offices/cro/getinvolved/disasterreliefefforts.
16. Debbie Cobb. "The Library and CFOL Respond to the Camp Fire." *Chico Carrel*, February 2019, http://www.chicolibrary.org/Carrel/2019%20Carrels/201902%20February%20Carrel.pdf.
17. Mel Lightbody. "Books to Evacuees: CFOL Member Acknowledged." *Chico Carrel*, February 2019, http://www.chicolibrary.org/Carrel/2019%20Carrels/201902%20February%20Carrel.pdf.
18. Jeff Munson. September 1, 2021. "Friends of Carson City Library Donate Books to Caldor Fire Evacuees." CarsonNow.org, https://carsonnow.org/story/09/01/2021/friends-carson-city-library-donate-books-caldor-fire-evacuees.
19. City of Tualatin, Oregon. 2023. "Friends of the Library Donating to the Texas Disaster Relief," https://www.tualatinoregon.gov/library/friends-library-donating-texas-disaster-relief.
20. Dolly Parton's Imagination Library. 2023. "Celebrating! 1 in 10 Children under the Age of Five in the USA Receives Imagination Library Books," https://imaginationlibrary.com/.
21. Dolly Parton's Imagination Library. 2013. "The Journey of an Imagination Library Book." YouTube, https://www.youtube.com/watch?v=IjxcK1ZZw3c&t=209s.
22. Cedar Rapids Public Library. 2023. "Home/Children," https://www.crlibrary.org/children/imagination-library.

23. Knox County Tennessee Public Library. 2023. "Seeds of Imagination Luncheon," https://www.knoxcountylibrary.org/dolly-parton-imagination-library/seeds.

24. Dolly Parton's Imagination Library. [n.d.] "How to Start a Program," https://imaginationlibrary.com/usa/start-a-program/.

25. Dolly Parton's Imagination Library. 2017. "Affiliates & Community Partners," https://imaginationlibrary.com/ilData/usrFiles/2021/04/USA_Affiliates-Community-reg2021.pdf.

26. Los Angeles Public Library. 2023. "Los Angeles Public Library Creators in Residence," https://www.lapl.org/creators.

27. Poudre River Public Library District. 2022. "Fort Collins Book Fest," https://www.focobookfest.org/.

28. Fulton County Library System. April 28, 2022. "Fulton County Library System and the Atlanta-Fulton Public Library Foundation Announce New Children's Book Festival This Spring." Press Releases, https://www.fulcolibrary.org/news/fulton-county-library-system-and-the-atlanta-fulton-public-library-foundation-announce-new-childrens-book-festival-this-spring/.

29. Knox County Tennessee Public Library. 2023. "Children's Festival of Reading," https://www.knoxcountylibrary.org/childrens-festival-of-reading.

30. West Virginia Book Festival. 2023. "A Celebration of Books," http://www.wvbookfestival.org/.

31. Madison Public Library. 2022. "Wisconsin Book Festival," https://www.wisconsinbookfestival.org/about.

32. Madison Public Library. 2022. "Show Your Support for the Festival." Wisconsin Book Festival, https://www.wisconsinbookfestival.org/give.

33. Madison Public Library. 2022. "Get Involved." Wisconsin Book Festival, https://www.wisconsinbookfestival.org/get-involved.

34. John Y. Cole. January 2005. "One Book Projects Grow in Popularity." Library of Congress, https://www.loc.gov/loc/lcib/0601/cfb.html.

35. Friends of the Clifton Park-Halfmoon Public Library. 2023. "Two Towns-One Book," https://friendsofcphlibrary.org/two-towns-one-book/.

36. Stewart's Shops, https://www.stewartsshops.com/.

37. Friends of the Clifton Park-Halfmoon Public Library.

38. Tulsa City-County Library. 2023. "One Book, One Tulsa: Crying in H Mart," https://downtowntulsa.com/do/one-book-one-tulsa-crying-in-h-mart.

39. Tulsa City-County Library. 2018. "One Book, One Tulsa' Community-wide Reading Initiative to Explore Mental Illness and Homelessness," https://www.tulsalibrary.org/press-release/one-book-one-tulsa-communitywide-reading-initiative-explore-mental-illness-and.

40. Tulsa City-County Library. 2018. "One Book, One Tulsa—Join the Conversation," https://www.tulsalibrary.org/press-release/one-book-one-tulsa-join-conversation.

41. Wege Foundation. [n.d.] "Is the Planet Worth Saving?" https://wegefoundation.com/.

42. Grand Rapids Public Library. 2023. "One Book, One City for Kids," https://www.grpl.org/kids/onebook/.

43. Knox Education Foundation. 2023. "One Book Read City," https://knoxed.org/initiatives/one-book-read-city/.

44. Oneida City School District. 2020. "One District, One Book," https://www.oneidacsd.org/district/special_projects/one_district_one_book.

45. Sam Northern. March 25, 2019. "One School + One Book = A Love of Reading." Knowledge Quest, Journal of the American Association of School Librarians, https://knowledgequest.aasl.org/one-school-one-book-a-love-of-reading/.

46. Oswego High School. 2023. "Oswego High School—One Book, One School," https://www.sd308.org/Page/20061.

47. University of Miami Libraries. 2023. "One Book, One U," https://www.library.miami.edu/one-book/.

48. University of Miami Libraries. 2023. "Friends of the Libraries," https://www.library.miami.edu/about/friends-of-the-libraries.html#:~:text=The%20University%20of%20Miami%20Friends,%2C%20alumni%2C%20and%20community%20leaders.

49. University of Miami Libraries. 2023. "One Book, One U."

50. Villanova University One Book. 2023. "One Book Villanova Program," https://www1.villanova.edu/villanova/onebook.html.

51. Villanova University One Book. 2023."One Book Villanova Nomination Form," https://www1.villanova.edu/villanova/onebook/nomination.html.

52. Villanova University One Book. 2023. "Get Your One Book!" https://www1.villanova.edu/villanova/onebook/onebookorders.html.

53. Friends of the Saint Paul Public Library. 2023. "One Book, One Minnesota," https://thefriends.org/minnesota-center-for-the-book/one-book-one-minnesota/.

54. Minnesota Department of Education. [n.d.] "State Library Services," https://education.mn.gov/MDE/dse/Lib/sls/.

55. Council of Regional Public Library System Administrators. [n.d.] https://www.crplsa.info/

56. Mackin. 2023. https://home.mackin.com/.

57. Minitex. 2020. https://minitex.umn.edu/about/about-minitex.

58. University of Minnesota Press. 2023. https://www.upress.umn.edu/.

59. Minnesota State Legislature. 2023. "Arts & Cultural Heritage Fund," https://www.legacy.mn.gov/arts-cultural-heritage-fund.

60. Maryland Humanities Council. 2023. "One Book, One Maryland," https://www.mdhumanities.org/programs/one-maryland-one-book/.

61. State Library of Iowa. 2023. "All Iowa Reads," https://www.statelibraryofiowa.gov/index.php/libraries/programs/all-iowa-reads.

62. Knopf Doubleday Publishing Group. 2023. "Reading Group Center," https://knopfdoubleday.com/one-book-one-community/.

63. Simon & Schuster, Inc. 2019. "Connect Your Community to a Great Read," https://www.simonandschusterpublishing.com/onebook/index.html.

64. Goodreads. 2023. "One Book One School Books," https://www.goodreads.com/shelf/show/one-book-one-school.

65. Friends of the L.E. Phillips Memorial Public Library. 2017. "Give a Kid a Book," https://www.ecpubliclibrary.info/friends/programs/give-a-kid-a-book/.

66. Friends of the Library, Alachua County Library District. 2022. "Snuggle Up & Read," https://folacld.org/m%5Epsnuggle.html.

67. Head Start. 2022. "About Us." U.S. Department of Health & Human Services, https://eclkc.ohs.acf.hhs.gov/about-us/article/head-start-program-facts-fiscal-year-2017.

68. CAC. 2022. Knoxville-Knox County Community Action Committee, https://www.knoxcac.org/newweb/.

69. Healthy Parkinson's Communities. January 20, 2021. "The What, Why, and How of Community Action Committees (CACs)." Davis Phinney Foundation for Parkinson's, https://healthyparkinsonscommunities.org/cacs/1062680/#:~:text=%E2%80%9CWhat%20is%20a%20Community%20Action,a%20difference%20in%20their%20community.

70. Friends of the Knox County Library. October 2018. "Brief History of the Involvement with Head Start." Report compiled by the Friends of the Knox County Library.

71. Oklahoma Library Association. [n.d.] "Henry & Anne Zarrow," https://www.oklibs.org/page/LegendsZarrow.

72. Tulsa Library Trust. 2017. "Zarrow Award," https://tulsalibrarytrust.org/program/zarrow-award/.

73. Tulsa City-County Library. 2023. "Anne V. Zarrow Author Award for Young Readers' Literature," https://www.tulsalibrary.org/programs-and-services/anne-v-zarrow-award-for-young-readers-literature.

74. Voices of Oklahoma. 2023. "Peggy Helmerich, Hollywood Starlet." Oklahoma Historical Society, https://voicesofoklahoma.com/interviews/helmerich-peggy/.

75. Tulsa Library Trust. 2017. "Helmerich Author Award," https://tulsalibrarytrust.org/program/helmerich-award/.

76. Tulsa City-County Library. 2018. "Sankofa Freedom Award," https://www.tulsalibrary.org/research/african-american-resource-center/sankofa-freedom-award.

77. Tulsa City-County Library. 2018. "American Indian Festival of Words," https://www.tulsalibrary.org/american-indian-festival-words.

78. Friends of the Clifton Park-Halfmoon Public Library. 2023. "Friends of the Library Scholarships," https://friendsofcphlibrary.org/friends-of-the-library-scholarships/.

79. Albert Wisner Public Library. 2019. "Albert Wisner Public Library Foundation," https://www.albertwisnerlibrary.org/content/albert-wisner-public-library-foundation.

CHAPTER 12

Library Support Groups Writing and Seeking Grants

FOR THOSE OF YOU who are unfamiliar with grants, especially for a library support group, I will start off this chapter with a helpful definition and description. A nonprofit grant, which is called a fundraising grant at times, is a financial donation given to an organization, usually by a foundation, corporation, or government agency known as grantmakers. Nonprofit library support organizations frequently secure funding by researching a wide pool of grant award options for open grants that may be a way to provide the money for the specific programs or initiatives they have targeted. However, grants are not given as a lump sum to pay for general operations, and grantmakers, in most cases, carefully specify how their gifts are to be used.

Grants typically come from large, established sources. They are important because they generally surpass the size of gifts from individual donors. These larger monetary gifts can permit your library support group to pay for programs, projects, or essential materials well beyond the means of your group's or your library's regular budget. A bonus is that when your group achieves a grant award and sees the funded goal through, it builds visibility, credibility, and a positive image which is especially attractive for impressing subsequent potential donors.[1]

Therefore, to supplement fundraising activities, donor memberships, donor drives, membership dues, and other forms of contributions, it behooves Friends, foundations, and trusts to include seeking grants as a way to aid their recipient libraries. However, many library support groups find the idea of researching, applying for, monitoring, and evaluating grants to be a daunting endeavor. It can be the opposite though, if board members follow a sensible and carefully planned process with knowledgeable and informed grant proposal leaders at the helm.

The guidance in this chapter will help those leaders who are tactically approaching the grant process and who include applying for grants to their overall strategic planning. It will benefit those who may already be experienced and who want some advice to make the process even more streamlined or complete, as well as those who have no previous experience with grants at all but who would like to give the option of incorporating grants a try.

The first step would be for boards to decide what unmet goals they have for completing their mission for their libraries and then targeting the kinds of grants needed to get there. Does a particular library collection need a big boost? Is a library community garden in an adjacent lot through which youth could be actively involved a highly desired library goal? Does the library require updated computers for its instructional lab? Is the library building in need of a revamp to allow for more meeting spaces? The ideas for grants can range from inexpensive to major as they aim to address your recipient library's most essential needs and wants but that have yet to be funded. The good news is that there are many wonderful resources available for investigating grants and their purposes, several of which I will be describing during this chapter.

Once you have used those resources and figured out a grant or grants for which you qualify and which you hope will suit your goals, the next step would be to create grant proposals for your grant applications. This is the most complex part of the process, but when it is done well, it not only helps grantmakers to bestow grant dollars but it can aid a library support group in creating a useful checklist for keeping tabs on how an awarded grant is properly put into action.

With the checklist handy, you can track grant progress by keeping vigilant records and other documentation. This is essential because you will be responsible for reporting back to the grant-giver about how the money was actually used and how it benefitted your organization in serving its library community. In the end, with all of your well-kept records at hand, you might even find that completing your final report to the grant-giver is rather rewarding. A winning report secures your positive impression with the grantor and, as a consequence, provides a stronger possibility of being awarded another grant from the same source in the future.

Grants and Grant-Finding Resources

As noted, the initial step is to decide and seek out what grant or grants would be the most suitable and logical for your purposes. Yet you may be confused about where to start looking. You might start off by expressing a need for a recommendation and asking your board members to let their personal contacts know that you are hoping to secure grants for particular uses. Those contacts may know of and be able to apply for grants to benefit your cause or suggest ones for which you can apply. There may be local grants available which may be fairly easy to get.

As an example, a situation where this proved successful occurred at the Friends of the Poudre River Public Library in Fort Collins, Colorado. Board member Robin Gard's daughter, Madeline, an employee of Waterpik in Fort Collins for a number of years, an outspoken library supporter, and a library volunteer as a youth, applied for a Church & Dwight Employee Giving Fund grant to benefit the Friends. A $4,500 grant was awarded in 2023 to boost the Friends' efforts in significantly supporting educational and children's programming at the Poudre River Public Library District. Church & Dwight, the parent company of Waterpik which is committed to giving back to the communities where their employees live and work, has distributed more than fifteen million dollars since its inception in 2005.[2]

If you do not have a connection like this one to help you find a grant, or you wish to seek additional funding, there are several resources available that can provide assistance.

One of the premier research tools for this purpose is Candid's Foundation Directory. It is very expensive to subscribe to this directory, but you can still access it for free. One way is by earning a Candid Gold Seal of Transparency, discussed earlier in this book. It offers a benefit of one year's free access, which would make searching easy from a home or office computer. However, even though after a year a library support group would then be required to pay the subscription rate to continue access, there may be another avenue for using this resource without charge.

Many public libraries provide free online access to Foundation Directory via their library website research sections, although there is a caveat. Because of the expense for a library to subscribe, most libraries cannot afford unlimited access for personal use outside a library building. Instead, a library card holder usually needs to go in person to a specific library branch and use an in-house computer at that branch to gain access. Still, this is a valuable and cost-effective way for library support groups to connect to this resource and do the research at their own libraries without charge. A bonus is that, because searching can be complex, in the library itself there is usually a librarian at hand to offer user guidance. It can definitely be worth a trip!

You may be wondering why Foundation Directory is so special. The reason is that it is a valuable resource for discovering pertinent and promising matches for what you hope a grant will accomplish while helping to avoid applying for grants that would most likely be rejected. It provides a huge and ever-expanding number of grantmaker profiles that are relevant to the needs of nonprofits.

To use the Directory, a searcher enters a phrase describing what type of grant aid is needed for a particular purpose. For example, if a Friends Foundation wants to provide new computers for a library branch that has outdated ones, or a Friends of the Library group would like to host a week-long artist-in-residence series at their local library for children during a spring break, then keywords, advanced searches, and filters can be applied as needed to find suitable grants that fund these sorts of endeavors. Searches deliver a results page that includes grantmakers, grants, and previous recipients. Profiles included give in-depth summaries of each potential funder's work along with pertinent details that allow searchers to target the best matches.[3] For a short overview of what the Directory offers to searchers, Candid has a YouTube video you can watch called "How to Know If a Funder Is Right for Your Nonprofit with Foundation Directory."[4]

GrantWatch is another resource that may be practical to find match possibilities for library nonprofits of all kinds, whether for public, school, or other library support. Many grants listed are state specific and the database of grants that are open for proposals is limited compared to Foundation Directory, but if Foundation Directory is unavailable, this may be worth checking. Though GrantWatch access requires a subscription, the cost may be manageable. Prices as of this writing range from eighteen dollars to use it for a week, to forty-five dollars for a month, ninety dollars for three months, and $199 for a year.[5]

A webpage that may be useful to library support group grant seekers is the Grants & Funding page on the ProLiteracy website. For more than sixty years, ProLiteracy has been "the largest adult and basic education membership organization in the nation [that] believes a safer, stronger, and more sustainable society starts with an educated adult population." Because of their strong focus on changing lives and communities through the power of literacy, they give links to about fifteen websites, including three of their own with different literacy funding purposes, so that those searching for literacy initiative grants have a free place to find prospective funding sources. The links to sites would be primarily useful for grant projects aimed at adult, student, and family literacy.[6] If your library support organization plans to seek a grant to aid your library with a program or project related to those areas of focus, you may find this page of use.

As an illustration of what can be accomplished through such a grant, one Friends of the Library organization applied to the Dollar General Literacy Foundation, listed among the ProLiteracy choices, for funding to support adult literacy. In 2017, the Friends of the Dallas Public Library received a ten-thousand-dollar grant to enrich High School Equivalency and English language classes held at the Dallas Public Library to bolster learning outcomes. Because these Friends have a mission to help people meet their lifelong learning needs by funding the library's free education and literacy resources, the grant was an appropriate fit and an award was received.[7]

Another example of a Friends group grant that helped to fund the efforts of their library was one awarded to the Friends of the Chesapeake Public Library in Virginia. In 2022, they received a one-thousand-dollar Judith F. Krug Memorial Fund Programming Grant from the Freedom to Read Foundation (FTRF), affiliated with the American Library Association. The FTRF distributes grants each year to organizations that support activities to raise awareness of intellectual freedom and censorship issues during the annual Banned Books Week celebrations in October. These are awarded to honor Krug who was a fierce proponent of education and a defender of First Amendment rights. Libraries, schools, universities, and nonprofit community organizations—such as library support groups with a mission to fund efforts toward these issues—can submit applications by the May deadlines. With the heightened, reactivated focus on censorship concerns and the need to defend intellectual freedom today, this is a particularly significant grant.

The ways that this grant was put into action in Chesapeake was exemplary. The money contributed to the efforts of library staff to make banned books the focal point of their third annual Black Ink festival, a daylong, all-ages festival which celebrated local authors of color. During the festival, writing workshops, poetry slams, panel discussions on the value of diversity in publishing, banned book giveaways, and a keynote speech from nationally honored, local author Kwame Alexander, a target of book-banners himself, were held. Since their local school district has been targeted for book challenges, the festival largely centered on middle and high school students, primarily the underserved, and highlighted the library's growing partnership with administrators and teachers at Chesapeake Public Schools.[8]

For school library support groups, also keep in mind the Laura Bush Foundation for America's Libraries. Its mission is to provide "grants to school libraries to expand, diversify, and update their collections."[9] This resource could be an excellent place for a school Friends or other group to apply for a grant to provide collection development assistance for their beneficiary school library or media center.

If your library support group wants to fund and/or partner for library endeavors to enhance literacy, focus on intellectual freedom, enlighten readers by giving them opportunities to hear prominent authors speak, build up a diverse children's book collection, create a teen book discussion or writing program, or any number of other meaningful goals, consider grants as an additional method to help pay for them. Hopefully, you are feeling persuaded to do so, and I will move on to the actual process of applying for and getting grants.

Applying for Grants with a "Mission Match"

For many years, Sharon Skinner, who has served as grants coordinator for the City of Mesa in Arizona, has advised: "Grant proposal writing is both a science and art. It is a form of persuasive writing that requires including hard data and a compelling story while following a logical sequence . . . [it] includes a narrative thread that ties the entire story together from the opening (executive summary) to the conclusion (budget narrative)." The central idea is to make your particular proposal shine above all the others that a grantmaker receives, allowing yours to win over reviewers, to garner more points, and to successfully gain the money that your library support group needs to enhance your mission.[10]

The following steps that Skinner recommends, adapted for library support groups, will take you on an effective path through applying for, securing, and evaluating grants:

- Keep in mind as you research grants that funders are looking for a *"mission match"* when they award money. Be certain to pursue only grants that specifically support the purpose or goals for which your library support group is aiming.
- Carefully read and understand the *specific requirements* given for developing a potentially successful grant application once you have found a grantmaker you believe can fulfill your needs through an award.
- Be aware that, in most cases, grant applications need to be completed and submitted electronically.
- When you are sure that you have targeted a grant that is a mission match, take note of and *apply the grantmaker's specific requirements* using the *proper formats and terminology* as you proceed toward applying, including adhering to deadlines.
- For you own use so you know you have covered everything asked for, *develop a checklist of requirements and applicant expectations* to review before sending off your submission.
- To boost making a good impression, have *details at hand on past programs and activities with positive outcomes* that your library support group has provided for your beneficiary library. Openly portray your community, your library, any partnerships in which you engage, and any successful earlier grant experiences. You will need to add *pertinent documentation* along with *letters of commitment and support*, as the grantmaker necessitates.
- When you *tackle the needs/problem statement*, pinpoint the issue or issues that the grant money would help your group to address; add whatever data you can that will validate the need, with citations; and meticulously describe the conditions where the funding would be impactful.
- After this, using visuals, timelines, or charts where appropriate, you will need to *explain in detail how funding would make a difference*—how it would enable your group to affect change, improve conditions, and heighten the experience of the library, the library users, and/or the overall community it serves.
- Next will come the *goals and objectives* piece where the *expected results and benefits* are explained. The most effective way to do this is through "SMART" goals, discussed in some previous chapters, which are specific; measureable; achievable; relevant; and fit a logical timeframe.

- A *budget* relaying the amount your group needs and a descriptive list of all the materials and other costs as they directly connect to your goals and objectives must also be added.
- The anticipated *progress and outcomes* of the programming, project, or activity that may be funded is given in the evaluation section. Besides aiding a grantmaker in the decision about whether or not to give an award, this would later serve as a guideline as you offer assessments and feedback according to your award agreement.
- Before final submission, have your organization's board members proofread and review the content and style of the application and make any necessary adjustments. Using your checklist of requirements as a gauge, ensure that they are all in agreement that the application is complete and ready to send in.[11]

Although these steps are rather clear-cut, there are some additional pointers and observations from June Ruther, Institutional Relations Manager at the Friends of the Saint Paul Public Library, that Friends and Foundations can keep in mind during the grant researching and application process. First of all, she states that there have been notable changes in funding that is offered and alterations in the means of securing that funding. In other words, a new level of flexibility in funding has evolved, so that if grantors say they will only fund educational endeavors, this can be expanded to include not only schools and school libraries but also public libraries and community centers that wish to offer any number of educational opportunities. This allows library support groups of all kinds to consider more types of available grants to suit their needs.

Another shift in the grantmaking scene is a very explicit focus on connecting with and meeting the needs of historically excluded populations. This means that in your grant proposals you will want to communicate an understanding of and satisfactory methods for reaching a diverse audience with your programming or project plans. It is not enough to simply say that grants will allow you to provide events or activities for "the entire community," but to specify how ethnic, cultural, socioeconomic, and other elements of equity blend into your plans. Furthermore, grantors are also considering whether the requesting library support nonprofit itself makes equality and inclusion a priority for its board and membership.

Besides these factors, grantmakers are looking to make awards for nonprofits that have solid vision and mission statements. They want to be sure that yours includes evidence that the programs you want them to fund are deeply integrated with your statements and that your mission supports the equitable activity they expect. That will require gathering information about your community, details about and demographics for who is using the library, quantifiable aspects of library-community relations, and relatable stories and examples gleaned from the library staff. The library itself can help you to collect much of this information and data. These elements will help you to create connected storytelling to substantiate your request for funding and to reflect a strong web of impact that grantors want to uphold.[12]

Ruther summed up this helpful information with an apt and encouraging statement for library support organizations that wish to seek grants to benefit their libraries as exemplified by the Friends of the Dallas Public Library grant described earlier:

> Libraries are uniquely suited to the kind of funding that is being offered by many community foundations right now. Interest in public spaces as social connectors, leadership in

the area of digital equity and inclusion, and the neighborhood-focused nature of most library programming makes educational partnerships and community learning an obvious step. And should you have recently undergone, say, a *strategic planning process*, well, you probably have the community connections, data, and vision you need at your fingertips.[13]

Consider that one side benefit of applying for grants and using money you have raised for doing good work in the community to promote books and literacy is that it highlights your existence and purpose. When that happens, your group might also find itself a surprised recipient of other kinds of special award money in addition to grants. An example of this type of award comes from the Friends of the Knox County Public Library in Tennessee. In 2023, the group was awarded a three-hundred-dollar First Book gift certificate by KPMG U.S. as part of their Family for Literacy Community Impact Day.

KPMG is a global network of professional firms providing audit, tax, and advisory services.[14] Making a positive difference in communities is a priority for them, and one of their goals is to empower and impact the next generation of leaders through equitable lifelong learning and quality education.[15] Because First Book is a nonprofit dedicated to providing a path out of poverty through quality educational materials, it made sense for KPMG to give the award to a Friends group that targets efforts toward that goal it its mission. By awarding the First Book gift certificate to such library Friends, KPMG has provided funds to access to the First Book Marketplace online store, which carries books and other classroom resources for educators and program leaders serving children and teenagers in need from ages birth to eighteen years.[16]

Following through with the purpose of the award, the Knox Library Friends immediately used the certificate to order eighty-one new books in Spanish to fulfill requests from several of their Books in the Community partners. The books were donated to a behavioral health agency, a juvenile detention center, and a refugee service facility. This scenario illustrates what library support groups can do on many levels to supplement its library's resources and literacy goals in the community they both serve.[17]

Figure 12.1. Members of the Friends of the Knox County Public Library in Tennessee dressed up as characters from the book, *Little Blue Truck's Christmas* by Alice Schertle, for the station WIVK downtown Christmas Parade in December 2022. *Credit: Mallory Nygard.*

Receiving Grant Awards and Documenting Grant Results

Imagine that you have followed all the protocols for submitting well-constructed and documented grant proposal, and after the deadline and consideration time passes you receive the notification you were hoping to get: "Congratulations! We have awarded you a grant!"

This is wonderful news, and now there are some more steps to be completed as an official grant recipient:

- **Call the grantor to express your thanks.** The person who calls should be the fundraising chair who may have been instrumental in the process of writing the grant, or it could instead be the chair or president of your organization, preferably on the same day that notification is received.
- Once the funds are received, **write a thank-you letter** on official stationery. This letter also needs to include language regarding tax-deductibility. The Internal Revenue Service has a booklet you will find useful with substantiation and disclosure requirements for charitable contributions, which a grant of $250 or more is considered for tax purposes.[18]
- Call your group's project manager to **plan a meeting to talk about the actual grant implementation** and invite everyone whom that person feels should be present. Flesh out and finalize your ultimate strategic plan now that the funding is at hand.
- **Get your calendar and add all the pertinent due dates and deadlines**, especially those for the interim and/or final reports the grant requires.
- **Spread the word** that your organization has received the grant and the reasons for it. Make sure the general membership, the volunteers, the board, the library being supported, the community, and anyone else connected are all notified via emails, personal messages, on your social media, in a newsletter, in local media, on your website, and so on.
- **Make communication a priority.** Depending on the scope of the program or project, have the project manager keep in good touch at least monthly with all essential parties from both the grantors' side and your group's side. Do this regularly to ensure the expected progress as it has been planned. However, if problems or concerns materialize about completion within the proposed timeline, inform your funder as soon as possible before or by the halfway mark. Do not delay in reporting and working to remedy stumbling blocks.
- As time passes, **continue updating your grantor**. Send messages with pertinent details about milestones and steps moving forward as your program or project unfolds.[19]

Once again, as a vital finishing touch to accepting a grant, you will have agreed to report back with end results to the funding provider, and therefore be prepared to keep good quantitative and qualitative statistics once a grant is awarded. Use the information you will regularly gather as progress is made toward your targeted outcomes. Figure out the most essential details to include and the methods to use as you convey the outcomes to the funders. The more carefully and comprehensively you provide your feedback, the stronger the chances are that you may be able to secure further grants in the future. Grantmakers appreciate knowing that the money they have invested in your cause was well used for a worthwhile venture.

What If Your Grant Proposal Is Not Successful?

Now imagine a different scenario from the one in the previous section. You feel certain that your organization has followed all the applicable advice and completed the application for a much-desired grant correctly, exactly as instructed. You and others have spent a lot of time and effort putting it all together. All the same, instead of meeting with success in being awarded the grant, you are met with a disappointing message saying that the money has been given elsewhere. Know that even though your group had hoped to be given an acceptance letter rather than a rejection, you can use the experience(s) to move forward in a positive manner and to learn how you may hopefully improve your future chances to obtain a grant.

The first factor to recognize is that rejection letters are part of the process in seeking a grant. Just about every nonprofit attempting to secure grants goes through some negative responses. The key takeaway though is to consider a "no" answer as a positive, potentially leading to successful future prospects. Truly, rejection letters can be a learning tool.

Most rejection letters are short and to the point which is a sign of respect and acknowledgment that disappointment will come following the receipt of the message. These messages are not meant to be harsh or critical and grantmakers want you to know that they appreciated your efforts. They also want to encourage future impactful projects and they will commonly include improvement and strengthening suggestions for another proposal from you. Realize that this feedback is valuable and take it to heart.[20]

Be aware that there could be several clear reasons that a rejection may have happened. One is that grantmakers commonly receive many applications asking for more money than they are prepared to distribute. When an application is turned down, it does not necessarily indicate that its particular proposal is without merit or carefully constructed. It most likely means that the available funding was given to other organizations with needs deemed more urgent than yours at the time.

On the other hand, there could be other reasons for some applications to face rejection. A submitter may have accidently missed a deadline within a grantor's application consideration cycle. Likewise, it could be that a proposal may not have contained a strong enough argument to support a major point for the grant's requirements or the fact was missed that only organizations in designated states, not the applicant's, would be considered.

There may be other causes for rejection that will need more vigilant attention next time. Maybe the applicant failed to research thoroughly and had asked for more money than the funder normally gives. Then again, perhaps a funder's strictly required application format was not adhered to or an application was poorly written and hard to understand, either of which gives an impression of carelessness. To avoid any of these mistakes, remember to have outside readers review your application, including its requirements, prior to submission.

The good thing is that most grantors will explain the reason(s) directly and concisely in your rejection letter. If your letter is missing those clues, you might want to call the grantmaker to help you comprehend the reason your grant was not successful and how you might have improved it. Some funders might even allow you to peruse the approved proposals, so you can ask if that opportunity is feasible in order to get a wider perspective. Furthermore, if, when you are ready to try again for a grant, you are worried that your group's goal for your library could possibly not gel with a particular grantmaker's priorities, before investing the time in applying you might want to contact the funding organization ahead of time with a query.

When any feedback is received, be sure to make note of the comments and suggestions since they will have been shared by a caring grant review committee that desires to receive further applications from the best possible contenders for their funds.

Besides looking for feedback, there is a last essential step to take after a funding rejection, and that is sending a sincere and gracious thank you letter addressed, if at all possible, to the person in charge of the review committee. In your letter, express appreciation for the grantor's time and consideration for your request and that you look forward to sending another request in the future. This special touch can make your group more memorable, help to build a positive relationship, and show interest and optimism.[21]

From what your group learns and how it grows through the rejection experience, you can work toward making your next application one that is finally accepted.

Notes

1. Kindful Nonprofit Glossary. [n.d.] "What Is a Nonprofit Grant?" Bloomerang, https://kindful.com/nonprofit-glossary/nonprofit-grant/#:~:text=A%20nonprofit%20grant%2C%20sometimes%20referred,%2C%20corporation%2C%20or%20government%20agency.

2. Poudre River Friends of the Library. January 2023. "Waterpik Grant." Poudre River Friends of the Library Newsletter, p. 3, https://mcusercontent.com/9a49e6d2f9f3b9dfd39b7e54d/files/2361ff32-5eea-ca93-9aea-3d2ebe50b12d/2023_01_Jan_Newsletter.pdf.

3. Candid. 2023. "Features of Foundation Directory," https://fconline.foundationcenter.org/welcome/features?_ga=1.17402425.1669982867.1445279741.

4. Candid. [n.d.] "How to Know If a Funder Is Right for Your Nonprofit with Foundation Directory." YouTube, https://www.youtube.com/watch?v=J6_Xp5Zzas8.

5. GrantWatch. 2023. "Grants for Nonprofits and Municipalities," https://www.grantwatch.com/grants-for-nonprofits.

6. ProLiteracy. 2023. "Grants & Funding," https://www.proliteracy.org/Resources-Publications/Grants-Funding#.

7. City of Dallas. 2017. "Friends of the Dallas Public Library Receives a $10,000 Grant to Support Adult Literacy." City of Dallas Office of Communications, Outreach, and Marketing, https://www.dallascitynews.net/friends-dallas-public-library-receives-10000-grant-support-adult-literacy.

8. Freedom to Read Foundation. April 5, 2023. "Judith Krug Fund Banned Books Week Event Grants," https://www.ftrf.org/page/Krug_BBW.

9. George W. Bush Presidential Center. 2023. "Laura Bush Foundation for America's Libraries," https://www.bushcenter.org/topics/education/laura-bush-foundation-for-americas-libraries.

10. Sharon Skinner. June 2018. "Grant Proposal Writing for Librarians: Tips for Scoring Points and Winning Big." *Voice of Youth Advocates*, p. 18.

11. Skinner, pp. 18–20.

12. June Ruther. February 24, 2022. "Strategic Planning & Grant Writing." *Library Strategies*, https://www.librarystrategiesconsulting.org/2022/02/strategic-planning-grant-writing/.

13. Ruther.

14. KPMG U.S. 2023. "KPMG in the US," https://www.kpmg.us/.

15. KPMG. 2023. "KPMG Community Impact," https://www.kpmg.us/about/community-impact.html.

16. First Book. 2023. "First Book: Our Mission/Our Impact," https://firstbook.org/.

17. Friends of the Knox County Public Library. July 13, 2023. Facebook posting.

18. Internal Revenue Service. 2016. "Charitable Contributions," https://www.irs.gov/pub/irs-pdf/p1771.pdf.

19. Library Strategies. May 21, 2017. "Following Up on Your Grant Proposal," https://www.librarystrategiesconsulting.org/2017/05/following-up-on-your-grant-proposal/.

20. Instrumentl. April 11, 2023. "Sample Grant Rejection Letters: Examples & What to Do," https://www.instrumentl.com/blog/sample-grant-rejection-letters.

21. Library Strategies. May 21, 2017. "Following Up on Your Grant Proposal," https://www.librarystrategiesconsulting.org/2017/05/following-up-on-your-grant-proposal/.

CHAPTER 13

Distributing Funds to, Advocating for, and Otherwise Supporting Your Library

ULTIMATELY, AS WE ALL KNOW, the bottom line of all library support group fundraising efforts, in whatever forms they take, is to provide financial backing for their organization's beneficiary library. To give this support, there must be good communication between support groups and the libraries. Libraries need to let those aiding them know their needs and how much money is required to satisfy those needs. Reversely, support groups need to keep their libraries informed about what additional ideas they might like to propose toward making their libraries stronger and sounder, then find out if the libraries want to move forward with them.

As discussed earlier in this book, attending one another's meetings is a helpful approach in this regard. Keeping each other in the loop with important messages and progress reports on fundraising and project goals is another. Using tiered wish list funding requests for upcoming fiscal years is one more. Through the wish lists, the library outlines their first, second, third, and fourth-tiered requested items for support group financial backing consideration.

In this chapter, I will take a closer look at the ways these interactions take place and the kinds of special funding nonprofit library support organizations can provide. I will start off by further discussing the very useful tools just mentioned, library wish lists.

Library Wish Lists and Special Requests

Library "wish lists" that Friends, foundations, and trusts aim to fulfill can be addressed in different ways. One approach is to ask beneficiary libraries for tiered lists as new fiscal years are approaching but not yet imminent. Library support group boards are then able to configure final lists of items they are able to cover, determine funding amounts based on what is available in their treasuries, and present recipient libraries with enough money to pay for the designated items.

Another method is to create wish lists based on library requests that are promoted by library support groups to the public on their and the libraries' websites and through other means. This is done in hopes that individuals will offer donations to provide or toward providing particular items. For example, at the Rochester Public Library in Minnesota, the library has a wish list page on their website that says: "These unbudgeted items are needed for various Library services. If you would like to purchase an item, please contact the Library Foundation at (phone number and email address)."

The message is followed by a list of items with details for each one. The items include updated library signage; new stacking chairs for programming; a van for youth services outreach; updated tools to enhance creating and recording abilities for programs and library services; and books and other materials in both print and digital formats. Each needed item listed gives a total targeted amount that the Foundation is hoping to finance through donations for it to be eventually purchased, for instance, the van. In addition, the cost of individual items within each need is listed independently in case donors prefer to fully contribute toward the purchase of one particular thing, such as one of the stacking chairs.[1]

In essence, wish lists are given to library support groups to hopefully satisfy needs and wants that are unmet through regular library budgets, and they may take the approach just described, or they may be accomplished via alternative means. For instance, a group might set up a wish list donation page on Amazon or another online purchasing website that they promote to their community and from which donors would be able to select books or other items that are desired and needed by their library.

As another approach, a wish list might be submitted to a library support group indicating potential funding areas that would best take place with grant money, accompanied by a request for help in writing grant proposals. The members of the Friends of Curry Public Library in Gold Beach, Oregon, did just that. They received a special project and program wish list from the library director that was taken on by the organization's Work Group committee members instead of using library staff time. The Work Group selected three of the desired programs and projects and began the task of applying for grants to hopefully fund each of them.[2]

Use your ingenuity and imagination to propose ways that the wish list concept could be employed to benefit your library. You might want to consult with the library staff to see if they have requests they would like to see addressed through wish lists. Then, brainstorm ways your library support group may be able to bring those requests to life. In the end, even if your organization may only be able to partially fund the requests that are received, with the existence of a solid library partnership, everyone involved would appreciate that the library support group has done its best to secure contributions to satisfy as many of the requests as possible.

Funding Summer Reading Challenges and Other Library Reading Events

In chapter 11, I discussed the concept of "one book" programs for communities that involve entire towns or schools or combinations of those. Library support groups can make a big difference in sponsoring and supporting these "community reads" programs in various forms. However, there are other important ways to offer reading promotion and support closer to home through summer reading programs and related library reading events.

In this section, I want to address the significance of these types of reading programs which are usually top-tier funding requests for library support groups. Most large-scale summer programming events need a large amount of financial backing, and to do them as meaningfully and effectively as possible, monetary enhancements to regular library budgets are frequently required. Through the years, it has become traditional for library support groups to pitch in with the dollars that these special library reading events call for to function effectively.

You might be unaware that "summer reading programs" are not a newfangled invention and today there are many names for them and facets to them. They actually began in the mid-1890s as a channel for encouraging school children, mostly in urban areas where they were not needed for summer farm work, to read during their summer vacations, to use their libraries, and to build solid reading habits.[3]

To pinpoint an exact year, it all began in 1896, when the first record of a newly established summer reading program can be found. Linda Eastman, who was the head librarian at the Cleveland Library, believed deeply in the value of children's literature. She created and distributed a list of suggested titles through the local schools so that children could work toward getting as far down the list as they were able during the summer recess.

This effort resulted in a record number of children visiting the library that summer and that outcome was enough evidence for the Cleveland Library board to support the development of the Cleveland Library League. Eventually, the organization grew to more than twelve thousand members who were grouped into smaller sized book clubs. While this was taking place, the concept of using reading logs was put into practice. Through them, children made lists of the books they had completed and they shared their reactions with one another.

When librarian Caroline Hewins at the Hartford Library in Connecticut considered the news about the reading program that had already been created, she realized that children needed to go beyond simply recording the books they read and to augment the process being used by them to review and recommend titles. She felt that interactive activities needed to be added to more deeply focus upon reading. Consequently, she developed another kind of summer reading program that added weekly discussion meetings, prizes for reaching targeted reading goals, and even a popular, related puzzle club. From her newly designed way of planning summer reading with its lively and interactive approach, she led the way for constructive summer reading that rapidly unfolded into the early 1900s with vacation reading clubs offering certificates of completion, opinion reports about books that were read, and book read-alouds at local playgrounds.

These early efforts, which promoted literacy as well as critical thinking, evolved into the comprehensive programs that we see today. By the 1990s, research had revealed further benefits. Summer reading programs helped to remedy the "summer slide" that children who did not read over summer vacations often experienced. Studies indicated that they were losing as much as 30 percent of what they learned during the school year. The biggest losses were noticed in lower-income students who were disproportionately affected because of a lack of access to the same books and encouragement as middle-income readers.

Research also showed that if children read four or five books during summer break they retained a high average of what they learned during the school year and many retained all and even strengthened their skills. After disclosing this research, summer reading programs boomed even more, and now over 95 percent of public libraries in the

United States hold summer reading programs through which reading is encouraged in an accessible, enjoyable manner.

As summer reading programs continued to evolve, they have become unique and varied, reflecting the needs and goals of each particular community.[4] They have also added annotated reading lists by age and grade levels; online registration options; paper, printable, and online reading logs/records; contests; and various rewards and prizes for meeting milestones. In addition, there are now challenging, educational, enlightening, and fun programs and activities offered in-person and virtually through which children are encouraged to learn and experience new things. The latest trend is to zero in on STEM (science/technology/engineering/math) learning and activities (with some libraries even expanding to STEAM or STREAM, adding art and advanced reading options).

Some libraries partner with their local school libraries and community organizations in these endeavors. Further, many libraries have added teen and adult summer reading programs in similar veins that target and engage their specific audiences. Often, they have also changed the names of summer reading "programs" to be more accurate and reflect these advances, such as calling them summer reading challenges, summer learning programs, summer reading adventures, or comparable titles.

In conjunction with and during the process of this growth and progress, in 1987, ten Minnesota regional library systems partnered to develop a summer library program for children by selecting a theme, creating artwork, and choosing cost-effective incentives that the libraries could purchase and use as they designed their summer offerings. This eventually became the Collaborative Summer Library Program (CSLP) which grew to include libraries throughout the country by providing inclusive, literacy-based programs with reproducible activities, a unified theme, shared resources, and available professional support that can be enjoyed by all ages.

Usually, state libraries and larger library systems are the guiding forces in developing high-quality CSLP summer reading challenge materials and activities to share. This is often accompanied by summer reading online and in-person training sessions for library staff members within their states so that libraries can create reading programs addressing children's, teen, and adult populations in their communities. As a final outcome each year, after documenting the results of their programs, participating librarians share more of their ideas, expertise, and costs with each other which keeps on improving the collaborative.[5] Directly related to the ability to share these outcomes is another useful resource, the Public Library Association's free, on-demand webinar for learning how to measure the success of summer reading programs.[6]

Many libraries are now adding winter reading events, spring break reading programs, and other creative additions to the tradition of summer reading programs. These can provide additional ways to participate for children as well as teenagers and adults and to keep readers active throughout the year.

How Library Support Groups Can Help with Reading Programs and Events

With all this background in mind, consider the importance and value of summer reading and other reading programs in your community and consult with your library about how your group can help to make such programs the best quality that they can be. When you do, you can follow the example of such Friends groups as the one serving the Sun Prairie Library in Wisconsin. With funding and through collaboration with the library, they have been able to provide the funding for a summer reading kickoff program with ice cream or snow cones; a juggling program; an evening end-of-summer-reading pool party at the community aquatic center; and Library Champion yard signs for each youth who completes the reading challenge to display at their homes.[7] Be creative and discover new ways to make summer reading meaningful and fun!

Here are a few suggestions you most likely will want to pursue to help make the summer reading challenge in your community the best it can be:

- Make funding requests for summer reading programs and events a top priority when deciding what your fundraising can support. Be sure to ask your library to submit its program requests well in advance.
- If your library would like you to apply for grants that may, if awarded, add spice to the schedules of summer and other reading programs and events, agree to do so if you are able—again, well in advance.
- Recruit volunteers from your membership ranks to help staff reading program registration and information desks and to assist librarians with programs and events.
- If you have a Junior Friends of the Library group, ask them to help raise funds or take volunteer roles as they are able.
- If you are a school library support organization, reach out to your public library to see if there are ways you may be of assistance to facilitate partnering for reading programs and events. Some schools are able to keep their media centers open during the summer as they collaborate with their public library's summer reading programs. Ensure that the school administrators and school board members get copies of a report about and maybe even presentations on what the program accomplished.
- Invite representatives from the library staff to attend library support group board meetings at which they share the outcomes of the reading programs after they conclude.

Funding Staff Development Opportunities

Library customers are, of course, significant recipients of library support group good works. However, there are other needs that libraries have to keep progressing. Library staff members are regularly wanting and needing to have educational opportunities to keep their skills current and to increase their knowledge and expertise. Regular library budgets are occasionally able to cover the cost of some special trainings and educational requirements. However, as with other needs, the demands for advanced learning opportunities to keep up-to-date and improve are usually limited by budget constraints despite being essential. Likewise, another required area of attention and need for many library administrators besides staff training is being able to provide affordable, special staff recognitions and honors. Once again, these are all circumstances where library support groups can often step in and offer aid.

As a for-instance, at the Tulsa City-County Library in Oklahoma, the Tulsa Library Trust has, as part of its philanthropic purpose, a goal to focus upon rewarding the librarians and other employees for their hard work all through the year. They provide awards to library staff members who go above and beyond their call of duty. The Trust also recognizes how much the staff depends on continuous training to keep the most relevant information, equipment, and technology available for Tulsa county residents. To that end, the Trust helps to support the important educational opportunities that are instrumental in leading the Library on its journey to be and to keep positively evolving into a dynamic and future-thinking library system.[8]

Here are some other examples of library support groups with similar goals for assisting their beneficiary libraries with staff education, training, and development that you may consider and perhaps decide that you would like to emulate or adapt:

- The Friends of the City Library in Salt Lake, Utah, funds events for the annual all-day staff training, provides support for the programming that is included, and serves refreshments to keep staff energetic as they learn.[9]
- The Friends of the Allen Public Library in Texas cover the expenses for library staff appreciations and professional staff development. They also show gratitude to the corps of one hundred teenage volunteers who join the VolunTeens group that provides indispensible help for the library's summer programming through a Teen Volunteer Scholarship and the End of Summer VolunTeen party—an exciting evening of food, games, and thanks.[10]
- At Ohio University, the Friends of the Libraries support the outstanding student library employees who provide exceptional service through such job duties as checking out books, serving as technology consultants, working with rare book collections, plus all other aspects of library operations. The Friends recognize the students' important contributions to the Libraries' essential operations and services and, through a special fund, bestows scholarships for their studies in a broad range of majors at the University.[11]
- Every spring, the Friends of the Summit County Libraries in Colorado award two $1,500 scholarships to high school seniors who have served as exemplary volunteers at the Summit County Libraries.[12]
- The Friends of the Durham Library in North Carolina award Durham County Library staff with scholarships toward tuition for their continuing education in graduate school to study library science or related fields such as digital communications.[13]
- Through the Betsy Moon Proctor Endowment Fund, held in reserve by the Madison Public Library Foundation in Wisconsin, scholarships are given to encourage and assist Madison Public Library employees who plan to further their careers in library and information studies. Also held in reserve under the auspices of the Foundation, the Professional Development Endowment Fund, which was created with a seed gift from library supporter Barb Arnold, library staff, and an anonymous donation, aids Madison Public Library staff in gaining career growth opportunities including conferences, workshops, and other training.[14]

Standing Up for Your Library: Advocacy, Promotional Activities, and Further Support

Now it is time to consider another kind of library support: advocacy. Advocacy is a powerful way to demonstrate camaraderie, speak up for, and to back a library, which can take place in any number of ways. In this section, I will illustrate some of those ways and how your library support group might decide to undertake similar library advocacy causes.

Advocacy efforts might be activities that take on several politically or community-oriented forms. They might encourage needed library funding and discourage budget cuts; foster speaking out for intellectual freedom and against censorship; stand up for sensible library privacy issues; let communities know what their libraries can do for them; promote library card sign-up activities, and much more.

As far as essential political advocacy activities go, lobbying to give voice to needs for strong library funding is vital. In the case of libraries that are publically funded, advocacy efforts targeting elected officials to remind them that private, nonprofit organizations exist to offer *additional* support to libraries rather than providing funding for general library operational costs are indispensable. In similar fashion, a school library support group can speak out to a school board about the necessity of funding a school library and its staff.

When you are thinking about lobbying like this, remember that, in general, lobbying is a legal activity for nonprofits if they *refrain from endorsing specific candidates who are running for elected offices* and they *spend less than 20 percent of their annual operating budget on lobbying activities*.[15] However, you will want to check with your library administrators, legal advisors, or others who are aware of limitations about the exact prohibitions and limits for your particular location.

One very helpful step for library support groups to take to spotlight advocacy is to create an "advocacy committee." At the Friends of the Knox County Public Library, there is an official Advocacy Committee with several designated work goals, including:

- To increase public awareness and support libraries with both government officials and local citizens.
- To stand up for a fully funded county budget as submitted by the library's executive director.
- To monitor issues, policies, and legislation relevant to the continuing health of public libraries at the local, state, and national level.
- To coordinate the Branch Liaison program that fosters a positive relationship between the Friends and the branch library staff.

These Friends also post a list of their advocacy accomplishments over the previous year, thereby demonstrating that they are turning their goals into actions. In 2023, those included securing a mayoral proclamation recognizing the Friends during National Friends of the Library Week; participating in a City neighborhood conference to share information about the Friends and library programming; celebrating National Library Week by presenting over 190 staff members with restaurant meal gift cards and personal notes; partnering with Friends of Tennessee Libraries to identify library advocacy and support opportunities; and attending the Knox County Commission meeting, at which the Friends president gave thanks for their library support.[16]

Notice that the goals merge with issues and topics of concern at other libraries in addition to the one for which the organization directly operates. This exemplifies that the finest advocacy efforts come from those organizations that see *beyond* the community in which they function with the understanding that we are all involved in and with an interconnected library world.

TEXTBOX 13.1
LEARNING ABOUT ADVOCACY AND PUTTING IT INTO ACTION

If you are wondering how your library support group can further investigate the topic of advocacy and develop an action plan like the Friends of the Knox County Public Library, there are several resources you can use to learn how.

Advocacy[1]

The Public Library Association provides this useful webpage with a large selection of resources to explore and use for an array of advocacy efforts.

Advocacy in Action: Local Library Awareness Campaigns[2]

WebJunction offers this step-by-step guide to planning and executing successful library awareness campaigns in local communities. The resources it contains will help you to showcase the value of your library throughout the community and bring to light critical funding issues libraries encounter every year. It is organized in five phases, with each one sequential so as to build momentum and create an impact.

Citizens Save Libraries: A Power Guide to Successful Advocacy[3]

United for Libraries gives a blueprint for advocacy action in this document, which tells how to set up and run an effective advocacy campaign.

Friends Groups: Critical Support for School Libraries[4]

United for Libraries has provided a PDF of this document, which explains the reasons school Friends of the Library groups are necessary under several circumstances. This could be if they are speaking out on behalf of school libraries when they are targeted for cuts and closures; if they wish to help and encourage the development of good collections and services; if they want to raise the profile of the school library or media center; if they hope to promote outreach efforts; if they want to assist with educating students and faculty about the library; or if they want to focus upon raising money, volunteering, and more.

Turning the Page: Supporting Libraries, Strengthening Communities[5]

The Public Library Association supports and promotes this free-to-use-and-share advocacy-training program for public libraries and library advocates. It offers an advocacy training curriculum and resources to aid you, whether you are addressing funding issues, policies, or other concerns.

Notes

1. Public Library Association. 2023. "Advocacy," https://www.ala.org/pla/advocacy.
2. WebJunction. 2023. "Advocacy in Action: Local Library Awareness Campaigns." OCLC, https://www.webjunction.org/explore-topics/advocacy-in-action.html.
3. Sally Gardener Reed, Beth Nawalinski, and Jillian Kalonick. May 2013. "Citizens Save Libraries: A Power Guide to Successful Advocacy." United for Libraries, https://www.ala.org/united/sites/ala.org.united/files/content/powerguide/united-power-guide.pdf.
4. Sally Gardener Reed. November 7, 2013. "Friends Groups: Critical Support for School Libraries." United for Libraries, https://www.ala.org/united/sites/ala.org.united/files/content/friends/orgtools/school-friends.pdf.
5. Public Library Association. [n.d.] "Turning the Page," https://www.publiclibraryadvocacy.org/.

If your library support group wants to get involved with advocacy initiatives and set up yearly advocacy goals, the following examples and information might inspire you to concentrate on like actions and to take similar steps:

- The Denver Public Library Friends Foundation has a forum to promote advocacy causes for the library via its blog. As an illustration, in 2021, there was a Speak Up for Denver Public Library blog post urging library fans to vote for an upcoming bond measure that would have permitted the construction of two new libraries and the renovation of a third that targeted three historically underserved neighborhoods.[17] The measure ultimately passed. Likewise, with Friends Foundation support in 2022, a referendum to create a designated tax to help fund the library was passed and put into place in 2023.[18] When vital library issues and concerns are on local ballots, library support groups can lend supportive hands by getting involved in similar and perhaps even additional ways.
- Discover the nonprofit, donor-funded EveryLibrary and get your organization and library familiar with its services for times when they may be needed. EveryLibrary is non-partisan, pro-library, and the first and only national organization dedicated to building voter support for libraries. It promotes public, school, and college/university libraries by advocating for support of public library funding and building public awareness of public funding initiatives. In addition, due to the upsurge in challenges to intellectual freedom that have materialized, they have built up their Fight for the First campaign program that gives direct aid to libraries and their supporters so that they may take action against book bans when they are occurring in their communities. EveryLibrary does even more, which you can learn about if you tune in to their website, join their email list, and connect on social media.

    All EveryLibrary consulting services for libraries and "Vote Yes" committees are offered pro bono with no chargebacks, fees, or other back-end financial arrangements. When travel is required to a particular community, some libraries are able, especially with the help of library support groups, to reimburse them for actual travel expenses so that they can make their pro bono consulting go farther. However, because of their donor contributions, it allows them to waive travel costs for library communities that are unable to afford them. In addition, their companion organization, EveryLibrary Institute, trains librarians on political literacy.[19]
- Libraries can help you to advocate for them by posting information on their websites about advocacy in addition to whatever you might post on yours. In general, promoting advocacy opportunities and about one another's advocacy efforts in this manner lets more members of the community know that they have a voice and can play a significant role in aiding the library. For instance, the Nassau Library System in New York does this by posting a page announcing the "Top 5 Ways You Can Advocate for Your Library." It begins with a statement, "Library advocates know that public libraries are essential to their communities. Help your neighbors and legislators understand the value of the library by being an advocate."

    First, they make clear that it is essential to speak up and speak out for the library. People can do this by sharing information with others face-to-face in any number of settings, or if they prefer, or as a further measure, they might want to write an opinion editorial on libraries for the local paper, submit a letter to the editor, or post a message on social media. After this, the library explains that citizens can go farther by contacting government officials, participating in library advocacy days at centers of government, registering with the state library as a library advocate if that option exists, and, most importantly voting for people and referendums that support libraries. Then, they encourage joining and contributing to a Friends, Foundation, or other library support organization and political action committees that support libraries. Finally, they advise library advocates to keep current about news in and surrounding the library world and library-related policy issues via reputable media and the American Library Association (ALA) website.[20]

- Speaking of the ALA website, they have a very helpful page specifically devoted to advocacy issues. It might be a great idea to check the page regularly to find out current news on the advocacy front and to find out ways your library support group might join in and promote advocacy efforts. The premise of the page is that "from privacy education to effective school library programs across the country, ALA advocates have been at the heart of our nation's greatest advances for libraries. Learn how you can be an advocate for every library across the country" as well.

   As you explore the page, a list of "Issues & Advocacy" links takes you to the targeted topics of banned books; equity, diversity, and inclusion; intellectual freedom; literacy; privacy; and public awareness. For each topic, there is an abundance of information and ways to advocate for the causes related to it. An additional section of the page takes you to the ALA eLearning Catalog which gives you icons to click for lists of advocacy courses, webinars, and customized eLearning content, some fee-based but many that are free.[21]

- For organizations supporting school libraries, there is a wonderful resource to explore and use for advocacy issues and concerns. At the Live Oak Middle School Library in Louisiana, there is a dynamo librarian who is also a great school library promoter and advocate. At the middle school website, there is a page devoted to the topic of school library advocacy called "School Libraries Make a Difference." It includes a lengthy list of links to school library advocacy resources and added information that you might find inspiring and useful. The highlight of the page is two shared videos that you can watch about the role of school librarians and why they are absolutely crucial.[22]

   Not only do the videos as advocacy tools demonstrate how essential school librarians and libraries are, but they also offer excellent examples for school library support groups that might want to consider creating advocacy videos to promote their own causes. As a matter of fact, library support groups of any kind could benefit from making similar videos as projects to promote their particular libraries and bring library issues of concern to light. The videos could be posted on websites, shared on social media, and shown during forums where they might substantiate an advocacy point being conveyed.

- San Jose State University (SJSU) in California has one of the best programs for library and information science students working toward a variety of library science-oriented degrees at several levels. To that end, the program is committed to instilling a library advocacy perspective by offering an active Library Advocacy Student Group that helps to build the concepts of library and related advocacy into student knowledge bases. A purpose statement for the group encompasses it best: "We facilitate educational opportunities and activities to influence decision-making at the local, regional, state, national, and international levels that result in funding or policy changes in support of public, school, and special libraries."

This mission is accomplished through a multi-faceted approach encompassing student groups, classes, internships, and opportunities for conference presentations when they are available. With the understanding that library advocacy goes beyond promoting the use of libraries, students work with notable fellow library advocates, legislatures, politicians, parents, students, and others to foster literacy, libraries, and equitable knowledge access. They demonstrate doing this by such projects as conducting a School Library Symposium to support legislative change in the state and nation; building a Virtual Reality Library; and running a Fill the Box Campaign to boost literacy and access to books for Native American children. They also have a Library Advocacy page on the SJSU School of Information website, which has information and links to podcasts, projects, resources, and other topics with library advocacy-related interest. You may want to check out their pages to get inspired, learn about some important approaches to advocacy, and perhaps engage some young people from your community to participate in library advocacy efforts following the SJSU students' examples.[23]

- Is your library support group ready to stand up for your library and speak up and out about intellectual freedom, preventing censorship, and fighting book ban attempts? If so, you will be glad to know about and use the Get Ready, Stay Ready: Community Action Toolkit. It was developed through the teamwork of parents and librarians who believe there is power in community and working together in a collective pushback against others who want to eliminate facts, meaningful stories, and historical realities. The toolkit includes scripts for public speaking and writing, helpful videos, and informational materials to educate supporters about the negative impacts of censorship in order to aid in resistance efforts. There are also resources for civic engagement and contacts for organizations throughout the country that aim to preserve rights to high-quality education through intellectual freedom and the right to read. In addition to all the helpful materials you can access through their website, you will find details about applying for $2,500 mini-grants to prepare for book challenges and to put the advice and recommended activities in the toolkit into action.[24]

Frontline Advocacy and Political Lobbying—Valuable Aspects of Advocacy

Again, many people in nonprofits, in particular for those in library support groups, are not familiar with the fact that one fundamental piece of their service can be advocacy, which allows them to lobby for their beneficiary libraries' needs. Frequently, even when library employees themselves are restricted from lobbying, the library support groups that are standing behind them are able to step in. Yet, there are even limited lobbying efforts that library staff members are able to take. It helps to be informed so that all parties know what is actually permitted. Lobbying is an essential component of library advocacy as long as participants adhere to the rules.

I remember several years ago having the opportunity as a library staff member to peacefully demonstrate outside our nation's capital at the conclusion of the American Library Association annual conference in support of intellectual freedom. Afterwards, many of us were scheduled to go in to the capitol building and meet with our state representatives to speak with them in their offices about library funding issues. It was an exciting and memorable day, and I was glad to be a part of a scene of hundreds of library workers calmly expressing our perspectives and spreading the word about the value and needs of libraries in our country without trying to politically influence them. For those of us who have experienced such participation, it reinforces the fact that speaking out to those in government at all levels about the crucial roles of libraries is a worthwhile and meaningful act.

Citizens who are not library employees and especially those who belong to established nonprofit library support organizations are in unique positions to state the cases for many aspects of libraries and library services. To help facilitate effective advocacy ability when library support group backing is at hand, library employees can make sure that the members of the groups know about supportive lobbying and what information they require to expound on the value of libraries from a non-employee standpoint. A library director in particular can be instrumental in organizing a support group's advocacy committee if one is nonexistent, and educating its Friends, foundation, and/or trust members about how to most effectively advocate for their library. However, any and all other library staff members can play a role in educating library supporters as well. This is called Frontline Advocacy.

The term *Frontline Advocacy* was coined by past ALA president Camila Alire during her 2009–2010 term. It means that, when suitable circumstances arise, all library staff members can and should be encouraged to impart information to library customers about the value of the library services to which they have access. Once customers are reminded of or realize this value, they can share their knowledge with fellow community members and potentially with elected officials. Frontline Advocacy specifically delineates that library staff members are spokespersons to their customers and others in the community—including members of nonprofit library support organizations—and not directly to elected officials. When Frontline Advocacy is matched up with political advocacy by library supporters, it can make a potent impact. It enables the support groups to help government officials realize that their nonprofit work to aid the library is for *enhancements* of what public funding provides, not to replace equitable, stable annual allocations or to cover budget cuts.

One central thing mentioned earlier in this chapter that bears repeating is to know and remember that lobbying by nonprofit library support groups is a *completely legal activity*. To help groups like those dedicated to libraries understand the limitations, the Internal Revenue Service has conveyed two basic guidelines. Those are that *nonprofit organizations cannot endorse particular candidates for public office*, and that *lobbying expenditures must be kept below 20 percent of an organization's total budget*.[25]

Even with these guidelines, an additional element to nonprofit lobbying that you may need to mull over in this digital age is what is and is not legal on websites and in social media. There are actually quite a few considerations for what is lawful when employing your virtual tools to empower your organization for online advocacy. Check with your legal advisor or the Internal Revenue Service if you are uncertain about what rules and regulations you need to follow to comply. You may be surprised to realize that there are many topics to consider surrounding not only websites and social media, but also blogs, email lists, media sites, and more.

The national association Bolder Advocacy, A Program of Alliance for Justice offers expert help in answering very specific questions about nonprofit online lobbying and related issues. They have a web page called, "Influencing Public Policy in the Digital Age: The Law of Online Lobbying and Election-Related Activities," which covers a large array of topics in a question and answer format. Just about any type of online posting a nonprofit must weigh for legality is included on the page. It would behoove library support nonprofits that are unsure of the legalities of particular virtual approaches and content to read and use this resource.[26]

TEXTBOX 13.2

CONDUCTING A LETTER-WRITING CAMPAIGN

To make an impact with city, state, and federal government officials at all levels, a well-run letter-writing campaign with many dedicated non-library employee advocates participating can sometimes do wonders. This textbox features a template you may wish to adapt for letter-writing campaigns to support your library. It is based on a template used by the Denver Public Library Friends Foundation.

First of all, before posting or publishing the template, place a note before it that begins by saying, "Do you know who your city council representative is, and who other governmental representatives are? Find out by scrolling to the bottom of this page." After you add the template, append a list of government officials and their contact information and be sure to keep it current.

Template for an Advocacy Letter

Dear [Name of government official]:

I am writing to encourage you to support the [name of library] in your work as a [name of government official's title]. The [name of library] is an essential part of our community, and it has over [number] of visitors each year. [Briefly add any other pertinent details about the library.]

The [name of library] addresses the community's most pressing needs through a variety of programs and services. It does the obvious things like providing books and other materials, and other, less obvious things, like [give examples].

Here are the reasons that the [name of library] is important to me as a citizen and library user. [Explain your personal reasons for library appreciation and support.]

Thank you for your service on/in [name the governmental body of service]. As you fulfill your role in that capacity, I want you to know that I believe the library is one of the most important places of public service and sources of information in our [city/town/community]. Once again, I encourage you to support the library. It is one of the best and most vital actions you can take for the good of [name of community].

Sincerely,
[Your Name]
[Your Street Address]
[City, State, Zip Code]
[Phone Number]
[Email Address][1]

Notes

1. Denver Public Library Friends Foundation. 2023. "Advocacy Update," https://www.dplfriends.org/how-to-help/advocate/.

Participating in Special Events to Promote Your Group and the Library You Support

A rather fun part of advocacy is participating in special events where your library support group can attract attention. When library support group members show up at special library events or important community events, it provides a unique forum to promote the organization to those in attendance. Bringing plenty of informational forms, documents, and publicity to place on a table and/or hand out to those drawn to take a look gives opportunities to explain the nonprofit organization, encourage new memberships, solicit donations, and offer contact information for later questions. These might be bookmarks listing details about upcoming book sales; membership brochures; copies of recent newsletters; a flyer summarizing the latest annual report; promotional material for upcoming events sponsored by your group; and any organizational swag as giveaways, such as "I Love My Library" stickers, bookmarks, or refrigerator magnets.

It is a good idea to invest in having at least one big banner of good quality made that names your organization, includes its logo, and adds its web address and phone number. The banner can be placed in front of a table, posted on walls at events, or carried while marching. Decide how you will be using any banners before getting them made. You might also consider adding feather flags, pop-up banners, or retractable banners, depending on your needs and how much you can afford to spend.

There are many online businesses that provide banner-making services and some are specifically aimed at nonprofits. You may also have local shops that sell banners and the nice thing about them is that you can meet with someone in person to help you design and create exactly the right banners for your cause.

If yours is a recently formed Friends of the Library or other library support organization, you might be trying to decide at what events you will be present and how you will need to display your banner(s). Consider these ideas:

- Parades: Community parades to celebrate holidays or other special occasions are a perfect place to show your library spirit and promote your organization. Find out what parades are going to be held in your city or town and how your members might participate. Do you need to create a float? Can you decorate a car and drive it with the parade? Are you able to simply march, perhaps in costumes and handing out bookmarks or candy to bystanders? You can carry your banner if it is appropriate or place banners elsewhere depending on how you will take part in the parade.
- Grand openings: Is your library having a ribbon-cutting ceremony to open a new building or library wing? Are you finally celebrating the christening of a just-purchased bookmobile? Especially when your library support group has contributed to the fundraising for whatever reason the celebration is taking place, you will definitely want to be represented. Maybe if your town is welcoming a new school to the district or a new independent bookstore, you might be able to set up a table at any celebratory events being held. Keep tabs on any and all events that may be coming up so that you can join the festivities when it is fitting.
- Library programs: When you have helped to get a guest author to come to your library and funded the expenses of the visit, you will want to have an informational

table set up at the event along with your banner. This is true for any special event or activity that you have sponsored for or with the library or in partnership with a local bookstore.
- Festivals: If there is a book festival, a children's summer reading kickoff event, or a special community event or celebration, your group will want to be represented and put up its banner if possible.
- National Library Week Events: When your library is celebrating during this designated week to highlight and commemorate libraries throughout the country, you will want to be involved and have an informational table at any related activities. The American Library Association offers a page on its website with in-depth details on how libraries and those supporting them can celebrate during the week, which is always held in April. The page provides an overall theme, tells ways to participate, gives days that highlight special library topics and services, and offers free tools and promotional materials. In 2023, there was Right to Read Day; National Library Workers Day; National Library Outreach Day; and Take Action for Libraries Day.[27] Find out how your library is planning to celebrate these events each year and how you can take part. By the way, often it is library support groups that provide tokens of special appreciation for the libraries they serve, so aim to budget for it and plan ahead.
- Book shops and book sales: Always have your banner(s) and lots of display materials at book sales and at your nonprofit's used bookstores. Many people ask questions at these spots that draw in book and library lovers, and library support groups are able to not only sell books and other materials at and through them, they are able to promote the group, entice new members, and engage potential donors as a secondary result.

Participating in all these special events means you will need to make sure you have a wide network of volunteers to create the required materials, help staff the tables, make floats and show up to march, and fill whatever other duties and actions are needed. You will want to incorporate training of the volunteers into your plans for scheduling them so that they know exactly how to proceed with the tasks at hand and they are primed to share information and answer inquiries. It is very important to enlist someone qualified to become the volunteer coordinator or for two astute people to team up as co-chairs because the job requires good planning skills, people skills, and adroitness. As always, make the persons in charge of and participating in the events beneficiaries of your sincere thanks.

Feedback, Follow-Up, and Thanks from the Library

On a final note, as one who has appreciated all the wonderful things library support groups did for me and the libraries at which I worked for several decades, one aspect of their kindness and service that I especially appreciated was when they extended thanks to us when we did things like providing teen volunteers for book sales or helping them in other ways. They were always prompt and considerate in sending thank-you notes and letters of gratitude. In turn, the libraries always made sure to extend the same appreciation back to them. When they gave us special treats and messages during National Library Week, our administrators made certain to send thank-you messages back to them in a timely fashion. When they funded our teen advisory group's attendance at an annual state literature conference for teenagers, we always promptly sent them thank-you notes and even had the teens attend their next board meetings for in-person expressions of gratitude and brief slide shows documenting the conference trips. Because we gave each other feedback, followed up, offered encouragement, and bestowed thanks, it always made our affiliation pleasant and very effective.

I have said in many areas of this book how essential it is to extend genuine and timely thanks to donors and other contributors to library support organizations. The same holds true of library and library support group partnerships. The following examples illustrate how libraries can extend gratitude to their library support group(s) and community donors through publicly expressing appreciation and offering kudos.

- At the Ames Public Library in Iowa, they gave a shout-out of thanks on their blog to what they consider to be their "sister organization," the Ames Public Library Friends Foundation. This was done to mark the occasion of National Friends of Libraries Week. The library expressed how the community donations and support they received through this partnership made a huge difference and impact. They explained what those contributions mean to the Library—that without them, STEM kits, author visits, Wi-Fi hot spots, a program to supply free summer meals for youth, new furniture for youth areas, and several technological improvements would simply have been unfulfilled but still much-needed enhancements. They also announced the hiring of a new development director position at the Friends Foundation, and they said what a boost it would give the library to have a new leader available to foster more community outreach, participation, and the facilitation of innovative community ideas for additional Friends Foundation support.[28]
- Several years ago, the Iowa City Public Library honored and thanked their Iowa City Public Library Friends Foundation with "Thanks a Million!" posters and balloons during Love Your Library month. Library visitors were invited to peruse the banner over the book return slot inside the front door. This recognition of the support group and its generous contributors was made after they met a million-dollar fundraising goal. The money was used for building improvements, new technology, a large number of new books for the collection, and programming for all ages of library users, including summer reading. Those who were already contributing were thanked and new donors were encouraged to participate in joining the cause via a drop box or online donation.[29]
- In response to a successful Colorado Gives Day, the Friends of Loveland Public Library Foundation published testimonials from a director, former director, teen services manager, and guest author poet through which they received praise for many of the ways that the group has supported the library. These included such things as a productive capital campaign; a partnership with local agencies to provide snacks and an author visit with free copies of signed books for teens in need or at risk; a poetry workshop; and funding advances for programs, materials, special projects, and other services.[30] Beneficiary libraries sharing gratitude testimonials like these is another way to demonstrate to library support groups that they are appreciated while allowing the groups to publicize the comments elsewhere and further their causes.

At that, I come to a close. As I mentioned in the introduction, and which you have seen throughout the text and will see in the appendixes, bibliography, and webliographies, there is a large amount of further reading and research you can pursue for any topics that would have been impossible for me to cover in their entirety in one book. I encourage you to explore and use the suggested additional resources I have incorporated when your own library support group might require much more in-depth information on specific topics.

Finally, thanks for reading and considering my ideas and examples along with those of others that I have represented here who are already doing wonderful things with and through their library support groups. Thanks for taking the time to imagine how, in your particular communities, you might start, expand, or enhance your own library support organizations. Our libraries are so important and exceedingly worthy of investments of our time, efforts, and monetary contributions. Best of luck in whatever endeavors on which you set forth, now and in the future.

Notes

1. Rochester Public Library. 2023. "Wish List," https://www.rplmn.org/about-us/library-foundation/wish-list.

2. Friends of the Curry Public Library. 2023. "What We Will Do," https://friendsofcurrypubliclibrary.org/what-we-will-do/.

3. American Library Association. May 16, 2019. "Summer Reading Programs," https://libguides.ala.org/summer-reading#:~:text=Summer%20reading%20programs%20began%20in,develop%20the%20habit%20of%20reading.

4. Ellie Wilkie. [n.d.] "A Brief History of Summer Reading Programs." *Reader Zone*, https://www.readerzone.com/post/a-brief-history-of-summer-reading-programs.

5. Collaborative Summer Library Program. 2023. "Mission Statement," https://www.cslpreads.org/about/mission-statement/.

6. Public Library Association. March 17, 2016. "Make a Splash with Project Outcome: Measuring the Success of Summer Reading Programs." Webinar, https://www.ala.org/pla/education/onlinelearning/webinars/archive/projectoutcomesplash.

7. Cynthia J. Mestelle. Email message to author, November 28, 2023.

8. Tulsa Library Trust. 2017. "Staff Development," https://tulsalibrarytrust.org/program/staff-development/.

9. Salt Lake City Public Library. 2023. "Friends of the City Library," https://services.slcpl.org/friends1-4550.

10. Allen Public Library. 2023. "Friends of the Allen Public Library," https://www.cityofallen.org/1714/Friends-of-the-Allen-Public-Library.

11. Ohio University. 2023. "Friends of the Libraries Scholarship," https://give.ohio.edu/funds/friends-libraries-scholarship.

12. Summit County Library. June 19, 2023. "Friends of the Library 2023 Scholarship," https://summitcountylibraries.org/programs-news/news/friends-library-2023-scholarship?vnrosnrosee=yes.

13. Durham County Library. December 8, 2022. "Friends of the Durham Library Award Scholarships to Durham County Library Staff," https://durhamcountylibrary.org/2022/12/09/friends-of-the-durham-library-award-scholarships-to-durham-county-library-staff/.

14. Madison Public Library Foundation. 2023. "Endowment Funds," https://mplfoundation.org/give/endowment-funds/.

15. Library Strategies. November 16, 2015. "10 Foundation Best Practices," https://www.librarystrategiesconsulting.org/2015/11/10-foundation-best-practices/.

16. Friends of the Knox County Public Library. 2023. "Advocacy," https://www.knoxfriends.org/advocacy/.

17. Denver Public Library Friends Foundation. 2021. "Speak up for Denver Public Library: Be an Advocate for DPL," https://www.dplfriends.org/news-events/blog/be-an-advocate-for-dpl/.

18. Joe Rubino. November 8, 2022. "Denver Referred Ordinance 2I: Library Tax Passes Comfortable, Unofficial Results Show," https://www.denverpost.com/2022/11/08/denver-referred-ordinance-2i-results-library-tax/.

19. EveryLibrary. 2019. "About," https://www.everylibrary.org/about-everylibrary.

20. Nassau Library System. [n.d.] "Top 5 Ways You Can Advocate for Your Library," https://www.nassaulibrary.org/about/top-5-ways-you-can-advocate-for-your-library/.

21. American Library Association. 2023. "Advocacy," https://www.ala.org/advocacy/.

22. Live Oak Middle Library. [n.d.] "School Libraries Make a Difference," https://www.lomlibrary.org/library-advocacy.html.

23. SJSU School of Information. [n.d.] "Committed to Library Advocacy," https://ischool.sjsu.edu/library-advocacy.

24. Get Ready, Stay Ready. 2022. "Community Action Toolkit," https://www.getreadystayready.info/.

25. Peter Pearson. September 17, 2015. "'Lobbying' Is Not a Dirty Word." *Library Strategies*, https://www.librarystrategiesconsulting.org/2015/09/lobbying-is-not-a-dirty-word/.

26. Bolder Advocacy. 2023. "Influencing Public Policy in the Digital Age: The Law of Online Lobbying and Election-Related Activities." *Alliance for Justice*, https://bolderadvocacy.org/resource-library/influencing-public-policy-in-the-digital-age-the-law-of-online-lobbying-and-election-related-activities/.

27. American Library Association. 2023. "National Library Week," https://www.ala.org/conferencesevents/celebrationweeks/natlibraryweek.

28. Sheila Schofer. September 25, 2023. "Spotlight on Library Friends Foundation." Ames Public Library Notes, https://www.amespubliclibrary.org/node/39319.

29. Iowa City Public Library. February 10, 2015. "Thanks a Million, Friends Foundation Supporters!" Iowa City Public Library News, https://www.icpl.org/articles/thanks-million-friends-foundation-supporters.

30. Colorado Gives 365. 2023. "Friends of the Loveland Public Library Foundation," https://www.coloradogives.org/organization/FriendsoftheLovelandPublicLibrary.

Appendix A

Friends of Libraries Section

FLS creates a network to connect and inspire Friends groups
in all types of libraries to support the New York library community.

Annotated By-Laws
What Should Be Included In By-Laws For Friends Organizations?

What are by-laws? *Robert's Rules of Order* states "Having a constitution and by-laws as separate documents is not necessary; one document suffices, generally referred to as the by-laws." By-laws are an organizing document, a formal statement defining the primary characteristics of the organization, how it operates and is governed, and the relationship of the members to the organization as a whole. By-laws contain a concise statement of purpose. By-laws state what rights the members have, who has power to make decisions, and the limits of that power. These key operational procedures and rules of the organization cannot be changed without previous notice to all the members and require a large majority for the vote. **It is not within the purview of the officers to change the by-laws at a monthly Board meeting.**

Before you begin: Consult a new edition of *Robert's Rules of Order*. The "simplified and applied" editions devote considerable coverage to constructing one of the most important documents of the organization. By-laws are legal documents and there are legal requirements for what should be included. The New York State Nonprofit Revitalization Act (NPRA) of 2013 has specified language and other considerations for by-laws for nonprofit organizations. For example, "**committees of the board**" has replaced "standing committees;" the Executive Committee or Finance Committee are examples. Other language includes "**committees of the corporation**," e.g., nominating committee, program committee, membership committee. The NPRA also outlines rules for remote participation in meetings (i.e., videoconference) and action taken by the Board without a meeting. As a nonprofit board, the Friends will need to adopt a conflict of interest policy that requires an annual review and disclosure statements signed by each Board member.

If you wish to incorporate your Friends group as a tax-exempt nonprofit corporation at a later date, the by-laws will need to be in place for that process. Incorporation of a Friends group is not required, but the process can lead to advantages for fundraising. Contributors to nonprofit groups can deduct donations from their income tax if the group has been granted tax-exempt status by the IRS. Consult with the library's attorney or an attorney with experience in the area of nonprofit law about the advantages and responsibilities for nonprofit organizations. There are very specific requirements for obtaining tax-exempt status from the Internal Revenue Service. See "Application for Recognition of Exemption" at www.irs.gov.

The organization should not need to go through a by-laws change every time a new membership category is established, or a new committee is appointed. It is best to make the by-laws as basic, concise, and flexible as possible. Broad, general statements like "the Executive Board will meet once a month" will serve better than stating "the second Tuesday of every month," given that the officers may change and have a conflict with a proscribed date.

All interested parties should have an opportunity to review the by-laws and make comments. If the Friends group is just beginning, the steering committee may write a draft, make it available for review (i.e., at the library or online), and then present it at the inaugural meeting of the Friends. Drafts should be sent to the library director and the library's Board of Trustees before they are formally adopted by the Friends membership.

Annotated By-Laws for Friends, page 2

*These **samples** of by-laws for the Friends of the Library contain comments to explain some of the nuances of language, sequence of the information, and sometimes cautionary notes. They are illustrative only and **not a complete set** of by-laws.*

Name of the Organization, Purpose, and Mission: The official name that is used on your legal documents (e.g., certificate of incorporation, application to the IRS for 501(c)(3) status) needs to agree, document to document. Be careful with your name: is it THE Friends of the Idyllic Free Library, or just "Friends of Idyllic Free Library"? Is there a THE before the library's name? That is, "Friends of the Anytown Public Library" or "Friends of Anytown Public Library"? Use the library's proper name, i.e., not just "Anytown Library". The organization's purpose and mission will guide future decisions on planning, programming, and spending the Friends funds. It defines who will be served by the group. The purpose should reflect long-term support for the library (rather than "raising funds for a new library building").

> **Article I: Name**
> The name of the organization shall be known as "Friends of the Anytown Public Library," hereafter referred to as the "Friends."
>
> **Article II: Purpose**
> The Friends is organized and shall be operated exclusively for charitable purposes, in general, as set forth in Section 501(c)(3) of the Internal Revenue Code of 1986 as now in effect or hereafter amended. The purpose of the Friends shall be to maintain an organization of persons interested in libraries, to encourage and receive funds for the benefit of the Anytown Public Library ("the Library"), and to support and cooperate with the Library in developing library services and facilities for the community.
>
> **Article III: Mission**
> The Friends of the Anytown Public Library supports cultural and educational programs for the community and assists the library with special projects and purchases not covered by the library's operating budget.

Members: There are two kinds of NYS nonprofit corporations (see Section 601 of New York State Not for Profit Corporation Law): (1) membership and (2) non-membership. Review the organization's incorporation papers to learn what type of corporation your Friends is. The by-laws indicate who can join the organization, what the membership categories are, how to join (e.g., pay dues), the duration of the membership year, and any privileges afforded to the members. The amount of membership dues should not be included. One consideration: do you want to accommodate rolling registrations or only bill members once a year for their memberships?

> **Article IV: Members**
> Section 1: Eligibility. Membership is open to any individual, family, organization, or business that has indicated their willingness to be involved in the Friends program by paying their membership dues.
> Section 2: Dues. There shall be a membership fee established by the Board of Directors for each class of membership covering the fiscal year of September 1 through August 31. Friends joining after May 1 shall be members for the following fiscal year.
> Section 3: Privileges. Members shall be entitled to attend all meetings of the Friends Board of Directors.

Governing Body: Officers, the Executive Board, and Committees: What officers will the group have (e.g., president or chairman)? How will they be chosen and what are their terms of office? Help the Board be self-perpetuating with staggered terms and limits for length of service. How many people will serve on the Board of Directors? The duties and their general responsibilities should be outlined (e.g., attend each meeting). How will vacancies be filled? The nomination and election process needs to be detailed along with committees.

Do not include the personal names of the officers. Rather than outline full job duties in the by-laws, other documents, like a Leadership Manual, can contain the operating details of the Friends group (e.g., officers' and committee chairs' job descriptions, a procedural manual for the book sale, any guide for day-to-day operations).

Article V. Officers and Elections

Section 1: The officers of the Friends shall be the President, Vice President, Secretary, and Treasurer.

Section 2. Officers shall be nominated by a nominating committee of no fewer than three members appointed by the Executive Board at least two months before the Annual Meeting. With the consent of each nominee, the nominations shall be submitted in writing to the membership at least one month prior to the Annual Meeting. Additional nominations may be made from the floor with the consent of the nominee.

Section 3. Officers shall be elected by a majority vote of those present at the Annual Meeting, for the term of two years, commencing upon election. An officer may not hold the same office for more than two successive terms.

Section 4. All requests for withdrawal from office prior to the end of the term should be submitted in writing to the Executive Board. The Executive Board may appoint a person to serve out the unexpired term of an office rendered vacant. Any officer, upon leaving office, must relinquish all documentation, monies, and other properties to his/her successor.

Article VI. Executive Board

Section 1: The Executive Board shall consist of the officers of the organization and the chairpersons of committees of the corporation. The Library Director shall serve or appoint a staff designee as an ex-officio member of the Executive Board without voting privileges.

Section 2: The Executive Board meetings to conduct the business of the Friends are held in accordance with a schedule approved at the annual membership meeting.

Section 3: The Executive Board shall transact business by a majority vote of the members present.

Section 4. A majority of the Executive Board shall constitute a quorum. A quorum will be required to approve all financial and business transactions of the organization.

Meetings: The by-laws do not note the meeting calendar dates for a specific year; the location does not need to be specified. They do outline how the meetings are scheduled, to whom they are open, and what notice must be given.

Article VII. Annual and Special Meetings

Section 1. An Annual Meeting open to the general membership shall be held each year, at a time to be determined by the Executive Board, for the purpose of electing officers as scheduled and hearing reports on the business of the organization from the previous year. Members shall be notified in writing at least one month prior to the date of the meeting. Voting at the Annual Meeting is open to each paid membership.

Section 2. Special Meetings may be called at any time by the President, by any three members of the Executive Board, or by fifteen members of the organization for the purpose of conducting business.

Fiscal Matters: The fiscal year needs to be defined, along with auditing procedures and how financial matters will be conducted. Research what state requirements apply to the financial governance of nonprofits.

Article VIII. Fiscal Year and Finances

Section 1. The fiscal year of the organization shall be concurrent with that of the Anytown Public Library. A budget for the fiscal year shall be approved by the Executive Board prior to the year's commencement.

Section 2. No officer, committee, task force, or individual member shall incur any expenses on behalf of the Friends unless duly authorized by the Executive Board.

Section 3. The official financial records of the organization shall be maintained at the Anytown Public Library. The Friends accounts are subject to the audit practices of the Library.

Annotated By-Laws for Friends, page 4

Section 4. The Treasurer shall present a financial status report and a budget status report at each Executive Board meeting.

Parliamentary Authority and Amendments: What rules will be followed in official meetings? How are the by-laws amended?

Article IX: Parliamentary Authority
In all instances when they are applicable and not inconsistent with the by-laws and any other special rules the organization shall adopt, the rules contained in the current edition of ***Robert's Rules of Order*** shall govern the proceedings of this organization.

Article X: Amendments
The proposed amendments may be ratified at the annual meeting of the general membership, by affirmative vote of two-thirds of the persons present who are eligible to vote. Each paid member shall be notified in writing one month prior to the meeting at which the voting is to take place and provided with a copy of the proposed changes to the by-laws with recommendations from the Executive Board.

Dissolution Statement: What happens to the organization's assets if the organization disbands? Where would the funds go? This provision is required by law.

Article XI: Dissolution
In the event of a dissolution of the Friends, after paying or adequately providing for the debts and obligations of the organization, the remaining assets shall be distributed to the Anytown Public Library or, if at the time of dissolution, the Anytown Public Library is no longer in existence, then said assets shall be distributed to an organization exempt under Section 501(c)(3) of the Internal Revenue Code upon majority vote of the Executive Board members present at the last meeting of the Friends. Further, no member of the Friends shall be entitled to share in any assets upon dissolution of the organization.

By-laws should be reviewed annually to make certain they accurately reflect the current way of work for the Friends. A task force may be appointed by the Executive Board to review the document, looking for points that are no longer relevant or detailed statements that could be generalized. Proposed changes are brought to the full Board of Directors for discussion. Ask a parliamentarian and an attorney with experience in nonprofit law to review your proposed changes. The by-laws are then amended by a vote of the members at the annual meeting.

Always keep a hard copy of the current by-laws. **The original date of the adoption of the by-laws for the organization should be noted**, followed by the date(s) of any revisions. The latest official by-laws should be signed by the current Board President and Secretary. Every board member should receive a copy of the current by-laws for their own reference. Consider posting your by-laws on the Friends website.

This information has not been reviewed by an attorney, does not consist of legal advice, and must not be relied upon as an alternative to legal advice. Ask a local attorney knowledgeable in nonprofit law to review your by-laws and incorporation papers.

Always be certain to check for any recent changes or updates in the tax law which might affect the accuracy of this information, which was prepared 9/18/21.
Compiled and written by Lisa C. Wemett. **All rights reserved.**
Contact FLS/NYLA at FLS.NYLA@yahoo.com.

---

file: Annotated Friends Bylaws 2021.docx

Appendix B

Friends of the Weathersfield Proctor Library

Bylaws

Name

The name of this corporation shall be Friends of the Weathersfield Proctor Library, Inc., hereinafter referred to as the Association.

Purpose

The purpose of the Friends of the Weathersfield Proctor Library shall be to maintain an association of persons interested in outstanding library service, to increase the facilities and service of the library, and to aid the Library Board of Trustees and the Librarian in their efforts to make Proctor Library a vital community resource; thus enriching the cultural and learning opportunities available to the citizens of Weathersfield and any visitors to the area.
The activities of the Association shall include sponsorship of special projects; informing the public of the resources and services of the library; securing funds for materials that are beyond the command of the ordinary budget; and, performing other services deemed helpful to the library.

Membership

Membership in this Association shall be open to individuals, organizations, and businesses in agreement with its purposes. There may be various categories of membership as determined by the Executive Board. Dues shall be determined annually by the Executive Board prior to the annual meeting.

Officers

The officers of the Association shall be President, Vice-President, Secretary, and Treasurer. The elected Executive Board shall include officers of the Association, (1) one member-at-large, and ex officious Proctor Library Director and Chairperson for the Proctor Library Board of Trustees. The (5) five elected Executive Board positions shall be staggered (3) three-year terms, not to exceed (2) two consecutive terms. A member may return to the Executive Board following a one year absence. Officer positions shall be (1) year in length with elections conducted at the annual meeting.

Duties of Officers

> **President:** The President shall preside over and conduct meetings, appoint all committees and be an ex officio member thereof, except as limited herein; to submit an annual report of the operations of the organization to the members at the annual meeting; and, report to the Executive Board all matters within his/her knowledge that should be brought to their attention in the best interest of the organization.

Vice-President: To perform the duties of the President in the absence of the President.

Secretary: The Secretary shall record attendance, take minutes of all meetings, and maintain a file of meeting minutes for reference at future meetings; maintain files which will include press releases, flyers, newsletters, announcements of programs and activities, and any other pertinent information relative to the Friends Association; conduct necessary correspondence for the Association; keep a list of the membership with addresses, phone numbers, and e-mail addresses, and shall notify the members of the time and place of meetings.

Treasurer: The Treasurer shall be responsible for the collection, safekeeping, and disbursement of all funds and assets; keep and maintain financial records of all financial transactions of the Association; submit a financial accounting of the Association's transactions and financial status at the annual meeting and at other times when requested; prepare or oversee any necessary documents for the IRS related to the finances of the Association, as required by federal and State statute or regulation.

Meetings

Section 1. Executive Board meetings will be held when necessary to conduct business of the Association with prior notification of (5) five business days. Business can be conducted if a quorum is present. A quorum shall be defined as no less than (3) three Executive Board members in attendance.
Section 2. The annual meeting of the Association shall be held at a time and date in the month of June to be determined by the Executive Board.
Section 3. Association meetings of the full membership may be called at any time by the President or by officers of the Association, with 48-hours notification, with the purpose of forwarding the business or mission with a minimum of five members constituting a quorum.

Funds and Liability

Section 1. All dues shall be established by the Executive Board and approved at the annual meeting by a two-thirds majority of those present.
Section 2. All funds shall be deposited to the account of the Friends of the Weathersfield Proctor Library and shall be disbursed by the Treasurer, as authorized by the President, acting on behalf of the membership.
Section 3. Records of accounts shall be maintained by the Treasurer.
Section 4. No member of the Association shall be liable except for unpaid dues, and no personal or financial liability shall in any event be attached to any member of the Association in connection with any of its undertakings.
Section 5. No part of the funds from the Association shall benefit any individual of the Association, except that the Association may pay reasonable compensation for services rendered and to make payments and distributions in furtherance of the purposes of the Association.
Section 6. Upon the dissolution of the Association after paying or making provisions for the payment of the liabilities of the Association, any remaining assets shall be disbursed in accordance with Article VIII of the Articles of Incorporation.

Section 7. Fiscal year shall be July 1 to June 30.

Conflict of Interest

Any possible conflict of interest on the part of any member of the Executive Board or membership shall be disclosed in writing to the Executive Board and made a matter of record through an annual procedure and also when the interest involves a specific issue before the Executive Board. Where the transaction involving any member of the Association exceeds ($500) five hundred dollars in a fiscal year, a two-thirds vote of the disinterested Executive Board is required. The minutes of the meeting shall reflect that a disclosure was made, the abstention from voting, and the actual vote itself. Every new Executive Board member will be advised of this policy and shall sign a statement acknowledging, understanding, and agreeing to this policy.

Amendments

Amendments to the Articles and Bylaws may be made at the annual meeting of the general membership by a two-thirds vote of those present, after a minimum of five business days notification prior to the meeting at which voting is to take place. Proposed changes to the Bylaws must be posted within the Library and to the website.

Parliamentary Procedure

Robert's Rules of Order, latest edition, shall govern the proceedings of the Association unless they are in conflict with the Articles of Incorporation and the Bylaws.

Created: 1/30/06
Revised: 6/19.06; 9/26/07; 04/23/2015; July 2015

Appendix C

The Friends of the Milford Public Library
Board Member Position Description

Position Title: President

Summary of Position: Leadership position for the Friends of the Milford Library. Ensures the mission of the organization is executed, its programs are carried out in support of that mission, its finances are managed to carry out that mission, and works with the Library Director, other board members, committee chairpersons, volunteers, and members.

Election/Duration of Position:

1. Shall be elected at annual meeting in accordance with Article IV, Section 2 of FOML by-laws.
2. Shall not be eligible for re-election after serving 2 consecutive 2-year terms until a lapse of at least one year has occurred.

Responsibilities:

1. Serves as the chief volunteer of the organization.
2. Oversees marketing, finance, fundraising, and advocacy activities.
3. Create agendas and presides at all board meetings of the organization. Calls meetings of the Board of Directors as required.
4. Provide input and guidance as needed to board members and committees
5. Serves as an ambassador for the Friends and the Milford Public Library. Public face and voice of FOML, contribute to press releases and newsletters, make statements for media release.
6. Contribute to member communications.
7. Respond to organization emails, manage organization electronic storage.
8. Project manage annual meeting for the general membership.
9. Represent the organization to other boards and organizations, such as Milford Library Board and Friends of the Connecticut Libraries.
10. Appoint standing or ad hoc committees as needed.
11. Serves as an ex officio member of committees and attends their meetings when invited.
12. Perform duties of Vice President Public Relations in the absence of the of Vice President Public Relations.

Qualifications:

1. Prior leadership experience preferred.
2. Success as a committee chair or board member preferred.
3. Organizational skills, excellent written and verbal communication skills required.
4. Familiar with Google applications, gmail, drive, etc.
5. Membership in FOML required.

Date Approved by Board: 8/27/2021

Appendix D

Board of Directors
Candidate Consideration Form

You have been referred for consideration as a director to the Friends of Knox County Public Library Board.

Name:

Address:

Email:

Phone Number:

Qualifications and Expectations

- Be a member of the Friends of the Knox County Public Library, or join now!
- Be a resident of or work in Knox County Tennessee.
- Attend monthly board meetings.
- Join and participate in a Friends Committee: Finance, Used Books, Book and Author, Advocacy, Communications, Board Development & Nominating, Charters & Bylaws, Membership, or other.
- Respond promptly to emails and telephone calls.
- Demonstrated ability to work collegially.

On a separate sheet, please tell us about:

- Your special skills and talents which will help grow Friends of the Knox County Public Library.
- Your experience in:
    - Not-for-profit volunteer organizations;
    - Not-for-profit organization governance or management; and/or
    - Fundraising.
- Anything else you would like to share with the Nominating Committee for your consideration, such as your resume.

Appendix E

THE ETHICAL DOZEN FOR FRIENDS OF THE LIBRARY
Adopted September 18, 2015

1. Friends of the Library is a group of individuals who value public library services to the community and who volunteer their time, talents, and efforts to promote and support the vision, mission, and objectives of their library in whatever way will be helpful.

2. Friends organize to help support the work of the library, not to engage in the work and responsibilities of the library trustee board members or the library staff. Friends of the Library cooperate with both, but do not interfere with either. Friends recognize that they do not perform a decision-making role for the library: they are familiar with and support the policies of the library. Friends provide input into the library's long-range planning process and remain knowledgeable as to the status of the plan.

3. Friends support quality library services in the community through fundraising, volunteerism, and serving as advocates for the library's program.

4. Friends work to ensure that the public has equal access to information, both as a Constitutional right and as the best way to sustain a democratic way of life.

5. Friends subscribe to and believe in the Library Bill of Rights, the Freedom to Read, and the Freedom to View statements.

6. Friends recognize that authority rests with the whole Friends board assembled in public meetings and shall make no personal statements or promises nor take any private action which may compromise the board. They support the actions taken by a majority of the board and clearly differentiate personal opinions from board decisions.

7. Friends do not interfere with the library operations of the library staff.

8. Friends promote the library program to the public.

9. Friends conduct fundraising which complements the library's mission. Friends' activities support library board long-range plans and policies. Friends decide how to spend their funds after conferring with the library director.

10. Friends follow legal, professional, and ethical practices in making decisions. They scrupulously avoid personal conflicts of interest and do not condone them in others. They say nothing in a board meeting that could be construed to violate anyone's civil rights.

11. Friends serve as advocates for local, state, and national library issues and represent the library program to legislators and funders.

12. Friends are open and welcoming to suggestions, questions, and communications from the library staff, trustee board members, and the public.

Friends of Tennessee Libraries
Website: friendstnlibraries.org
Email: info@friendstnlibraries.org

Appendix F

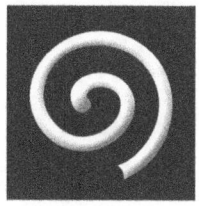

286 APPENDIX F

Who We Are

The Junior Friends of the Groton Public Library is a group of young people who organize service projects and fundraisers that benefit the Library and the community.

Becoming a Junior Friend is a great way to show your appreciation for the Library and give something back to the community.

What We Do

The Junior Friends actively support the Library through volunteering, fundraising and sponsoring events that involve and inspire young people. The Junior Friends:

- Help clean and decorate the Library and outside play area
- Sponsor fundraisers that support the purchase of supplies and special events
- Host movie and craft programs
- Take on projects that benefit charitable groups within the community

How to be a Friend to the Library

- Show Respect — take good care of the books, computers and toys in the Library
- Keep It Down — use a quiet voice in the Library
- Say Thanks — show your appreciation for the Library staff and volunteers
- Spread the Word — tell your friends that the Groton Public Library is a great place to visit

Join Today

Becoming a member of the Junior Friends is easy! Complete the form below, detach and return it to the Groton Public Library.

Once you become a Junior Friend, you will receive a membership card and regular emails listing Junior Friends' meetings and events.

_____
Name

_____
Address

_____
City / State / Zip Code

_____
Phone

_____
Email

☐ I give the Groton Public Library, its representatives and employees permission to take photographs or videos of me at Junior Friends Events.

I allow the Groton Public Library to copyright, use and publish the same in print and/or electronically.

I agree that the Groton Public Library may use such photographs or videos of me with or without my name and for any lawful purpose, including such purposes as publicity, illustration, advertising, and Web content.

_____
Signature

Appendix G

The Junior Friends Of Uniondale Public Library
Sponsored by the Friends of Uniondale Public Library

Who are the Junior Friends?
The Junior Friends are a subdivision of the Friends of Uniondale Public Library. The group is comprised of ambitious tweens/teens in grades 6-12.

What do they do?
These community service oriented teens promote and sponsor library programs while voicing their ideas and developing valuable leadership and organizational skills.

How can teens get involved?
All young adults in grades 6-12 are welcome to join the group. **Fill out the membership application below and return it to the Head of Teen Services.**

When do they meet?
The teens meet once per month, check the monthly library calendar and the newsletter for the dates and times of the monthly meetings.

$2.00 Annual Membership Fee is due at the time of the submitting the membership form.

Date: _____

Grade: _____ School: _____ Expected HS Graduation Year: _____

Name: _____

Complete Home Address: _____

Telephone: _____

Email address: _____

APPENDIX G ▲ 289

Appendix H

OUR PURPOSE

We are an association of people interested in books and libraries - specifically the St. Clair Shores Public Library.

We assist in promoting knowledge of and participation in Library programs.

We provide funds to meet special library needs outside of the public budgetary resources.

We support and cooperate with the library in developing library services and facilities for the community.

We encourage gifts of books, endowments and bequests.

We provide a channel for individuals and organizations to express ideas and make suggestions for library use and service.

FOLLOW US ON FACEBOOK & INSTAGRAM

FACEBOOK.COM/SCSLIBRARYFRIENDS
INSTAGRAM.COM/SCSLIBRARYFRIENDS

SCAN QR CODE TO VISIT OUR WEBSITE

WEBSITE:
SCSFRIENDS.MAILCHIMPSITES.COM

EMAIL US:
SCSFRIENDSOFTHELIBRARY@OUTLOOK.COM

Last revised Dec. 2022

FRIENDS

OF THE ST. CLAIR SHORES
PUBLIC LIBRARY

22500 ELEVEN MILE ROAD
ST. CLAIR SHORES, MI 48081

JOIN THE FRIENDS TODAY

Friends of the St. Clair Shores Public Library is a non-profit, 501(c)(3) organization, established in 1983 under the leadership of its first President, William Gilstorf. It is guided by a 12-member volunteer Board of Directors who plan and execute the fundraising efforts of the group. Dues and contributions may be tax deductible.

To date, the Friends through fundraisers, book sales and membership fees have contributed over **$400,000** to our local St. Clair Shores public library.

MEMBERSHIP BENEFITS

- **One free book** at our used book sales
- **One week free** on rental books
- Bi-monthly newsletter mailed to your home
- 50% discount on rental fee of $2 videos *(no limit)*
- Check out up to five $1 videos from Youth Services *(free of charge)*
- Satisfaction in helping your local Library

WHAT WE DO

The Friends of the St. Clair Shores Public Library is a busy group who could use your help!

- We maintain a large, year-round Used Book Store
- We offer periodic used book sales and various fundraising sales, including puzzles, accessories and more

HOW WE MAKE A DIFFERENCE

Our contributions to the St. Clair Shores Public Library are many. Currently, we support the following programs, activities and services:

- Adult & Children's Summer reading programs
- Free copies of Book Page monthly magazine
- Copy machines, Overdrive Reader and self-checkout facilities
- Community-wide Free Little Libraries
- Subscriptions to various newspapers and periodicals
- Large print books

FRIENDS OF THE ST. CLAIR SHORES PUBLIC LIBRARY MEMBERSHIP APPLICATION

☐ New Member ☐ Renewal

☐ Senior 62+ $10.00
☐ Individual $15.00
☐ Family $20.00
☐ Contributor $40.00
☐ Benefactor $100.00
☐ Patron $250.00
☐ Life $500.00

Please print clearly or use an address label

NAME: _____ DATE: _____

ADDRESS: _____

CITY: _____ STATE: _____ ZIP CODE: _____

PHONE: _____ EMAIL: _____

VOLUNTEER: ☐ Book Sales ☐ Membership
☐ Program Coordination ☐ Volunteer Coordination

Please make checks payable to "Friends of the St. Clair Shores Public Library"

As a 501(c)(3) non-profit organization, dues and contributions are tax deductible and also qualify for a Michigan tax credit.

Appendix I

Your Membership Supports:

- Public programs.
- Exhibits of Division collections.
- Partnerships with library, archival and cultural organizations.
- Research stipends.
- Florida History Day awards.

Will You Join Us?

info.florida.gov

500 South Bronough Street, MS 9
Tallahassee, Florida 32399-0250

850.245.6614
info@dos.myflorida.com

The Friends of the State Library and Archives of Florida Inc. is a nonprofit organization whose purpose is to provide financial and administrative support for the services and programs of the Florida Department of State, Division of Library and Information Services.

FLORIDA DEPARTMENT of STATE

Friends of the State Library and Archives of Florida

Supporting the mission of the Division of Library and Information Services.

Our Mission

The mission of the Friends of the State Library and Archives of Florida, Inc. is to enrich library, archives and records management services for the benefit of Florida's residents by promoting and supporting the programs and services of the Division of Library and Information Services.

info.florida.gov/about-us/friends/

Underwater photography by Bruce Mozert (MOZ00044). The Friends of the State Library and Archives of Florida sponsored an opening exhibition of his work, recently acquired by the State Archives of Florida, at the R.A. Gray Building in January 2020.

Become a Member

Benefactor	$500
Business friend	$250
Affiliate organizations	$100
Family	$40
Individual	$25
Senior	$20
Student	$10
Other Donation	$____
Total	$____

Name/Business/Organization
_____

Address
_____
_____

Email Address
_____

Map cases in the State Library and Archives research room funded by the Friends of the State Library and Archives of Florida.

Division Services

Your membership supports the Division of Library and Information Services.

The Division exists to provide services such as:

- **Access and technical assistance** related to collections of the **State Library and the State Archives of Florida**.
- **Support and consultation** to libraries across the state.
- **Records management consultation services** and training to government agencies and businesses.
- Managing state and local government records through off-site storage and servicing at **the State Records Center**.

Detach this form and return to:

Friends of the State Library and
Archives of Florida Inc.
R.A. Gray Building
500 South Bronough Street, MS 9
Tallahassee, Florida 32399-0250

Appendix J

Poudre River Friends of the Library
FOL Used Book Sale Guidelines Rev. Apr 2023

PRESALE ACTIVITIES

Schedule book sales as far in advance as possible – currently scheduled for all 2023 sales
Contacts: Coordinate with Jennifer Zachman, children's librarian at Harmony and with the Answer Center 970-555-6740

Monica, Phil & Robin: Monitor book inventory every 4 weeks

Volunteer signup –Char
    Volunteer caller begins filling shifts-at current book sale for next sale
    Use emails and SignUp Genius to send to caller list from previous sale that includes non-member volunteers in addition to current membership list, contact new members early

Groups to contact:
    Fiji Fraternity for book loading: Reily: xxxxx@gmail.com
    National Charity League – Char schedules

NOTE: It is very helpful if possible to have a sorting center volunteer on each shift to resolve pricing and category problems.

Sale supplies:

- Phil brings signs, sign supports, cash boxes, safe and office supplies, Target sacks and boxes
- Large purple Rubbermaid has office supplies and master file of forms, including laminated sales tax tables, membership forms, bulk buyer and tax exempt registration, set-aside invoices, volunteer sign ins, Webster House donation maps, cash & material donation receipts and floor boss ASK ME signs

Promotion – Robert Micek

- Coloradoan calendar listing
- Loveland Reporter-Herald
- booksalefinder.com
- KFRC: send to calendar@krfcfm.org with who what where when & phone contact
- KUNC
- Pirate Radio/ radio@pirate935.com
- Whofish
- Facebook on FOL and PRPLD sites. Katie Aumun does all PRPLD promo and Robin does Facebook posts and event listing, Robert does Facebook targeted marketing and media
- Post poster and next sale info on FOL web site – Bob Viscount & Samantha Ye
- FOL newsletter – Naomi Lederer

Facilities Liaison: Rob Stansbury/Book Transport: Phil Sullivan & Mike Gard

- Coordinate Harmony sales with Molly Thompson and FRCC security – call upon arrival and before leaving
- Truck rental–2-4 weeks ahead – Phil Sullivan & Mike Gard   Midtown U-haul, 24 ft,
- If using tents at Harmony, notify FRCC so they can shut off sprinklers at night
- Week of sale, contact appropriate library manager and exchange contact info
- Week of sale, contact Harmony coffee cart folks to let them know sale dates
- Harmony Shop is closed during book sale/annex is open if staff there wants it to be

SALE SET-UP

- MAKE SURE ALL TABLET COMPUTERS ARE CHARGED AND UPDATED!
- Bring extension cord for tablets
- Thursday is setup day for our normal Friday-Sunday sales
- For Harmony – move chair carrels Thurs a.m. into northeast corner of library for sale duration
- For Old Town – get door fob from Rob, use loading dock area as staging.
- Rob brings down extra tables from other libraries, outside tents for Harmony July & Nov

- Deploy tables according to room layouts
- Assemble signs into supports and fine-tune book placement so incoming books can be immediately placed on tables
- Setup cashier's tables and apportion supplies
- Hang miscellaneous signs on designated borders in room: next sale info, bookfinder.com, tally table reminders, etc.
- Put beer boxes under table near entrance for book customers, Target sacks at cashier tables

ACTUAL SALE ACTIVITIES

Daily:

- At Old Town: post sign on front and rear door asking volunteers to report to rear door
- At Harmony, use red phone to let Security know you have arrived and have them de-activate door alarms
- Opening Day – talk to pre-sale crowd and vendors about set-asides and thank them for coming
- Maintain pre-sale crowd in orderly line
- Floor bosses monitor book supply and let Robin or Phil know when we need re-supply
- Monitor tablet battery levels
- Monitor beer box supply for customers
- Opening: check form & receipt supply, turn on and log in to tablet computers
- Closing: turn off tablet computers and plug in overnight to charge
- Harmony: drape outside children's and lobby books
- Sunday is always HALF PRICE day

Finances Treasurer

- Set up cash/cash boxes – see attached
- Treasurers (Barbara & Maya) collect and count money as needed
- Square reports immediately available for daily totals

POST SALE ACTIVITIES

- Tabulate expenses and give receipts to treasurer
- Treasurer formulates sale revenue reports
- Volunteer coordinator totals hours and sends to library

Thank-yous:

- by President to volunteers (Monica & Char),
- on Facebook (Robin)
- by email to staff and Front Range Community College (Robin)

CURRENT CONTACTS

Specials–Carol Smith, 555-0262
Book Shop – Terrie Batty-555-1269
Tents/Canopies–Rob Stansbury
Mowing/sprinklers – xxxxx@frontrange.edu
Library Communications Manager – xxxxx@poudrelibraries.org
Library Volunteer Coordinator – Audrey Glasebrook 555-6183
Library Staff for IRS/Jr FOL/Teens–555-8403 (teen librarian)
FOL Newsletter Editor – Naomi Lederer xxxxx@hotmail.com
FOL Membership – Amy Gage
Book transport–Phil Sullivan, 555-8152/555-0844, Mike Gard 555-4927
Old Town Library -, Old Town Library Manager, Kristen Draper, 555-6678
Harmony – Molly Thompson, Harmony Library Manager 555-6670

Attachments:

- Poster distribution list
- Table Layouts

Appendix K

How We'll Play

The Moderator will pronounce each word, use it in a sentence, and repeat the word. After the Moderator says the word a second time, each team will have 60 seconds to discuss their answer and write it on the dry-erase board. After 30 seconds, each team will hold up their answers. The word will then be projected onto a screen for everyone to see.

If you have spelled the word incorrectly, you'll lower one of your flags and prepare for the next word. If you spell a word incorrectly and it is your THIRD incorrect spelling, your team is eliminated unless you wish to purchase a MULLIGAN. If not—you'll lower your third flag and remove your team name sign.

You may proceed with play if you purchase a Mulligan —Extra Chance ($30). A Mulligan gives your team ONE flag back (you are back in the competition until you misspell another word. At this point your team is out...unless you purchase another Mulligan). Only THREE Mulligans are allowed per team, and a Mulligan can only be purchased during regular round play (NOT during the Championship Round). If you'd like to purchase a Mulligan, act quickly because teams must be ready to spell the next word called by the Moderator. When there are five remaining teams left, the Spelling Bee enters the Championship Round (no more mulligans).

Single Elimination Round: teams will be eliminated with the first word misspelled, until there is only one team left. If all remaining teams misspell the same word, only these teams will be allowed to try again and spell a new word. If there is a tie, the Moderator will continue to offer words until there is a clear winner.

Judges make the final decision on all questions. There will be no appeals.

HOSTED BY:

BENEFITING:

Selected Bibliography and Webliography

Beard, Jason, et al. *The Principles of Beautiful Web Design*. 4th edition. Melbourne: SitePoint, 2020.

Bertinelli, Lina et al. *All Ages Welcome: Recruiting and Retaining Younger Generations for Library Boards, Friends Groups, and Foundations*. Chicago: ALA Editions, 2020.

Beyond Book Sales: The Complete Guide to Raising Real Money for Your Library. Susan Down, ed. Chicago: ALA Neal-Schuman, 2013.

Bray, Ilona. *Effective Fundraising for Nonprofits: Real-World Strategies That Work*. Berkley, CA: NOLO, 2022.

Bryson, John M. *Strategic Planning for Public and Nonprofit Organizations: A Guide to Strengthening and Sustaining Organizational Achievement*. Hoboken, NJ: Wiley, 2018.

Burk, Penelope. *Donor-Centered Fundraising*. Second edition. Chicago: Cygnus Applied Research, 2018.

Feld, Brad et al. *Startup Boards: A Field Guide to Building and Leading an Effective Board of Directors*. Hoboken, NJ: Wiley, 2022.

Felke-Morris, Terry Ann. *Basics of Web Design*. 6th ed. London: Pearson, 2021.

Fletcher, Adam F.C. *Steps to Youth Leadership in Modern Times*. Olympia, WA: Freechild Institute for Youth Engagement, 2023.

Fuller, Joy L. *Strategic Planning for Public Libraries*. Chicago: ALA Editions, 2021. (Available in a digital version or as a print/ebook bundle.)

Hammerman, Susan Summerfield. *Researching Prospective Donors: Get More Funding for Your Library*. Chicago: ALA Editions, 2014.

Jennings, Karlene Noel, and Joyce Gerczynski. *Fundraising for Academic Libraries: A Practical Guide for Librarians*. Lanham, MD: Rowman & Littlefield, 2020.

Karle, Melody. *A Social Media Survival Guide*. Lanham, MD: Rowman & Littlefield, 2020.

Kihlstedt, Andrea. *Capital Campaigns: Strategies That Work*. 4th edition. Sudbury, MA: Jones & Bartlett Learning, 2017.

La Piana, David. *The Nonprofit Strategy Revolution: Real-Time Strategic Planning in a Rapid Response World*. Nashville, TN: Turner, 2018.

Lehn, Carla. *From Library Volunteer to Library Advocate: Tapping into the Power of Community Engagement*. Santa Barbara, CA: Libraries Unlimited, 2018.

Mon, Lorri, and Christie Koontz. *Marketing and Social Media: A Guide for Libraries, Archives, and Museums*. Lanham, MD: Rowman & Littlefield, 2021.

Reed, Sally Gardner. *The Good, the Great, and the Unfriendly: A Librarian's Guide to Working with Friends Groups*. Chicago: ALA Editions, 2017.

Reed, Sally Gardner et al. *101+ Great Ideas for Libraries and Friends*. New York: Neal-Schuman, 2004.

Reed, Sally Gardner, and Beth Nawalinski. *Even More Great Ideas for Libraries and Friends*. New York: Neal-Schuman, 2008.

Renner, Allison. *Library Volunteers: A Practical Guide for Librarians*. Lanham, MD: Rowman & Littlefield, 2019.

Thomsett-Scott, Beth C. *Marketing with Social Media*. Chicago: ALA Neal-Schuman, 2020

Wood, M. Sandra. *Successful Library Fundraising*. Lanham, MD: Rowman & Littlefield, 2014.

Webliography

Academic Friends: Resources for Getting Started. 2023. United for Libraries, https://www.ala.org/united/friends/academic.

American Library Association. 2008. "Library Advocate's Handbook," https://www.ala.org/ala/issues/2008LAH.pdf.

American Library Association. 2023. "Frontline Advocacy for Public Libraries," https://www.ala.org/advocacy/frontline-advocacy-public-libraries.

American Library Association. 2023. "State Legislative Toolkit," https://www.ala.org/advocacy/state-legislative-toolkit.

American Library Association Public Programs Office. 2003. "One Book, One Community: Planning Your Community-Wide Read," https://www.ala.org/tools/sites/ala.org.tools/files/content/onebook/files/onebookguide.pdf.

Balsamiq. 2022. "Design Tips for a More Effective Nonprofit Website." Webinar video. Balsamiq Wireframing Academy, https://www.youtube.com/watch?v=fwjvlxn9QX4.

Bertin, Stephanie. A History of Youth Summer Reading Programs in Public Libraries. A Master's Paper for the M.S. in L.S degree. May, 2004. 71 pp. Advisor: Brian Sturm. https://ils.unc.edu/MSpapers/2977.pdf.

Blue Avocado. 2022. Nonprofits Insurance Alliance, https://blueavocado.org.

BoardSource. [n.d.] "Nonprofit Strategy and Planning," https://boardsource.org/fundamental-topics-of-nonprofit-board-service/nonprofit-strategic-planning/.

BoardSource. 2021. "Putting Purpose First: Nonprofit Board Leadership Today." https://boardsource.org/product/putting-purpose-first/. (72 pp., available as a PDF or in print.)

Candid Learning. 2022. Candid, https://learning.candid.org/.

EveryLibrary. 2019. EveryLibrary Institute, https://www.everylibraryinstitute.org/.

Fairfax County Public Library, Virginia. 2019. "Friends of the Library Handbook," https://www.fairfaxcounty.gov/library/sites/library/files/assets/documents/pdf/friends-handbook.pdf.

Freechild Institute for Youth Engagement, https://freechild.org/.

Friends of Tennessee Libraries, Resources. 2022. https://www.friendstnlibraries.org/resources/resources-by-topic/.

George W. Bush Presidential Library, 2023. Laura Bush Foundation for America's Libraries, https://www.bushcenter.org/topics/education/laura-bush-foundation-for-americas-libraries.

Hanson, Charles D. August 2013. "Academic Library Friends: A Toolkit for Getting Started—You Can Do This!" United for Libraries, https://www.ala.org/united/sites/ala.org.united/files/content/friends/orgtools/academic-library-friends.pdf.

Illinois Library Association. [n.d.] "Advocacy Toolkit," https://www.ila.org/content/documents/ila-advocacy-toolkit-013112.pdf.

Internal Revenue Service. 2022. "Charitable Organizations." United State Government, https://www.irs.gov/charities-non-profits/charitable-organizations.

Library Strategies. 2021. Friends of the St. Paul Public Library, Library Strategies Consulting Group, https://www.librarystrategiesconsulting.org/.

Mattison, Allen. 2011. "Influencing Public Policy in the Digital Age: The Law of Online Lobbying and Election-Related Activities." Alliance for Justice, https://bolderadvocacy.org/wp-content/uploads/2012/01/Influencing_Public_Policy_in_the_Digital_Age_paywall-1.pdf.

National Head Start Association, https://nhsa.org/.

Nonprofit Quarterly, https://nonprofitquarterly.org/.

Nonprofit Works, https://www.nonprofitworks.com/resources/.

Public Library Association. 2023. "Advocacy," https://www.ala.org/pla/advocacy.

Public Library Association. [n.d.] "Understanding Advocacy." Turning the Page, https://www.ala.org/pla/advocacy.

Raise Funds, https://www.raise-funds.com/.

Reed, Sally Gardner. November 2013. "Friends Groups: Critical Support for School Libraries Toolkit." United for Libraries, https://www.ala.org/united/sites/ala.org.united/files/content/friends/orgtools/school-friends.pdf.

Reed, Sally Gardner. August 2012. "Libraries Need Friends: Starting a Friends Group or Revitalize the One You Have." United for Libraries, https://www.ala.org/united/sites/ala.org.united/files/content/friends/orgtools/libraries-need-friends.pdf.

Reed, Sally Gardner, Beth Nawalinski, and Jillian Kalonick. May 2013. "Citizens Save Libraries: A Power Guide to Successful Advocacy." United for Libraries, https://www.ala.org/united/sites/ala.org.united/files/content/powerguide/united-power-guide.pdf.

Ryan, Janice M. and Meredith K. McCoy. 2019. "The Dos and Don'ts of Lobbying for Nonprofit Organizations." PowerPoint. Venable, https://www.venable.com/-/media/files/events/2019/02/dosanddontofnonprofitorganizations.pdf.

United for Libraries. 2022. American Library Association, https://www.ala.org/united/.

United for Libraries. 2023. "Citizens-Save-Libraries Power Guide," https://www.ala.org/united/powerguide.

WebJunction. 2023. "Advocacy in Action: Local Library Awareness Campaigns." OCLC, https://www.webjunction.org/explore-topics/advocacy-in-action.html.

Yoke, Beth, with Linda Braun. "Adopting a Summer Learning Approach for Increased Impact: A YALSA Position Paper." Adopted by YALSA's Board of Directors, April 16, 2016. https://www.ala.org/yalsa/adopting-summer-learning-approach-increased-impact-yalsa-position-paper.

Youth.gov. 2023. United States government official website, https://youth.gov/.

Webliography of Library Support Group Sample Websites

LIBRARY SUPPORT GROUPS represented in this supplementary webliography are provided for quick access to user-friendly and comprehensive examples and ones that may include links to beneficial approaches, sample applications, and event ideas. They represent the various types of library support organizations mentioned in this book. These may give you ideas about potential ways to move toward the creation or redesign of your own group's website depending on its focus. Population estimates for the service areas of the beneficiary public libraries are given for each organization in order to demonstrate what library support groups in small, medium, and large communities can do.

Public Library Friends, Friends Foundations, Library Trusts

Friends of the Boca Raton Public Library, Boca Raton, Florida (City population 101,000)
https://www.bocalibraryfriends.org/

Friends of the Brainerd Public Library, Brainers, Minnesota (City population 15,000)
https://www.wineandwordsandfriends.com/

Carmel Public Library Foundation, Carmel, California (City population 3,200)
https://carmelpubliclibraryfoundation.org/

Chapel Hill Public Library Foundation, Chapel Hill, North Carolina (Metro Durham-Chapel Hill population 650,000)
https://chplfoundation.org/

Chester County Library Trust, Exton, Pennsylvania (County population 534,000)
https://chescolibraries.org/about/how-you-can-help/chester-county-library-trust/

Poudre River Friends of the Library, Fort Collins, Colorado (City population 169,000)
https://www.prfol.org/

Great Falls Public Library Foundation, Great Falls, Montana (Metro population 84,000)
https://www.gfplf.org/

Friends of the Knox County Public Library and Knox Public Library Foundation, Knoxville, Tennessee (County population 487,000)
https://www.knoxfriends.org/
https://www.knoxfriends.org/library-foundation/

Los Angeles County Library Foundation, Los Angeles, California (County population 9.83 million)
https://www.lacolibraryfoundation.org/

Friends of the Library, Montgomery County, Maryland (County population 1,055 million)
https://www.folmc.org/

Friends of the New Orleans Public Library, New Orleans, Louisiana (Metro city population 1.27 million)
https://friendsnola.org/

Friends of the Metropolitan Library System and Library Endowment Trust, Oklahoma City, Oklahoma (Metro population 1,018 million)
https://friendsnola.org/
https://supportmls.org/let/

Pacific Grove Public Library Friends and Foundation, Pacific Grove, California (City population 15,000)
https://www.pglibraryfriends.org/

The Library Foundation, Portland, Oregon (Metro population 2.6 million)
https://www.libraryfoundation.org/

Friends & Foundation of the Rochester Public Library, Rochester, New York (Metro population 749,000)
https://ffrpl.libraryweb.org/

Friends of the Saint Paul Public Library, Saint Paul, Minnesota (City population 311,000)
https://thefriends.org/

Seekonk Library Trust, Seekonk, Massachusetts (Town population 15,000)
https://seekonklibrarytrust.org/

Friends of the Thompson Public Library, Thompson, Connecticut (Town population 9,400)
https://thompsonpubliclibrary.org/about-us/friends-of-the-library/

Friends of the Torrance Public Library, Torrance, California (City population 147,000)
https://www.friendsofthetorrancelibrary.org/

Tulsa Library Trust, Tulsa, Oklahoma (City and Metro area population 791,000)
https://tulsalibrarytrust.org/

Friends of Westlake Porter Public Library and Westlake Porter Public Library Foundation, Westlake, Ohio (City population 34,000)
https://www.westlakelibrary.org/friends
https://wpplfoundation.org/

Wood Memorial Library Trust, South Windsor, Connecticut (Town population 27,000)
https://www.woodmemoriallibrarytrust.org/

Friends Foundation of Worthington Libraries, Worthington, Ohio (City population 15,000)
https://worthingtonlibrariesfriends.org/

School, College, and University Library Support Groups

Friends of the Library, Angelo State University, San Angelo, Texas
https://www.angelo.edu/give/join/friends-of-the-library-membership.php

Friends of the University Libraries, Bowling Green State University, Bowling Green, Ohio
https://www.bgsu.edu/library/about/ULFriends.html

Double Eagle Elementary School Friends of the Library, Albuquerque, New Mexico
https://doubleeagle.aps.edu/our-school/library/friends-of-the-library

Friends of the Oakland Public School Libraries/Oakland Literacy Coalition, Oakland, California
https://fopsl.org/

Rancho Bernardo High School Friends of the Library, San Diego, California
https://www.rbhsfriendsofthelibrary.org/who-we-are/

Friends of Southern Methodist University Libraries, Dallas, Texas
https://www.smu.edu/libraries/join/friends

State Friends of the Library, Foundations, and Trusts

Friends of the State Library & Archives, Division of Library and Information Services, Florida Department of State, Tallahassee, Florida
https://dos.myflorida.com/library-archives/about-us/friends/

Friends of Libraries Section, New York Library Association, Guilderland, New York
https://www.nyla.org/4DCGI/cms/review.html?Action=CMS_Document&DocID=144?MenuKey=fls

Friends of Tennessee Libraries, Knoxville, Tennessee
https://www.friendstnlibraries.org/

Trust for Montana Libraries, Missoula, Montana
https://www.mtlibrarytrust.org/

Friends of the Library of Hawai'i, Honolulu, Hawai'i
https://friendsofthelibraryofhawaii.org/

Indiana State Library Foundation, Indianapolis, Indiana
https://www.indianastatelibraryfdn.org/

Friends of Libraries in Oklahoma, Tulsa, Oklahoma
http://www.okfriends.net/

For further information about state Friends organizations:

State Friends Groups (list), American Library Association, United for Libraries
https://www.ala.org/united/friends/statefriends

Index

Page numbers in italics refer to figures.

academic libraries, support groups in: examples of, 27–28; reasons for, 21, 26–27
accrual accounting systems, 92
acknowledgment, donor gift, 191–94
adult spelling bees, planning, 170–72
advocacy: initiatives, examples of, 258, 260–62; online resources for, 259; overview of, 7, 257; political, 258, 262–64; special events, 265–66
advocacy committees, 258
ALTA (Association for Library Trustees and Advocates), 22
American Library Association (ALA): advocacy and, 261; United for Libraries, 22–23, 58
Ames Public Library Friends Foundation, Iowa, 267
annual budgets. See budgets
annual reports, 207
application for membership, 118–20
applying for grants. See grant-finding resources; grant writing
appreciation for library support groups, examples of, 139–40, 266
articles of incorporation, nonprofit establishment and, 45–46
Atlanta-Fulton Public Library Foundation, Georgia, 218, 219
author events: examples of, 182–88; fundraising through, tips for, 180–81
awards programs and honors, 237–39

balance sheet, purpose of, 93
Balentine, Kimmerle, 133
banners, tips for purchasing, 265
bequests, 201
Bloomerang + Kindful (website), 194
Blue Avocado (website), 37
board leadership team. See leadership team
board meetings. See meetings
Bolder Advocacy, 263
book balls, examples of, 177–78
book bundles: book sales and, 159–60; examples of, 162–65. See also book sales, unique examples of

book festivals: children's, examples of, 218–20; examples of, 217–21; planning, online resources for, 222
book nooks, 162–65
book sales: breweries, partnering with, 166–68; coffee houses, partnering with, 168; continuous, examples of, 162–65; online, tips for, 166; traditional, in-person, 156–59; unique, examples of, 159–68
book shops, 162–65
breweries, fundraising events held at, 168–70. See also fundraising, examples
brochures, promotional, membership solicitation through, 119–20
budgets: aspects of, 91; defined, 90; preparing, 91–92; resources for learning more, 94–95; wish list prioritization and, 90–91. See also financial statements
budgets, library: supplementing, library support groups and, 7; using wish lists to supplement, 252–53
button-making machines, 179
button-sales fundraising, 179
bylaws, nonprofit establishment and: creating, 46, 65–66; leadership team members and, 43–44, 69

Candid Learning (website), 37, 94
Candid's Foundation Directory, free access to, 244
Capital Campaign Pro (website), 199
capital funds campaigns, 195–98; designing and implementing, 197–98; hiring consultants for, 196; online resources for, 199
cards, greeting, fundraising with, 176–78
Cary Memorial Library Foundation, Inc., Massachusetts, 204
cash accounting systems, 92
Cedar Rapids Public Library, Iowa, 215
challenges faced by library support groups: board vacancies, 104–8; conflict over objectives, 100–102; declining support, 97–99; group efforts overlapping, 102–4; solutions for, 98–104, 107–9; volunteer resignations, sudden, 108–9
charitable gift annuities, 201

▲ 309

charitable organizations, establishing. See nonprofit, establishing as a
charters, nonprofit establishment and, 45–46
Chattanooga Public Library Foundation, Tennessee, 164
Chico Friends of the Library, California, 212, 214
Children's Book Festival, Atlanta, Georgia, 218, 219
children's book festivals, examples of, 218–20, 219
Children's Festival of Reading, Knoxville, Tennessee, 220
City of Mesa Library, Arizona, 1, 77, 166
Clawson, Erin, 29–31
Clawson, Karen, 29–31
Clawson, Patrick, Jr., 29–31
Collaborative Summer Library Program (CSLP), 255. See also summer reading programs
community involvement: book festivals, 217–22; creators in residence programs, 216–17; Disaster Relief Fund (ALA), 214–15; donating books, 210, 212–14; emergency giving, 214–15; Head Start programs, 234–36; Imagination Library Program participation, 215–16; Little Free Libraries, 211–12; reading programs, 223–33; special awards programs and honors, 237–39
community reading programs: in academia, 231–32; examples of, 224–28, 230–33; overview of, 222–24; resources for starting, 233–34; statewide, 233; youth-focused, examples of, 226–31
community volunteers, partnering with, 146–47
conflict-of-interest policies, 59–60
contributors, attracting and securing, 111
creators in residence programs, 216–17
credit card payments, accepting, setting up, 123–24
crowdfunding platforms, 198
crowdsourcing, defined, 198

Denver Public Library Friends Foundation, Colorado, 15–16, 18, 64, 122, 157, 167, 260, 264
development planning, 82–83
development strategic plans, 83–84
digital platforms, 114–16
Disaster Relief Fund (ALA), contributing to, 214–15
dismissals of board members: preventing, 107–8; process for handling, 106–7
Dollywood Foundation, 215–16
donation buttons. See donation pages, online
donation pages, online: alternatives to, 200; best practices for, 193–94; example of, 121–22; setting up, 200
donations: accepting materials as, 160–62, 162; donation levels, setting, 121–22; legacy giving and, 200–201; recurring, payment collection and, 123–24; soliciting for, 121–22. See also conflict-of-interest policies
donor appreciation: annual reports and, 207; gift acknowledgement, 191–94; overview of, 147–48
Donor Bill of Rights, 60–61
Donorbox Blog (website), 94
donor relationship management: importance of, 192–93; online resources for, 194
DonorsChoose (website), 198

DonorSearch (website), 202
dues, membership, collecting: online, 118, 123–24; raising additional funds through, 120–22; setting rates and, 118–19; volunteering in lieu of, 118

electronic giving, online donation page best practices, 193–94
endowments: distribution of, 203; library support through, 200–201; soliciting for, 203–4
estate planning, library support through, 200–201
ethics statements: creating, 58–59; example of, 59; history of, 58–59. See also conflict-of-interest policies
events, ticketed, fundraising through, 182–88
EveryLibrary (website), 260
Excel software, using for budgeting purposes, 90
executive board. See leadership team
ex officio board members, 43–44, 74

federal tax code, establishing nonprofit status under, 45
Felburn Foundation, 20
filing taxes. See tax filing
financial officers. See treasurers
financial statements: legal requirements of, 92–93; overview of, 92–93; types of, 93
flamingos, plastic lawn, fundraising with, 174–76, 175
FOLUSA (Friends of the Library USA), 22
Form 990, 92
Form 1099-NEC, 94
forming a library support group, 38–40. See also nonprofit, establishing as a
Form W-937, 94
Fort Collins Book Fest, Fort Collins, Colorado, 217–18
Fort Vancouver Regional Library District, Washington, 19–20
Fort Vancouver Regional Library Foundation, Washington, 19–20
Foundation Directory, free access to, 244
foundations: defined, 13; overview of, 13–14. See also library support groups; merging support groups
Freechild Institute for Youth Engagement, 127
free libraries, 7–9
Freewill (website), 202
Friends Foundation of the Birmingham Public Library, Alabama, 60
Friends Foundation of Worthington Libraries, Ohio, 168
Friends groups. See Friends of the Library groups
Friends of Chapel Hill Public Library, North Carolina, 163
Friends of Curry Public Library, Oregon, 253
Friends of Johnson County Library, Kansas, 160–61, 163–64, 205
Friends of Lancaster Public Library, Pennsylvania, 183
Friends of Loveland Public Library Foundation, Colorado, 267
Friends of Snow Library, Massachusetts, 52
Friends of Tennessee Libraries, 59, 258
Friends of the Ada Public Library, Idaho, 118
Friends of the Allan Hancock College Library, California, 28
Friends of the Allen Public Library, Texas, 257

Friends of the Austin Public Library, Minnesota, 174–76, 175, 182
Friends of the Blackstone Public Library, Massachusetts, 99–100
Friends of the Beacon Falls Library, Connecticut, 169
Friends of the Boca Raton Public Library, Florida, 114–15
Friends of the Boynton Beach City Library, Florida, 176–77
Friends of the Brainerd Public Library, Minnesota, 182–83
Friends of the Brooks Library, Central Washington University, 97–99
Friends of the Campbell Library, Minnesota, 165
Friends of the Carson City Library, Nevada, 214
Friends of the Chesapeake Public Library, Virginia, 245
Friends of the City Library in Salt Lake, Utah, 257
Friends of the Clifton Park-Halfmoon Public Library, New York, 224–25, 238
Friends of the Dallas Public Library, Texas, 245, 247–48
Friends of the Dover Public Library, New Hampshire, 157–58
Friends of the Duke University Libraries, North Carolina, 27
Friends of the Durham Library, North Carolina, 257
Friends of the Ferguson Library, Connecticut, 164–65
Friends of the Joseph T. Simpson Public Library, Pennsylvania, 58
Friends of the Knox County Public Library, Tennessee, 80, 112–13, 113, 145, 153, 161, 163, 166–67, 167, 213–15, 220, 227, 234–36, 248, 248, 258
Friends of the L.E. Phillips Memorial Public Library, Wisconsin, 234
Friends of the Libraries, Ohio University, 257
Friends of the Libraries Section of the New York Library Association, 66
Friends of the Library, Montgomery County, Maryland, 162–63, 179
Friends of the Library at Alachua County Library District, Florida, 234
Friends of the Library at Mill Springs Academy, Georgia, 33
Friends of the Library at the Double Eagle Elementary School, New Mexico, 33
Friends of the Library at the Georgia O'Keeffe Elementary School, New Mexico, 33–34
Friends of the Library Foundation of Kanawha County, West Virginia, 220
Friends of the Library groups: defined, 11; dues collecting and, 118–19; establishing, 12–15; membership applications, 118–20; on the state level, 21–22. See also library support groups; merging support groups
Friends of the Library of Hawai'i, 165
Friends of the Longview Public Library, Washington, 168, 178
Friends of the Metropolitan Library System, Oklahoma, 204
Friends of the Milford Public Library, Connecticut, 184, 184
Friends of the Millis Public Library, Massachusetts, 185
Friends of the Olathe Public Library, Kansas, 185, 186
Friends of the Palo Alto Library, California, 213
Friends of the Saint Clair Shores Public Library, Michigan, 120
Friends of the Saint Paul Public Library, Minnesota, 233, 247
Friends of the Salado Public Library, Texas, 118–19
Friends of the San Diego Public Library, California, 52
Friends of the San Francisco Public Library, California, 201
Friends of the Santa Maria Public Library, California, 101–2
Friends of the Saratoga Springs Public Library, New York, 168
Friends of the State Library and Archives of Florida, 120
Friends of the St. Charles City-County Library, Missouri, 161
Friends of the Summit County Libraries, Colorado, 257
Friends of the Sunnyvale Public Library, Texas, 54
Friends of the Sun Prairie Public Library, Wisconsin, 75–76, 78–79, 256
Friends of the Thompson Public Library, Connecticut, 20
Friends of the University of Northern Colorado Libraries, 27–28
Friends of the Wichita Falls Public Library, Texas, 213
Friends of Tualatin Library, Oregon, 214
Friends of Weathersfield Proctor Library, Vermont, 20, 158, 180
Friends of Williamsburg Regional Library Foundation, Virginia, 57
Frontline Advocacy, 263
Fuller, Lisa, 136
funding matches, library giving days and, 196
Fund Libraries, 198
fundraising: background of, 153; capital funds campaigns, 195–98; donor-centered vs. traditional, 190–91; legacy giving, 200–204; online resources of ideas, 155–56; strategic planning and, 154; teen service organizations and, 206–7
fundraising, examples: adult spelling bees, 170–72; book sales, traditional, 156–59; book sales, unique, 159–70; grocery store donations, 204–5; ideas, additional, 174–88
fundraising strategic plans. See development strategic plans
funds distribution: library prioritization of, 252; staff development opportunities through, 256–57; summer reading programs and, 255–56; wish lists and, 252–53

galas, examples of, 182–88
gift cards, 162–65
gifts, donor acknowledgement and, 191–94. See also donations; donor appreciation
giveaway books, 212–14
goal setting: grant writing and, 243; membership drives and, 143–44; SMART strategic plans, using, 86; terminology used, 82–83
grab bags. See book sales, unique examples of
Grand Rapids Public Library Foundation, Michigan, 226–27
grant-finding resources: Candid's Foundation Directory, 244; GrantWatch, 244; ProLiteracy Grants & Funding page, 244–45
grants: defined and described, 242; examples of, 245; receiving and accepting, 248–49. See also grant writing
GrantWatch (website), 244
grant writing: grant-finding resources, 243–45; overview of, 243; proposals, steps to writing, 246–47; rejected proposals, handling, 250–51; tips, additional, 247
grocery store sales percentage donations, 204–5

Hart's Ladder of Children's Participation, 128
Head Start programs: supporting, 234–35; tips for starting, 236
Hilbert College Friends of the Library program, New York, 28
Huntley Area Public Library Friends Foundation, Illinois, 18–19, 50
Huntsville-Madison County Library Foundation, Alabama, 170, 183, 195

Imagination Library Program, 215–16
individual retirement accounts (IRAs), as legacy gifts, 201
Infopeople (website), 116
Internal Revenue Code, section 501(c)(3), 45. See also nonprofit, establishing as a
Iowa City Public Library Friends Foundation, Iowa, 267

J. Frank Dobie Library Trust, 15
job descriptions, leadership team: board member or member-at-large, 73–74; committee chairperson, 73; considerations when creating, 69–70, 74; executive director, 71; ex officio member, 74; junior board members, 78–79; president or chair, 71–72; secretary, 73; treasurer, 72–73; vice president or vice chair, 72
Johnson County Public Library Foundation, Indiana, 177–78, 205
junior board members, 76–79
Junior Friends of the Groton Public Library, Connecticut, 120, 131–34, 132, 134, 145–46
Junior Friends of the Joseph H. Plumb Memorial Library, Massachusetts, 135–36
Junior Friends of the Library groups: establishing, 130–31; examples of, 132–35; fundraising through, 206–7; reasons for joining, real-life accounts, 136
Junior Friends of the Uniondale Public Library, New York, 135

Keela (website), 194
Kempworth, Pamela, 18–19
Kindful (website), 194
K is for Kids Foundation, 29–31
Kroger Community Rewards, 205. See also grocery store sales percentage donations

Lake Forest Library Foundation, Illinois, 204
Lanier Library, North Carolina, 20
Larson, Terry, 79
Laura Bush Foundation for America's Libraries, 245
Laurel Oak Elementary Friends Foundation, Florida, 29–31
Lawrence Public Library Friends & Foundation, Kansas, 16–18, 17, 183
leadership roles, overview of, 42–43
leadership team: culture, creating, 55; ex officio members, 43–44, 74; job descriptions, creating, 69–70; junior board members, 76–79; members aging out, concerns around, 137; officers, 42–43; recruiting new members, 74–76; training and orientation, 79–81. See also job descriptions, leadership team
Leander Library Foundation, Texas, 54

legacy gifts, 200–204
legal assistance, free of charge options, 10
letter-writing campaigns, tips for and template, 264. See also advocacy
library advocates. See advocacy
Library Foundation of Kanawha County, Inc., West Virginia, 220
Library Foundation of Los Angeles, California, 57, 164, 216–17
Library Foundation of Spokane County Library, Washington, 169
Library Giving Day: background of, 195; best practices for, 196. See also capital funds campaigns
library staff, Frontline Advocacy and, 263
library staff, partnering with, 81–82, 129. See also ex officio board members
Library Strategies (website), 37–38
library support groups: advocacy and, 257–66; background of, 6–10; funding by, 255–57; including youth members, 127–31; leadership of, 42–43, 65–66; promoting, 139–40; soliciting donations for, 120–22. See also challenges faced by library support groups; nonprofit, establishing as a
Lied Scottsbluff Public Library Teen Advisory Council, Nebraska, 206
life insurance, as a legacy gift, 201
LinkedIn (website), 194
literacy promotion: community reading programs, 224–33; Head Start programs, 234–36
Little Free Libraries, 211–12
Live Oak Middle School Library, Louisiana, 261
Livingston County Library Charitable Trust, Missouri, 14
logos: designing, tips for, 112; examples of, 112–13; importance of, 111–12
Los Angeles Public Library Creators in Residence, 216–17

Madison Public Library Foundation, Wisconsin, 196, 221, 257
marketing: logos, 111–13; website redesigning, 113–14
matching funds, library giving days and, 196
meetings: budget overview, 91; minutes, creating effective, 41–42; organizing and running, tips for, 40
member recruitment: ideas for, 140–43; online promotion and, 113–14; setting goals for, 143–44; tips for, 98–100; younger and middle-aged adults, 137–39; youth opportunities, 127–30
membership: application forms, designing, 119–20; online services for, 118
membership drives: evaluating, 144; overview, 139; planning for, 143–44. See also SMART goal setting
membership libraries. See subscription libraries
Memorandum of Understanding (MOU), 15–16, 64–65, 101–2, 103
merging support groups: examples of, 15–19, 17; library participation in, 18–19; reasons for, 15–19, 103–4. See also Memorandum of Understanding (MOU)
Mesa Public Library Board of Trustees, Arizona, 77
Mestelle, Cynthia J., 76

Metropolitan Library System Library Endowment Trust, Oklahoma, 54, 204
Middle Country Library Foundation, New York, 57
mission statements: creating, 51; defined, 51; examples of, 50, 52

Nassau Library System, New York, 260–61
National Friends of Libraries Week, 139
New Rochelle Public Library Foundation, New York, 203
newsletters, 12
nonprofit, establishing as a: assistance with, 10, 37–38, 45, 94–95; documentation needed, 44; leadership, role of, 42–43; legal considerations for, 44–45
Nonprofit Strategic Planning (website), 87
notecards, historical, fundraising with, 178

officers, board. See leadership team
officers-in-training, 42–43. See also junior board members
One Book, One City for Kids, Grand Rapids, Michigan, 226–27
One Book, One Minnesota, 233
One Book, One School, Oswego High School, Illinois, 230–31
One Book, One Tulsa, Oklahoma, 225–26
One Book, One U, University of Miami, Florida, 231–32
One Book movement, origination of, 222–23. See also community reading programs
One Book Read City, Knox County, Tennessee, 227
One Book Villanova, Pennsylvania, 232
One District, One Book, Oneida School District, New York, 227–28
One School, One Book, Simpson Elementary School, Franklin, Kentucky, 230
online donation pages: best practices for, 193–94; setting up, 200
online lobbying, nonprofits and, guidelines for, 263
online privacy notices, 62–63
online resources, selected: advocacy, 259; book festivals, 222; budget creation and support, 94–95; capital funds campaigns, 199; donor management assistance, 194; fundraising ideas, 155–56; logo creation, 112; nonprofit support, general, 37–38; planned giving, 202; social media presence, building, 116; strategic planning, 87; tax code instruction, 45; websites, building, 116
online sales: book selling through, 166; collecting payments through, 123–24
orientation and training: packets for new members, 79–80; welcome letter sample, 81, 145–46
outreach efforts, promoting support groups through, 126

Parent-Teacher Associations (PTAs), 9–10, 29
parliamentary authority, nonprofit establishment and, 46
partnering with community volunteers, ideas for, 146–47
Parton, Dolly, 215–16
payments, receiving and processing: selecting online platform(s) for, 123–24; self-service options, 124
Pima County Public Library, Arizona, 61–62

planned giving: donors, individual, 120–22; online resources for, 202
PlannedGiving (website), 202
political lobbying, library support groups and, 262–64
Polk County Community Foundation, North Carolina, 20
Poudre River Friends of the Library, Colorado, 1, 12, 47–48, 59–60, 63, 77–79, 81, 84, 123–24, 157, 162, 217, 218
Poudre River Friends of the Library Board of Directors, Colorado, 77–78, 84, 117, 159
Poudre River Library Trust, Colorado, 1, 14, 138–39, 217–18
ProLiteracy (website), 244–45
PTAs (Parent-Teacher Associations), 9–10, 29

Raise Funds (website), 38
Rancho Bernardo High School Friends of the Library, California, 32–33
reading programs, youth-focused: examples of, 226–31; guidelines for, 228–29
recognition, library support group, ideas for, 139–40, 266
recruiting: leadership team members, 74–76; teenage leadership team members, 76–79; younger and middle-aged adult members, 137–39; youth engagement and, 127–30. See also member recruitment; membership drives
resignations of board members: preventing, 107–8; process for handling, 104–6
retained life estates, 201
Return of Organization Exempt from Income Tax, 92
Rochester Public Library Foundation, Minnesota, 253
rules, special, nonprofit establishment and, 46–47
rules, standing, nonprofit establishment and, 47–48

sales percentage donations, 204–5
San Jose Public Library, California, 63
San Jose State University, California, 261–62
scholarship programs, community support through, 238
school libraries, support groups in: examples of, 29–34; reasons for, 21, 28–29
search engine optimization (SEO), 116–17
Skinner, Sharon, 246–47
SMART goal setting, 86, 143–44
Smartsheet (website), 95
Smith, Natalie, 236
social media, lobbying and, considerations for, 263
social media presence: considerations for, 61–62; creating, 114–16; tools for building, 116
social media sites. See social media presence
spelling bees, adult, fundraising through, 170–72
staff development, funding for, 256–57
statement of activity, purpose of, 93
statement of cash flows, purpose of, 93
statement of functional expenses, purpose of, 93
statements (ethics, mission, values, vision): significance of, 49–51, 55; utilizing digital platforms to share, 114. See also ethics statements; mission statements; values statements; vision statements
state statutes, nonprofit establishment and, 44–45

St. Charles Public Library Foundation, Illinois, 187
steering committees, 39–40
STEM (science, technology, engineering, math) programs. See summer reading programs
Stillwater Public Library Foundation, Minnesota, 52
strategic planning: essential steps for, 154; grant writing and, 243–51; online resources for, 87; terminology, 82–83; types of, 85
subscription libraries: examples of current, 20–21; history of, 7–8
summer reading programs: funding and collaboration, ideas for, 255; history of, 254;
youth development and, 254–55
summer slide, 254
support groups. See library support groups

tax-exempt status. See nonprofit, establishing as a
tax filing, 92–94
Techboomers (website), 116
technology, modern, utilizing, 111, 114. See also social media presence; websites
Techsoup (website), 116
teen advisory groups: fundraising in partnership with, 206–7; recruitment and, 77
teenage board members: including, 76–79; partnering with library staff to find, 129; voting and, 76–77
texting, donations and, best practices for, 193–94
thank-you letters, tips for writing, 191–92
The Helpful Professor (website), 49
training and orientation: new member packets, 79–80; welcome letter sample, 81, 145–46
treasurers: assistant treasurers, using, 88; importance of, 87–88; job description for, 72–73; newly elected, installing, 88–90
Trust for Montana Libraries, 15
TrustLaw (website), 10
trusts, overview of, 14–15. See also library support groups
Tulsa Library Trust, Oklahoma, 52, 121–22, 225–26, 237–38, 256–57
Two Towns—One Book, Clifton, New York, 224–25

United for Libraries, 22–23, 58. See also National Friends of Libraries Week
University of Pennsylvania, 15

vacant board positions, managing, 104–8
values statements: creating, 56; defined, 56; examples of, 57–58
vision statements: creating, 53; defined, 53; examples of, 54
volunteer appreciation: annual reports and, 207; benefits of, 151; best practices for, 148–49; ideas for, 149–50; overview of, 147–48; thank-you template, 151
volunteering in lieu of paying dues, 118–19
volunteer management, 138–39, 147–48
volunteer recruitment, 113–14, 146–47

Wallace Foundation (website), 95
Walmart Spark Good, 205. See also grocery store sales percentage donations
Weathersfield Proctor Library Fundraising Committee, Vermont, 158, 180, 187–88
website maintenance: importance of, 115; search engine optimization (SEO) and, 116–17; soliciting volunteers for, 115–16; tips for, 117
websites: donation pages, 193–94, 200; membership services, 118; as promotional tools, 113–14; redesigning, 113–14; tools for creating, 116; as virtual library branches, 113. See also website maintenance
welcome letters, examples of, 81, 145–46
West Palm Beach Library Foundation, Florida, 52
West Virginia Book Festival, Charleston, West Virginia, 220
Wisconsin Book Festival, Madison, Wisconsin, 221
wish lists, making, 252–53. See also budgets; funds distribution

Ye, Samantha, 78, 117
youth engagement: benefits of, 127–30, 130; fundraising and, 206–7. See also Junior Friends of the Library groups; officers-in-training; teenage board members
Youth.gov (website), 129–30
YouTube (website), 87, 116, 199, 202

About the Author

A former English teacher and high school drama director/coach, **Diane P. Tuccillo** earned her MLS degree from Rutgers University in 1980. After serving as young adult librarian at the Rutherford (New Jersey) Public Library and the Reading (Massachusetts) Public Library, she became the longtime young adult coordinator at the City of Mesa Library in Arizona, where she led a dynamic, nationally known library teen advisory group for twenty-seven years. Most recently, she was teen services librarian at the Poudre River Public Library District in Fort Collins, Colorado, from 2007 until 2017, where she co-led a vibrant Interesting Reader Society teen advisory group.

Tuccillo has been actively involved in and has received awards from several professional organizations, including the Young Adult Library Services Association, the Assembly on Literature for Adolescents of the National Council of Teachers of English, and the Arizona Library Association; has been a book reviewer and article contributor for professional journals such as *School Library Journal* and *Voice of Youth Advocates* (*VOYA*) magazine; has contributed to books such as Nilsen & Donelson's classic *Literature for Today's Young Adults*; and has been a regular and an emeritus member of the *VOYA* advisory board. Her second book, *Teen-Centered Library Service: Putting Youth Participation into Practice*, was published by Libraries Unlimited in 2010; her third book, the completely revised and updated second edition of *Library Teen Advisory Groups* (the first edition originally published by Scarecrow in 2005), was published by Rowman & Littlefield in 2018; her fourth book, *Totally Tweens & Teens: Youth-Created and Youth-Led Library Programs*, was published by Rowman & Littlefield in 2020; and her fifth book, *The Teen Library Internships Handbook*, was published by Rowman & Littlefield in 2021. Her article on teens in charge of library fundraisers, "Teens at the Helm: Library Fundraisers," was published in *Voice of Youth Advocates* magazine in June 2018, and her books discuss how teens and librarians can partner with their Friends of the Library groups.

During her long librarianship career, Tuccillo worked closely with Friends of the Library members to gain support for youth library programs and activities; has gotten teenagers involved with the Friends as volunteers; and helped to get teen representatives serving on library trustee and Friends boards of directors. During the two years between her early retirement from the Mesa Library position and securing the one at the Poudre

River Public Library District in Colorado, she freelanced around the country providing librarian education workshops at libraries large and small; taught library science courses; and served on the Board of Directors of the Friends of the Mesa Library. Later, she served on the Board of Directors of the Poudre River Friends of the Library and as a Poudre River Public Library volunteer for four years after her final retirement.

Diane Tuccillo now lives with her husband in Tennessee, where she currently serves as a member of the Knox County Friends of the Library and on its board of directors.

www.ingramcontent.com/pod-product-compliance
Lightning Source LLC
Chambersburg PA
CBHW080534300426
44111CB00017B/2722